The Pocket Lawyer for Filmmakers

This no-nonsense reference helps independent filmmakers recognize and solve the critical legal issues they might face throughout the course of making a film.

Author Thomas A. Crowell, TV producer turned entertainment lawyer, will help you understand and negotiate crucial production contracts, handle actors and their agents, and navigate the perils of copyright infringement and other lawsuits. Updated throughout to address important changes to the law and incorporating discussion of online distribution, crowd funding, social media marketing, and international productions, this expanded third edition will provide you with the skills to:

- Protect the copyright to your work.
- Finance your film and watch out for common financing traps.
- Understand how tax credits and other incentives are used in film financing.
- Work with other screenwriters and protect your script ideas.
- Adapt a book or comic into a screenplay.
- Know how to spot the difference between copyright infringement and fair use.
- Hire crew members, actors, and post-production staff.
- Draft a production services agreement or a license to use someone else's work.
- License music for soundtracks.
- Negotiate a distribution agreement or understand how to distribute your film alone.
- Learn how to best position your film for Netflix.
- Make money from YouTube.

And much more!

Written for accessibility and ease of reference, this book is a vital resource for any student or independent filmmaker wanting their films to be successful and free of legal disasters.

Thomas A. Crowell, Esq., is a practicing lawyer and law professor specializing in entertainment law and intellectual property rights issues. He is the editor of the Focal Press Pocket Lawyer series and author of *The Pocket Lawyer for Comic Book Creators* (Focal Press, 2014). For more information, see www.ThomasCrowell.com.

The Pocket Lawyer for Filmmakers

A Legal Toolkit for Independent Producers

3rd edition

Thomas A. Crowell, Esq.

Routledge
Taylor & Francis Group
NEW YORK AND LONDON

Cover image: Dorothy Shi

Third edition published 2023

by Routledge
605 Third Avenue, New York, NY 10158

and by Routledge
4 Park Square, Milton Park, Abingdon, Oxon, OX14 4RN

Routledge is an imprint of the Taylor & Francis Group, an informa business

First edition published by Focal Press 2007

Second edition published by Routledge 2011

Library of Congress Cataloging-in-Publication Data

A catalog record has been requested for this book

ISBN: 9781032132822 (hbk)
ISBN: 9780367562489 (pbk)
ISBN: 9781003228479 (ebk)

DOI: 10.4324/9781003228479

Typeset in Akzidenz Grotesk

by Apex CoVantage, LLC

DISCLAIMER

This is a book written by a lawyer, so of course it has to open with a disclaimer. Here goes:

As you will note by its rectangular shape and paper pages, this is a book and *not* an attorney. Nothing in this book is intended as legal advice or to substitute for the personalized advice of a lawyer. Only your lawyer can tell you which laws apply to your particular situation. Laws change all the time and may be subject to numerous exceptions that are not covered by this book. There are no guarantees as to the accuracy or applicability of the information presented herein.

Furthermore, this book uses examples that feature character and company names. These names are fictitious, and any similarity to actual people, living or dead, or actual companies is purely coincidental. I have also used several real trademark and business names to illustrate certain legal issues. The use of these names and marks does not imply any approval, sponsorship, endorsement by, or affiliation with the owners of these trademarks. All views expressed are mine and do not necessarily reflect those of either the publisher or anyone I consulted while writing this book.

DEDICATION

To my wife, Natali; my sons, Connor and Xander; my parents, Caleb and Sheila; and to frustrated filmmakers everywhere.

CONTENTS

PART 9. CONCLUSION

ACKNOWLEDGMENTS

This book has been shaped by many people.

First, I could not have written this book without the help of two very special people: my parents. As published authors many times over, they inspired in me a love of writing and a love of the law.

My warmest thanks go out to my beautiful wife Natali, for fighting through the various drafts of my manuscript and for putting up with the crazed schedule of a lawyer/author/husband, and my sons Connor and Xander, for keeping me sane. They faithfully reminded me that no matter how much work I have, I must always take time to hang out with them and enjoy life.

Special thanks to contributing attorney Victoria Jade Bennett, Esq.; Victoria's knowledge of international film law proved invaluable to this addition. Older editions of this book would not have been possible with the help of Matt Savare, Esq., and the tireless efforts of Paolo Macchi, Esq.

I'm grateful for the help of my editor, Katherine Kadian, and her editorial assistant, Alyssa Turner, for handing me the reins on this book and trusting me to write the book I envisioned.

I am forever indebted to Sheafe B. Walker, Esq., whose tireless research and writing skills and passion for the law shaped early editions of the book that focus on employment and labor law.

My heartfelt thanks go to my old friend, theatrical agent Victoria Kress, who heads up the youth division of the Don Buchwald & Associates agency. Victoria provided valuable insight, tips, and humor on how to handle actors and their agents.

Thanks to William Patry, Esq., for inspiring in me a love of copyright law, and to Jeffrey M. Liebenson, Esq., and my former colleagues at KMZ Rosenman, LLP, for their support during the early years of my legal career. My former law partner, Ivan Saperstein, Esq., deserves special recognition, both as a mentor and a friend. A special shout out to Marshall M. Kolba, Esq., for showing me at an early age that you can be a lawyer and still be cool at the same time.

And because this is a book for artists, a big shout out to illustrator Alan Norico, whose awesome illustrations (prepared for my other book "The Pocket Lawyer for Comic Creators") grace a few of these pages: they were so cool, I just had to reuse them. If you are making a movie based on a comic or graphic novel, you may want to pick up a copy (to the best of my knowledge, it is the first dedicated legal guide for the comic book industry)

One of the fun things about being an attorney is that you are always learning. Every new client brings a fresh set of legal issues to explore. Every new student gives me a new perspective. I am, therefore, grateful to all my clients and students for allowing me the opportunity to learn from them and to help them make their wonderful films.

ABOUT THE AUTHOR: THOMAS A. CROWELL, ESQ.

Thomas counsels clients on a wide range of entertainment law and intellectual property rights issues in practice areas that range from film and television to comic book publishing, music, video games, manufacturing, and the graphic arts.

A seasoned negotiator, Thomas spearheads deals for client content appearing on Nickelodeon, Discovery, Starz, DIY Network, TLC, SyFy, DreamWorks, WE, Smithsonian Channel, and others. With a solid background in both narrative and unscripted television, Thomas has worked with the Dominican Republic Film Commission to harmonize the Dominican Republic's motion picture legislation with that of the United States.

He is a co-creator and the former Director from Practice of the Indie Film Clinic at the Benjamin N. Cardozo School of Law, and the Executive Director, emeritus, of the New Jersey Volunteer Lawyers for the Arts. Since 2015, Thomas has taught continuing legal education courses on comic book legal practice at "comic cons" across the country.

An avid writer, Thomas is the series editor of the Focal Press "Pocket Lawyer for . . ." series of legal guides for artists and is also the author of the first dedicated legal guide to the comic book industry, *The Pocket Lawyer for Comic Book Creators* (Focal Press, 2014). His own comic book stories appear in the pages of Waxwork Comics.

Before becoming an attorney, Mr. Crowell was a television producer and the head of business development for one of Japan's premier satellite television news companies, the Science Technology Network. Mr. Crowell managed the company's Development and Acquisitions department and supervised the production of its weekly science news program. Mr. Crowell created the children's video series

Professor Potto's Videolabs, which was awarded a National Parenting Center Seal of Approval.

Mr. Crowell received his Juris Doctor from the Benjamin N. Cardozo School of Law, where he graduated cum laude and was awarded membership in the Order of the Coif, the national legal honors society. Mr. Crowell earned his Bachelor of Fine Arts degree from New York University's Tisch School of the Arts in Film and Television Production. He is admitted to the practice of law in New York and New Jersey and before the bar of the US Supreme Court.

For more on Thomas's lectures and publications, please see his personal website at **www.thomascrowell.com**.

1

INTRODUCTION

This book is intended to provide you with a grasp of many of the key legal issues you will face during the course of making your independent films. The material in this book can help you understand and negotiate crucial production contracts, steer you through the choppy waters of handling actors and their agents, and navigate your production past the perils of copyright infringement and other lawsuits. Most importantly, it can help you protect that most valuable of properties: the rights to your film.

When I was approached to write the first edition of this book, I wanted to create something filmmakers would use on a daily basis—something that I would have used when I was a producer. Before sitting down to write, I surveyed the market and found that books on film law generally fell into two broad categories: contract form books and textbook-style legal treatises. What was missing was a pocket guide that could help the first-time filmmaker spot critical legal issues right away without having to first sort through a lot of legal theory or read through a stack of contracts. Filmmakers needed a quick reference to reach for when they were on the phone with an actor's agent or waiting to go into a pitch meeting. I wanted to write a book that would sit in the producer's bag just as *The American Cinematographers Manual* is carried by every camera operator.

THE AUDIENCE FOR THIS BOOK

This book is aimed at the independent filmmaker who wants to make money by selling their film. You, the reader, may be an industry professional, a recent film school graduate, or an amateur who wants to break into "the biz." Regardless of who you are, if you want a chance at selling your film, you must have artistic passion and *you must be prepared to treat your film project as a business!*

The book's premise is simple: you can't sell something you don't own, and unless you take care of the legal aspects of filmmaking, you could wind up not owning or not being able to sell your movie.

Furthermore, paying careful attention to a film's legal housekeeping will go a long way toward convincing a distributor that the filmmaker is a professional whose project is worth considering. The opposite is especially true: a filmmaker who ignores the legal aspects of their film will almost certainly scare a distributor away from picking up an otherwise marketable film! Even if you decide to self-distribute your film, you need to safeguard against lawsuits, cost overruns, and the failure to properly protect your rights.

WHY THIS IS NOT A CONTRACT FORM BOOK

A quick thumb through this book will show you that there are few contract forms within these pages. This is intentional.

I was an independent producer for many years before I became an attorney. Like many producers, I was very hands on: I was much more comfortable wrapping cable than reading contracts. When it came time to negotiate a contract, I would pull a contract form book from the shelf and fill in the blanks. After all, I figured, a lawyer wrote the form book, so the contracts it contained had to be good.

However, since then, so much has changed: Filmmakers looking for a contract would never dream of copying one from a book—that's what the Internet is for!

What I and many other producers fail to realize was that these form contracts are only good for a particular deal . . . and no two deals are exactly the same. Contractual language that works for one situation may leave you woefully unprotected in another; contracts are *not* one size fits all.

That's where this book comes in handy. Rather than giving you form contracts, I have taken key contracts and broken them down into their important deal points. This allows you, the filmmaker, to concentrate on negotiating the deal without having to read and understand a lot of legal language.

It is also the way the pros do it. The distributor who negotiates a distribution agreement with the filmmaker is almost never the same person who drafts the contract. It is easier to come to an agreement when you are concentrating on what the deal *is* rather than on *how* to draft the agreement. (That being said, of course crafting the contract matters. "The devil is in the drafting," as they say, and the wording of a defined term or a net profit clause may make all the difference.)

Don't get me wrong: both contract form books and textbooks are good and valuable resources in their own right. In fact, it is my sincere belief that the filmmaker is best protected by using this book in conjunction with a contract form book when negotiating contracts and by using a textbook when trying to figure out *why* the law is the way it is.

A list of useful books that contain examples of film contracts may be found at the back of this book. Books by Mark Litwak, John W. Cones, and Philip H. Miller may be particularly helpful. (See "Bibliography and Resources," p. 501.)

HOW TO USE THIS BOOK

This book is organized roughly chronologically, according to the life cycle of a film. Nevertheless, it is also intended to be a flexible resource, allowing the filmmaker to access information in a variety of ways:

- The book is designed for easy access for the filmmaker who needs to jump right in and find an answer without having to first read the book cover to cover. To help these nonlinear readers, I have repeated some key information from section to section, particularly in the sections covering contracts' deal points.

- The book may also be read straight through like any traditional book. In fact, readers may get the greatest benefit from starting at the beginning and continuing until the end. Not only will such a reader know what to anticipate, but they will have a greater understanding of how all the legal puzzle pieces fit together.
- Extensive cross-references have been included in the text. These references provide the section and page number where a related topic may be located. (See "Setting Up the Production Company," p. 43.)
- A section featuring frequently asked questions (FAQs) may help you zero in on particularly pressing issues. (See "Filmmaker FAQs," p. 8.)
- Two appendices are included at the end of the book, forming a portable law library. These sections will provide you with separate, handy guides to intellectual property, contract law, and common contract clauses.

– Appendix A: "A Filmmaker's Guide to Intellectual Property Law," p. 401.
– Appendix B: "The Clause Companion," p. 475.

IMPORTANT TIP: **Regardless of how you use this book, you should first read the section entitled "Legal Building Blocks." This section is critical to understanding the rest of the guide.** **(See "Legal Building Blocks: Contract and Intellectual Property," p. 21.)**

VIDEO VS. FILM

Years ago, there were two camps: videographers and filmmakers. Today, thanks to excellent inexpensive video cameras, production-quality mobile phones, and affordable computer editing programs, the distinction between film and video has largely been eliminated. Some independent producers shoot on hi-def video and transfer to film for theatrical distribution, and every project shot on film is transferred to video at some stage of its distribution. More and more theaters have facilities for projecting video media, and virtually every film has its own online trailer. Because producers tend to refer to their projects as "films" regardless of the medium in which they are shot, I have adopted that convention here. From a legal perspective, the choice of label is largely irrelevant. I have used the term *filmmaker* or *producer* to describe creative artists working in either film or video and the term *film* to describe the project or medium in which they are working, even if that medium is video.

LEGAL ISSUES

This book is designed to help you spot legal issues common to most film and video productions. Generally, these legal issues will typically fall into one or more of the following categories:

- Copyright and intellectual property law.
- Contract law.
- Labor and employment law.
- Finance and business.

Most issues involve several of these topics—for instance, working with a professional actor involves both contract and labor law; raising money for a film involves finance, business, and contractual legal issues; distributing a film involves contractual, copyright, and finance issues.

Key Areas of Law Impacting The Filmmaker

Contract Law	• Negotiating, drafting, and defending agreements
Copyright	• Protects original works of expression
Employment Law	• Federal and State labor law
Securities laws	• Federal and Stateinvestment laws
Tax and Production Incentives	• Help film financing through tax credits and other incentives
Rights in Ideas	• Protects unique ideas as property (tough protection to get)
Trademark	• Protects titles, labels, slogans, etc. against consumer confusion
Rights of Publicity	• Protects the right to commercially exploit likenesses
FTC Truth in Advertising	• Protects consumers from unfair or deceptive advertising, marketing, and endorsements
Defamation	• Liability for statements that damage a person's reputation

STRUCTURE OF THE BOOK

The book follows a roughly chronological organization that tracks the life cycle of a film. You will learn how to deal with such issues as:

- ***Setting up your production company and financing your film.*** Filmmaking is a business and needs to be treated like one. This section will help you:
  - Choose and create the right type of company. (See "Setting Up the Production Company," p. 43.)
  - Select and hire professionals such as lawyers and accountants. (See "Your Professional Team," p. 53.)
  - Learn what kinds of insurance you need to have in place before you make your movie. (See "Insurance," p. 59.)
  - Decide how to finance your film and watch out for common financing traps. (See "Financing Your Movie," p. 63.)
  - Identify whether you have potential securities law issues. (See "Investors and Securities Laws," p. 67.)
  - Understand how tax credits and other incentives are used in film financing. (See "Film Tax Credits and Other Production Incentives," p. 77.)
  - Learn how to borrow money against tax credits in order to partially fund your film. (See "Credits into Cash," p. 83.)
- ***Development.*** During development, the script is chosen and acquired, the writers are hired, and the film property is protected. This section will help you:
  - Protect your script ideas. (See "Idea Rights," p. 91.)
  - Work with other screenwriters. (See "Writing Collaboration," p. 108.)
  - Buy or option a screenplay. (See "Acquiring Screenplay Rights," p. 121.)
  - Adapt a book into a screenplay. (See "Screenplay Adaptations," p. 142.)
  - Acquire somebody's life story. (See "Life Story Rights," p. 150.)
  - Protect your script through copyright registration. (See "Copyright Registration," p. 164.)
- ***Pre-production.*** During pre-production, the filmmaker is primarily concerned with hiring the cast and crew and preparing for production. This section will help you:
  - Negotiate a product placement deal. (See "Product Placement," p. 189.)
  - Become familiar with labor and employment law. (See "Federal and State Labor and Employment Law," p. 199.)
  - Hire a producer. (See "Above-the-Line Services Agreement," p. 215.)
  - Hire a director. (See "Above-the-Line ," p. 215.)

- Hire a crew member. (See "Crew Services Agreement," p. 233.)
- Draft an actor's letter of intent to help secure financing. (See "Letters of Intent," p. 241.)
- Hire an actor. (See "Performer's Services Agreement," p. 256.)
- Deal with the Screen Actors Guild. (See "Working with SAG-AFTRA," p. 243.)
- Get a script to an actor. (See "How to Get a Script to a SAG-AFTRA Actor," p. 266.)
- Negotiate a production services agreement. (See "Production Services Agreements," p. 178.)

- ***Production.*** When you shoot your film, you need to be concerned with locations, extras, and avoiding infringing other people's intellectual property. This section will help you:
  - Identify when you need a release from an extra. (See "Depiction Releases," p. 275.)
  - Negotiate a location agreement. (See "Major Deal Points: Location Agreement," p. 287.)
  - Know when you need a shooting permit. (See "Shooting Permits," p. 285.)
  - Keep your art direction from infringing someone's copyrights. (See "On-Set IP Infringement," p. 293.)
  - Negotiate a license to use someone else's artwork. (See "Artwork License," p. 298.)
- ***Post-production.*** When the shooting stops, the post-production begins. Here you need to be concerned with editing and scoring your film. This section will help you:
  - Hire post-production staff. (See "Post-Production Staff," p. 311.)
  - License music. (See "Music Licensing," p. 315.)
  - Hire a composer. (See "Commissioned Music," p. 330.)
  - Obtain stock footage and film clips. (See "Film Clips and Stock Footage," p. 335.)
- ***Distribution.*** When the film is completed, you will probably want to sell it. To do that, you either need to work with a distributor, or you will need to distribute your film yourself. This section will help you:
  - Learn about the different kinds of distribution deals. (See "Types of Traditional Distribution Deals," p. 356.)
  - Understand how the audience's dollars make their way from ticket sales all the way to the producer's pocket. (See "The Money Pipeline," p. 358.)
  - Learn how to negotiate a distribution agreement. (See "Major Deal Points: Distribution Agreement," p. 362.)

– Understand how to distribute your film online, by yourself or with others. (See "Putting Your Film Online," p. 379.)
– Put your film in a theater by yourself. (See "DIY Theatrical Distribution," p. 373.)
– Make money from putting your film on YouTube. (See "Making Money from YouTube," p. 387.)
– Learn how to deal with copyright issues on YouTube. (See "YouTube and Copyright Takedowns," p. 393.)

The chronological portion of the book is followed by a Law Library in the form of appendixes, which provide an overview of the following:

- Copyright, rights of publicity, defamation, privacy law, and moral rights; see Appendix A, "A Filmmaker's Guide to Intellectual Property Law," p. 401.
- Typical contract clauses found in most film and video contracts; see Appendix B, "The Clause Companion," p. 475.

E-Z TABS

The E-Z tabs allow you to quickly locate the section you're looking for. The tabbed sections are:

1. Part 1: FAQs and Introduction.
2. Part 2: The Production Company.
3. Part 3: Development.
4. Part 4: Pre-Production.
5. Part 5: Production.
6. Part 6: Post-Production.
7. Part 7: Distribution.
8. Part 8: Intellectual Property.
9. Part 9: Contracts.

Just put your thumb over the appropriate tab on the back cover and flip until you find the section you need. No muss. No fuss. No endless searching. It's just a pity I couldn't make it lemon-scented for you.

FILMMAKER FAQS

Do you have a burning legal question that needs to be answered right now? The following frequently asked questions are designed to help you jump right into the book and get answers.

However, to get the most from this book, you should first read the section "Legal Building Blocks: Contract and Intellectual Property" on p. 21.

Business and Finance

Starting a production company and financing a movie are critical first steps to any successful production. As you begin, you might have one or all of the following questions:

- Why do I need a company? Can't I just make a movie? (See "Setting Up the Production Company," p. 43.)
- What kind of business should I set up? What's the difference between a corporation and an LLC? (See "Types of Business Entities," p. 45.)
- Do I need a lawyer? An accountant? (See "Your Professional Team," p. 53.)
- What kind of insurance do I need when I make a movie? (See "Insurance," p. 59.)
- What are the different ways to raise money for my film? (See "Financing Your Movie," p. 63.)
- I am going to be raising money from investors. What do I need to know? (See "Investors and Securities Laws," p. 67.)
- How do I use Kickstarter or other crowdfunding platforms to fund my film? (See "Crowdfunding," p. 72.)
- I have an actor interested in my project, but the film isn't funded yet. How do I use the actor's interest to help secure funding? (See "Letters of Intent," p. 241.)
- I want to work with an actor who has his or her own "loan-out" company. Can you tell me more about that? (See "Loan-Out Companies," p. 51.)
- I heard that film tax credits are a great way to finance my film. How do I take advantage of them? (See "Film Tax Credits and Other Production Incentives," p. 77.)

Development

Development is the stage in a film's life cycle that deals with the creation and acquisition of the script, life story, and other rights needed to make your picture.

- I haven't written a script yet and I want to pitch a few ideas to a production company. How do I protect my ideas so the production company won't steal them? (See "Idea Rights," p. 91.)
- How do I copyright my script? (See "Copyright Registration," p. 164.)
- I want to write a script with somebody else—what do I need to do? (See "Writing Collaboration," p. 108.)
- How can I base my script on a comic book or novel or other work that somebody else has written? (See "Screenplay Adaptations," p. 142.)

- How do I hire a writer? (See "Hiring a Screenwriter," p. 136.)
- I want to buy another writer's script; how do I do that? (See "Acquiring Screenplay Rights," p. 121.)
- I'm still raising money. Is there any way I can reserve the right to a script so that no one else can buy it first? (See "The Screenplay Option/Purchase," p. 124.)
- Can I base my script or movie on someone's life story? (See "Life Story Rights," p. 150.)
- I was inspired by someone else's work. How do I determine whether I can be sued for copyright infringement? (See "Copyright Infringement," p. 429.)
- I want to work with a writer who's a member of the Writers Guild of America. What is that? (See "Writers Guild of America," p. 115.)

Pre-Production

In pre-production, you should be concerned with preparing for the shoot. A huge part of that is hiring the cast and crew:

- How do I get money for putting a company's product in my film? (See "Product Placement," p. 189.)
- Someone wants to hire my production company to shoot a program for them. How do I do that? (See "Production Services Agreement," p. 178.)
- How do I work with sponsors to help me fund my YouTube channel? (See "The Sponsorship Deal," p. 194.)
- I want to shoot my film outside the United States. How do I create an international co-production? (See "International Co-Productions," p. 185.)
- When I hire cast and crew, what legal areas do I need to worry about in addition to the contracts? (See "Hiring Cast and Crew," p. 199.)
- How do I hire an actor who is a member of the SAG-AFTRA? (See "SAG-AFTRA," p. 243.)
- How do I hire a director? (See "Above the Line: Producers and Directors," p. 213.)
- How do I hire a crew member? (See "Crew Services Agreement," p. 233.)
- I want to work with a famous actor. How do I get the actor interested in my project? (See "How to Get a Script to a SAG-AFTRA Actor," p. 266.)
- Can I hire only independent contractors and not employees? (See "Independent Contractor or Employee?," p. 201.)
- I need to cast children in my film. Are there any special legal requirements I have to worry about? (See "Working with Minors," p. 207.)

Production

Production is the stage in a film's life cycle when you shoot the film:

- I need to shoot in a restaurant/store/house. How do I get permission? (See "Getting Permission to Use a Location," p. 285.)
- I just want to shoot a couple of scenes on the streets. Do I need to get permission from anybody? (See "Shooting Permits," p. 285.)
- Why do I need a location release or permit? What happens if I don't get one? (See "Why You Need a Location Release," p. 283.)
- I want to film passersby on the street or patrons in a business. Do I need them to sign releases? (See "Depiction Releases," p. 275.)
- My art director wants to decorate the set with a really cool poster/statue/painting they bought. Do I need to get permission from somebody to use it? (See "On-Set IP Infringement," p. 293.)
- I am shooting a scene in a kitchen/grocery store. Do I have to get permission from the manufacturers every time I show a product label on screen? (See "Trademarks on the Set," p. 300.)

Post-Production

Post-production is the stage in a film's life cycle when you edit, score, and assemble all the pieces into a finished film:

- Do I need contracts when I work with editors, music supervisors, and engineers? (See "Post-Production Staff," p. 311.)
- I want to use a popular song in my movie. Whose permission do I need? (See "Using Prerecorded Music," p. 315.)
- I want to hire a composer. How do I do that? (See "Commissioned Music," p. 330.)
- Can I rerecord my own version of a popular song? (See "Rerecording an Existing Song," p. 318.)
- I want to insert footage from another movie. How do I do that? (See "Film Clips and Stock Footage," p. 335.)

Distribution

Distribution is the stage in a film's life cycle when you license and sell the film. This is the money-making stage (hopefully):

- How does a film make money? (See "The Money Pipeline," p. 358.)
- What kind of contract will a distributor offer me? (See "Distribution Rights Acquisition Agreement," p. 362.)

- I've worked with a SAG-AFTRA actor. Are there any distribution concerns? (See "Assumption Agreement," p. 372.)
- I think I got all the copyright permissions I needed when I made the film. If I didn't, will there be any problems with distribution? (See "Legal Issues in Distribution," p. 346.)
- How do I land a distributor for my film? (See "Film Festivals, Markets, and Meeting Distributors," p. 348.)
- Help! I can't get a distributer to pick up my film! What do I do now?!? (See "DIY Distribution," p. 373.)
- How do I get my film into a movie theater without a distributor? (See "DIY Theatrical Distribution," p. 373.)
- How can I get my film to Netflix, Hulu, Amazon Prime, and other OTT exhibitors? (See "Content Aggregation and Over-The-Top Television," p. 379.)
- Can I make money by putting my film on YouTube? (See "Making Money from YouTube," p. 387.)
- How do I work with sponsors on YouTube (or other websites)? (See "The Sponsorship Deal," p. 194.)
- How do I respond to/file a copyright claim or strike on YouTube? (See "YouTube and Copyright Takedowns," p. 393.)

Copyright

Copyright law protects artistic works such as films, books, paintings, etc.:

- If I own the copyright to my film/script, what rights do I have? (See Appendix A, "Copyright Rights," p. 403.)
- How long does my copyright last? (See Appendix A, "Copyright Duration," p. 406.)
- Does copyright protect every part of my film? (See Appendix A, "Limitations on Copyright Protection" p. 408.)
- How do I hire a cast or crew member and ensure that I keep the copyright to their work? (See Appendix A, "Work Made for Hire," p. 418.)
- What is "fair use"? Can't I just use anybody's work in my film as long as I don't sell the film? (See Appendix A, "Fair Use," p. 433.)
- Aren't there certain books/films/plays/music/photographs that aren't protected by copyright law? (See Appendix A, "Public Domain," p. 409.)

ROADMAP TO KEY LEGAL ISSUES

These handy-dandy adventure maps can alert you to legal perils in your path to production. Okay, maybe they're just flowcharts, but beware, for beyond their boundaries . . . here be dragons[1]!

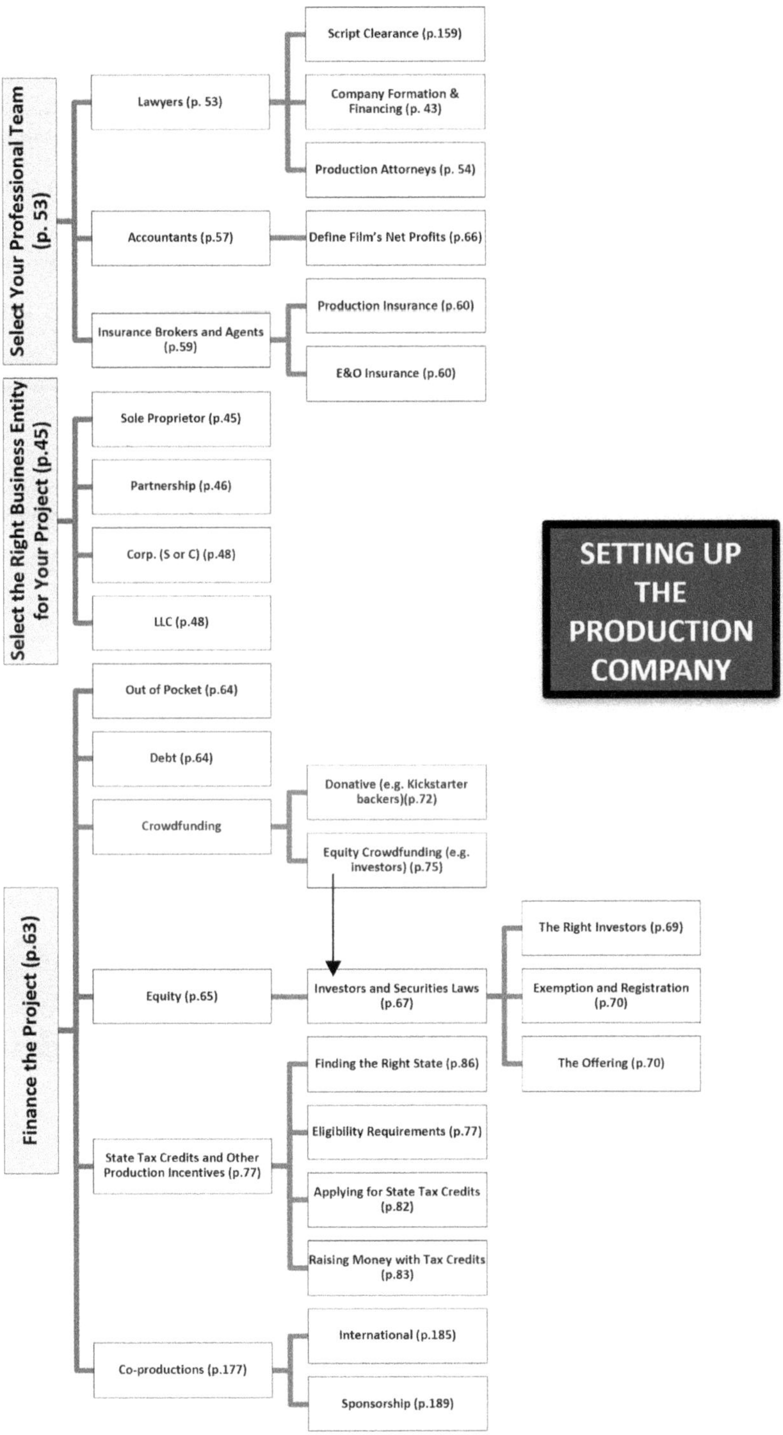
Select Your Professional Team (p. 53)
Lawyers (p. 53)
Script Clearance (p.159)
Company Formation & Financing (p. 43)
Production Attorneys (p. 54)
Accountants (p.57)
Define Film's Net Profits (p.66)
Insurance Brokers and Agents (p.59)
Production Insurance (p.60)
E&O Insurance (p.60)
Select the Right Business Entity for Your Project (p.45)
Sole Proprietor (p.45)
Partnership (p.46)
Corp. (S or C) (p.48)
LLC (p.48)
SETTING UP THE PRODUCTION COMPANY
Finance the Project (p.63)
Out of Pocket (p.64)
Debt (p.64)
Crowdfunding
Donative (e.g. Kickstarter backers)(p.72)
Equity Crowdfunding (e.g. investors) (p.75)
Equity (p.65)
Investors and Securities Laws (p.67)
The Right Investors (p.69)
Exemption and Registration (p.70)
The Offering (p.70)
State Tax Credits and Other Production Incentives (p.77)
Finding the Right State (p.86)
Eligibility Requirements (p.77)
Applying for State Tax Credits (p.82)
Raising Money with Tax Credits (p.83)
Co-productions (p.177)
International (p.185)
Sponsorship (p.189)

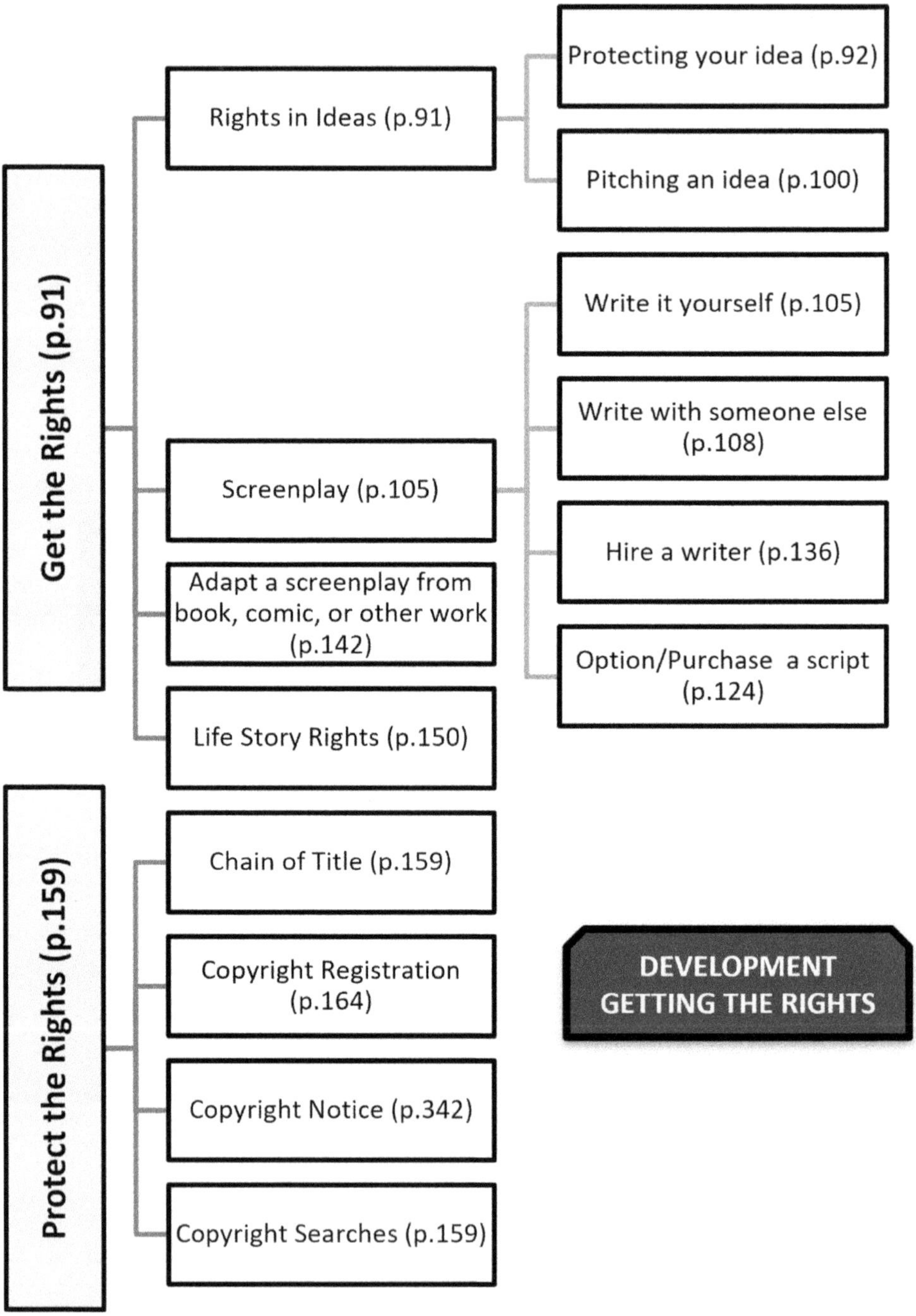
Get the Rights (p.91)
Rights in Ideas (p.91)
Protecting your idea (p.92)
Pitching an idea (p.100)
Screenplay (p.105)
Write it yourself (p.105)
Write with someone else (p.108)
Hire a writer (p.136)
Option/Purchase a script (p.124)
Adapt a screenplay from book, comic, or other work (p.142)
Life Story Rights (p.150)
Protect the Rights (p.159)
Chain of Title (p.159)
Copyright Registration (p.164)
Copyright Notice (p.342)
Copyright Searches (p.159)
DEVELOPMENT
GETTING THE RIGHTS

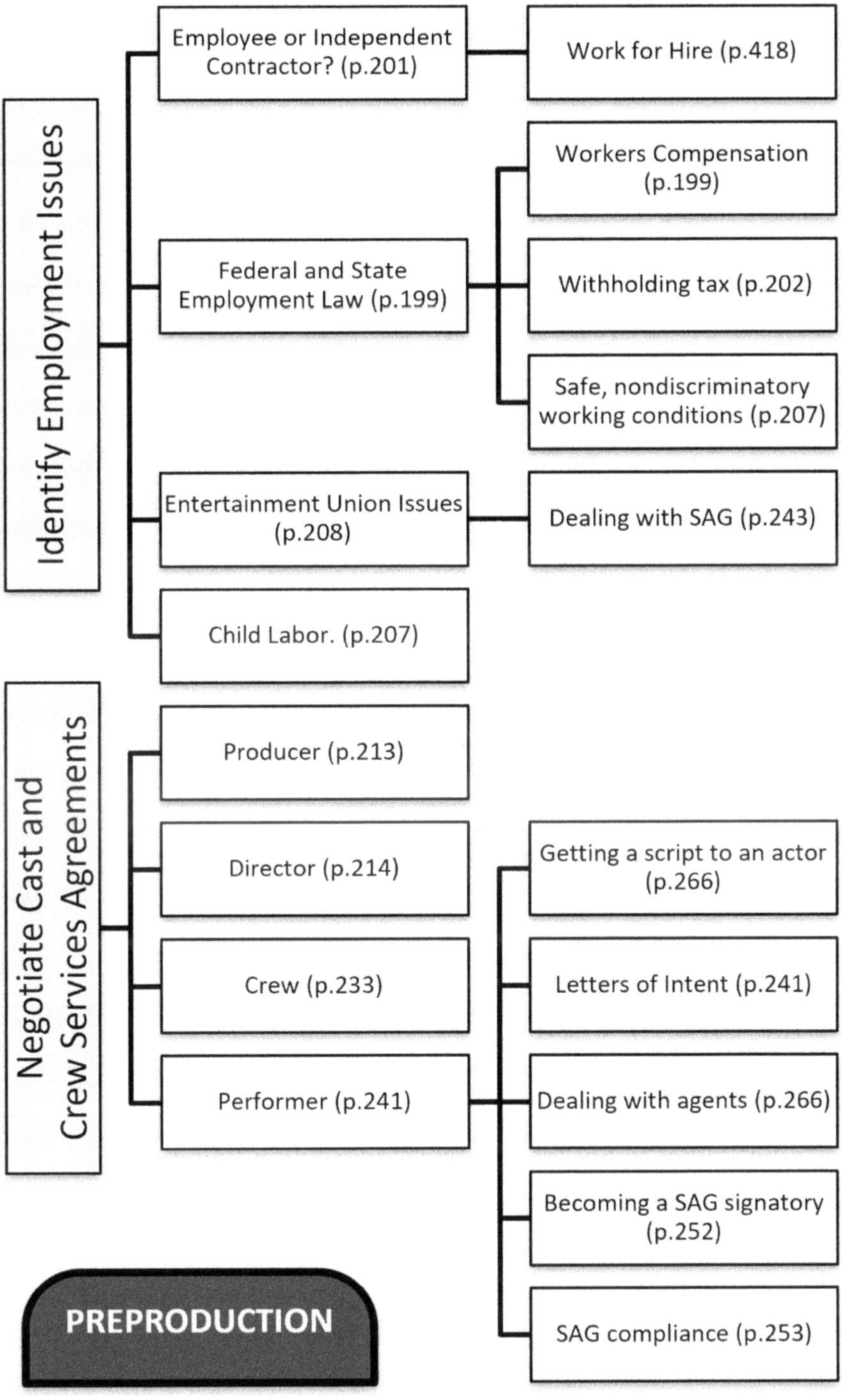
Identify Employment Issues
Employee or Independent Contractor? (p.201)
Work for Hire (p.418)
Federal and State Employment Law (p.199)
Workers Compensation (p.199)
Withholding tax (p.202)
Safe, nondiscriminatory working conditions (p.207)
Entertainment Union Issues (p.208)
Dealing with SAG (p.243)
Child Labor. (p.207)
Negotiate Cast and Crew Services Agreements
Producer (p.213)
Director (p.214)
Crew (p.233)
Performer (p.241)
Getting a script to an actor (p.266)
Letters of Intent (p.241)
Dealing with agents (p.266)
Becoming a SAG signatory (p.252)
SAG compliance (p.253)
PREPRODUCTION

FAQs/
INTRO.

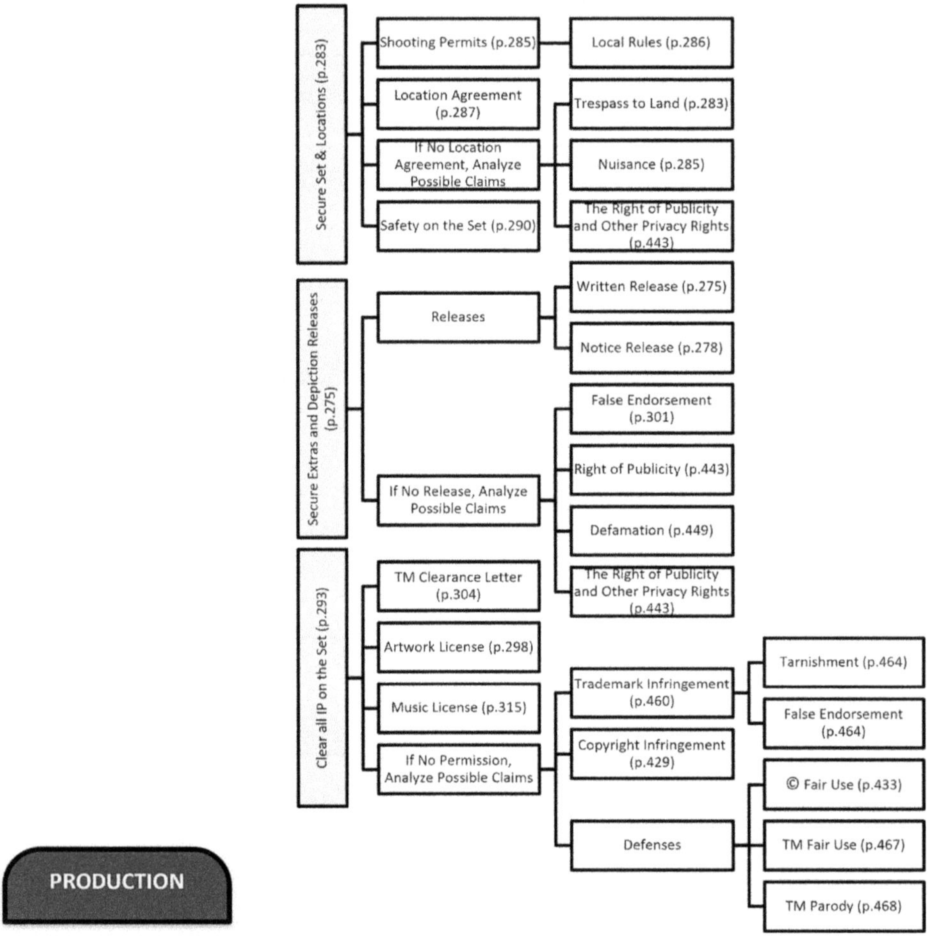
Secure Set & Locations (p.283)
Shooting Permits (p.285)
Local Rules (p.286)
Location Agreement (p.287)
If No Location Agreement, Analyze Possible Claims
Trespass to Land (p.283)
Nuisance (p.285)
The Right of Publicity and Other Privacy Rights (p.443)
Safety on the Set (p.290)
Secure Extras and Depiction Releases (p.275)
Releases
Written Release (p.275)
Notice Release (p.278)
If No Release, Analyze Possible Claims
False Endorsement (p.301)
Right of Publicity (p.443)
Defamation (p.449)
The Right of Publicity and Other Privacy Rights (p.443)
Clear all IP on the Set (p.293)
TM Clearance Letter (p.304)
Artwork License (p.298)
Music License (p.315)
If No Permission, Analyze Possible Claims
Trademark Infringement (p.460)
Tarnishment (p.464)
False Endorsement (p.464)
Copyright Infringement (p.429)
Defenses
© Fair Use (p.433)
TM Fair Use (p.467)
TM Parody (p.468)
PRODUCTION

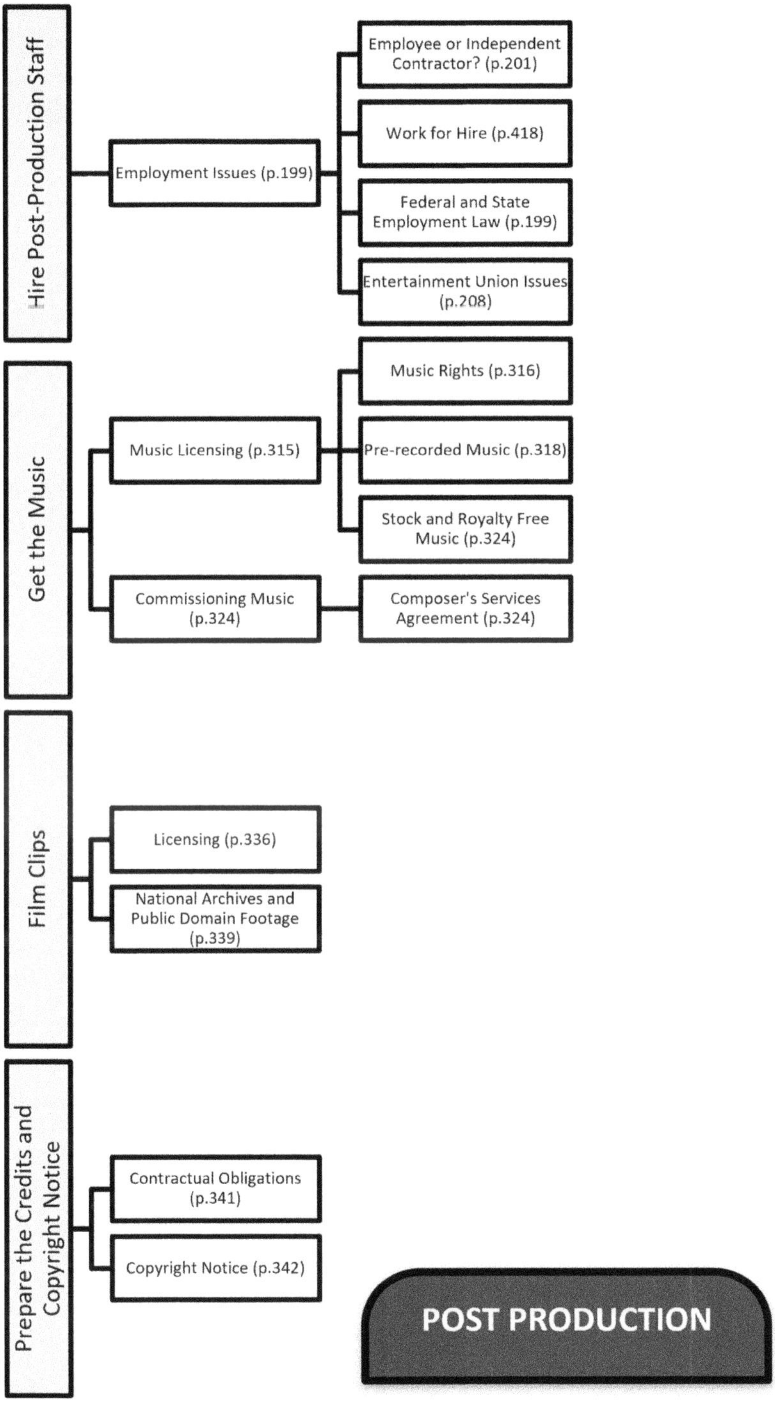
Hire Post-Production Staff
Employment Issues (p.199)
Employee or Independent Contractor? (p.201)
Work for Hire (p.418)
Federal and State Employment Law (p.199)
Entertainment Union Issues (p.208)
Get the Music
Music Licensing (p.315)
Music Rights (p.316)
Pre-recorded Music (p.318)
Stock and Royalty Free Music (p.324)
Commissioning Music (p.324)
Composer's Services Agreement (p.324)
Film Clips
Licensing (p.336)
National Archives and Public Domain Footage (p.339)
Prepare the Credits and Copyright Notice
Contractual Obligations (p.341)
Copyright Notice (p.342)
POST PRODUCTION

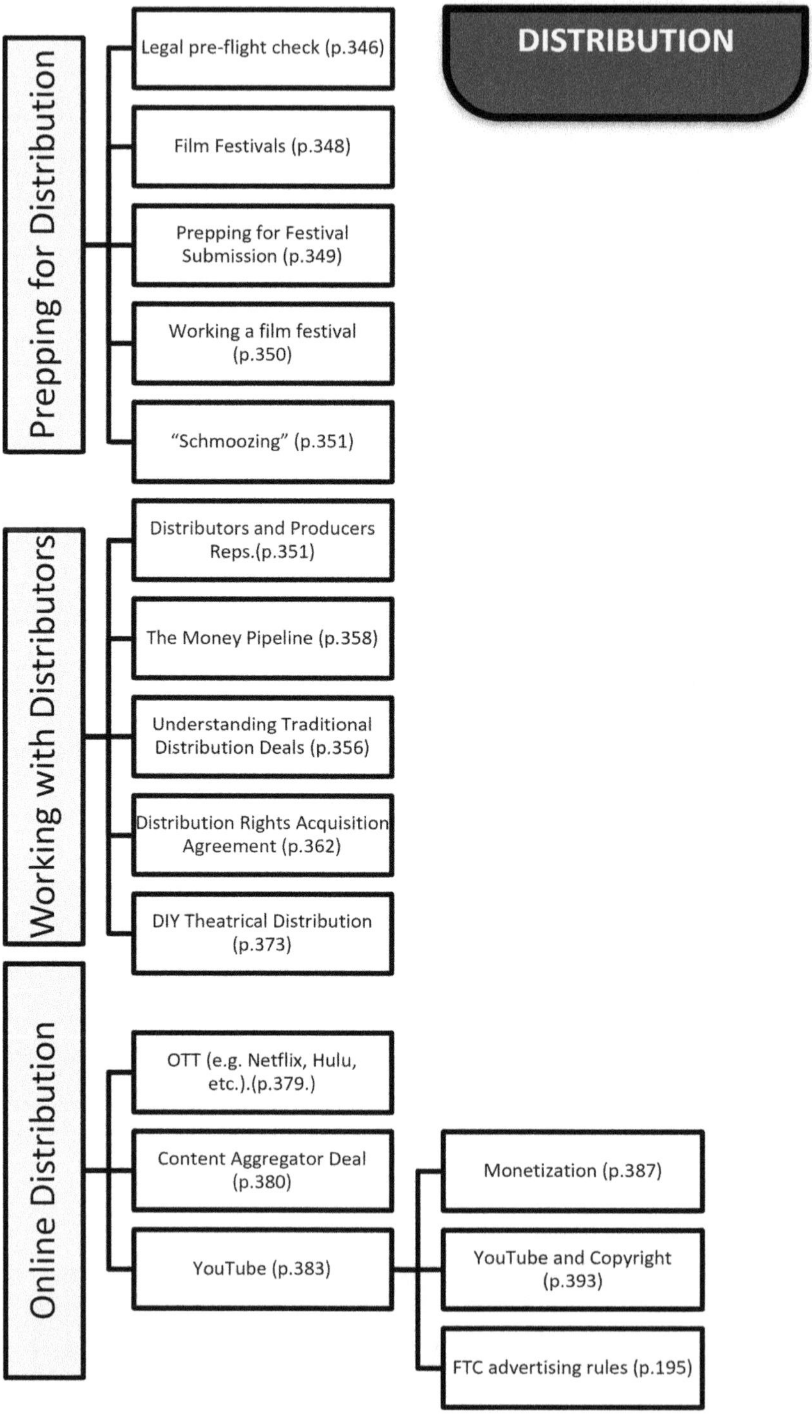
DISTRIBUTION
Prepping for Distribution
Legal pre-flight check (p.346)
Film Festivals (p.348)
Prepping for Festival Submission (p.349)
Working a film festival (p.350)
"Schmoozing" (p.351)
Working with Distributors
Distributors and Producers Reps.(p.351)
The Money Pipeline (p.358)
Understanding Traditional Distribution Deals (p.356)
Distribution Rights Acquisition Agreement (p.362)
DIY Theatrical Distribution (p.373)
Online Distribution
OTT (e.g. Netflix, Hulu, etc.).(p.379.)
Content Aggregator Deal (p.380)
YouTube (p.383)
Monetization (p.387)
YouTube and Copyright (p.393)
FTC advertising rules (p.195)

A word about references to URLS referenced in this book: hyperlinks change all the time (I've lost track of how many times I've updated the ones in this book as I've been writing). If it looks like a link is broken, try instead to search the title of the document; it may just have moved.

NOTE

[1] Or if you want to sound fancy and use the Latin: "hic sunt dracones!"

2

LEGAL BUILDING BLOCKS: CONTRACT AND INTELLECTUAL PROPERTY

READ THIS SECTION FIRST!

Two key legal areas every filmmaker must become acquainted with are *intellectual property law* and *contract law*. These are the building blocks of every agreement used in motion picture and video production. You will get the most benefit from this book if you first read the following section before diving into the rest of the book.

A more detailed discussion of intellectual property and contract law can be found at the back of the book in:

Appendix A: "A Filmmaker's Guide to Intellectual Property Law," page 401, and

Appendix B: "The Clause Companion," page 475.

1

COPYRIGHT AND INTELLECTUAL PROPERTY

All film deals are built on the foundation of intellectual property. One of the key jobs performed by most of the contracts you'll be dealing with is the protection and/or transfer of such intellectual property rights as copyrights, trademarks, rights of publicity, or rights in ideas.

WHAT IS INTELLECTUAL PROPERTY?

The term *intellectual property* refers to a collection of laws that protect products of the mind or personality, such as copyright, trademarks, rights in ideas, rights of publicity, and privacy rights. The laws that protect patents and trade secrets are also part of intellectual property, but these are generally less important to the filmmaker. Intellectual property is often referred to by its abbreviated label, IP.

WHAT IS A COPYRIGHT?

The most important intellectual property law for filmmakers is *copyright law*. Copyright is actually a collection of legal rights, all of which protect "original works of authorship fixed in any tangible medium of expression [. . .]."[1]

Copyright protects all of the following:

- Literary works, such as screenplays, novels, magazine articles, and poems.
- Motion pictures, television shows, and other audiovisual works.
- Musical works, including any accompanying words.
- Dramatic works, including any accompanying music.
- Pantomimes and choreographic works.
- Pictorial, graphic, and sculptural works.
- Sound recordings.
- Architectural works.
- Websites.
- Other works of original authorship fixed in a tangible medium of expression.

Copyright is one of the easiest forms of intellectual property protection to obtain: just create an original work of authorship, write it down or record it in some way, and you have a copyright in that work. Only a minimum amount of creativity is required. You don't even have to fill out a form or put a "C" in a circle to get copyright protection; however, you get more legal protection if you do. (*See* "Copyright Registration," p. 164.)

EXCLUSIVE RIGHTS UNDER COPYRIGHT

For filmmakers, copyright law gives the copyright owner the *exclusive* right to take his or her work and:

1. ***Make copies of it***. Zeus Pictures, Inc., owns the copyright to the film *Wombats in Love*. Only Zeus Pictures, or someone with that company's permission, can authorize Dupe Co. to press Blu-ray discs of that film.
2. ***Distribute it***. Once the film prints for *Wombats in Love* are made, only Zeus Pictures, or someone with that company's permission, can authorize Dingo Distributors, LLC, to license the picture for domestic theatrical distribution. However, once a Blu-ray copy is sold (as opposed to licensed), Zeus Pictures has no more control over to whom that particular copy can be sold.
3. ***Publicly perform that work***. Only Zeus Pictures can authorize an exhibitor or broadcaster to show *Wombats in Love* to the public.

4. ***Publicly display that work***. Only Zeus Pictures can authorize a website or other public display of production stills from *Wombats in Love*.
5. ***Make derivative works based on the original work.*** Only Zeus Pictures can commission a remake or sequel to *Wombats in Love* or authorize the manufacture of action figures, video games, and other licensed products based on the movie.

Of course, Zeus Pictures can *license* or *sell* any of these rights to a third party. In fact, that's how films make money.

THE FILM PROPERTY

When you own intellectual property, you have the exclusive right to sell, license, dispose, possess, and exploit it. When you sell intellectual property, you are really selling these rights. This holds true for all forms of property, whether you're selling your house, your car, or the copyright to your screenplay. If you plan to sell or publicly exhibit your film, you must treat it and protect it as the valuable property it is.

The *film property* is the collection of property rights in the film and the screenplay on which it is based. The term usually refers to a collection of rights necessary for owning a motion picture, which includes:

- The copyright to the screenplay.
- Ownership of treatments and synopses on which the screenplay is based.
- The right to adapt the screenplay from another work, such as a book.
- The copyright and other property rights in the resulting motion picture.
- Any trademark rights in the film's title or images of its characters.
- The right to authorize the use of clips or likenesses of the film's actors for promotional tie-ins.
- The right to create another work (e.g., a video game, television series, action figure, etc.) based on the film property.

These rights, especially copyright, can be divided up and licensed in several ways. Typically, rights are granted and divided up by the following categories:

Medium, such as:

- Film.
- Television.
- Literary.
- Theater.
- Video game.

- Digital.
- Home video.
- Merchandising.

Means of exhibition and distribution, such as:

- Theatrical exhibition.
- Cable television.
- Over-the-top television (OTT).
- Video on demand (VOD).
- Pay-per-view (PPV).
- Satellite.
- Free over-the-air broadcast.
- In-flight movie.
- Closed circuit.
- Internet download.
- Internet streaming video.

Duration, such as:

- Perpetual.
- Specified time.
- Specified number of broadcasts, performances, exhibitions.

Territory, such as:

- North America.
- Europe.
- The universe.

As a result, it is possible for a screenwriter to convey the theatrical rights in a script to a production company while retaining the rights to write a novel from the screenplay. That is why it is critical for filmmakers and writers to be aware of exactly which rights they are receiving and granting.

Being able to control the property rights to a screenplay is the foundation on which you will construct your film property. To sell, distribute, or exhibit most films, you must first have secured the property rights to the screenplay on which they are based.

You protect your film property by ensuring that you:

1. Own or control the copyright to the screenplay. (*See* "Creating a Screenplay," p. 105, and "Hiring a Screenwriter," p. 136.)

2. Don't infringe on someone else's copyright. (*See* "Copyright Infringement," p. 429, and "Copyright Searches and Permissions," p. 159.)
3. Register and maintain a clean copyright chain of title. (*See* "Chain of Title," p. 159.)

GOT A FEW MINUTES? GET SOME COPYRIGHT LAW UNDER YOUR BELT!

Now might be a good time to acquaint yourself with the basics of copyright law; after all, you will be dealing with copyright issues at every stage of your film project. Get yourself up to speed by reading through the copyright law section in the "Law Library" portion of this book. (*See* Appendix A: "Copyright Law," p. 402.)

Because copyright is such a tricky subject, it is easy to get into trouble, either by (1) failing to adequately protect one's work or (2) inadvertently infringing somebody else's copyright. *Keep in mind that you don't have to intend to infringe a copyright to be held liable for copyright infringement.*

The United States Copyright Office has a very helpful website. Its FAQ page can help answer some basic questions about copyright law: www.copyright.gov/help/faq/.

NOTE

[1] See 17 U.S.C. § 102(a)(2020).

2

THE CONTRACT ENGINE

Copyrights and other IP may be the heart of your work, but a **contract** is the engine that drives the deal. Without a contract to define the duties and obligations of each party, a collaboration can quickly spiral out of control, ending up in a thicket of thorny legal problems. And like an engine, unless you understand how one works, you're not going to be able fix one when a working relationship starts to sputter and seize up.

My goal throughout this book is to give you the tools to help you navigate your agreements so you can understand your contractual obligations well enough to steer clear of those scary areas that would put you in breach of contract. Hopefully, you'll find that the better able to read a contract you are, the less boring they will appear. I don't want to oversell it—you're not going to find reading a license agreement as adrenaline-spiking as the latest blockbuster movie, but you will find that when you know what each clause in your agreement means and how it functions, you'll be able to see how exactly it applies to *you*. It will become personal . . . and *that* will make it interesting.

THE COMPREHENSIBLE CONTRACT

Understanding legal mumbo-jumbo can be tricky, but it really helps if you imagine how you would be affected by each clause. So, if you feel your eyes glazing over, think: "What does this clause stop *me* from doing? What does it require *me* to do? What does it make *me* responsible for?" As they say in Hollywood trailers, "This time, it's personal!"

WHAT IS A CONTRACT?

A contract is a legally enforceable agreement that determines the rights and obligations of each contracting party. In order to be a valid contract, you need:

- An offer that is accepted.
- Terms that are definite and specific, not vague or ambiguous (although sometimes these terms can be implied).

DOI: 10.4324/9781003228479-4

- Consideration—something that each party gives or gets for entering into the contract.
- Legal capacity—each party must be competent to enter into a contract.
- Legal purpose—a contract to do something illegal is no contract at all.

KEY CONTRACT CONCEPTS

An **express contract** is one where all the terms are stated, as are the contract formation steps of offer, acceptance, and consideration.

An **implied contract** is one that is formed through the behavior of the parties or assumed by the circumstances. When certain key terms are not discussed in an implied contract, a court may fill them in with "reasonable" terms. For the most part, you want to be very careful to avoid creating implied contracts, since by definition, their terms are uncertain. However, if you're pitching an idea to a production company or studio, you may want there to be at least an implied contract for its protection.

When one party does not perform their duties or fulfill their obligations under a contract, they are in default or have **breached the contract**. We will deal with contract breach more fully in "Breach of Contract," p. 496.

THINGS THAT LOOK LIKE CONTRACTS BUT MAY NOT BE CONTRACTS

A Proposal

A proposal, by contrast, is merely an offer to enter into a contract. If someone sends you a proposal, they are essentially saying "here are the terms which, should you accept them, will form our contract." You may receive a proposal with a signature block at the end and a statement that says something like: "sign below to indicate your intent to be bound by the above." If you sign on the dotted line, then that proposal may in fact be transformed into a contract. In fact, even **if it isn't signed**, if you behave as if there is a contract in place (e.g. using a writer's script after receiving such a proposal), then a court may find that a contract was formed between the parties. The downside to a proposal is that it's often extremely cursory and doesn't contain many important clauses that a more fully expressed contract would. As a result, if this is the only agreement in place, the parties may soon find themselves fighting over what exactly their agreement is. Furthermore, if the proposal doesn't address key deal points and is too vague, a court might find that it's not a contract at all.

A Deal Memo

A deal memo is a short memorandum outlining the major deal points of a contract. It is often a more complete agreement then a proposal. Signed by both parties, the deal memo is often (but not always) a binding contract. It is often used as a quick agreement to get the parties working together until a more complete agreement (a "long-form" agreement) can be drafted and signed by the parties.

Memorandum of Understanding

A **memorandum of understanding** (MOU),[1] by contrast, is "an agreement to agree," or a set of parameters for the contract the parties will negotiate eventually. It *usually* not legally binding. Keep in mind that people unfortunately use the terms MOU and deal memo interchangeably. Whether a document is binding is controlled by its terms and the parties' mutual assent, not by its title.

Deal Points

Deal points are those terms that everyone must agree on before negotiating the rest of a contract. These are the terms that would appear on a deal memo or short form contract. Major deal points are usually the points that are negotiated first between the parties; as a result, these are the clauses on which this book will focus on the most.

Promises Are Not Always Contracts

While a contract is an agreement that a court will enforce, not all agreements are contracts, and not all agreements are enforceable. In your professional career, you should have at least a rough idea of what constitutes a contract. Here are some examples:

- A distribution company executive approaches you at a film festival and says, "Your film looks great. I think we may want to distribute it." You would have a hard time claiming there is a contract at this point. There are no terms and no definite obligation on the distributor's part.

- Your sweet grandmother says to you: "I'm going to give you $100,000 to make your movie. No strings attached." Wonderful news, but if your grandmother reneges a couple of days later, after her losing streak on the slots in Vegas, you can't make her cough up the money. Promises to make a gift are generally not enforceable. And besides, Grandma's broke and hiding from her bookie.
- Even if the parties are agreed on the key terms, if they are still negotiating the agreement, there is likely no contract.[2]

READ IT OR WEEP!

The fact that you didn't read your contract or that you didn't understand what you read is no defense to the enforcement of the contract. As the Supreme Court of Montana pointed out:

"One who executes a written contract is presumed to know the contents of the contract and to assent to those specified terms, in the absence of fraud, misrepresentation, or other wrongful act by the other contracting party. Absent incapacity to contract, **ignorance of the contents of a written contract is not a ground for relief from liability.**"

Quinn v. Briggs, 172 Mont 468, 476, 565 P2d 297, 301 [1977]

The Contract "Themes"

Just as movies often tackle big dramatic themes, contracts confront important business themes in the paragraphs between introduction and signature block. Most contract clauses deal with one or more of the following themes:

CONTRACT THEMES
1
2
3
4
5
6
7
Who are the parties?
What are the parties getting?
What are the parties giving in exchange for what they're getting?
What promises are being made about the IP?
What protections do the parties have?
What rules govern the business relationship between the parties?
What happens when something goes wrong?
CONTRACT

As you'll see, these concepts are interdependent. Any given contract clause may deal with several concepts, each one affecting the other. Once you learn to view each paragraph of an agreement through one of these thematic "windows," the parts of the contract should start to appear more integrated in your mind. Let's look at each of these themes in greater depth, from a creator's point of view.

Who Are the Parties?

The parties are the people or companies bound by the contract. This is not as straightforward as it may seem; the cinematographer you're hiring may, in fact, want their loan-out company to be party to the contract (see "Loan-Out Companies," p. 51), or the script that you're acquiring may be based on a novel written by someone other than the author of the script, and that original author may have rights to receive money if that script is made into a film. Furthermore, a contract may have more than two parties, each of whom may have a different set of duties and obligations toward the others.

What Are the Parties Getting?

What you're getting depends on the kind of deal you're negotiating. From a producer's perspective, you will generally be acquiring the following:

- **Rights**. Contract clauses that deal with intellectual property rights are often the most critical part of your contract. And as we saw in the last section, controlling IP rights is the key to maintaining control of your property. (See also Appendix A, "A Filmmaker's Guide to Intellectual Property Law," starting on p. 401.) If you hire a writer, director, or other creator to work on your movie, you will need contract clauses that deal with:
  - Your right to use the copyright in that creator's work. (See Appendix A, "Copyright," p. 402.)
  - Any idea rights that the writer, director, crew members, or performer may have in your project. (See "Protecting Ideas," p. 91.)
- **Services**. Virtually anybody you or your company hires is performing services for you. You'll be getting the right to direct their creative input and to require them to deliver certain creative assets to you (like scripts, performances, soundtracks, etc.).
- **Property**. The lease of equipment, the purchase of materials to create your film, props and wardrobe, etc.
- **Money**. Money to fund your film, your services as an artist, or the net profits from a film's exploitation—these are just a few examples.
- **Credit**. Credit obligations control more than just the job title: they also specify the order in which the person's name must appear, whether it's on

a single card or shared, whether it must appear in advertising, and many other critical aspects. Not surprisingly, it's one of the most important clauses in any filmmaking agreement.

What Are the Parties Giving in Exchange for What They're Getting?

This is the flip side of the above:

- **Services**. If you're a writer hired by a production company, you're trading your services as a writer (and the copyright) to the screenplay in exchange for a fee.
- **Property**. Prop and set builders, costume designers, and special effects make-up artists all create property for a fee. Make no mistake about it: if you sign a work-for-hire agreement, your right to keep your physical artwork must also be in writing, or you may end up with a paycheck and little more.
- **Intellectual Property Rights**. Artists trade a portion (or all) of their IP rights to the producers and companies who hire them. As we've seen, these rights could be non-exclusive, exclusive, or work for hire. Producers also grant rights, such as the right to distribute the film in a certain territory, the right to manufacture Blu-ray discs, or the right to create a television series based on their film property. One important aspect of granting intellectual property in a movie property is that producers need the right to further assign those rights to persons and entities which are not part of the initial contract between producer and artist.
- **Money or the right to receive money** if the film makes a profit is usually what a production company gives an artist in exchange for the artist's IP rights, services, and property created for the project. Obviously, compensation comes in many forms: salaries, deferred compensation, profit participation, bonuses, royalties, licensing fees, buyouts, option prices, and so on.

HIRING AN ARTIST? PUT THE IP IN THE CONTRACT!

If you're hiring another artist to work on your book, your contract with them **MUST** address their IP rights in the project. Do you own the IP rights to their work, or are they just licensing them to you? And regardless of which of you owns the work, you also must have the right to license and assign all or part of the IP rights in your movie to studios, distributors, merchandisers, and other third parties . . . or you'll never be able to exploit your film. As you can see, IP clauses can be both tricky and critical. Tread carefully. (See "Hiring Cast and Crew," p. 199.)

WHAT PROMISES ARE BEING MADE ABOUT THE IP?

In addition to the exchange of services or property for money, what other promises are being made by the parties about the IP (and other critical areas)? For instance, you might be promising:

- That you have the right to enter into the contract with the other party and that you have all the necessary IP rights to the film to offer. (See Appendix B, "Representations and Warranties," p. 482.)
- That you will agree to the production company's restrictions on your ability to publicize your work. (See Appendix B, "Publicity," p. 492.)
- That your script or film will not defame anybody or infringe anybody's copyrights or trademarks. (See Appendix A, "Libel and Defamation," p. 449.)

WHAT PROTECTIONS DO THE PARTIES HAVE?

Smooth business relationships require more than promises between the parties; they require each party to be able to protect his or her valuable assets. For example:

- How often can you check the other party's accounting to make sure that you have been paid what you were promised? (See Appendix B, "Audit and Accounting," p. 485.)
- Who has approval over a creative or business decision? (See Appendix B, "Approvals," p. 475.)
- Who pays the legal bill if you are sued for somebody else's mistake or breach? (See Appendix B, "Indemnification," p. 488.)

WHAT RULES GOVERN THE BUSINESS RELATIONSHIP BETWEEN THE PARTIES?

In a sense, the entire contract is a rulebook for the relationship between the parties. That being said, many provisions determine important housekeeping functions that are separate and apart from the quid pro quo issues at the heart of the contract.

For example:

- How do you communicate with the other parties? (See Appendix B, "Notice and Cure," p. 486.)

- Can you assign your rights or duties under the contract to other people? (See Appendix B, "Assignment and Delegation," p. 484.)
- How long is the contract in effect? (See Appendix B, "Term," p. 483.)

WHAT HAPPENS WHEN SOMETHING GOES WRONG?

If something goes wrong, you can always sue, right? Perhaps not. It is quite common for contracts to contain clauses limiting a person's right to sue in court, requiring that person to arbitrate instead. Several kinds of clauses govern how the parties must solve their disagreements. The following questions might be addressed, for example:

- Can the parties sue, or must they arbitrate disputes? (See Appendix B, "Remedies," p. 492.)
- Do the parties have time to cure problems before they are in breach of contract? (See Appendix B, "Notice and Cure," p. 486.)
- What happens if something goes wrong and it's nobody's fault (e.g., an earthquake, flood, riot, fire, or pandemic)? (See Appendix B, "*Force Majeure*," p. 487.)
- Where must a lawsuit or arbitration be initiated? (See Appendix B, "Choice of Law," p. 485.)

CLARITY, CLARITY, CLARITY!

You should always draft your contracts so that they can be read and understood by somebody who was not part of the negotiations. Contracts are very often assigned to third parties who were not present during the initial deal making. As a result, if the language of the contract is not clear, these third parties may not understand how to interpret the contract. You want to make sure that there are no hidden assumptions as to what each party was supposed to do. The best contract is a detailed roadmap and set of instructions for a business transaction, written in a way that the parties to the contract can easily understand their obligations to one another.

RULES OF THUMB FOR CONTRACTS

1. **Some kinds of contracts must be in writing**—sometimes a handshake just won't do. A good example is any contract which deals with an

exclusive copyright. It doesn't matter that the screenwriter whom you hired as an independent contractor to design your film's website promised that they will create your website design as a work for hire; unless that designer signed the contract with you which *says* it's a work for hire, it's just not a work for hire. In fact, they may still have some rights to use their design on other sites and in other media, because they own the copyright and have—at best—only granted you a license to use the design for your site.

2. **Some kinds of contracts don't need to be in writing**—contracts for the protection of an idea, for instance, don't need to be in writing. Neither do many contracts to perform services for a certain amount of money. What this means is that you need to be very careful when brainstorming with somebody about working on their concept or negotiating with somebody about the possibility of their working with you. You need to understand when you're forming a contract and when you're not. This is why, for clarity's sake, the best practice is to get all contracts in writing.
3. **Especially when you're working with your friends, you need a contract**. When you're working with your friends, feelings can get easily hurt; it's best to have a written contract that both buddies can reference to determine what duties each one owes the other. It's just human nature; people remember their obligations towards others in a way that's most favorable to themselves. Written contracts can preserve friendships.
4. **A contract should be clear**. A good contract should be so clear and understandable that even people who were not involved in its negotiation should be able to follow it. It's true that there's a lot of bad contract drafting out there; many lawyers are sesquipedalian when they should be plainspoken (see what I did there?). As a matter of fact, there are very few "magic legal words" needed in a contract. If you can state each party's duties and obligations to each other in plain language, you will have a more effective contract.
5. **Watch out for "defined terms."** Words don't always mean what you think they do, especially if a contract defines them very differently from the dictionary meaning. So, if you've written a screenplay and a producer gives you a contract which defines the term "Film," to mean: "*that audiovisual work based upon the Screenplay produced by the production company, as well as any audiovisual or other work derived therefrom*," well then, guess what? For purpose of the contract, the term "Film" could also include *any sequel, TV show, or remake based on your script*! Not something you want to suddenly find out when you turn on the TV and find your scintillating work of genius has been repurposed as a mediocre sitcom!
6. **Know what you're representing, warranting, and indemnifying**. Every professionally drafted production agreement has both "representations and warranties" and "indemnification" provisions. Among other

things, the representations and warranties are promises that you are making to the production company about the ownership of the work you are making for them or licensing to them. If you don't own everything free and clear, and the production company gets sued, the indemnification clause may stipulate that you have to pay all of their legal bills and other damages . . . as well as the legal bills and damages of the studio, distributor, theater, television station, merchandiser, etc. in the chain.

7. **Hiring a lawyer to negotiate and draft a contract is cheaper than hiring a lawyer to litigate a breach of contract**. I know lawyers can be expensive. Still, they can save you a lot more money than they cost. And while it might cost a couple of grand to negotiate a potentially lucrative publishing agreement, it would cost you tens of thousands of dollars to litigate the same agreement. Studios have lawyers; shouldn't you?
8. **A "click-wrap" agreement is binding**. Yes, I hate it too. But the fact remains that when you click "I Agree" before you register with a website or purchase a piece of editing software, you have likely formed a binding agreement. Yes, I know there was no negotiation. Yes, I know you don't have time to read the darn thing. Yes, I know you don't have any choice if you want to use the service. Bottom line: a click can consummate a contract.
9. **When negotiating with somebody, don't take their word for what the contract says**. Production companies use contracts that they are very familiar with, and it may be tempting to have the well-meaning development executive explain your contract to you. But the fact is, that exec is not your attorney (and may not be an attorney at all). In short, they may think the contract means one thing for you when in fact it doesn't. Furthermore, there will be language in that contract which says, in effect, that the only legally binding agreement is what's on the page and not what has been explained to you. I sincerely hope this book will help you interpret your contracts, but as I said before, nothing can replace the advice of an experienced lawyer who has actually read your agreement.
10. **You will be bound by a contract even if you didn't understand it and even if you didn't read it**. Saying you didn't understand your contract when you signed it is not a defense. And saying that you didn't even *read* your contract before you signed it is not a defense to anything. . . . Except the allegation that you treat your work as a professional.

Now that you have an overview of some of the issues involved in contract law, how about a crash course in the particulars?

THE BOTTOM LINE: **Written, well-drafted, and signed contracts are the *only* way to safeguard your right to receive money, credit, the film's copyright, and, by extension, the entire film property.**

THE CLAUSE COMPANION

You will get more out of the rest the book if you flip to the back and work your way through "Appendix B: The Clause Companion," p. 475. It's a great place to start if you need to get familiar with the function and definition of typical contract clauses. So, if you're uncertain as to the difference between an "indemnification" and an "inducement" provision or need to know how to troubleshoot "defined terms," this is the place to go. In fact, it's a good idea to bookmark this section as a handy guide to understanding the clauses we will refer to in the rest the book.

NOTES

1 For a cogent description of MOUs, see http://internationalbusinesslawadvisor.com/memorandum-of-understanding-and-letter-of-intent-whats-the-difference/ (Accessed October 30, 2020).

2 *Weinstein Co. v. Smokewood Entertainment Group, LLC*, 664 F.Supp.2d 332, 346 (S.D.N.Y., 2009). ("It is fundamental to contract law that mere participation in negotiations and discussions does not create binding obligation, even if agreement is reached on all disputed terms.") However, a court can find that parties have entered a preliminary agreement to negotiate in good faith based on the following factors: "(1) the language of the agreement; (2) the context of the negotiations; (3) the existence of open terms; (4) any partial performance; and (5) the necessity of putting the agreement in final form, as indicated by the customary form of such transactions." Weinstein at 356, internal citations omitted.

3

PROD. CO.

THE PRODUCTION COMPANY AND FINANCING YOUR MOVIE

FILMMAKING IS A BUSINESS

If you're planning on making a film for your own amusement and have no intention of trying to make money from it, you can probably skim through this section. Or if you've already set up your company and have financed your project, jump ahead to "Development," p. 89.

But if you're like most filmmakers, you would like the possibility of selling or licensing your film someday. Whether you hope to see your film in theaters, on cable, Netflix, or on Blu-ray discs distributed worldwide, you'd like some return on your financial investment. It should come as no surprise, then, that if you want your film to make money, you need to treat your production as a business.

This part covers many of the key issues involved in setting up and financing your production company:

- How to choose and create the right type of company. (See "Setting Up the Production Company," p. 43.)
- How to contract with loan-out companies commonly used by actors and other artists. (See "Loan-Out Companies," p. 51.)
- How to select and hire professionals such as lawyers and accountants. (See "Your Professional Team," p. 53.)
- How to ensure your company retains ownership of the film property. (See "The Company as Owner of the Film," p. 49.)
- Learn what kinds of insurance you need to have in place before making your movie. (See "Insurance," p. 59.)
- What to do if someone threatens to sue your company. (See "Cease-and-Desist Letters and Lawsuits," p. 56.)
- Decide how to finance your film and watch out for common financing traps. (See "Financing Your Movie," p. 63.)
- Learn how to structure a successful crowdfunding campaign. (See "Crowdfunding," p. 72.)
- Identify whether you have potential securities law issues. (See "Investors and Securities Laws," p. 67.)
- Raise money from tax credits and other state production incentives. (See "Film Tax Credits and Other Production Incentives," p. 77.)

3

SETTING UP THE PRODUCTION COMPANY

The first step in forming a production company is often to create a *business entity*, such as a limited liability company (LLC), limited partnership (LP), or corporation. There are many advantages to setting up a business entity:

- You can divide the financial risk among several people. The members, partners, or shareholders of a business share in the company's profits and losses.
- Your company is considered a *legal person* and as such can enter into contracts, bring lawsuits, and hold intellectual property rights, such as the copyright to a film.
- You can separate your personal finances from the company's finances.
- You may die someday, but your company doesn't have to. Some kinds of businesses can last forever, and ownership interests in those companies, such as shares or membership interests, can be passed down from generation to generation.

And perhaps most important:

- You can avoid personal lawsuits! If your company breaches a contract or infringes a copyright, it will be the company that will pay the damages, *not* the company's officers or individual members. However, this *limited liability* protection is only offered with certain kinds of business entities (see the information that follows).

BUSINESS CONCEPTS

Limitation of Liability

Some business entities, such as LLCs, corporations, and LPs, allow their members to limit their liability to the amount that they are invested in the company. The members of such companies are not personally liable for the debts or other legal claims against the company.

So, for example, if an LLC or corporation is sued for breach of contract, the most that each member or shareholder can lose is the amount of his or her investment in that company. If the company is bankrupt and has no more assets, the company's creditors cannot collect the company's unpaid debts from the personal assets of its members.

DOI: 10.4324/9781003228479-6

It is important to note, however, that the limitation of liability a company's owners (its members, shareholders, or partners) might enjoy is not ironclad. There are situations in which a court will allow creditors to "pierce the corporate veil" (a term used for LLCs and LPs as well as corporations) and hold the company's owners personally liable for the debts of the company. Courts may pierce the corporate veil:

- If the company's members or shareholders have used the company to commit fraud.
- If the company's members or shareholders have treated the company as their alter egos—in other words, if the members fail to keep proper company records, mix their personal finances in with the assets of the company, or undercapitalize the company, leaving it without sufficient assets to perform normal business functions.

Respondeat Superior

Keep in mind that an employer, such as a production company or producer, is generally legally responsible for the actions of its employees and agents performed during the scope of their duties.[1] This is the *respondeat superior* doctrine.

This means that if your employee gets into a car accident while picking up cast and crew members, your company is responsible for paying the damages from any lawsuit that may arise. Similarly, if your art director infringes somebody's copyright in creating a painting for your movie set, your company is responsible. Furthermore, if your employee or agent enters into a contract with a third party on your company's behalf, your company may be bound by that contract. Here the employee vs. independent contractor distinction really matters. (See "Independent Contractor or Employee?," p. 201.) Liability for the actions of independent contractors, unlike employees, often doesn't transfer to the contracting party, except for:

- Inherently dangerous activities.
- Activities that can't be delegated.
- Where the contracting party exercises control over the manner in which the independent contractor performs the work.[2]

If you have a limited liability entity (such as an LLC, LP, or corporation) and your company hires an employee, your *company*, and *not you personally*, will be responsible for paying the legal damages that result from your employee's actions. On the other hand, if the employee was hired by you rather than by your limited liability business, *you personally* will be responsible for paying all claims, legal costs, and damages.

It is extra work to set up and run a limited liability business, but it may save you from having to sell your house to pay for a lawsuit caused by an employee's actions.

Keep in mind that it's not always clear just who is an employee and who is an independent contractor. And in some states, like California or New Jersey, the default status for a worker is that they are employees, unless you can establish otherwise. Bottom line: you may think you are working only with independent contractors, but you could in fact be managing employees. For help with these distinctions, see, "Independent Contractor or Employee?" p. 201.

TYPES OF BUSINESS ENTITIES

The first step in establishing your business is selecting the type of company you will establish. In the United States, producers typically do business as one of the following kinds of companies:

- Sole proprietorship.
- General partnership.
- Limited partnership.
- C corporation (C corp).
- S corporation (S corp).
- Limited liability company (LLC).

Some business entities, such as the sole proprietorship or the general partnership, do not require any legal formalities to start up. Other kinds of businesses, such as the LLC, the LP, or the corporation (S or C corp), can only be created by filing and registering with the state government.

***TIP:* This book cannot cover all the legal requirements for creating a business; there are entire books devoted to that subject alone. The filmmaker is encouraged to seek an attorney who is experienced in setting up business organizations.**

Sole Proprietorship

The *sole proprietorship* is the default form of business. You are sole proprietor—automatically—the moment you start doing business by yourself, without having formed another kind of company.

There are some advantages to being a sole proprietor:

- Virtually no legal paperwork is involved.
- Decision making is easy because there is only one member of the company—you.

However, there is one *huge* disadvantage to sole proprietorships:

- There is no limitation of liability. If your business is sued, you are sued. If the business defaults on its debts, you personally must pay the debts.

WHAT'S IN A NAME? THE DBA CERTIFICATE

The law begins with the presumption that sole proprietors do business under their own name (e.g., "Sasha Collins"). However, if you want to operate your sole proprietorship under a name that is different from your own (e.g., "Bongo Monkey Pictures"), depending on where you live, you will need to file a *fictitious name statement* with either the city government where your business is located or with county clerk's office. These are also known as *DBA certificates* (which stands for "doing business as"). Additionally, you should also perform business name and trademark searches to make sure that your proposed name is not currently being used by another company.

General Partnership

A *general partnership* may be formed when two or more people work together to own and operate a business for profit. There is usually no government filing required to create a general partnership, although it is recommended that partners have a *partnership agreement* or other contract which lays out the partners' respective rights and duties.

A partnership carries with it certain legal implications, such as:

- *Fiduciary duty*. Each partner has a heightened legal duty of loyalty and good faith toward his or her partners.
- *Unlimited personal liability*. Generally, each partner is personally liable for the debts and obligations his partners incur within the scope of the partnership business.
- *Partnership property*. Unless there is a partnership agreement that says otherwise, the partnership—and not the individual partners—will own all property acquired by partnership funds, brought into the partnership, or contributed to the partnership.
- *Partnership proceeds*. Unless there is a partnership agreement that says otherwise, all partners will share equally in the income and losses of the partnership, regardless of the amount of work they actually perform in the management of the business.

Two or more people who work together in a common business enterprise are often surprised when the court determines that they are in fact partners in a general partnership.

One variation on the general partnership is the limited liability partnership (LLP), not to be confused with the limited partnership (LP) (discussed in a moment). Because the right to form an LLP is often restricted to professionals, such as doctors, lawyers, and architects, it will not be discussed in this book.

CAUTION! Be very careful when deciding to do business as a general partnership! Because general partners must answer for the debts of the other partners incurred during the scope of the business, choosing the wrong partner can get you into personal financial trouble.

For example, Carlos and Kim are general partners in KimCarlos Productions, a start-up motion picture company hoping to find financing for their first motion picture, *Broken Beer Bottle Blues*.

For the film, Kim decides that she needs to do extensive research on the effects of drinking and depression. Over a two-month period, she lives in a neighborhood bar, pounding back expensive imported beer and videotaping herself with the latest high-definition video camera, purchased with an eye toward using it for the film. Needless to say, she runs up quite a bar tab and electronics bill. When her creditors come a-knockin', they can attempt to collect the debt from Kim personally, as well as from KimCarlos Productions ...and Carlos personally, *even though he didn't personally incur the debt.*

Joint Ventures

A *joint venture* is a special type of general partnership, one formed for a particular and limited purpose. Producers and writers often use joint ventures to combine the forces of two existing production companies for a particular project, such as co-producing a film, writing a screenplay, or creating a television pilot.

To have a joint venture, the joint venture partners must have (1) a common business purpose, such as the writing and exploitation of a screenplay; (2) shared profits and losses; (3) an express or implied contract to work together; and (4) an equal hand in controlling the relationship.

Limited Partnership (LP)

A *limited partnership* is a partnership in which *some* of its partners may enjoy liability protections:

- The business is owned by two classes of partners: *general partners* and *limited partners*.
- Only the general partners are personally liable for all the debts of the business. For this reason, there must at least one general partner.
- Only general partners may obligate the business (authorize the business to enter into contracts, authorize loans, settle lawsuits, hire and fire, etc.).

- Limited partners are liable only to the extent of their investments, but they have no management authority.
- A person may be both a general and a limited partner at the same time.
- A state government filing of articles of organization is required to form an LP.
- Though not generally required, a partnership agreement is recommended.

Corporation

There are two types of for-profit corporations: *C corporations* and *subchapter S corporations* (a.k.a. "S corps"). The features common to both kinds of corporations are:

- The corporation is owned by its shareholders and managed by its board of directors and officers.
- Someone can be both a shareholder and a director or officer.
- Directors, officers, and managers legally obligate the business (they can cause the business to enter into contracts, authorized loans, settle lawsuits, hire and fire, etc.).
- All shareholders enjoy limited liability status.
- A corporation is created by filing articles of incorporation with the state government.
- Ownership interests are conveyed by the corporation issuing shares or by a shareholder transferring shares to another person.

Bylaws dictate how the corporation governs itself.

The two big differences between the S corp and the C corp are as follows:

- The C corp can have an unlimited number of shareholders, whereas the S corp is limited to 75 shareholders.
- The C corp is subject to "double taxation," which means that the corporation is first taxed and then the individual shareholders are taxed. S corps, like partnerships, LLCs, and sole proprietorships, are only taxed at the individual income level.

Limited Liability Company (LLC)

The limited liability company, also known as an LLC, has become the business entity of choice for most small film production companies. This is because it has the limited liability advantages of the corporation with the flexibility of a partnership. Its features include:

- The LLC is owned by its "members."
- The LLC may be managed directly by the members (in the case of a "member-managed" LLC) or by managers whom the members appoint (in the case of a "manager-managed" LLC).

- Like the shareholders of a corporation, the members and managers enjoy limited liability status.
- State filing, called the *articles of organization*, is required to form an LLC.
- Taxation is on the individual member level, similar to the S corp, the partnership, or the sole proprietorship.
- The rules dictating how the business is run are largely driven by the *operating agreement*, which is a very flexible and highly customizable contract between the members of the LLC.
- In addition to contributing cash, members may also agree to contribute services to the company, such as directing the movie or writing the script, or to contribute property, such as the copyright to the screenplay, the ownership of the camera, or the use of an editing system.

FORMING AN LLC

- LLCs are typically formed by filing articles of organization with the secretary of state in the state in which your business is located. At this point, you will need to elect whether your LLC is a member-managed or manager-managed LLC.
- An *operating agreement* should be negotiated, agreed upon, drafted by a lawyer, and signed by the LLC's members. The operating agreement usually governs the company's structure, the duties and obligations of each of the company's members, the amount and manner of the members' contributions to the LLC, the way finances are handled, and the way voting is determined. Many states require the operating agreement to be signed within a certain time after the articles of organization have been filed.
- If you are planning on raising money with your LLC (usually done by offering LLC membership interests to investors), you should have your securities attorney carefully review, and preferably draft, your operating agreement. See "Investors and Securities Laws," p. 67.
- Some states have an additional formation requirements. New York, for instance, requires LLCs to publish their formation in two local newspapers within 120 days of formation, designated by the county clerk. Failure to do so results in a suspension of your ability to do business in New York![3]

The Company as Owner of the Film

Regardless of which business entity the producers ultimately form, the filmmakers must conduct all business related to the making of the film in the name of the company. This means that:

- Everything should be paid for out of a company bank account, not a personal bank account.

- The copyright and other film assets should be transferred to and owned by the production company.
- When making the movie, it is the company that should enter into contracts required for making the film. It is critical that you first form your LLC and execute your operating agreement before entering into contracts on behalf of the company! Make sure to sign all contracts in your capacity as company owner, partner, member, manager, shareholder, and so forth. Do not sign them without indicating your company status.

  Example: "Don Simmons, Managing Member, Sprocket Films, LLC."
- The company, and not the individuals who own the company, should rent, own, or purchase all the equipment.
- The company should hire all performers and crew members.
- Records of membership, partnership, or shareholder interests must be meticulously kept. Each owner's percentage of ownership must be tracked and records adjusted as new owners join the company. Ownership interest increases and decreases each time owners invest more capital in the company.

Failure to adhere to these and other critical rules could erase the limited liability protections that the company enjoys.

LOAN-OUT COMPANIES

Loan-out companies are often used by actors and above-the-line crew members. A loan-out company is a company formed for the sole purpose of providing the services of an artist to a production company. Loan-out companies are typically either LLCs or subchapter S corps.

When a production company is hiring an artist who has his or her own loan-out company, the production company is actually hiring the loan-out company, which in turn is providing the services of the artist.

Any contract with that artist must be drafted so that the contracting party is, in fact, the loan-out company. *Example:* "Production Company, Inc., agrees to employ Lender, Actor's Loan-Out, LLC, f/s/o the Performer, Andie Actor."

Additionally, all contracts with loan-outs should include an *inducement clause* at the end of the contract. (See Appendix B, "Inducement Clause," p. 489.)

Keep in mind that loan-out companies should still be required to transfer copyrights and other intellectual property to the production company that engages them under production contracts, just as individuals are required to do. (See "Work Made for Hire," p. 418.) *Example:* Davida Director has a loan-out company, Dodo, LLC. Peanut Pictures, Inc., engages Dodo, LLC, to provide the directing services of Davida for the film *The Laughing Legume*. Under its director's services contract with Peanut Pictures, Inc., Dodo, LLC, must still agree that all work done by Davida is done as a work made for hire with Peanut Pictures as the copyright owner.

If the production company is seeking financing in the form of state production incentives, such as tax credits, hiring an actor or director through their loan-out company may require additional guarantees from those workers that their respective loan-out companies will be registered to do business in the state granting the tax credits. (See "Eligibility Requirements," p. 78).

Loan-out company terminology:

- *f/s/o* is a common abbreviation for the term "for services of."
- *Lender* is typically the defined term that refers to the loan-out company.
- *Inducement* is a promise by the artist that she will perform the services required by the production company as though she were hired directly by the company rather than through her loan-out company.

THE BOTTOM LINE: **Before you open your doors as a production company, you should form a limited liability business to protect your personal assets.**

NOTES

[1] *Texas Integrated Conveyor Systems, Inc. v. Innovative Conveyor Concepts, Inc.*, 300 S.W.3d 348, 368 (Tex. App.-Dallas, 2009) ("Under the doctrine of respondeat superior, a principal or employer may be vicariously liable for the tortious acts of an agent or employee if the acts are within the course and scope of employment").

[2] *Celia Hendricks v. Pepperidge Farm, Inc.*, Holiday Supermarkets, Hellendale Distributors, Inc., and Gale Grunigen, 16 Phila.Co.Rptr. 164, 167 (Pa.Com.Pl. 1987) ("in order to hold a master vicariously liable for the negligence of a servant, it must be shown that the master has the right to control not only the results of the servant's work but also the very manner in which the work is to be done").

[3] N.Y. LLC. LAW § 206.

4

YOUR PROFESSIONAL TEAM

To create your company and get your business up and running, you will need to work with several different types of professionals: attorneys, accountants, and insurance agents and brokers.

ATTORNEYS

One of the first things you should do is establish a relationship with a good entertainment attorney, preferably one with experience in setting up businesses.

Although the process of forming a company is not brain surgery, creating the company's internal documents can be tricky and is a task better left for your attorney. After all, you should be worrying about developing a screenplay, not how to draft the operating agreement provision on tax treatment of membership interests. It is important to bring in your attorney early in the process of establishing your company. No, I'm not shilling for lawyers here. You will actually save money on legal fees by making sure that everything is done right from the beginning rather than bringing in a lawyer after the fact to clean up problems.

Because film and television are highly specialized industries, you will need a lawyer who is familiar with both IP law and with the particular deals and agreements routinely used by production companies in the film and TV industries. In other words, your average general practitioner might not be the best person for the task of negotiating and drafting film contracts.

Some filmmakers prefer to use several attorneys: a general business attorney to help them set up and run their production company and an entertainment attorney to help with the legal issues involved in shooting a movie. Additionally, if a filmmaker is looking to raise money for a film from investors, she should seek the advice of an attorney who has securities law experience. (See "Investors and Securities Laws," p. 67.)

In the beginning, your attorneys can:

- Form your business with the state.
- Prepare internal company documents (e.g., operating agreements, bylaws, partnership agreements, etc.).

DOI: 10.4324/9781003228479-7

- Help you protect movie ideas when they are still in the "concept" phase; see "Idea Rights," p. 91.
- Advise you regarding employees and independent contractors.
- Help you with the company's financing documents and investor solicitation process.

Once your business is set up, the entertainment attorney does most of the heavy lifting during development and pre-production. Your attorneys should:

- Prepare a screenplay clearance report, alerting you to potential legal issues contained in the script (see "Screenplay Clearance Report," p. 162).
- Negotiate or help in the negotiation of key cast and crew agreements.
- Draft the cast, crew, and other necessary contracts.
- Help advise on union issues and labor and employment law.
- Advise you on choosing the most favorable state in which to shoot for your tax credit needs (see "Tips for Selecting a Good Tax Credit State," p. 86).
- Work with the financiers, agents, and lending institutions in setting up and managing escrow accounts.

ESCROW ACCOUNTS

An *escrow account* is a bank account set up for a special purpose, such as holding an actor's or director's salary. The money is deposited in a bank (the *escrow agent*) and released by the bank to the actor or director under the terms stated in the escrow agreement. The escrow account provides a level of reassurance to the actor or director because the money is literally in the bank and can't be taken out by the production company in violation of the terms of the escrow agreement. With increasing frequency, filmmakers are using online transaction settlement services like the well-known Escrow.com.

Be careful here. There have been more than a few "scam" sites set up to dupe the unwary investor. These sites are often elaborately designed to look like the legit escrow sites, but once your investor's money has been wired there, neither you nor they will ever see it again. Make sure to do your research before using an unfamiliar escrow service.

How to Find the Right Attorney

The best way to select the right attorney or attorneys is through references from other producers: go to a popular filmmaking forum, like Stage32.com and ask other producers for their recommendations. You can also contact your state's bar association for help in finding an entertainment attorney in your area or use attorney locator sites, like LegalZoom.com.

Once you've located an entertainment attorney, sit down with them and discuss your project. Don't be afraid to interview the attorney before you retain them. Make sure that they are a good fit for you by asking such questions as:

- How much experience do you have representing production companies?
- How much of your practice is devoted to representing production companies?
- How long have you been practicing law? What law school did you graduate from?
- Have you ever worked in film or video production?
- Have you ever been sued for malpractice or brought up on disciplinary charges?
- Do you have any relationships with distributors?
- Can you estimate how much legal fees will be, given the size and nature of my production?
- Do you charge by the hour, or do you offer any services at a flat rate?

Attorney's Fees

Most attorneys either charge by the hour or as a percentage of the final film budget. It is not unusual for an entertainment attorney to charge $350+ an hour or 2–5% of the film's budget for films that have been funded. Remember, the more information you give them and the more homework you are willing to do, the cheaper it will be for you in the long run.

After the initial conversation with your attorney, they will probably bill you every time they talk to you over the phone—and many attorneys charge in either 6- or 15-minute blocks of time.

Some attorneys can quote you a flat rate for certain services. This means that you will pay a fixed fee for the particular legal service, regardless of how long it takes the attorney to perform that service. Attorneys often charge flat fees for routine tasks such as:

- Copyright and trademark registration application filings.
- Business formation (state filings).
- Simple contract preparation (where little or no negotiation is required).
- Initial consultations.

***TIP:* There are two phases in creating a contract: the negotiation and the drafting. If you are an experienced producer, you may save time and money by negotiating the initial deal points yourself and**

then turning the contract over to your attorney to draft. However, if you are uncomfortable or inexperienced with negotiating a particular deal, you may be better off having your attorney handle the negotiations. Remember to budget for both your attorney's negotiation time and their drafting time.

CRITICAL TIP: It is almost always cheaper to hire an attorney to review, draft, and negotiate a contract than it is to have them litigate a breach of contract. Hire an attorney early on to spot and prevent trouble!

If you simply can't afford an attorney, contact your local Volunteer Lawyers for the Arts Organization. These non-profit organizations provide volunteer attorneys to low-income artists and arts organizations. However, unlike paid attorneys, they are not always "on call" for you. A volunteer attorney may handle a contract or two but is unlikely to take on the arduous task of becoming a production attorney for the entire film production.

VOLUNTEER ATTORNEYS

Organizations that supply pro bono attorneys to filmmakers, such as Volunteer Lawyers for the Arts, can usually be found with a simple Internet search under your state plus the phrase "pro bono attorneys for the arts." They tend to help artists located or doing business in the organization's home state. If you're in:

- California: www.calawyersforthearts.org
- New York: www.vlany.org
- National directory: https://vlany.org/national-directory-of-volunteer-lawyers-for-the-arts/

Check your state bar for the arts-focused pro bono legal organization nearest you.

Cease-and-Desist Letters and Lawsuits

If you are sued, don't panic. Before a lawsuit is filed against you, you will probably receive a "cease and desist" letter from your adversary's attorney. This is a letter that tells you (in your adversary's opinion) what you have done wrong and what rights you have violated. The letter also lets you know what you can do to rectify the problem. *Keep in mind: receiving a cease-and-desist letter is not the same thing as being sued.*

Example: Let's say that you are being accused of infringing the copyright in a painting that you have used as a background prop in a scene in your film. (See "On-Set IP Infringement," p. 293.) The cease-and-desist letter will begin by telling you that the copyright to that painting is owned by your adversary. It will then inform you that you have infringed the adversary's copyright by depicting that painting in your film. In the letter, your adversary will demand that you remove any scenes containing the painting from the film, and they will then probably demand some form of payment for the unauthorized use of the painting. The letter will usually conclude by saying that you have a certain time period within which to respond, and it will threaten further legal action (a lawsuit) if you do not comply with the terms of the letter.

If you have received a cease-and-desist letter, do not try to answer it yourself! Unless you are an attorney, you might not know how to write your response so as to avoid admitting facts that could be used against you in a lawsuit. On more than one occasion, I have personally had to clean up a mess left by a client who has responded to a cease-and-desist letter before contacting me.

Hopefully, if you follow this book's advice, you will already have a lawyer who can respond to the letter that you've received. But if you have not hired a lawyer already, now is definitely the time to do so.

If you don't respond to the terms of the cease-and-desist letter or if you can't reach an agreement with your adversary, your adversary's next step may be to file a lawsuit.

If you are sued, stop talking directly with your adversary. Let your lawyer do the talking. Once you have a lawyer, your adversary's attorney should only talk with your attorney and not to you personally (unless your attorney gives permission). If you can't afford a lawyer, try to get one through your local Volunteer Lawyers for the Arts or similar pro bono legal organization.

ACCOUNTANTS

Managing money, handling taxes, and supervising payroll is a full-time job. If you are dealing with budgets in the thousands of dollars, *especially if that money belongs to other people*, you should hire an accountant.

There are several kinds of accounting projects your production company will face: (1) general business accounting and tax preparation for the production company itself, (2) accounting for the film production, (3) audits of production and production company expenses for lenders and state production incentive agencies, and (4) audits of production company and distributor accounting records for a production's investors. Many producers choose to hire a production office accountant in addition to their company's accountant. The production office accountant keeps track of the *film's* expenses.

The production company accountant keeps track of the *company's* income, expenses, taxes, and accounting to the company's investors.

You should bring in your accountant as early as possible in the creation of your business. Ideally, the accountant and the attorney will work together in forming your company.

In the beginning, your accountant should:

- Get a federal tax ID number (also called an employer identification number, or EIN).
- Set up payroll and income tax withholding for employees.
- Work with your attorney to set up special bank accounts, such as escrow accounts.

As your business begins to take in money from investors, lenders, and other sources, your accountant should:

- Create and keep track of account ledgers recording everybody's investments.
- Help prepare the budgets and other financial documents needed to apply for state film production incentives. (See "Applying for State Tax Credits: An Overview of the Process," p. 82.)
- Organize and prepare cash flow schedules, financing documents, and budgets to submit to tax credit lenders. (See "Working with Asset-Backed Lenders," p. 84.)

  As pre-production gears up, money is spent fast and furiously. Both your business accountant and your production office accountant should be monitoring your cash flow on a daily basis and generating weekly reports. They will need to:

  - Prepare income and expense reports and create budgetary forecasts based on spending patterns.
  - Keep a tight rein on costs, alerting the production company at the earliest possible moment to potential cost overages.
  - Collect and record business expenses and receipts.
  - Disburse payroll, possibly in conjunction with a payroll company, making sure that the appropriate withholdings have been taken into account.
  - Ensure that payroll checks are sent to the appropriate parties. Often this is an agent or a manager who takes his or her commission before passing the remainder on to the actor or crew member. If this is the arrangement, you must double-check that there is language in that cast or crew member's contract permitting you to disburse the funds directly to his or her agent or manager.

The accountants will continue to work after the film is in the can. They will:

- Make sure that the production company is meeting its obligations to investors, lenders, and state production incentive-granting agencies by providing them with budget reports, tax documents, audited statements, etc.
- Track royalties, licensing fees, film rental fees, and other sources of income derived from the licensing of the film property.
- Ensure that an audited final budget is properly prepared and submitted to the state issuing any state tax incentives.
- Prepare the company's tax filings and other tax documents.

ABOVE-THE-LINE AND BELOW-THE-LINE COSTS

A film's production budget is often separated into three broad categories: above-the-line, below-the-line, and other expenses.

Above-the-line costs include all the creative elements and key personnel: salaries and fees for principal actors, producers, writers, directors; literary property acquisition; and screenplay development costs.

Below-the-line costs include other expenses required to put the film in the can: crew labor, equipment rental, studio rental, film stock, art direction, wardrobe, post-production, and so forth.

Other costs include legal expenses, insurance, publicity, contingency, overhead, etc.

INSURANCE

Productions require several different types of insurance. Establish a good working relationship early on with an insurance broker or agent who is experienced in the film industry. The need for insurance comes into play early in the game: for instance, you'll need to have workers' compensation insurance the moment you start hiring employees.

Insurance Coverage

Production companies need to take out entertainment insurance policies covering the following:

General liability. This policy pays third parties for damage caused by the production company. For instance, if you accidentally destroy a stove while shooting on location in a restaurant, general liability insurance should pay this claim.

Workers' compensation. This is a legal requirement if you are employing people. It covers work-related injuries to employees. Along with general liability insurance, this should be one of the first insurance packages you obtain. (See "Labor and Employment Law," p. 199.)

Errors and omissions insurance (E&O). This policy pays claims arising from intellectual property disputes, such as copyright infringement, defamation, trademark tarnishment, idea misappropriation, invasion of privacy, or the like. Although E&O is costly, distribution companies, broadcasters, and exhibitors typically require production companies to have an E&O policy in place prior to distributing or exhibiting a film. Securing an E&O policy often takes a lot of work. To get insurance, production companies are required to provide chain of title to the screenplay, copies of production agreements, proof of intellectual property licensing, and a script clearance report. (See "Chain of Title," p. 159.)

Production insurance packages. Insurance brokers who service the film and television industry commonly offer production insurance packages that include some or all of the following types of insurance:

- *Negative film and videotape.* This insures the exposed film negative or videotape stock against damage. When your footage is damaged, payment on this claim will fund your reshoots.
- *Faulty raw stock and camera.* This insures you against faulty film, tape, and other materials prior to exposure and is usually purchased in conjunction with negative film and video tape insurance, above.
- *Talent insurance: essential element cast.* This will compensate the production company for losses incurred as a result of actor's injuries or illnesses.
- *Equipment insurance.*
- *Car insurance.*
- *Third-party property damage liability.*
- *Props, sets, wardrobe.*

Keep in mind that an insurance company will pay out a claim only up to a certain coverage limit, as defined in the insurance policy. That's why it often pays to purchase the highest limit the production company's budget can afford.

ADDITIONAL INSUREDS

During the course of your film project, you will be adding many *additional insureds* to your insurance policy. These are people or companies whose interests will also be protected by your insurance policy. For instance, when you get a shooting permit from a city, the city will be added as an additional insured to your general liability policy so that if they are sued from someone injured by your film production, the city will be covered by your insurance policy.

Completion Bonds

A *completion bond* is like an insurance policy that guarantees the film will be made on time and on budget. The completion bond is granted by the *completion guarantor* for a fee, which is often around 3–5% of the film's budget.

Prior to issuing a completion bond, the completion guarantor reviews elements of the film package, including the shooting script, the production budget, the shooting schedule, the chain of title, résumés of key cast and crew personnel, production insurance packages, critical production contracts, and bank accounts. Producers and directors may also have to sign agreements stating that they will stay within budget and on schedule and that they have secured all the necessary permissions required for making the film.

Once the completion bond has been granted, the film's investors are protected in that the film is now guaranteed against the production going over budget. Such protection, however, comes at a huge creative cost: if the film begins to go over budget or fall behind schedule, or if other requirements of the completion bond are not met, the completion bond company may seize creative control over the film, substitute its own director and producer, and finish the film in the cheapest and quickest possible way. Needless to say, the threat of being pulled off the job and replaced by a substitute whose primary concern is the film's financial bottom line gives a tremendous incentive to directors and producers to stay on budget and on time.

LOOKING FOR SOMETHING?

LA 411 and NY 411 are great print and online resources to help you find production insurance brokers, completion bond guarantors, expert tax credit accountants, and even an extra roll of gaffers' tape. Check out the following resources:

- https://la411.com/
- https://ny411.com

THE BOTTOM LINE: **You should have your attorneys, accountants, and insurance brokers or agents in place to help you form your business properly. Above all, don't take anybody else's money until you've hired your professional team.**

5

FINANCING YOUR MOVIE

Getting the money: this is, without a doubt, the single trickiest part of making a movie. Unless you're a trust fund baby or a Hollywood movie star, finding the money to make your film will probably be the biggest barrier between you and the realization of your creative vision.

Fortunately, digital technology has enabled producers to shoot professional-quality feature films at dime-store prices. Unfortunately, given the fact that many feature films routinely cost $50 million, that "dime-store price" can still be in the tens to hundreds of thousands of dollars. Furthermore, although digital technology may give you the tools required to capture an image on tape and then edit it, it will not help you pay for locations, cast and crew, hotel and travel, meals, music licensing, rentals, or any of the other items required for making even the smallest film.

If ownership of the final project is not critical, filmmakers may get their films made by co-production agreements or by selling the project to a third party, such as a studio.

- *Co-production agreements*. Co-production agreements allow filmmakers to partner with another entity, usually a production company with studio facilities and/or equipment. In exchange for providing production services and/or studio facilities to the filmmaker, the co-producer receives an ownership position in the film itself. Depending on the deal, that co-producer may own equity in the filmmaker's company, a portion of the copyright in the film, a percentage of the profits of the film, or, most likely, some combination thereof.
- *Selling the film*. Filmmakers often pitch a film package—script, stars, and hot director—to a more established studio. If the studio likes the film, it will offer to buy the package. Sometimes this sale is treated as a co-production, but the copyright to the final project and, therefore, ownership of the film itself invariably rests with the studio. Despite the lack of ownership of the final film, many filmmakers would be more than willing to sell their projects to a major studio. The problem is that you usually have to be an established film producer to attract the interest of a movie studio. However, in both the world of television and online video, it can be easier to strike a deal with a media company in which you shoot your program on their dime (see "Production Services Agreements," p. 178). But, like the movie studio, the television company will usually want to own all the rights to the final film or program.

DOI: 10.4324/9781003228479-8

None of that sits well with most indie filmmakers, who want an ownership position in their films. Therefore, they tend to finance their films in one or more of the following ways:

- Pay for the film out of pocket.
- Incur debt.
- Bring in investors.
- Crowdfund their films.
- Use state production incentives, such as tax credits, to partially fund the film.

PAY FOR THE FILM OUT OF POCKET

This idea is fairly straightforward: cash in some stocks and bonds, sell something to raise money, allocate a portion of your weekly paycheck, or dip into your savings account—in other words, *use money you already have to make the film*. This is the most expensive, most risky, but potentially the most lucrative route; it also has the advantage of being the least troublesome from a legal point of view. Of course, most people don't have hundreds of thousands of dollars lying around with which to fund their movies!

Some producers decide what to write and shoot based on the resources they already have. However, some pictures don't lend themselves to that low-budget approach. Furthermore, if you want to give yourself the best chance of selling the film, you will want to have known actors in your lead roles, and, unfortunately, most name actors would rather stay in a hotel than the director's mom's basement.

DEBT

If you don't have the money lying around, you can always try to borrow it. Loans are either *secured* by collateral or *unsecured*.

- If a debtor defaults on a secured loan, the lender can take the property that serves as collateral for the loan.
- If the debtor defaults on an unsecured loan, the lender will have to sue the debtor to recover the money lent.

Independent filmmakers typically borrow money in several ways:

- *Credit cards*. Credit cards are a form of debt. The high interest rates that credit card companies charge makes them one of the most expensive forms of debt to carry. Yet filmmakers love their credit cards. Whether they're renting lights or paying for an actor's meal, the film's costs are routinely paid for by plastic. Many a tale has been told of filmmakers who pay for their feature films by racking up huge credit card bills and using new cards to float the balance as long as they can. As you can imagine, card-financing success stories are rare, and bankruptcy is often the outcome of this approach.

- *Personal loans.* This kind of loan, typically from a bank, requires you to put up some form of collateral to guard against the possibility of your defaulting on the loan. A second home mortgage is an example of this kind of loan. If you can't repay the loan, the bank takes your car, house, or other collateral you used to secure the loan.
- *Promissory notes.* These are debt instruments that your production company may grant to another company or individual, called the *noteholder* or *lender*. A promissory note is an *unconditional promise to repay* the borrowed amount at a specific time plus interest. Even if your company has not made any money on the film—in fact, even if the company has *lost* money—your company is still obligated to repay the loan. Many filmmakers use promissory notes to avoid securities issues. (See "Investors and Securities Laws," p. 67.) *Be careful here! Promissory notes may still be classified as securities, especially when the lender is given a percentage of the profits of the film.*
- *Borrowing against state tax credits.* Producers who apply for state tax credits can borrow money against the resale value of the credit by working with a lender. (See "Credits into Cash," p. 83.)

EQUITY

As opposed to a loan, which obligates the borrower to return the money loaned (plus interest), an *equity* investment represents an *ownership* interest in the company. Examples of this kind of financing include shares in a corporation, units in a limited partnership, or membership interests in a limited liability company (LLC). If the company fails to make money, so do the investors, but if the company makes money, the investors share in the profits. Since net profits are so important to equity investors and other profit participants, let's spend a little time exploring that concept.

Net Profits

The term *net profits* is often seen as the illusory end product of Hollywood "creative accounting." Yet such profits do exit (sometimes), and investors expect to receive them (most of the time). In fact, the list of people who want to share in a film's net profits (the *net profit participants*) also includes writers, directors, producers, and lead talent. The order of priority in which investors, deferred salaries, and other back-end participants are paid is often called the film's "waterfall," which is a pretty good metaphor: money pouring in to the production company from ticket sales and other receivables "fills up" higher-priority recipients before tricking down to the next group of recipients.

So, what is a net profit? "Hollywood accounting" aside, in most businesses, net profits are simply revenue minus expenses.

> ***Example:*** Glop-Pop Inc. sells $1 million worth of oatmeal-flavored lollipops. The combined costs of producing the lollipops (ingredients, salaries, factory costs, etc.) and running Glop-Pop Inc. (salaries, overhead, taxes, advertising, etc.) are $750,000 per year. At the end of the fiscal year, Glop-Pop declares its net profits: the company has made a net profit of $250,000 on the fibrous confections.

In the film industry, however, net profits are a highly defined term of art that can change from deal to deal. In other words, a film's net profits are what the parties to the contract define them to be, and in the case of a movie studio, that definition can run for 40 pages or more. Furthermore, the formulae for computing net profits differ drastically depending on whether you are a vertically integrated major studio/distributor or an indie filmmaker. Since most of this book's readers are probably indie filmmakers, that is the net profit model we'll emphasize.

Indie Film Net Profits

A threshold question is: what kind of net profits are you talking about—the net from the exploitation of the film by the distribution company(s) or your production company's net profits once all the costs of making the film have been deducted?

It might be helpful to keep two broad definitions in mind as you look at the contracts in this book:

- The *film's net profits* are the monies that are given to the production company after the distributors have deducted their expenses and have been paid their distribution fees. (See "Traditional Distribution," p. 335.) This is also the level at which investors and other net profit participants usually take their cuts. *This is the net profit definition we will refer to most often in this book.*
- By contrast, the *production company's net profits* are what's left over after the production company has paid its investors, the profit participants (those people sharing in the net profits), deferred salaries, and other the costs of making and promoting the film. If such profits exist at all, they're the final pile of money left on the table. It's similar to the net profits in our earlier oatmeal-popsicle example.

Example: Pizzicato Pictures has made its first picture, *Sax and Violins*, a gripping drama about a jazz musician caught up in the rough and tumble world of the chamber orchestra. When it was raising money for the film, Pizzicato promised its investors and screenwriter a portion of the *film's net profits*. The film is distributed and the distribution company deducts expenses and pays itself a distribution fee. The remaining monies are sent to Pizzicato; these monies become the *film's net profits*. the investors and the screenwriter(s) are paid their share from the film's net profits, as are all the deferred salaries; finally, Pizzicato pays the cost of production and all its other debts. Any monies left over become the *production company's net profits*.

For a detailed description of distribution expenses and other deductions, see "How Does the Money Get From a Movie Theater to the Producer?," p. 358.

INVESTORS AND SECURITIES LAWS

From the investor's point of view, an equity investment has tremendous upside potential: if you invest several thousand dollars in a company that is producing a low-budget film that turns out to be as successful as *The Blair Witch Project*, *Super Size Me*, or even *Monty Python and the Holy Grail*, you will reap many times the value of your initial investment. Each one of those films cost a thousand dollars to shoot and yet made millions worldwide.

For the producer, the biggest advantage with this kind of financing is that if the film never sells and the company loses money, there is no obligation to repay the investor's capital. You might be thinking, "Wait a minute; let me see if I understand this: investors put money into my company, and I have no obligation to return that money unless my film makes money? Where do I sign? Better yet, where do I get my investors to sign?"

Before you rush out and offer shares or membership interests in your company, take heed: you must be extremely careful using this kind of financing, because it is quite easy to run into problems with both state and federal securities laws. Despite both your and your investor's willingness to enter into a seemingly fair deal, *failure to adhere to a complex system of state and federal securities laws may expose you and your company to civil and criminal penalties.*

What Is a Security?

When most people hear the word *security*, they think of stock in a large public company, such as a share of Microsoft. Filmmakers are often very surprised when they learn that their efforts to raise money for their films may be violating state and federal securities laws, because what the filmmaker is offering to investors is also considered a security. The reason is that virtually any kind of investment can be subject to scrutiny under these laws.

Under federal law, a security is defined as follows:

> Any note, stock, treasury stock, security future, bond, debenture, evidence of indebtedness, certificate of interest or participation in any profit-sharing

> agreement, collateral-trust certificate, preorganization certificate or subscription, transferable share, investment contract [. . .].[1]

In other words, an investment doesn't have to be labeled "Stock Certificate" to be regulated as a security.

Film Investments as "Investment Contracts"

Producers typically run into problems when they offer membership interests in an LLC, units in an LP, or shares in their corporation to potential investors in exchange for money to make the film (a process called an *offering*). That exchange of money for the expectation of profits may create an *investment contract* and thus a security.

In one famous case,[2] the US Supreme Court held that an investment contract (and thus a security) exists if the following elements are present:

- A person invests money in a common enterprise or scheme.
- That investor expects profits.
- Such profits are derived solely from the efforts of others.

As a result, if a person gives you money for your film project, and if that person is expecting a profit, and if he or she does not participate in the making of the film or the management of the film company, then that person's interest is probably a security.

> ***Example:*** Fred Filmmaker is trying to raise money for his feature film. He has created an LLC and is now seeking investors. The following crew members give him money in exchange for membership interests in his LLC: Carlo the cinematographer, Donna the director, William the writer, Gary the grip, and Peter the production office supervisor. Fred's Aunt Agatha and his barber, Betty, also give him money to invest in the film. Fred does not want to register his membership interests as securities or file for an exemption to securities registration. *Fred may have violated the securities laws.* Because neither Aunt Agatha nor Betty the barber contributed to the running of the business of the LLC or the making of the film itself, their membership interests were securities and as such would need to be registered or exempted from registration.

If the investment is a security, it must be either *registered* with the state and federal governments or *exempted* from registration *before* prospective investors are even asked if they want to invest in the film.

When a production company offers securities without registering or exempting them from registration, the company is probably breaking the law. If *both* state and federal securities laws are not complied with, the filmmaker can risk severe civil and criminal penalties from both the state and federal securities agencies.

CAUTION! You should always seek the help of an attorney who has experience in securities law before you solicit any investors or offer any securities!

Accredited and Nonaccredited Investors

Not only do the securities laws control the registration and exemption of securities, they also regulate whom you can solicit and how. Furthermore, the amount of information that must be disclosed is affected by whether the potential investor is an accredited or a nonaccredited investor.

An *accredited investor* is an officer of the company issuing the securities or a person or institution that has a lot of money. Anyone who is not within the category of accredited investors is, by definition, a *nonaccredited investor*.

The following are among the categories of accredited investors:

- A director, executive officer, or general partner of the company selling the securities.
- An individual, either alone or with his or her spouse, with a net worth that exceeds $1 million at the time of the purchase.
- An individual with income exceeding $200,000 in each of the two most recent years or joint income with a spouse exceeding $300,000 for those years and a reasonable expectation of the same income level in the current year.

If a potential investor is an accredited investor under the securities laws, he or she is presumed to have enough financial knowledge and experience to adequately assess the risks of the investment.

Every nonaccredited investor, however, must be given adequate information with which they can evaluate and make a decision about investing in your film. Nonaccredited investors must be given the same kinds of information that would be given by issuers of a registered security to its investors. The amount of disclosure is actually quite high: investors must be apprised of risk factors, both with the company and of the film industry in general.

CAUTION! As a rule of thumb, proceed with caution when making an offering to nonaccredited investors. You can reduce certain risks by making offerings only to accredited investors. If you do need nonaccredited investor money (and many of us do), be sure to seek the advice of an attorney who is experienced in the nuances of nonaccredited investor financing.

Exemptions From Registration

Registering securities in a film is expensive, time consuming, and usually not necessary for low-budget films. However, if you're not registering your security, you *must exempt* your security from registration. Filmmakers typically take advantage of one of the registration exemptions offered by SEC Regulation D:[3]

- *Rule 504 offering.*[4] Under Rule 504, production companies can offer to sell up to $10 million of securities within a one-year period. There is no limit to the number of investors who can be brought on board with this offering; however, companies generally cannot advertise or solicit the public. A company using this rule must comply with state securities laws and regulations in the states in which securities are offered or sold. Offers should only be made to persons with whom the company has a preexisting relationship.
- *Rule 506 offering.*[5] Under Rule 506, there is no limit to the amount of money that the production company can raise. But the offering must only be made to offerees with whom the company has a preexisting relationship. In addition to the investors being *accredited, financial sophistication* is a prerequisite for all nonaccredited investors. Under Rule 506, the disclosure requirements are the strictest of all.

Companies seeking to exempt their securities from registration must file a Form D notice of exempt offering with the SEC. Regulation D can be found on the SEC website at www.sec.gov/about/forms/formd.pdf.

Note: Form D must be filed within 15 days after the first sale of securities in the offering![6]

NO FRAUD ALLOWED!

All securities offerings, even those exempted under Regulation D, are subject to the antifraud provisions of the securities laws. This means that any false or misleading statement made by the company offering the securities is subject to civil and criminal penalties.

The Offering

These documents contain:

- An investor questionnaire, in which, ideally, the potential investors warrant that they are accredited investors.

- A securities disclosure document, such as a private placement memorandum (PPM), which contains such key points as these:
  - An overview of the company, its managers, and their experience.
  - Risk factors and disclosures—essentially telling investors that film investments are extremely speculative, and they may lose their money.
  - Capitalization—how the company is raising money.
  - How the money raised will be used.
  - How the investors' interests will be affected if other investors contribute money.
  - Description terms of the securities offered.
  - Audited financial statements of the company.
  - An LLC operating agreement or other organizational documents.
  - A "Description of Business" section, which should include information on the state of the film industry and the relevant markets in which you plan to shop your film.
- The script (or at least a synopsis).
- Subscription agreement—the agreement for the sale of securities to the investor.

STEP BY STEP: SECURITIES COMPLIANCE

To issue securities, production companies must:

- Work with an attorney experienced with private placement and securities laws, preferably film offerings.
- Either register their securities or file for Regulation D exemption by submitting a Form D.
- Comply with their state securities laws (called Blue Sky laws) regarding offering securities.
- Identify appropriate investors—the best practice is to make sure all the potential investors are accredited investors.
- Have an attorney create offering documents for your film project.
- Submit offering documents to potential investors.

***THE BOTTOM LINE:* If you plan on raising money from equity investors, you should seek the advice of an attorney who is experienced in securities and private placement law-*before* you even ask anyone if they are interested in investing! This is one area where it simply does not pay to try to do it yourself.**

CROWDFUNDING

Crowdfunding is a way to raise small amounts of money from a large group of people, typically through an Internet crowdfunding portal like Kickstarter. There are two fundamentally different kinds of crowdfunding:

- **Donation-based crowdfunding**

  Also known as "token crowdfunding," this kind of crowdfunding is based on the principle that "backers" to a project are not investors. Rather, they are giving donations to a creator's company in exchange for "rewards." The more money you give, the greater the reward level. Kickstarter and Indiegogo are prime examples of this kind of model. Backers contribute, and all the campaign founders are obligated to give the backers are the rewards promised rather than profits from the film.

- **Equity crowdfunding**

  This is a much newer way to raise money. A crowdfunding campaign is established, much like Kickstarter; however, in this model, the backers are actually investors who stand to share in the profits from your film's success. A word of caution: many of the legal requirements that apply to outright securities issues also apply here (See "Investors and Securities Laws," p. 67). In other words, equity crowdfunding is much more than just "Kickstarter with investors" and more like "Offering securities online."

DONATION CROWDFUNDING BASICS

Raising money on crowdfunding platforms requires the creation of a "campaign": a financial solicitation game plan which combines the elements of a business plan, an ad campaign, a preview of coming attractions, and an e-commerce store. Don't kid yourself that this is quick and easy—it's far easier to set up an Etsy store to sell re-creations of classic sculptures fashioned out of dryer lint than it is to create a crowdfunding campaign. This is real work, and with a little bit of luck, can earn you some real money.

Donation crowdfunding offers benefits outside of just raising money—it can also raise awareness for your film. Backers are often the best promoters for your project—once someone has donated money, they are psychologically incentivized to root for your project and to share campaign updates on social media, potentially bringing in additional backers.

Donation Crowdfunding Platforms

There are numerous donation crowdfunding platforms, but we're just going to concentrate on a few of the biggies: Kickstarter, Indiegogo, and Seed &

Spark.[7] Keep in mind: for *donation* crowdfunding, you CANNOT offer securities. Your backers are not investors—you can't promise them profits—they are donors, who get their "rewards" regardless of whether your film makes money.

- *Kickstarter.com:* probably the most famous of all token crowdfunding sites. Its biggest advantage is that it's so widely known and trusted. Its biggest drawback is that a campaign finance goal must be fully met in order for creators to receive any of the money (if you don't reach your target financial goal, funds are not taken from potential backers). Kickstarter's fee is about 5% of a financed campaign's earnings and a little more than 3% for payment processing fees.
- *Indiegogo.com:* popular with both filmmakers and inventors, Indiegogo allows the campaign creators to choose either an all-or-nothing financing model (like Kickstarter) or a more flexible model, allowing the creators to keep whatever money is raised. For the most part, Indiegogo's fees are similar to Kickstarter's.
- *Seed & Spark:* was set up with filmmakers in mind. It allows you to work with fiscal sponsors, takes 2% of the money you raise, and allows you to keep funds once you've reached 80% of your campaign goal. Note: S&S requires filmmakers to provide "an inclusion statement that clearly articulates how they/their project is increasing representation in entertainment. No crowdfunding campaign can launch without this element."

FISCAL SPONSOR

A fiscal sponsor is a nonprofit organization—typically a 501(c)(3)—that offers to shepherd a project that is part of their organization's mandate by providing fiscal management, oversight, tax exempt status, and other help. It is an especially important relationship for documentary filmmakers making films that reinforce a charitable organization's mission, often allowing the filmmaker to benefit from the charity's donations. While the distinctions between types of fiscal sponsorship relationships are beyond the scope of this book, filmmakers need to be aware of two different fiscal sponsorship categories: **comprehensive** and **pre-approved grant**.

In a comprehensive fiscal sponsorship, the non-profit organization has the most control, assumes the most risk, and is owned by the non-profit company. In a pre-approved grant relationship, the filmmaker accepts grant monies from the non-profit but is responsible for liabilities, tax reporting, and other duties. In a pre-approved grant relationship, the film may be owned by the filmmaker or jointly with the non-profit.

CREATING A CROWDFUNDING CAMPAIGN

As you might imagine, each crowdfunding platform has a slightly different process, but they all require you to go through some variant on the following steps.

1. Create an account with the crowdfunding platform. *Make sure to read through all of the prerequisites.*
   a. For instance, Kickstarter will only allow you to create a campaign if you're in one of 22 countries (the United States being one of them). They all require you to have a bank account and be over 18 years old. Some platforms have restrictions on the type of film content that can be funded.
2. Structure your campaign strategy and reward levels. The greater the donation, the better the reward should be. Keep in mind that most campaigns "stack" rewards, so backers at higher donation levels often get the lower donation level rewards as well. Really do your math here. When deciding how much money you need to raise, make sure to account for the platform and the payment processing fees as well as reward level costs. Some typical rewards filmmakers offer include:
   a. "Special thanks" and backers' names in the credits.
   b. Access to "behind-the-scenes" online production diaries and videos.
   c. Free downloads and physical copies of the finished film.
   d. Experiences like a visit to the set, lunch with the cast, private screenings with the director, walk-on parts, etc.
3. Design explanatory materials for your crowdfunding campaign landing page. DO NOT SKIMP ON THIS. For many potential backers, this will be the first time they are encountering your project; make sure your artwork and text capture the flavor of your project and make everything as clear as possible. Do your research and review other landing pages for other successful crowdfunding campaigns for inspiration. Think of this step as a combination of writing ad copy and giving a pitch.
   a. Perhaps the most important aspect of the crowdfunding campaign landing page is the trailer/explainer video. For film campaigns, this is usually a combination of eye candy footage representative of the project and a personal appeal for funding from the filmmaker. Show your personality, why this film is important to you, how much of your project has already been completed, how the backer money will be spent, your production timeline, and an overview of the (hopefully) awesome rewards the backers will receive.
4. Make sure to keep in frequent communication and engage with your backers so you can turn your bakers into promoters for the project. Stay on top of this! Nothing ruins goodwill faster than "radio silence" from campaign creators.

CROWDFUNDING TIPS AND TRICKS

- Try to have your campaign at least 30% funded *before* it goes live! Have family and friends be ready to donate in the first few minutes/hours of the campaign starting up to demonstrate campaign momentum.
- Put in as much effort into your pitch video as you do to your film itself. You are a filmmaker; people will judge the potential quality of your film on the quality of your pitch video.
- Make sure to pay off your reward levels! Nothing will kill future campaigns faster than poor follow-through on past campaigns.

EQUITY CROWDFUNDING

Thanks to the JOBS Act[8] and the SEC's Regulation Crowdfunding (Reg CF),[9] you can now raise investor capital through websites like StartEngine.com, WeFunder.com, us.trucrowd.com, and other online crowdfunding portals.

But be careful: an equity crowdfunding may look like a Kickstarter campaign, but that is just on the surface. Functionally and legally, it is actually much more like traditional equity investing (see "Equity," p. 65). You will still need to create all the materials for your equity crowdfunding portal landing page (project and reward description, movie trailer, etc.) similar to those created for a donation crowdfunding campaign (see "Donation Crowdfunding Basics," Pg. 72), but additionally you MUST create securities offering documents and deal with securities registration exemptions and the host of other issues critical to a business offering securities.

You will need to work with an attorney to:

- Create a securities offering memorandum and business plan.
- Exempt (or register) your securities with the SEC.
- Create and issue different classes of shares or membership units to investors.
- Comply with myriad other securities regulations for offerings like yours (see "Equity," p. 65).

> ***CAUTION!*** Like any securities issue, you should work with both qualified attorneys and CPAs to help you with the equity crowdfunding process! If you get it wrong, you could face both civil and criminal penalties!

NOTES

[1] Section 2(1) of the Securities Act of 1933, as amended.

[2] *SEC v. W.J. Howey Co.,* 328 U.S. 293 (1946).

[3] www.investor.gov/introduction-investing/general-resources/news-alerts/alerts-bulletins/investor-bulletins-31

[4] www.sec.gov/answers/rule504.htm

[5] www.sec.gov/answers/rule506.htm

[6] www.sec.gov/smallbusiness/exemptofferings/formd (Accessed May 12, 2021).

[7] These are the big ones as this book is going to press and will undoubtedly change over time.

[8] 17 CFR Parts 200, 227, 232, 239, 240, 249, 269, and 274.

[9] www.sec.gov/smallbusiness/exemptofferings/regcrowdfunding (Accessed May 20, 2021).

6

FILM TAX CREDITS AND OTHER PRODUCTION INCENTIVES

PRODUCTION INCENTIVES DEFINED

PROD. CO.

How would you like to be paid by a state (and sometimes also a city) just for shooting there?

Who wouldn't?!

One indispensable method of funding films is through the use of state *production incentives*, the most significant of which are *tax credits*. Broadly speaking, a tax credit is money paid by a state to the filmmaker for shooting (and incurring expenses) in that state. Cities and states offer these incentives to encourage film production within their borders; in fact, production incentives are conditional upon a certain percentage of the film's budget being spent in that state. In addition to tax credits, other state production incentives include relief for sales, gross receipts, use, and other local taxes. Some states also offer *rebates*, which are paid to filmmakers for certain qualified expenses incurred within that state.

Depending on the kind of tax credit, the filmmaker may use this money to:

- Put the money back into the film.
- Borrow money from a lender with the credit as collateral.
- Offset their state tax obligations.
- Sell the credit to someone else to offset that buyer's state tax obligations.
- Put the money toward the film's marketing and promotion.
- Pay back equity investors.

Example: Jared is shooting his film, *The Wrath of Grapes*—a cross between *Sideways* and *Saw*—in which a sommelier turns psychotic killer (tagline: "I prefer red, but not always wine."). His budget is $5 million. If his production company spends $5 million on applicable expenses in a state with a 30% *refundable tax credit*, Jared will receive a check for $1.5 million from that state—even if the film's production company doesn't owe any taxes there!

DOI: 10.4324/9781003228479-9

Production incentives have become one of the most significant factors producers consider when determining where to shoot their films.

—Matthew Savare, entertainment attorney,
Lowenstein Sandler, PC

FINDING THE RIGHT STATE

Most states have active *film commissions* whose function is to encourage in-state film and television production by helping filmmakers find local crew and supplies; recommending production-oriented state policy and legislation; and providing information on state permits, production incentives, and regulations on the use of public land for production. These organizations will be able to give you detailed information on that state's film incentive programs and eligibility requirements and supply you with the forms you need to get the process started. A quick Internet search will give you a state-by-state list of film commissions.

You may also want to search production company payroll websites, which typically have up-to-date information on state incentives. Keep in mind that state production incentives are a volatile landscape. A state that granted favorable production incentives one year may no longer offer them the following year, which is why I've avoided talking about any particular state's incentives in this chapter.

The federal government has also provided a film incentive under §181 of the Internal Revenue Code (IRC). The primary benefit of the federal program is to allow producers and other financial participants to deduct the first $15 million of expenses in the year the expense occurs. However, this IRC section may expire in 2025.[1]

ELIGIBILITY REQUIREMENTS

The states that offer tax credits give them to production companies only for *qualified productions* and only for *qualified production expenses*. For instance, some states won't give a tax credit to a webisode series or short film that is distributed exclusively on the Internet.[2] Nor does stock footage qualify for a state tax credit in some states. So much for being able to pay for your honeymoon with state tax credits by shooting background footage!

Qualified expenses typically include only those costs incurred in the credit-granting state, such as:

- Cast and crew salaries.
- Equipment rentals.

- Lodging, transportation, and other location fees.
- Set construction and production studio rentals.

Example: Jared shoots a sci-fi sequel to *The Wrath of Grapes*, called *Planet of the Grapes*, and needs a jungle location. He decides to shoot in Hawaii (who wouldn't!?) and wants to use the state's tax incentives. He registers for business in Hawaii (a requirement), buys production insurance in New York, and flies to Maui with his cast and crew to shoot. Although the salaries for cast and crew for services rendered in Hawaii may qualify for the tax incentives, the production insurance purchased in New York would not.

In addition to making sure your key expenses are incurred within the crediting state, you need to make sure that you spend a threshold amount within that state.

Example: Fiona is shooting in a state that requires that 60% of the production company's total production expenses be incurred within the state. If she spends 45% of her production budget on equipment and studio rentals outside that state, she will receive no tax credit.

Here are some tips for taking advantage of state tax incentives:

- Some states do *not* let you include above-the-line costs (e.g., salaries for writers, directors, producers, principal cast) as qualifying production expenses.
- State residency requirements are important. You will often qualify for a higher tax credit if you hire state residents rather than an out-of-state crew.
- Many states offer additional incentives for filmmakers who shoot in economically undeveloped areas.
- States often have specific rules regarding loan-out companies, state registration, and local taxes.
- As you might be able to gather, these credits and rebates are designed to bring film productions into a particular state and incentivize them to spend the majority of their production budgets on local crew, cast, and production expenses. For this reason, they may not be applicable for a filmmaker who is shooting all over the map.

QUALIFIED PRODUCTION EXPENSES AND LOAN-OUT COMPANIES

Be careful when an actor or director is working through a loan-out company (see "Loan-Out Companies," p. 51). Typically, payments to loan-out companies, such as an actor's salary, only count toward qualified production expenses if that actor's loan-out company is registered to do business in your production state and files an income tax return in that state. If the actor has a loan-out company, you might need to include a provision in the performer's services loan-out agreement that requires:

1. The loan-out company to register to do business and file a tax return in the production state.
2. Giving your production company the power of attorney to register the loan-out company to do business in the production state if the loan-out company fails to do so within a certain period of time.

TYPES OF PRODUCTION TAX CREDITS

There are three types of film tax credits that are offered by various states, some of which are more beneficial to filmmakers than others:

Refundable credits. If you have applied for and have been accepted by a state that offers filmmakers a refundable tax credit, you will receive a tax refund from that state. That's right, the state cuts you a check equal to a percentage of the qualifying expenses incurred in that state! These funds can reduce your tax liability below zero; in other words, even if you have no state tax liability, you may be eligible to get money back!

> ***Example:*** Moira is shooting her first noir feature, *Lamprey on Me*, about the adventures of a jawless detective in a state which offers a refundable tax credit of up to 40% for filmmakers who spend at least $50,000 on qualified expenses in that state. Assume that after Moira applies for that state's state film production credit, she spends $100,000 in expenses in that state. Once she files her business tax return in that state at the end of the year, she can expect to receive a $40,000 refund check from that state.

Refundable credits are often preferred by both filmmakers and lenders; unlike *transferable* credits (see below), they don't need to be sold to a third party in order for the filmmaker to get their money. As a result, a filmmaker with a refundable tax credit will usually receive more money from a lender than if the filmmaker had a transferable tax credit.

Transferable credits. Transferable tax credits are used to offset state tax liability. They are not refundable. In other words, if you don't owe any taxes in the state in which you shot, you do not get cash back from the state. What you can do, however, is sell the transferable credit to someone else for them to offset their state tax liability. Filmmakers typically use *tax credit brokers* to sell their transferable tax credits for them. Of course, the sale is always for less than the face value of the tax credit; in fact, this credit nets a filmmaker less money than the refundable tax credit because both the broker and the lender take a cut before the filmmaker receives her money (see "Credits into Cash" later in this chapter).

> ***Example:*** Moira is shooting the next film in her detective trilogy, *Lampreying Mantis*, in a state with transferable tax credits of up to 30% for filmmakers who spend at least $100,000 in qualified production expenses within that state. Assume that after applying for the film production credit, Moira spends $100,000 in qualified expenses in that state. Unlike the refund check she received for her first film (which was shot in a refundable tax credit state), this time she will receive a tax credit certificate, which she can either use to offset her state taxes or sell to a third party in that state for them to offset their state taxes.

Nonrefundable and nontransferable credits. This is the least flexible tax credit arrangement: filmmakers don't get a refund and don't get to sell their credits.

All they get to do is to offset their own or their production company's state taxes with these credits. However, for a company that does business in a state over several years, these nonrefundable and nontransferable tax credits can carry over from year to year.

> ***Example:*** Moira is shooting her last crime thriller, *Predator and Lamprey*, in an abandoned lighthouse in her production company's home state. However, her home state only offers nonrefundable and nontransferable credits of 5% for filmmakers who spend at least $75,000 on qualified production costs in that state. She spends $100,000 in qualified production costs. When she files her state tax return and attaches the Tax Reimbursement and Credit Certificate she's received from the state's Department of Economic and Community Development, she will receive a tax credit of 5%, which she can use to reduce her state taxes by $5,000. She must use this credit herself and cannot sell this credit to any third party.

By now you're probably thinking: "Free money from the state? What's the catch?" The catch is that due to the popularity of these programs, states can quickly run out of funds, so it pays to get applications in early in the state's fiscal year. Credits are usually offered on a first-come, first-served basis. Furthermore, state tax credit programs are in constant flux, and a state that offered a great incentive one year may end up curtailing its program simply because popularity among filmmakers has drained the tax credit funds dry. It's a constantly changing market, one that requires serious attention to financial detail and reporting. Check the production incentives of your state and its neighbors before deciding where to shoot.

APPLYING FOR STATE TAX CREDITS: AN OVERVIEW OF THE PROCESS

Because the processes and types of incentives differ from state to state, a detailed account of each state's procedures is not possible here. However, the following steps are fairly common:

1. Research the tax and rebate incentives in the states in which you may be shooting. If those states offer transferable tax credits, you might want to get in touch with a tax credit broker to understand what the market is like for selling the credits.
2. Contact the state film commission offices in states in which you will potentially be shooting. They can supply you with information on that state's production incentive programs, how to apply for them, and which state agency administers them.
3. Most states have a minimum budget threshold and, for big-budget films, a cap on the amount of credit available. Prepare a detailed budget that lists the qualified expenses you intend to incur in your target state. Make sure to include details on hiring local cast and crew.
4. States have requirements detailing the percentage of a production or minimum number of shooting days that must take place in the target state. Prepare a shooting breakdown that lists the in-state locations and facilities where you plan to shoot to demonstrate the percentage of the shoot that will take place in-state.
5. You will be asked to submit an application form, sometimes no less than 10 days in advance of shooting. The application form will probably ask you to submit:
    a. A budget, as in Step 3, that lists the qualified expenditures.
    b. A shooting schedule.
    c. Production facility and location information.
    d. List of wages for both resident and nonresident employees; some states exclude above-the-line expenses (writer, director, producer, speaking performers) from the definition of qualified expenses.
    e. Evidence of a completion bond, if needed.
6. After you submit the initial application, you may be required to schedule an appointment to discuss your application. It's important to note that you may be required to have the producer and the production office accountant at the meeting.
7. Some states will issue a "conditional approval" of the film. You will receive a certificate of conditional eligibility from the state. Note that this approval is *conditional* in nature, and if you fail to adhere to the very specific tax credit budgetary requirements, *your approval will be revoked, and you will be responsible for repaying any monies loaned to you by lenders (see*

below) based on the tax credit. You may also end up forfeiting your film itself if the film's copyright was used as collateral to secure the loan.

8. Once you've received conditional approval, you'll be required to notify the state production office and keep them updated on your:
    a. Shooting schedule.
    b. Cast and crew call sheet for first day of production.
    c. Current budget.
9. Once the film has wrapped, and typically after post-production has also been completed, you will need to submit a final application to the state office in charge of administering the film incentive program. This typically includes:
    a. State government final application tax credit forms.
    b. Finalized versions of the following:
        - Accounting for the film.
        - Film budget.
        - Shooting schedule.
        - Cast and crew list.
        - Payroll reports.
    c. An independent audit.

Failure to submit all the proper materials at this stage can cause you to lose the film tax credit that you worked so hard to gain!

Make sure to keep copies of all records, expenses, reports, and receipts. State film offices may audit you up to several years after your production has wrapped, and many states require an audit. Be sure to hire production accountants who are familiar with the processes of the states in which you are shooting, since nuanced rules could disqualify certain expenses. This point cannot be emphasized enough!

CREDITS INTO CASH

Having an entitlement to a future tax credit is all well and good, but how do you turn it into cash you can use *now* for your production? Your quickest option is to *borrow* money against the resale value of the credit by working with a lender such as a bank or an *asset-backed lender* (ABL). Both these types of lenders evaluate your tax credit and offer you less than the face value of the credit (hey, they have to make money, too). ABLs may offer a loan of only 80% or 90% of the credit's value, whereas a bank will charge interest and processing fees. Be prepared to pay either lender's legal expenses as they set their legal team to analyzing your tax incentive and preparing the loan documents.

You may get more money borrowing against a rebate or refundable tax credit rather than a transferable one. The reason is simple: you get the rebate or refund, and the bank deals directly with you. For a transferable credit, if you can't use it, you have to sell it to recoup its value. As a result, the lender may lend against 86% of the tax certificate's value. (Production companies often receive 82–88% of the face value of the credit from the sale.)

> ***Example:*** Tomislav is producing the film *The Naked Mole Rat's Revenge* in a state which offers a 20% *transferable* tax credit. He submits his paperwork and receives a provisional notice that his tax credit will be $200,000, which he brings to an ABL to borrow against. The ABL agrees to lend him 90% of the value of the tax credit certificate, but because the tax credit is transferable, it will have to be sold to a taxpaying entity in that state, which in turn will also pay less than the face value of the tax credit certificate (perhaps only 88%). As a result, the ABL will lend Tomislav 90% against the already discounted purchase price of the tax certificate, for an up-front amount of 79.2% of the credit (88% × 90% = 79.2%). So, if he shoots in that state, he will receive a loan of $158,400 for his $200,000 tax credit certificate.

Now, for contrast, let's assume that Jarrett had shot in a state where the tax credit is a *refundable* 20%. Tomislav receives his $200,000 tax credit certificate. Because the tax credit is refundable and not transferable, it doesn't have to be sold to a third party in order for the ABL to get its money. Now the ABL might issue a loan of 90% of the value of the tax certificate, with no third-party deductions. Here's the breakdown: Tomislav gets a loan of $180,000 (90% × $200,000), as opposed to the $158,400 he would have received for shooting in the transferable tax credit state . . . more than enough for to spend on those CGI mole rat effects he really wanted!

WORKING WITH ASSET-BACKED LENDERS

ABLs are often more flexible and quicker in their lending policies than banks and will usually lend against both transferable and refundable tax credits, whereas a bank may only lend against a refundable credit. It all depends on where you are shooting, however; if you are shooting in Canada and using Canadian tax credits, a bank may be the way to go, since banks have largely dominated Canadian tax credit lending for years.

The ABL Lending Process

1. It's a good idea to establish a relationship with a lender early on. ABLs may help you with the initial stages of selecting a favorable tax credit issuing state. You should approach them at least two to three months prior to principal photography.
2. You will be asked to fill out a financing application. Be prepared to supply the lender with the following information:

a. Production company contact info (as well as any co-production companies).
b. Detailed information on the production itself:
   - Shooting schedule, expected start and wrap dates.
   - Locations.
   - Above-the-line crew.
c. Contact information for the production company's:
   - Bank.
   - Production attorneys.
   - Completion guarantors, if any.
   - Insurance agents.
d. In addition to the application, you will likely be asked to provide:
   - A complete budget.
   - A detailed financing plan.
   - Cash-flow schedule.
   - Your shooting schedule.
   - Biographies of your producer and director.
   - Correspondence between the production company and the state film incentive program.
   - Synopsis of the project.
   - An estimate of the amount of tax credits being sought.

3. The ABL will review your application and materials, and if you pass muster, it will issue a *term sheet* detailing the conditions of the loan. Make sure to have your attorney review this document carefully. You may also be asked to give the ABL a deposit to cover its legal expenses.
4. If you are shooting in a transferable tax credit state, the ABL usually has relationships with tax credit brokers and will facilitate the process between you and the broker.

BE ORGANIZED AND PREPARED

Nothing will kill a potential lender's interest in you more quickly than disorganization. This is a process that requires you to work closely with accountants, financiers, lenders, and maybe brokers. It simply can't be done at the last minute or "by the seat of the pants."

Remember, lenders aren't lending you money because they have a passion for your film. They are lending you money because they believe they can recoup *even more* money from the tax credits that you will receive when you successfully comply with the issuing state's requirements. If the lender gets the sense that you may fail to qualify for the state tax credits, either through your mismanagement or your lack of understanding of qualified production expenses, they will not lend you money. And nothing gives them the willies faster than a disorganized producer.

Remember:

- You should work with a qualified accountant, preferably one with experience in film production and tax credits.
- Your cash-flow schedule, financing documents, and budget should all line up. Nothing is worse than showing a lender a budget of $2 million and a cash-flow schedule of $1.75 million.
- You need to really understand the qualified production expense rules of the incentive-granting state. For instance, some states require you to order camera equipment rentals through a local vendor to qualify as a production expense. If you receive a loan from the lender and then fail to qualify for the state tax credits or you have them revoked, *the lender may be able to seize your film as collateral to satisfy the debt.*

TIPS FOR SELECTING A GOOD TAX CREDIT STATE

From a tax credit perspective, there are a number of factors you want to consider when selecting the best states in which to shoot:

- *The nature of the tax credit itself.* Refundable? Transferable? Nonrefundable and nontransferable? Bottom line: are the tax credits sellable? In other words, does your production company need to use them itself or can it sell them to a third party?
- *Are the tax credits subject to recapture?* What happens if someone buys your tax credits, and after the purchase, the credit-issuing state discovers that you've been fast and loose with your accounting or were just plain mistaken about how much money you spent in qualified production expenses? The answer depends on the state: in some states, your credit may be subject to *recapture* by the issuing state, which will revoke the credit. So, not only can the state bring a claim against you, but so can the purchaser, who

has effectively purchased a worthless tax credit. Since there is an inherent risk on the part of the purchaser in recapture states, film tax credits sell for less money in these states. Other states are "clean states," meaning that a good-faith purchaser for value of your film tax credit gets to keep the film tax credit you sold them while the issuing state is bringing you up on charges of fraud.

- *Is it the right location?* Don't lose sight of the fact that your audience will not see your tax credits; they will only see the location where you decided to shoot. You might like the Massachusetts tax credit program, but if you're shooting a western, you might find it hard to make Martha's Vineyard look like Montana's badlands. You also need to take into account whether it is worth the cost of transporting and lodging cast and crew just for the sake of a few more percentage points of tax credit.
- *Is my film's content right for the state?* Some states scrutinize the content of the films seeking state production incentives to ensure that they portray the location state in a favorable light. If a state's laws stipulate that "movies under-written by the state should help promote it as a tourist destination,"[3] a movie that (1) paints a negative picture of the location state or (2) contains patently offensive material might be rejected for production incentive funding by that state's film commission. For instance, the Michigan film commissioner rejected the film *The Women*, in large part because it depicted "realistic cannibalism."[4] I guess some states don't like films about people who love people. . .
- *Other incentives.* In addition to state tax credits, some states offer other production incentives such as grants to filmmakers and waiving of sales tax.
- *Contact the state film offices.* Most states have a film office set up to encourage production in that state. They're wonderful resources to find up-to-the-minute information about that state's film incentives.
- *Consider federal incentives as well.* Currently, the federal government offers a tax incentive[5] for investors who invest in films with budgets that range between $1 million and $20 million and with at least 75% of its production completed within the United States. This incentive allows an investor to deduct money invested in a qualifying film from the investor's passive income earned in that same year.

> Incentives change every day. It is important to work with people who have up-to the minute information and the experience to help a producer select the right combination of incentives that will best serve the film's production and financing needs and maximize the upfront credit amount.
>
> —Michael Hansen, managing director, Three Point Capital, an asset-backed lender

NOTES

[1] See 26 U.S.C. §181(g).

[2] However, see www.ep.com/production-incentives/jurisdiction-comparison/?menu=Production%20Incentives%20Home

[3] See Michael Cieply "State Backing Films Says Cannibal Is Deal-Breaker," *New York Times*, June 15, 2010, at www.nytimes.com/2010/06/15/movies/15credits.html

[4] Id.

[5] Internal Revenue Code: Sec. 181: Treatment of Certain Qualified Film and Television Productions. See www.dga.org/~/media/Files/Initiatives/DGAIFTASection181Brochure.ashx (Accessed May 15, 2021).

4

DEVELOPMENT: CREATING, ACQUIRING, AND MANAGING THE FILM PROPERTY

During development, ideas and concepts are turned into screenplays; literary rights are acquired; life stories are purchased. In short, this is the stage of a film's life cycle in which the film property first takes shape.

No matter what kind of audio-visual production a filmmaker wants to make—a narrative film, a television commercial, a documentary, an industrial video—the filmmaker will need to have the legal right to tell that particular story. To put it bluntly, this is one of the most important legal issues facing filmmakers: neither a distributor nor exhibitor will pick up a film for distribution or exhibition if the story rights have not been obtained! Even if you plan on distributing your film by yourself on YouTube, you will need have all the necessary rights to distribute the film.

Of critical importance during development is the protection of the copyright in the screenplay. You need to make sure that the copyright is properly registered, that the script does not use anybody else's copyrighted material without permission, and that any writers you have hired have properly transferred their copyrights to your production company.

When you are collaborating with another writer, hiring a screenwriter, or acquiring literary, life, or other rights, you must have signed contracts. A handshake deal will not legally transfer the copyright or create a work made for hire.

This section covers legal issues concerning:

- How to protect rights in ideas. (See "Idea Rights," p. 91.)
- Writing the screenplay by yourself. (See "Writing the Screenplay by Yourself," p. 105.)
- Collaborating with other writers. (See "Writing Collaboration," p. 108.)
- Acquiring the rights to somebody's life story. (See "Life Story Rights," p. 150.)
- Optioning and purchasing a screenplay. (See "Acquiring Screenplay Rights," p. 121.)
- Adapting a screenplay from another work. (See "Screenplay Adaptations," p. 142.)
- Hiring a screenwriter. (See "Hiring a Screenwriter," p. 136.)
- Protecting the copyright in your screenplay. (See "Chain of Title," p. 159.)

7

IDEA RIGHTS

Protecting Your Pitches and Avoiding Idea "Theft"

It's a producer's worst nightmare: you pitch an idea to a studio, and they pass. Then a couple of years later, you see some variant of your idea on the big screen . . . released by the same studio to whom you pitched. How can you avoid this? If you've been following along with this book so far, you may be tempted to think the answer lies in copyright law. Buzz! Wrong answer.

Don't misunderstand me: without a doubt, a copyright is the best way to protect a *screenplay* from being stolen. However, a filmmaker may have only an *idea* for a film or television program—a concept that has yet to be turned into a screenplay—and copyright law *does not* protect ideas. In fact, even though they are valuable to the filmmaker, ideas can be very hard to protect *legally*. As the United States Supreme Court wrote over a hundred years ago: "The general rule of law is, that the noblest of human productions—knowledge, truths ascertained, conceptions, and ideas—become, after voluntary communication to others, free as the air to common use."[1] This is because the law sees artistic ideas as building blocks for expressive works. Anyone who had exclusive rights to an idea would have a monopoly over that idea, which would frustrate the policy of copyright law, which is to encourage authors in the creation of new expressive works.

Although we can't use copyright law to safeguard our ideas, we still have one superpower in our arsenal that will help us: the Almighty Contract.

In general, here's how it works: if someone agrees not to exploit your idea and then they do, you may be able to sue them for breach of contract.

That's the basic idea, anyway. But from here on it becomes more nuanced. For instance, the kind of contract you have matters (**express** or **implied**), as does when you enter the contract (**pre-disclosure** or **post-disclosure**), as does the *novelty* of your idea. But wait, there's more: states, to differing degrees, offer contract protection for ideas, but because it's on a state-by-state basis, the laws differ drastically throughout the country. Make sure you know which state's law controls your contract for the protection of your pitch.

Confused? I don't blame you. We will try to demystify this complex subject in this chapter. The big takeaway is that certain kinds of contracts can

DOI: 10.4324/9781003228479-11

sometimes protect movie and television pitches. I'm not going to sugarcoat it: it's far easier to protect a fully expressed screenplay via copyright than it is to protect a pitch through contract.

HELPFUL DEFINITIONS

A **pre-disclosure agreement** is a contract you make with a party before you tell them your idea.

A **post-disclosure agreement** is a contract entered into with the party after they have heard your idea.

An **express contract** is one in which all the elements and terms of a contract (offer, acceptance, consideration, etc.) are specifically stated. An express contract is usually, but not always, in writing.

An **implied contract** is an agreement that arises based on circumstances or by the actions or behavior of the parties. In other words, the contract may be created because the parties are acting as though a contract is in place, even though the terms of the agreement were not fully discussed. When you pitch an idea to somebody in a business meeting, and the industry practice is that people who pitch ideas are expected to be paid for them, you may be entering into an implied contract with the person to whom you're pitching the idea.

For more on the elements of a contract, see "The Contract Engine," p. 29.

DEGREES OF CONTRACT PROTECTION FOR A PITCH

Say you want to pitch your idea for a new comic book series to a production company. Let's take a look and see how and when your idea might be protected when it might not.

No Contract

Let's start first with the worst-case scenario. You don't have a contract with somebody, and you tell them your idea. Then they then decide to make their own film based upon your concept. Unfortunately, you have an almost impossible task ahead of you if you try to sue them for misappropriation of your idea (using your idea without permission): you would have to prove to a court that your idea is so unique and original that it should be treated as your private property. However, in practice, this often amounts to having to prove that your idea was so unique that no one else in the world had have ever conceived it! As you can imagine, that's the very definition of a losing proposition.

Express Pre-Disclosure Agreements

Okay, now that we've gotten the most depressing scenario out of the way, let's turn to a few ways in which your concept might be protected. These involve agreements between you and the person you're pitching to that are entered into *before* you disclosure idea. The timing on this is critical.

Let's say you're about to pitch your film idea to a production company, but before you tell them your concept *you both discuss and agree to specific contractual terms* under which you will disclose your idea, including:

1. That they will treat the idea that you're about to disclose to them as your proprietary property,
2. They will not use it or disclose it to others without your permission, and
3. If they exploit your idea, they will pay you an agreed-upon amount of money by a certain date or triggering event (like the movie's release).

Congratulations! You may have formed an express pre-disclosure contract with the production company. Feel free to pitch away. If the production company uses your concept after they've agreed not to, you can sue them for breach of contract. However, they may still have some defenses against your breach of contract suit, such as:

1. **Independent development**: they had developed an idea similar to yours through independent means (in other words, they didn't copy your idea but got it another way).
2. **Generic**: your idea was so generic that, as a matter of law, it should not be protectable. After all, they didn't know what the idea was before they heard it. If your pitch is "Two people meet, fall in love, tragic flaws keep them apart until the big climax when they come together and live happily ever after. Oh, and they're superheroes!" it's likely that your pre-disclosure agreement will fail because it is so generic the production company is not getting anything of value for its promise to pay you for the idea.

And stop and think about this for a moment. How likely is it that a production company is going to expressly agree not to exploit your idea no matter what it is before they've heard it? Furthermore, most people just go to pitch meetings and pitch their idea without ever talking about contracts beforehand. Therefore, to the extent that there is a contract in place, it is often an implied-in-fact contract.

The NDA and the Submission Release

Two common types of written express agreements which deal with idea disclosure are the non-disclosure agreement—also known as an "NDA"—and a submission release form. These contracts are virtually opposites of each other.

Someone who signs an NDA is promising not to disclose or exploit an idea they receive unless they have a written agreement with the party telling them the idea.

Someone who signs a submission release form, by contrast, is giving up the right to sue for idea misappropriation or breach of contract if an idea similar to theirs is used by the receiving party. Production companies often require writers and producers to sign a submission release form before they're allowed to pitch an idea to them.

Nondisclosure Agreements

If possible, the filmmaker should have the production company sign a *nondisclosure agreement* (NDA), which at a minimum should contain the following terms:

- **Proprietary information**. The production company agrees that the filmmaker's pitch is unique, valuable, and the filmmaker's proprietary property.
- **Confidentiality**. The production company must agree to keep the disclosed ideas confidential. It is standard to extend to the production company the ability to disclose the pitch to its professional advisors, like attorneys and agents, and to further circulate it within the production company itself.
- **Definition of Confidential Material.** The confidential information is usually defined in terms of both (1) those materials, oral and written, that a filmmaker submits to the production company and (2) those materials the production company itself creates in order to evaluate the project.
- **Exclusions from the Definition of Confidential Material.** This section defines what is *not* considered confidential or proprietary to the filmmaker (and thus is unprotected by the contract). Typically *excluded* from the definition of confidentiality in this section is:
  - Material that the filmmaker discloses to others on a nonconfidential basis.
  - Material that the production company can show it developed independently of the filmmaker.
  - Material that becomes publicly known.
  - Material that is in the public domain (e.g., clichéd concepts, common plots, stereotypical characters, etc.).

- **Agreement to Evaluate**. The production company agrees that it is receiving the confidential information for the purpose of evaluating the material for possible production. If the production company passes on the project, it agrees not to use the material. If the production company wants to use the material, it must agree to enter into an agreement with the filmmaker for its purchase and/or exploitation.
- **Representations and Warranties of Authorship and Indemnification.** The filmmaker must promise that they are the sole creator of the idea and that they will indemnify the production company if the production company is sued by somebody else laying claim to the idea.

REALITY CHECK

A filmmaker generally does not have the leverage to make a Hollywood studio sign an NDA; in fact, handing an NDA to a development executive prior to your pitch will almost certainly end the meeting. However, filmmakers may be able to convince a smaller production company or a local advertising agency to sign one.

As a former development executive myself, I also need to point out that a studio's aversion to filmmakers' NDAs is not because production companies and studios are in the business of ripping off artists, after all, it's far cheaper to pay an artist for an idea than to litigate. It's precisely *because* the production company wants to avoid frequent litigation that's behind their aversion to NDAs. A development executive may hear dozens of pitches a day, five or six days a week. You can be sure that whatever concept you're pitching, they've likely heard a variation on that theme. What makes a studio or production company want to buy a pitch is rarely the concept alone; it's the combination of a number of factors, including their perception of the filmmaker's ability to deliver the film or the show, any elements the filmmaker may have attached the project, the strength of the screenplay or treatment, the potential budget for the project, how competitive the market is for similar properties, the value of the filmmaker's identity (and how popular they are online), and, finally, the concept.

So, in practice, NDAs are rarely used by when pitching to the larger studios. More typically, the studio or production company has the leverage in the situation and will require filmmakers unrepresented by agents and attorneys to sign a *submission release* before hearing the filmmaker's pitch. Which is pretty much the exact opposite of the NDA.

Submission Release

The submission release is a document that largely exonerates the production company if it exploits an idea similar to the one the filmmaker is pitching. A filmmaker signing a submission release generally agrees to the following:

- **No Liability for Exploiting Similar Ideas**

The production company will not be held responsible if it exploits a similar idea to the one which the filmmaker has pitched. *Note:* In film contracts, the term *exploits* usually means "to develop or sell a property" (e.g., a production company exploits an idea by commissioning a screenplay based on it).

- **No Contractual or Fiduciary Relationship**

The filmmaker agrees that she has not entered into a contract with the production company for the sale of the idea, nor is there a fiduciary relationship between the parties that would require the production company to act only in the filmmaker's best interests.

- **Representations and Warranties of Authorship and Indemnification**

The filmmaker must promise that she is the sole creator of the idea and that she will indemnify the production company if the production company is sued by somebody else laying claim to the idea. (See Appendix B, "Representations and Warranties" p. 482.)

- **Free Use of Nonprotected Property**

The production company may freely use anything the artist discloses that is not protectable as "literary property." Because ideas are not protected by copyright, and the production company has not agreed to a contract that protects the filmmaker's ideas, this paragraph may mean that the production company is free to use any ideas pitched or disclosed by the filmmaker!

THE BOTTOM LINE: **Once you start telling people your idea without the benefit of a contract, you may have given up any property right you have in that idea**.

The Implied-in-Fact Pre-Disclosure Contract

This is the scenario in which you pitch your idea to a production company, but no agreement regarding your idea is fully discussed first. Or maybe you talk about some aspects of the business relationship but not all of the key terms. However, industry practice suggests that creative types, such as yourself, only pitch ideas to production companies if there's an expectation that if the production company uses your idea, you will be compensated. Now,

even though you didn't discuss it, you may be able to argue that there was an implied-in-fact contract for the protection of your idea. However, for a court to find an implied-in-fact contract, you'll have to show:

1. "That you submitted an idea to the production company, which the company received; and
2. That *before* you submitted your idea to the production company, you clearly conditioned your disclosure upon the company's agreement to pay for any of your ideas that the company used; and
3. That the company knew, or should have known, this condition upon which the disclosure was being made before the disclosure was made; and
4. That the company voluntarily accepted the submission on your terms and thereby impliedly agreed to pay you the reasonable value of any of your ideas it used; and
5. That in production of the film, the production company actually used your ideas; that is, that the project was based substantially upon your ideas rather than on the company's own idea(s) or those from any other source(s); and
6. The ideas the company used had value."[2]

Now here's where the states start to disagree. In California, if you prove these elements, that may be enough to support a pre-disclosure implied contract for the protection of an idea. However, across the country in New York, an additional element is needed: **novelty**.

New York law, and that of many other states, require that your idea also be novel, i.e., *new* and *unique* as opposed to a mere rehashing of generic concepts.

The "Novelty" Requirement

Many states agree that to receive any protection at all, an idea must be novel, i.e., new and unique,[3] if it is to be protected by an implied contract. Let's take a look and see how this works in practice. Say a screenwriter wants to pitch an idea for a movie to a production company.

If there is a contract between the creator and the production company for the protection of the idea, the creator's idea only needs to be novel *to the production company* or other party who is hearing the idea for the first time. In other words, as long as the production company had never heard this particular idea before, the fact that other companies might have heard it would not destroy the contract between the creator and the production company. Again, the important thing is the contract is entered into *prior* to the idea being disclosed.

However, without a contract between the creator and the production company, the creator must prove that his idea was so novel that no one else in the world had ever conceived of it!

To make things even tougher, some ideas are deemed so lacking novelty that even a contract won't protect them.

Determining an Idea's Novelty

So how do you figure out whether an idea is novel enough to be protected? One New York court[4] listed the following factors as among those courts will use to judge the novelty of an idea:

- The idea's specificity or generality; i.e., is it a generic concept or one of specific application?
- How common an idea is; i.e., how many people know of this idea?
- How unique the idea is; i.e., how different is this idea from generally known ideas?
- The commercial availability of the idea; i.e., how widespread is the idea's use in the film and television industries?

However, as the court pointed out, an idea will not be considered novel if:

- It is merely a clever or useful adaptation of existing knowledge, or
- It is merely a variation on a basic theme.[5] For instance, the "idea of a reality television show where people compete for a prize is a basic staple of modern television programming."[6]

Furthermore, just as in copyright law, the studio or production company will not be liable to the writer/producer if it can prove that it came up with its similar concept through its own initiative or through wholly independent means.[7] (See "The Doctrine of Independent Creation," p. 442.)

NOT EVERY GOOD IDEA IS A "NOVEL" IDEA

One well-known case involved the idea for *The Cosby Show*.[8] A producer pitched NBC on the idea of "combining the family situation comedy theme with an all-black cast." NBC turned him down and then went on to develop *The Cosby Show*. When the producer sued, he lost. The court stated that the producer's idea was not novel and therefore not subject to legal protection from unauthorized use because he had "merely combined two ideas which had been circulating in the industry for a number of years—namely, the family situation comedy, which was a standard formula, and the casting of black actors in nonstereotypical roles."

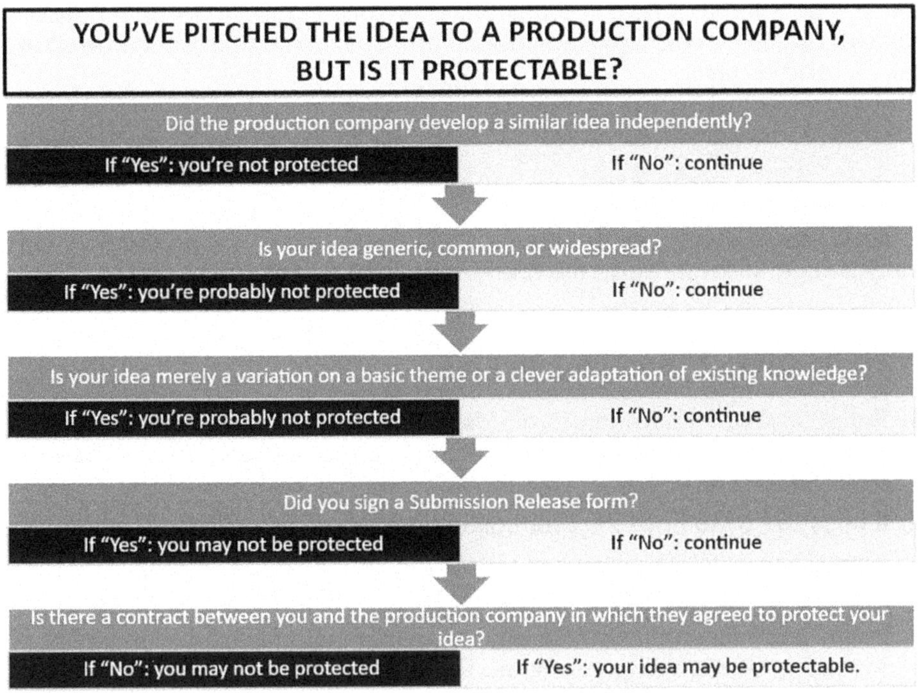

Post-Disclosure Agreements

And, finally, there's the scenario in which you pitch an idea to somebody, and *after* they hear it, they agree to compensate you if they exploit it. In other words, they enter into a contract with you after they've heard the idea: a post-disclosure agreement. In this scenario, courts don't really look at novelty, which makes sense: since the receiving party has already heard your idea before entering into a contract, they can judge its novelty and value for themselves. For these reasons, courts often uphold post-disclosure agreements.

BUSINESS ISSUES: FINANCES AND COSTS

Whether a filmmaker can demand that a production company sign an NDA prior to the filmmaker's disclosure depends on the filmmaker's leverage.

Generally, neither a submission release nor an NDA requires one party to pay the other as part of that contract. However, in the case of any implied or express contract that the filmmaker may try to create orally during the meeting, the production company should agree to compensate the filmmaker a *reasonable amount* if it ends up using the filmmaker's idea.

Other than attorney's fees in drafting and negotiating the NDA or submission release, the only costs incurred here are the costs of sending a follow-up letter via certified mail.

NEGOTIATION TIPS AND TRICKS

Often a filmmaker's agent or attorney can negotiate with the production company and get them to waive the requirement of a submission release.

Step by Step: Protecting an Idea

1. Put your idea into written form. Make it as full, complete, and expressive as you can, and register it with the US Copyright Office. (See "Copyright Registration," p. 164.)
2. If possible, try to have the production company sign an NDA.
3. If obtaining an NDA is not possible, have your agent or attorney negotiate a waiver of the submission release form.

4. In the pitch meeting, try to create a contractual obligation contingent on the movie studio using your idea. Don't try to "sound like a lawyer" here, just be clear, casual, and enthusiastic. It's really a question of finesse. If you sound like you're "playing lawyer," they will bring in their own attorney or, more likely, stop the meeting right there.

   Note: I am emphatically not suggesting that you trick them into agreeing to anything; in fact, there needs to be a "meeting of the minds" of all parties in order for a contract to be formed. No, what I'm saying is that now is the time be especially friendly and clear that you expect to be paid for the use of your idea. Use all of your people skills here.

   Example: Say something like, "I'm really excited about pitching my show to you. But, before I do, I just want to make sure that you guys are going to treat it as my property until we have a more formal deal in place and you're not going to discuss it with anybody outside your company and, of course, if you do decide to use it, I'm going to be paid a reasonable amount for it. We can work out the other details later."
5. If the movie studio executive agrees, you may have a contract. You should wait for the executive to show that she agrees with your requirements, either verbally or with some physically gesture, such as a nod. Generally, mere silence is not assent.
6. Follow up with an e-mail and certified letter restating the terms of the oral contract. Your claim to ownership of your idea will be strengthened if the production executive to whom you pitched agrees to your terms again after she has heard your pitch.

Example: "Thank you for taking the time to hear my pitch concerning my proposed screenplay. As we discussed after I pitched, you have agreed not to use my ideas without compensating me a reasonable amount. Thanks, too, for agreeing to keep my ideas confidential. I look forward to the possibility of working with you and your company in bringing my idea to the screen."

7. As a bonus, your ownership claim will be further reinforced if you can get the studio to state that they've never heard an idea like yours (notice how I rephrased the "novelty" requirement).

   Example: "It was so great to hear you say that you thought my idea was unique. I think so too, but it's nice to hear it confirmed by someone whose opinion I respect." Generally, you should only introduce the issue if they've mentioned it at the meeting, after being blown away by your perfect pitch, of course.

8. Follow-up. Once the filmmaker has pitched his or her idea, the next step is for the production company to either offer the filmmaker a deal or to "pass" on the project—that is, turn the filmmaker down.

   a. *If the movie studio has offered to pick up the project*, the kind of deal it will offer will depend on the nature of the project and the reputation of the filmmaker.

      - The production company might want to commission the filmmaker to write a screenplay. (See "Hiring a Screenwriter," p. 136.)
      - The production company may want to purchase a finished screenplay from the filmmaker. (See "Acquiring Screenplay Rights," p. 121.)
      - The production company may want to option the finished screenplay (an option is the exclusive right to purchase the screenplay). (See "The Screenplay Option/Purchase," p. 124.)
      - If you own a production company and have pitched to a studio, you may be offered a production services agreement. (See "Production Services Agreement," p. 178.)

- *If the movie studio has passed on the project*, the filmmaker should request the return of all their materials, or alternatively, the materials destruction. This helps to protect the filmmaker against the uncontrolled disclosure of their materials and, hopefully, the filmmaker's ideas.

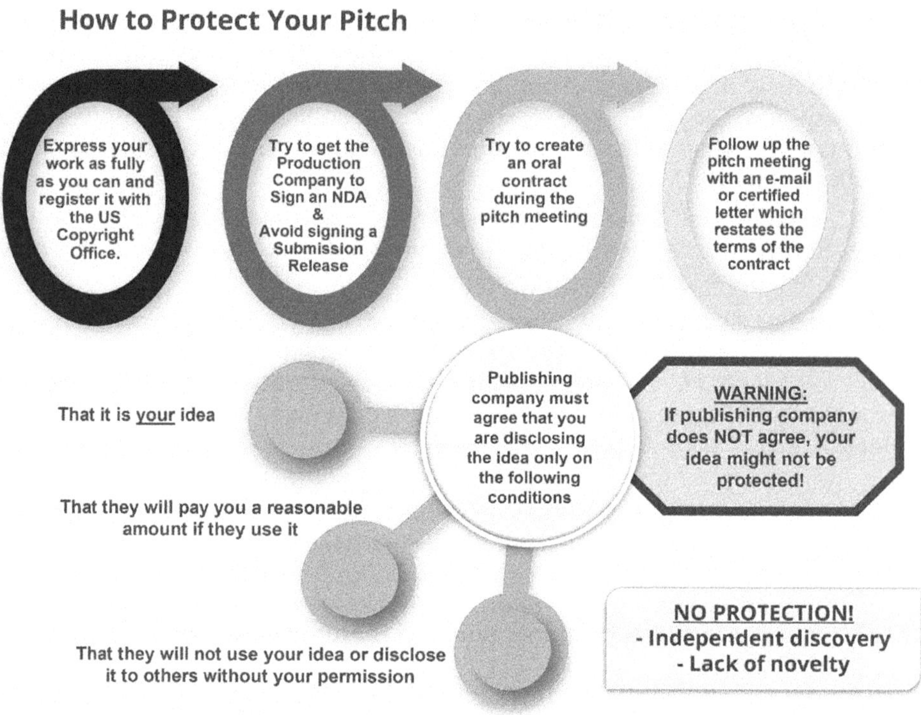

CAUTION!

- Be careful how you phrase your oral contract; be sensitive with your approach and tone. Sometimes sounding too much like a lawyer can turn an otherwise friendly business negotiation into an adversarial relationship.
- Listen and look for the production company's response; the production company must acknowledge and agree that you are disclosing the idea to them with the understanding that you expect them to pay you at least a "reasonable value" for your work, should they decide to use it.
- Even with a contract, your idea should be novel to the recipient. The idea "need not reflect the flash of genius, but it must show genuine novelty and invention, and not a merely clever or useful adaptation of existing knowledge."

NOTES

1 *Intl. News Serv. v. Associated Press*, 248 U.S. 215, 250 (1918).

2 William O. Knox, The Role of Novelty in A California Idea Submission Case, 11 *UCLA Ent. L. Rev.* 27, 28 (2004) (citing to *Mann v. Columbia Pictures, Inc.*, 180 Cal. Rptr. 522, 533 n.6 (Cal. Ct. App. 1982).

3 California doesn't require novelty for a pre-disclosure implied contract for the purchase of an idea; New York, New Jersey, and many other jurisdictions do.

4 *Nadel v. Play-By-Play Toys & Novelties, Inc.*, 208F.3d 368 (2d Cir. 2000).

5 *Alliance Sec. Products, Inc., v. Fleming and Co.*, 290 Fed.Appx. 380 (2nd Cir. 2008). ("When 'an idea consists in essence of nothing more than a variation on a basic theme [...]. novelty cannot be found to exist'.")

6 *Rodriquez v. Heidi Klum Co.,* No. 05 CV 10218, 2008 WL 4449416, at *4 n.11 (S.D.N.Y Sept. 30, 2008).

7 *Hollywood Screentest of America, Inc., v. NBC Universal, Inc.*, 151 Cal.App.4th 631, 646, 60 Cal. Rptr.3d 279, 290 (Cal.App. 2 Dist., 2007).

8 *Murray v. NBC,* 844 F2d 988 (2d Cir., 1988).

8

CREATING A SCREENPLAY

Creating and protecting a screenplay can be both artistically and legally challenging:

- Legally, the simplest route is to write it yourself. (See "Writing the Screenplay by Yourself," p. 105.)
- Even if you are the sole author of a screenplay, if you're adapting another person's work, you will need his or her permission to do so. (See "Screenplay Adaptations," p. 142.)
- If you are writing with another person, you should be aware of the legal implications of collaborative writing and joint authorship. (See "Writing Collaboration," p. 108.)
- If you are basing the script on someone's life story, you will need to secure the rights. (See "Life Story Rights," p. 150.)
- Regardless of how the screenplay is written, you should protect it by registering the copyright. (See "Copyright Registration," p. 164.)

but:

- If, instead of writing the screenplay yourself, you are buying or optioning the screenplay, you have a slightly different set of concerns. (See "Acquiring Screenplay Rights," p. 121.)

WRITING THE SCREENPLAY BY YOURSELF (SOLE AUTHORSHIP)

From a legal perspective, writing a screenplay by yourself is the easiest scenario. Assuming that the screenplay is wholly original with you, meaning that you haven't adapted it from someone else's work, you haven't written it with anyone else, and you haven't been hired to write it, the question of ownership of the screenplay's copyright is simple: You own it.

- You will still need to register the copyright to your screenplay. (See "Copyright Registration," p. 164.)
- Additionally, you'll need to assign the screenplay copyright to the production company that shoots the script, even if the company is yours. (See "Copyright Recordation, Assignments, and Transfers," p. 168.)

DOI: 10.4324/9781003228479-12

SOLE AUTHORSHIP

Woodrow Writer is finishing up his documentary screenplay, *Food for Worms: The Exciting World of Compost.* He has not based the film on another work, such as a graphic novel or a play.

Woodrow did get the *idea* for the script from watching several farming documentaries made in the 1950s, but because he only used *ideas* from these films, rather than scenes, dialogue, or other *expressions*, Woodrow does not have to worry about those filmmakers suing him for copyright infringement.

Woodrow did take a few pages of voiceover narration directly from *The Encyclopedia of Vermont Farming*, published in 1897, but because the copyright to that book has long since expired and the book is now in the *public domain*, he may freely use any part of that book (of course, so can anybody else). (See Appendix A, "Public Domain," p. 409.)

Having had a hard time finding other filmmakers interested in writing about controlled decomposition of organic matter, Woodrow has written the entire screenplay by himself. Copyright law considers Woodrow the sole author of the screenplay, and thus Woodrow is the script's sole copyright owner. In fact, anyone who wants to take the script and make a movie from it, write an article or book based on it, or turn it into a first-person-shooter video game must first get Woodrow's permission.

But:

If Woodrow had been employed by a production company when he wrote the script, and writing the script was part of the scope of his duties there, the script would be considered a work made for hire. Even if Woodrow worked as an independent contractor for the production company, the script would be a work made for hire if the company signed Woodrow to a work-made-for-hire agreement. In both these scenarios, the production company would own the copyright to the screenplay, and the company would be the only one authorized to license the screenplay for others to use. (See "Work Made for Hire," p. 418.)

Registering the Copyright to Your Work

The moment your script is finished, register it with the US Copyright Office. Don't be fooled into thinking that mailing a copy of your script to yourself or depositing it with the Writer's Guild is the same as registration. It's not. Only registration with the federal government will allow you to take full advantage of copyright protection. Besides, it's only $45 if you are the only author, it's not for-hire use, and you are only registering one work.[1] Check out the newly revamped Copyright Office online registration system (https://copyright.gov/registration/). Don't get me wrong, the site still looks like it was coded sometime in the 1990s, but now there are explanatory videos to help you with the process.

For a guide to registering your screenplay, see "Copyright Registration," p. 164, or download Circular 45, "Copyright Registration for Motion Pictures Including Video Recordings," from the US Copyright Office at www.copyright.gov/circs/circ45.pdf.

GOALS AND DEALS

As the sole author, you alone get to decide whether to sell your script or to accept or reject a particular deal. Oh, the power! Some of the deals you could face include:

- Producing your own script (see "Production," p. 273).
- Selling your script for movie production (see "The Screenplay Option/Purchase," p. 124).
- Optioning your script (see "The Screenplay Option/Purchase," p. 124).
- Licensing your script for novelizations, comic books, or other adaptation (see "Screenplay Adaptations," p. 142).
- If it's a television program and you own a production company, a television network may want to pay you to produce it (see "Production Services Agreement," p. 178).

Step by Step: Writing the Screenplay by Yourself

1. As you write your original screenplay, be aware of the sources you are drawing your work from. It's okay to be inspired by another work, but you must always be sensitive to the line between inspiration and copying. (See Appendix A, "Copyright Infringement," p. 429.)
2. If you are copying a portion of another person's work, even in part, you should analyze your use under copyright law to see whether you need to obtain permission. (See "Copyright Law," p. 402; "Screenplay Adaptations," p. 142; "Copyright Searches and Permissions," p. 159.)
3. Once your screenplay is written, you should register its copyright with the US Copyright Office. (See "Copyright Registration," p. 164). All copies of the script should have a prominently displayed copyright notice on the cover. (See "Copyright Notice," p. 342.)

Example: *Food for Worms: The Exciting World of Compost* © 2023 Woodrow Writer.

4. Before your film is shot, you will likely need to assign the script's copyright to the production company that shoots it. Be sure you understand which rights you are granting (at a minimum, the theatrical motion picture right) and which rights, if any, you are retaining. (See "Copyright Assignments," p. 424 & 169; "Option/Purchase," p. 124.)

WRITING COLLABORATION (WRITING PARTNERS AND JOINT AUTHORSHIP)

Whether you are writing a screenplay that you plan to produce or are writing one that you hope to sell, at some point you may decide to collaborate with other writers. Writing partners can be a great way to ease the burden of creating a 120-page screenplay. They help each other through writer's blocks, share in the actual workload, and bring new and fresh perspectives to each other's material. But, as with any business relationship, working with a writing partner can create legal problems, especially if certain issues are not dealt with *before* the partners start writing together.

Problems with collaborators typically occur over issues of screenplay ownership, the sharing of profits and expenses, and how to decide whether to accept offers for the screenplay's purchase. The best way to prevent these issues from disrupting an otherwise beneficial working relationship is to have the writing relationship governed by a writers' collaboration agreement, which is a contract that defines the duties and rights of each coauthor as well as the way in which the business of selling or exploiting the screenplay is managed, and how each collaborator is paid.

Under US copyright law, unless they have a contract that says otherwise, script writers who work together writing parts of the same script may be considered *joint authors*. (See "Joint Authors and Joint Works," p. 415.) Without a writers' collaboration agreement, copyright law will supply the default provisions that govern the ownership of the script's copyright. These default provisions often run counter to the expectations of one or more of the joint authors. For instance, in the absence of a contract that says otherwise, if the screenplay is sold, copyright law assumes that all joint authors will share equally in the script's profits and ownership—even if one of the writers originated the idea and did 95% of the work!

THE BOTTOM LINE: **Without a written and signed agreement between you and your cowriters, they may own more of the script than you would like and be able to license it without your permission.**

JOINT AUTHORSHIP

Connor Concept has an idea for a screenplay—a comic love story about two cannibalistic Elvis impersonators he has titled *Love Me Tender . . . and Juicy*. Connor sees himself primarily as an idea guy, and he decides to turn his story into a screenplay with the help of William Wordsmith. Because William is an experienced writer, Connor is hoping to help him flesh out the script outline and then let William do the majority of the actual writing.

They start writing together without an agreement between them. Because the two writers are each contributing copyrightable sections to the script (in other words, not just ideas), they are joint authors.

William writes the first 12 pages, and they are brilliant. Unfortunately, he then accepts the job writing for a television series, leaving Connor to finish the other 108 pages of the screenplay. Finish it he does.

Fortunately for Connor, his idea is so strong, despite his mediocre writing, that the script sets off a heated bidding war. Big Studio, Inc., is the winner, offering Connor $1.5 million to purchase the screenplay. There was no contract between the two writers, so Connor figures William should get about 10% of the money: after all, the screenplay was Connor's idea and William only wrote 10% of the final script. William, however, demands 50%.

Unfortunately for Connor, as a joint author under copyright law, William is entitled to a full 50%. If this is not the result Connor wanted, he should have protected his interests with a contract that specified how the monies and copyright ownership should be split.

The Writers' Collaboration Agreement: Goals and Deals

With a writers' collaboration agreement, each collaborating writer wants to establish their rights and obligations with respect to:

- Copyright ownership.
- Screenplay sales and licenses.
- Allocation of compensation and expenses.
- Resolving disagreements.
- Work schedule and distribution of writing tasks.

For definitions and explanations of common contract clauses, see Appendix B, "The Clause Companion," p. 475.

DEAL POINTS

A writers' collaboration agreement determines the rights and duties of each writer in a writing relationship. The agreement should contain sections that determine the following aspects of the relationship.

The Ownership of Rights

The ownership of rights is often affected by which author came up with the idea on which the screenplay is based (to keep things simple, many writers opt to share the rights equally, despite one of them being the idea person). Ownership issues typically include:

- Who will own the rights to the screenplay? Do the writers intend to be joint authors?
- If the writers do *not* want to be considered joint authors, the agreement should specify that.
- If they *do* intend to be joint authors, they should include a provision saying so, as well as language stating that in the event that one of the author's contributions is deemed not copyrightable, the author with the copyrightable contribution assigns a copyright interest to his writing partner.
- Are any rights held by only one writer, such as the idea person retaining the exclusive right to create a video game based on the screenplay?
- Who gets the rights in the event the writers can no longer work together? Does the idea person retain the exclusive right to turn her concept into another screenplay? If so, does she have to pay the other writers under this agreement?
- What if the screenplay can't be sold? Can either writer use portions of the work in their own separate works? Often writers require that their coauthor seek written permission before being allowed to use material from the joint work in separately, nonjointly authored works.
- Can either writer assign their own portion of the copyright? Generally, writers may want to restrict the transfer of the copyright to the transfer of the right to receive money from the copyright. Writers may want to restrict each other from granting to third parties the right to change or modify the screenplay.
- What promises are being made about the material each author contributes? Each author should represent and warrant that they created the material that they added to the screenplay. Each author should indemnify the other author for a breach of this provision.

The Working Relationship

- How do the writers decide when and to whom to sell the screenplay? It is often a good idea to restrict all the writers' abilities to individually grant any kind of license in the screenplay. Typically, the agreement requires the written permission of all or of the majority of the writers before the screenplay can be licensed.

- How is the income from exploiting the screenplay divided? For joint authors, the law presumes that they share the money equally, no matter which author came up with the idea, *unless* the agreement specifies otherwise. One typical formula is to have the right to income mirror the copyright ownership interests of the writers. However, the income from sales and licenses might be shared in other ways if the joint authors so chose:
  - For instance, the writer who came up with the idea might receive 60% of any money from a screenplay sale, the coauthor 40%.
  - The income could also be parsed by media form; for instance, income from the screenplay rights are split 50–50, but the money from literary adaptations (i.e., books) might be split 60–40, with the higher percentage going, again, to the idea person.
- When is the screenplay scheduled to be finished? Will work be done according to a schedule? If one writer is not meeting deadlines, is that a default? If so, does the defaulting writer have time to cure the default (e.g., ten days) before it is considered a breach of contract? It is a good idea to include mechanisms that allow the parties to cure defaults before they become breaches of contract. One method is to require a notice to be sent to the defaulting party for that party to be considered in default of their obligations. Once the defaulting party has received the notice, he or she is typically given some time to correct his or her default ("cure") before it is considered a breach of contract.
- In the event of a breach of contract, is arbitration mandatory?
- If any writer withdraws from the agreement before the screenplay is finished, how is the withdrawing writer's ownership affected? Is his percentage reduced by the amount added by other writers to fill the gap that the departing writer leaves behind? Typically, any withdrawal requires the creation of a *termination agreement*, which redefines the rights of the respective parties in terms of what each owns in the absence of the collaboration agreement. If the parties can't agree on the termination agreement, does the dispute go to arbitration or to court?
- How long does the agreement last? You might want to assert a time limit of a year or two here; if you can't write the screenplay in that time, there may be problems with the working relationship. Of course, that time period can be extended by all parties agreeing to do so. But distinguish between the term of the writing relationship and the ownership and duties with respect to the copyright of the screenplay, both of which are usually for the life of the copyright in the work.
- How will the writing team pay for the expenses of shopping the screenplay? Usually, writers pay for their own individual expenses.

- Are all business decisions decided by a majority vote? Some decisions, such as whether to admit new members into the writing team or whether to sell the screenplay, often require a unanimous vote.
- What happens if one writer's actions or unpaid debt causes the writing team to be sued (which can happen under the rules of joint and several liability)? The writer at fault should have a duty to indemnify their cowriter. (See "Indemnification," p. 488.)
- How will each writer be credited? How will writers be credited if they withdraw from the collaboration? One solution is to determine credit in accordance with the Writers Guild of America (WGA) rules. Even if none of the parties are members of the union, this way gives some structure to the formulation of writing credits. (See "WGA Credits," p. 117.)

Law: Joint Authors and Joint Works

Joint authors have certain rights under copyright law; if the authors want to change these rights, they need to do so by a contract between them, such as a writers' collaboration agreement.

When two or more authors work together to create a screenplay, copyright law may consider them *joint authors*.

Example: Remember William and Connor from the beginning of this section? William and Connor each wrote portions of the screenplay, with the intent that their individual contributions become part of the same screenplay. They are joint authors under copyright law, and their screenplay is considered a *joint work*.

To become a joint author, each coauthor must:

- Contribute expression to the joint work. For example, a would-be joint author would have to contribute more than just ideas, because ideas are not copyrightable.
- In addition to adding expressive elements, each potential joint author must also *intend* to merge his or her own contributions *inseparably* or *interdependently* with the contributions of the other coauthors to form a unitary whole. For example, a novel or screenplay may involve *inseparable* contributions, because the different authors' contributions generally do not stand alone, as in "Okay, Jenny, which sentences did you write again?" A motion picture, by contrast, generally has *interdependent* contributions, which can stand alone but are meant to be merged together to a new form, as in "I directed and shot the film that you wrote, and I never signed a work-for-hire agreement; I guess we're joint authors of the film."
- Finally, if it is unclear if the parties intended a joint authorship relationship, a court may assess who is the "dominant author" of the work.[2] An author is most likely to be the dominant one if they have decision-making authority, how they are credited, and whether they have the power to enter into written agreements with third parties regarding the work.[3]

CAUTION! As a screenwriter, you want to have a say in how your screenplay is licensed, but unless there is a contract between you and your other joint authors specifying how and to whom a screenplay must be licensed, any joint author can grant nonexclusive licenses to the script without having to first seek the permission of the other joint authors!

More details on how copyright law treats joint authors are found in Appendix A, "Joint Authors and Joint Works," p. 415.

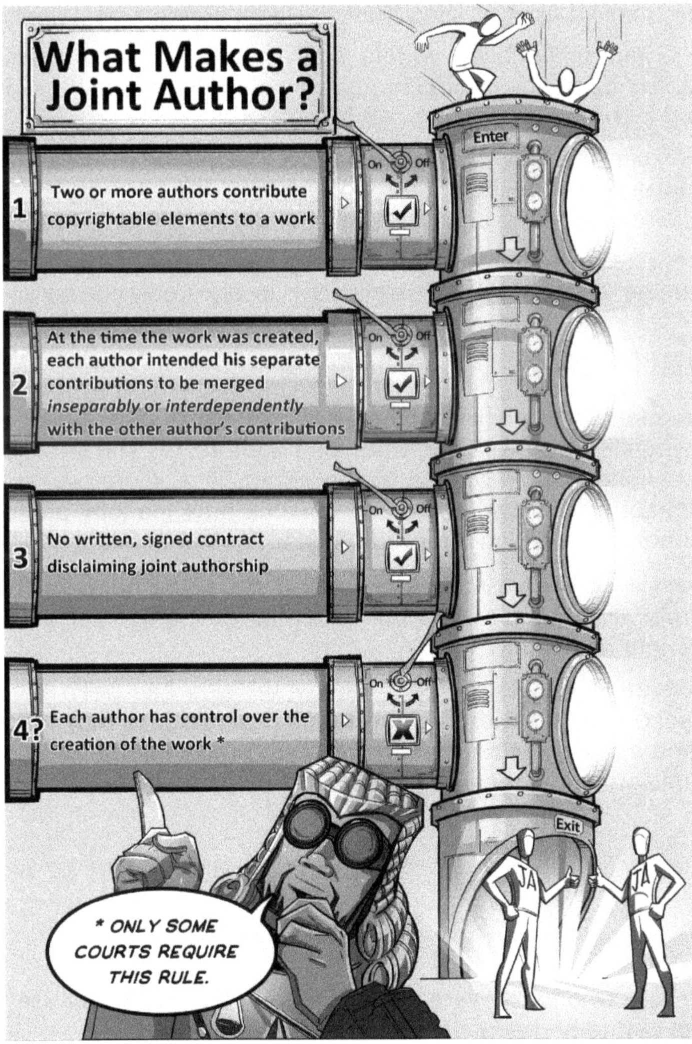

Business Issues

Entering into a writing collaboration is more than just a sharing of creative capital. If you plan to sell the final screenplay, you must recognize that you are going into business with your coauthor.

Deciding on a Business Organization

- The organizational form that a business relationship takes should be determined in advance. Although a writers' collaboration agreement focuses on the screenplay and defines how each writer will act with respect to the script—its creation and exploitation—there are numerous business aspects it does not cover (e.g., taxation, voting rights, etc.). As a result, it may be advisable for writing collaborators to also form a business. (See "Setting Up the Production Company," p. 43.)
  - *LLCs*. Given its flexibility, writers often create a member-managed limited liability company issuing membership interests to all cowriters. (See "Limited Liability Company," p. 48.)
  - *General partnerships*. Writers who work together to create and sell a screenplay might be surprised to learn that the law may treat them as having *already* formed a partnership.
  - *Joint ventures*. Alternatively, the law may treat cowriters as being part of a joint venture, especially if their relationship involves only one script or project.

Intellectual Property

Without a contract specifying otherwise, (1) each joint author owns the whole copyright—jointly with the other joint authors, (2) and each joint author can grant a nonexclusive license to the script. It is, therefore, advisable to have a contract that, at the very least, governs how the joint authors decide whether or not to accept an offer to purchase the rights to the script.

- If one author has single-handedly created the script concept (but not the script itself), that author may want to argue for a greater share of income and copyright ownership.
- The converse is also true: The screenwriter who has been brought in to write a second or third draft of an existing screenplay may want to avoid the collaboration agreement altogether and argue that he or she is a joint author, entitled to share equally with the other joint authors.

STEP BY STEP: WRITING COLLABORATION

Before Starting to Write

1. Choose your writing partners with the same care you would use to choose business partners—because that is what they are.

2. Decide whether to form a business organization. (See "Types of Business Entities," p. 45.) If you decide to form a member-managed LLC, many of the aspects of the writers' collaboration agreement can be dealt with in the agreement that governs your business entity (e.g., the LLCs operating agreement; the partnership agreement for a general partnership).
3. Negotiate, draft, and execute a writers' collaboration agreement, paying special attention to the issues of ownership of rights; who can grant licenses to the joint work; how to resolve disputes, deadlines, marketing strategies, expenses, and profits and losses.

While Writing

1. Keep track of each author's financial contributions and expenses.
2. Together, develop a strategy for trying to sell or make the screenplay.

After Your Work Is Written

1. Register the copyright with the US Copyright Office. (See "Copyright Registration," p. 164.) If you and your partners have decided to form a company, assign the copyright to the company and register the assignment with the US Copyright Office. (See "Copyright Recordation, Assignments, and Transfers," p. 168.)
2. Together, continue to implement a strategy for trying to sell or produce the screenplay.

CAUTION

- *It is critical to have a collaboration agreement, signed by all authors.* Without a contract to restrict them, joint authors may grant non-exclusive licenses to the screenplay without first getting the permission of their coauthors.
- To qualify as a joint author, you must contribute something more than just the idea or concept for a screenplay.
- Choose your writing partners carefully. Not only are they your writing partners, but they are also your business partners.

THE WRITERS GUILD OF AMERICA (WGA)

Working with Union Writers

The Writers Guild of America (WGA) is the union for professional screenplay, television, and certain "new media" writers. If you want to hire a writer or buy a script from a writer who is a member of the WGA, you might need to become a signatory with that union. A *signatory* is a company that has signed and therefore agreed to abide by the collective bargaining agreement of the WGA, known as the WGA Theatrical and Television Minimum Basic Agreement (MBA). If anything in your contract with the writer you hire conflicts with the MBA, your conflicting terms disappear and the MBA's terms govern in their place.

> ***Example:*** Even though the signatory producer wants to give three people "story by" credit, the MBA limits the number of writers able to receive that credit to two. Since the film is done under the WGA contract, only two writers may be given "story by" credits in the final film.

In general, the MBA controls minimum deal terms. For example, it controls:

- Minimum payment for WGA writers.
- Qualification for credits.
- Separation of rights.
- Reacquisition of the rights to the screenplay.
- Rules governing "new media" projects that fall within its jurisdiction.

Separation of Rights

Writers who are members of the WGA have special rights called *separated rights*. These are additional rights granted to WGA members who create original works under the WGA MBA. If a professional writer creates an original screenplay or teleplay or contributes a substantially new story to preexisting material that has been assigned to him or her, the writer may be entitled to a separation of rights.[4] Separated rights differ depending on whether the initial work was created for theatrical or television release. These rights, which stem from copyright, would not automatically flow to the writer for hire in the absence of the MBA. In fact, in non-union films, these rights are almost always reserved by the production company, leaving the writer with no separated rights or copyright interest whatsoever.

Separated rights can include:

- Publication rights.
- Dramatic stage rights.
- Sequel rights and payments.
- Mandatory rewrites for authors selling an original screenplay to the signatory production company.
- Meeting with a production executive.

- Reacquisition of the screenplay that has not been produced within five years by repaying to the production company the amount of money the writer was paid for her services.
- Sequel movie of the week (MOW) rights.
- TV series rights.
- Merchandising rights.
- Radio rights.

Who Receives Separated Rights?

If a WGA member writer is working for a WGA signatory company, that writer may receive separated rights as follows:

- *Motion picture.* A writer will receive separated rights if she is entitled to a "story by," "screen story by," or "written by" credit.
- *Television show.* A writer will receive separated rights if he is entitled to a "story by" or "written by" credit (and in some cases, he may be eligible if he receives a "television story by" credit as well).

Since the award of separated rights is driven by what WGA credit the writer receives, let's turn to WGA credits.

WGA Credits

If the film is subject to the WGA rules and jurisdiction (in other words, the production company is a signatory and the writers are union members), the WGA will determine the writing credits. As the WGA points out in its handy *Credits Survival Guide:*

> *The Guild has the sole authority to determine writing credits on theatrical and television projects written under its jurisdiction. A [production] company cannot guarantee that you will receive writing credit, or any particular form of writing credit.*[5]

How a writer is credited by the WGA affects his or her right to residuals, separated rights, and other rights under the WGA MBA.

When principal photography is over, the production company must send to both the WGA and to all of the writers:

- A notice of tentative writing credits.
- The final shooting script.
- The production company's proposed credits.
- Any source material for the script.

The way writers are credited by the WGA is set out in the WGA Screen Credits Policy:

- The WGA defines a screenplay as consisting of "individual scenes and full dialogue, together with such prior treatment, basic adaptation, continuity, scenario, and dialogue as shall be used in, and represent substantial contributions to the final script."[6]
- A "story" is "distinct from screenplay and consisting of basic narrative, idea, theme, or outline indicating character development and action."[7]
- "*Story by*" *credit* is given when "1) the story was written under employment under Guild jurisdiction; 2) the story was purchased by a signatory company from a professional, writer, as defined in the MBA; or 3) when the screenplay is based upon a sequel story written under the Guild's jurisdiction."[8] No more than two writers can share a "Story by" credit.
- "*Screen story by*" *credit* may be given to writers who furnish "source material of a story nature but takes from it only a springboard, a characterization, an incident, or some equally limited contribution, creating a substantially new and different story from the source material."[9]
- "*Screenplay by*" *credit* is given when there is "source material of a story nature (with or without a 'screen story by' credit) or when the writer(s) entitled to 'story by' credit is different than the writer(s) entitled to 'screenplay by' credit." Screenplay by credits can't be shared by more than two writers.
- "*Written by*" *credit* is given when the "writer(s) is entitled to both the 'story by' credit and the "screenplay by' credit."

HANDY WGA LINKS

- WGA: www.wga.org
- WGA Separation of Rights Guide: www.wga.org/contracts/know-your-rights/understanding-separated-rights
- WGA Screen Credits Manual: www.wga.org/contracts/credits/manuals/screen-credits-manual
- WGA Credits Survival Guide: www.wga.org/contracts/credits/manuals/survival-guide
- New Media Credits Procedures Guide: www.wga.org/contracts/credits/manuals/new-media-credits-procedures

NOTES

[1] If you're working with another author, it's $65. www.copyright.gov/about/fees.html
[2] See *16 Casa Duse, LLC v. Merkin*, 791 F.3d 247, 260 (2d Cir. 2015).
[3] Ibid.
[4] www.wga.org/contracts/know-your-rights/understanding-separated-rights
[5] WGA Credits Survival Guide: www.wga.org/contracts/credits/manuals/survival-guide
[6] WGA Screen Credits Manual, p. 14 (https://www.wga.org/contracts/credits/manuals/screen-credits-manual).
[7] Id. at 13.
[8] Ibid.
[9] Id. at 14.

9

ACQUIRING SCREENPLAY RIGHTS

In the last chapter, we covered how to protect the script you wrote or co-wrote. But what if you haven't written your own screenplay? This chapter is for those of you who want to:

- Option or purchase a screenplay written by someone else. (See "The Screenplay Option/Purchase," p. 124.)
- Negotiate a shopping agreement or attachment. (See "The Shopping Agreement," p. 134.)
- Hire a screenwriter to write or re-write a script. (See "Hiring a Screenwriter," p. 136.)
- Write a script that's based on someone else's novel, short story, or comic book. (See "Screenplay Adaptations," p. 142.)
- Purchase the right to someone's life story. (See "Life Story Rights," p. 150.)

THE RIGHT RIGHTS

One of the producer's primary jobs is the acquisition of the rights to turn a book, screenplay, comic book, or other underlying work into a film or television program. When you acquire literary property, such as the rights to a screenplay or the right to turn a book into a movie, you must pay special attention to the legal formalities of acquiring that property's copyright. All parties involved will need to know exactly who owns which of the many rights involved. For instance, even though the production company is buying the right to turn the screenplay into a movie, the writer of an original screenplay might want to keep a portion of the copyright rights, such as the right to turn the script into a stage play. (See "Screenplay Purchase Agreement: Reserved Rights," p. 129.) Or perhaps you want to adapt a comic book into a movie. Even if the comic book writer has given you permission to write a script, you may still need to get rights from any of the comic's co-authors as well as its publishing company. And no matter how the copyright is shared or owned, one thing is certain: The production company *must* have a signed contract granting it the right to make a motion picture (and other rights). (See "Screenplay Purchase Agreement: Rights Granted," p. 128.)

It's simple: If a copyright to a screenplay or book is not properly sold or licensed to you, you don't have the right to turn that script or novel into a

DOI: 10.4324/9781003228479-13

movie. This is not something that will "slip under the radar." When it comes time to distribute your film, the distributor will double-check that the copyright has been properly assigned to you or your production company, and if it hasn't been, you will lose the deal. Even if you're self-distributing, you could be sued by a writer, publisher, or other rights holder in the underlying work who has not properly granted you the rights you need.

CAUTION! THE WRITER IS NOT ALWAYS THE RIGHTS HOLDER!

Whether you're trying to negotiate an option purchase agreement, shopping agreement, and attachment or license of a literary property, you must make sure that you are contracting with all of the necessary parties; to put it simply: anybody who has an exclusive right to any of the copyrights in the property should be considered.

It's not always obvious at first glance. For instance, you may be trying to make a film based on a comic book property and have received assurances from both the comic book writer and their publishing company that the audiovisual rights are free and clear to grant to you. However, what about the merchandising rights? If you plan on trying to get the backing of a major studio or other media company, they will undoubtedly want the right to be able to make merchandise based on your film. However, most comic book publishers keep the merchandising rights to the books they produce. In this scenario, you would most likely need to negotiate from the publishing company the right to make merchandise based upon the filmed version of the comic while leaving the publishing company the right to make merchandise from the comic book itself. Make sure to thoroughly investigate all of the copyright ownership permutations, especially when it comes to publishers, jointly authored works, and anything created as a work made for hire.

Examples

- **PUBLISHERS**: Warren has written the comic book *Maggot Man: Carrion-Eater of Justice!*, which was published by Ursula Publishing. Like many comic book publishing companies, in addition to the right to publish the comic book miniseries, Ursula Publishing also acquired the audiovisual rights to Maggot Man. Pablo the producer is Warren's friend, and Warren would love him to make the movie. However, because Warren transferred the audiovisual rights to Ursula Publishing in the publishing agreement for the comic book, it is Ursula Publishing, not Warren, that is the underlying property rights holder.

- **JOINT AUTHORS**: Warren wrote the initial draft of his screenplay for *Zombie Sharks in Love*, back in film school with his ex-girlfriend Wanda. They broke up and Wanda became an investment banker with nothing to do with the film industry. Warren stayed in the film industry and wrote another draft of *Zombie Sharks in Love*, which Pablo the producer is interested in shopping. However, because the initial draft of the screenplay was written by both Warren and Wanda, they are likely joint authors and joint owners of the copyright to the original script, which was the basis of Warren's latest draft. As result, if Pablo wants the exclusive right to purchase or shop Warren's latest draft, he will need both Wanda and Warren's written permission to do so, as they are both the underlying rights holders.

- **WORK FOR HIRE**: Warren is employed as a screenwriter for Pugnacious Pictures. The employee handbook for Pugnacious Pictures specifies that the scope of his employment includes all screenplays he writes during the term of his employment. During nights and weekends, Warren works on his own script: *The Ballad of Millard Fillmore*, which Pablo the producer is interested in optioning. Because Warren's scope of employment encompassed all screenplays he creates while employed by them, the copyright to the ballad of Millard Fillmore is owned by Pugnacious Pictures as a work for hire. Thus, if Pablo wants to option the material, he must negotiate with Pugnacious Pictures as the underlying rights holder.

THE RIGHT CONTRACTS

As part of the development and financing stage, the producer needs the right to raise money based upon the underlying work, even if they have not yet purchased it. Unfortunately, there's a lot of confusion as to how to best do this, made even more unclear by the fact that many producers use the terms "**option**," "**shopping agreement**," and "**attachment**" relatively interchangeably; however, they are NOT interchangeable agreements.

The confusion arises because option/purchases contracts, shopping agreements, and attachments all have similar goals:

- **The producer wants**
  - To set up a project inexpensively. Producers need to be able to set up a property with a studio or financiers prior to committing to the full purchase price of an underlying property.
  - Exclusivity. Producers need exclusive rights to set up a property for a period of time and assurances that the rights may be purchased if a studio or financiers are interested.
  - To be attached to the project. Producers need certainty that they will be attached to the project if they use time, energy, and contacts setting it up.

- **The literary property owner wants**
  - Reasonable compensation. Underlying property owners need certainty that they will be compensated reasonably both for selling their rights as well as for "taking it off the market" while it is being shopped.
  - Ownership of their IP until sold. Underlying property owners need ownership of their intellectual property until it is sold and transferred.
  - Termination. Underlying property owners need to be able to disengage the property from producers who are not able to set up the project while it is still viable.

There are fundamental differences in how option/purchases, shopping agreements, and attachment contract address each of the above issues.

THE SCREENPLAY OPTION/PURCHASE

A filmmaker who wants to make a movie using someone else's script must buy the motion picture rights to that script in order to make the movie. If you can, you should try to buy the entire copyright to the script, not just the motion picture rights. Remember, the more rights you own, the more ways you can exploit those rights. To purchase the rights to a screenplay, the filmmaker should use a *screenplay purchase agreement.*

However, producers usually don't want to buy a script unless they know that they can get it made. After all, you need a little time to secure funding, interest actors, and hopefully, set up a distribution deal. However, the producer can't attach all those elements (financiers, talent, distributors) to the project unless they have the right to make the film from the screenplay. This is where the *option agreement* comes in handy. **An option agreement is a contract that gives the filmmaker the *exclusive* right to *buy* the screenplay copyright during a defined period of time** (e.g., 12 months from the execution of the option).

If the producer *options* the screenplay, they have *not* yet purchased all the rights to the screenplay. Purchasing a screenplay during the option period is called *exercising the option.* If the filmmaker chooses not to exercise the option and the option expires, the right to sell the screenplay *reverts* back to the screenwriter.

Always Negotiate a Purchase Agreement With the Option!

When you negotiate the option agreement you must, at the same time, also negotiate the purchase price and other key terms of the screenplay sale. A filmmaker who has negotiated the option agreement to a screenplay but not the purchase agreement holds a *worthless option.* It is worthless because although the filmmaker may exercise the option, the price and other sale terms have not been agreed on and, therefore, the screenwriter is not obligated to sell the script to the filmmaker for a certain price. In the case of a worthless option, what the filmmaker really has is not a right to *buy* the script, but only the right to *negotiate* for its sale. The screenwriter may demand as much money for the script as he or she wants, and the only choice the filmmaker has is either to agree to pay it or not to buy the script.

FAILING TO NEGOTIATE THE SCRIPT PRICE

Wendy Writer has written a script called *King Axolotl*, a monster flick about a giant fire-breathing aquatic salamander, which Petra Producer is very interested in making.

Suppose Petra *didn't* negotiate a purchase agreement when she negotiated the option agreement for the script. It's now six months later, and Petra has a backer interested in funding the picture. Petra tells Wendy that she wants to buy the script for $65,000. Wendy, knowing that Petra has an interested financier whom she doesn't want to lose, decides to hold out for a higher purchase price—$100,000. After all, Wendy figures, she is not obligated to sell the script to Petra at any certain price, so she might as well hold out for a higher price. Petra has lost her leverage over bargaining for the purchase price.

Without a purchase agreement tied to an option, the option is worthless.

MAJOR DEAL POINTS: THE OPTION AGREEMENT

For definitions and explanations of common contract clauses, see Appendix B, "The Clause Companion," p. 475.

The Parties

- *Producer*. The producer wants to "test drive" the script before they buy it—that is, to be able to shop the screenplay around to see if anybody is interested in financing, co-producing, staring in, or distributing the movie before the producer purchases the rights to the script outright. To that end, the producer will seek to get the longest possible time (the "*option period*") in which to shop the script. The producer will also seek to pay the smallest amount of money for the option and to make that amount applicable against the purchase price.

- *Writer*. It is often in the writer's interest to make an outright sale of the script, as the purchase price of a script is greater than its option price. However, the writer should also consider whether the producer can actually get the film made. The more of the writer's films that get made, the more money the writer can demand for their next film. The writer, therefore, should give the producer enough time to shop the script around to financiers, production companies, distributors, and so forth. For that reason, an option may make sense to the writer as well. The writer will seek to limit the term of the producer's option period to give the writer some time to seek other potential buyers for the script while the screenplay is still reasonably fresh.

The writer may work for their loan-out company, which would then be a party to the agreement. (See "Loan-Out Companies," p. 51.)

Grant of Option

This is the heart of the option—it grants to the producer the *exclusive* right to purchase the script by a future date according to the terms of the purchase agreement. As previously mentioned, a purchase agreement must be coupled with the option. (See "Purchase Agreement," p. 128.)

Option Price

This is the amount paid for the *option*, *not* the purchase price for the script itself.

- Option prices range from a token amount, such as $50 on the low end, to 10% of the purchase price on the high end.
- Will the option price be deducted from the final purchase price? If so, the option price is *applicable* against the purchase price; if the option price is not deductible from the purchase price, it is *nonapplicable*.

Option Period or Term

This governs the *duration* of the option:

- Most options are for at least a year, and often for 18 months.
- Often producers are given the right to renew the option prior to its expiration. If the option is renewed, the writer usually gets an *extension payment*. This payment is typically *not* applied against the purchase price.

Exercise of Option

This clause details how the producer may exercise the option and purchase the script pursuant to the purchase agreement.

- A notice sent via certified mail is a common device for exercising options. So is e-mail. The key is the notice must be sent in a way that is specified in the option agreement, and it should be in writing.
- This clause should reference the purchase agreement, requiring that the writer sign the purchase agreement when the producer exercises the option. Make sure to give the producer the power of attorney to execute the purchase agreement on the writer's behalf if the writer fails to exercise the purchase agreement.
- The writer should also be obligated to sign other documents such as copyright assignments and certificates of authorship that transfer the copyright and other rights in the script to the producer.

Right to Development and Pre-Production

A producer will likely need to develop the project prior to purchasing the script: to attract investors or studios, the producer may want to have the script re-written, commission storyboards, create websites, and produce sizzle reels and trailers and other "development materials" for the purpose of raising money for the film. You must ensure there is a clause in the option agreement which gives the producer the right to create such development materials. If you leave it out, any development of the film based on an unpurchased script might infringe the writer's copyright in the screenplay. However, problems occur when the ownership of the intellectual property of these development materials is not effectively dealt with in the option agreement. From the writer's standpoint, development materials are usually derivative works of the original optioned script, and the ownership of them should transfer with the purchase of the script. However, the producer may argue that they have added (and typically paid for) a substantial amount of new expression (new characters and perhaps entirely new plot lines, artwork, designs, etc.), and thus the producer may want to physically own these development materials as well as the copyright to any material the producer added *even if the option is never exercised*. To "square this circle," writers and producers often agree to "freeze" the rights in these derivatives if the option isn't exercised, allowing the rights and ownership of the materials to be "unfrozen" when the producer has been repaid for their actual costs (usually by the new producer on the project).

Reversion

This clause underscores the fact that the rights will revert back to the writer if the option is not exercised either during the term of the option or during any renewal periods.

This clause should require the producer to grant the power of attorney to the writer for executing any documents conveying the rights back to the writer.

MAJOR DEAL POINTS: THE PURCHASE AGREEMENT

Rights Granted

This section outlines the specific rights granted to the producer. In short, the producer needs the right to make a motion picture or pictures in whatever medium, to be distributed in any manner, throughout the universe, in perpetuity.

Remember, copyright can be divided in a number of ways, so the rights must be defined in terms of their:

- *Medium* (e.g., motion picture, television).
- *Duration* (e.g., perpetual).
- *Geography* (e.g., the universe, North America).
- *Motion picture rights.* At a minimum, the producer needs the exclusive right to make a motion picture from the script. The producer needs to make sure that this right extends to all media in which that motion picture will be exploited, such as theatrical release, television, video, Blu-ray, online media, VOD, mobile devices, and "any exhibition medium, now known or hereinafter developed."
- *Merchandising rights.* The producer is granted the right to make T-shirts, action figures, and so forth from the characters and events in the script. The writer is usually granted a portion of the money the producer receives from these sales.
- *Other rights.* Other rights are subject to negotiation but frequently granted to the producer, such as the right to make derivative works such as television shows, podcasts, sequels, remakes, video games and mobile apps, comic books, plays, amusement park rides, and "novelizations" of up to 7,500 words. *Novelization* does not involve the right to make a full-blown novel but rather the right to make a short literary version of the script for promotional purposes.
- *Right to make changes.* The producer must have the unfettered right to make changes to the script.

Keep in mind that the rights the screenwriter is optioning should be *exclusive* to the producer if the option is exercised. In fact, during the option period, only the producer should have the exclusive right to shop the screenplay around to potential financiers, studios, performers, co-producers, etc. Often, the writer wants to be able to shop the script around as well, and depending upon the writer's status in the film industry, that may be very helpful. However, the writer's ability to shop their own script must be spelled out in the option purchase agreement, and all deals should be subject to the producer's approval.

Reserved Rights

Reserved rights specify which rights the writer keeps. These are the rights the producer does *not* get. The rights the writer keeps are the subject of negotiation.

Often, the writer keeps the following:

- *Book rights* (the right to make a novel of the screenplay).
- *Radio rights*.
- *Comic book rights*.
- *Stage rights* (the right to turn the script into a play).
- If the writer is a WGA member and the producer is a signatory, the writer may also have *separated rights*. (See "Separation of Rights," p. 116.)
- The producer may ask for a holdback period for the *reserved rights* (often 5–7 years). This means that for the holdback period, the writer *cannot* exploit those reserved rights that are subject to the holdback.
- Even though the rights are reserved by the writer, the producer will often ask for the *right of first negotiation/right of last refusal* for any sale or exploitation of the rights. (See Appendix B, "Right of First Negotiation," p. 492.)

Copyright

This clause governs the mechanics of ownership and transfer of the script's copyright.

- It is *critical* that the producer perform a copyright search with the US Copyright Office to ensure that the acquired property is not owned by anybody else other than the stated owner(s) or that it is not in the public domain.
- The script's copyright information should be listed in the agreement, including the script's title, registration number, and year of publication.
- The producer typically gets the granted rights forever, along with an agreement by the writer to transfer of any copyright renewal rights. (But see Appendix A, "Termination of Transfer," p. 427.)
- The writer must promise to execute any additional documentation necessary to transfer the copyright to the production company.

Reversion of Rights

Frequently the writer will negotiate a return of the rights granted if they are not used by the producer within a certain period of time (called a *reversion*). The writer usually wants the rights to revert back to them if the film has not begun principal photography within five years from the date of the screenplay purchase.

Purchase Price/Compensation

This is where the purchase price for the script is specified. Different rights (theatrical, television, etc.) are compensated at different rates. If the writer is a WGA member, the minimum amount the producer can pay the writer will be determined by that union's *rate schedule*. Make sure to check with the Guild to get their current rates.

- *Rights transfer*. Should be conditional upon payment of the purchase price. Payment is usually due when the option is exercised or on first day of principal photography, whichever is earlier.
- *Sequels*. If a movie spawns a sequel, the writer typically receives 25–50% of theatrical purchase price of the script.
- *Remakes*. If the movie is remade, the writer typically receives 33–50% of theatrical purchase price of the script.
- *Net profits*. The writer commonly contracts for a portion of the film's net profits—often 5%. (See "Net Profits," p. 66.)
- *Bonus compensation*. Writers sometimes get bonuses if the motion picture is produced and released.
- *Agents*. Sometimes the writer will try to negotiate a 10% increase in the fee to pay the writer's agent's commission.

Accounting

If the writer is a net-profit participant or will receive any form of deferred or contingent compensation, this paragraph will delineate how often the writer may expect to receive accounting statements. This is coupled with the right to audit the production company, usually no more frequently than once a year.

Representations and Warranties

Representations and warranties are the promises that the writer is making to the producer and are coupled with an indemnification clause in which the writer states:

- The writer is the sole owner of the screenplay and nothing in the script infringes the rights of anyone else.
- Copyright registration is up to date and accurate.
- No other motion picture, dramatic, or other version of the script has been made or authorized.
- None of the granted rights are or have ever been granted to anyone else.
- By selling the script, the writer will not be violating any third-party rights (e.g., copyrights or rights of publicity).

- Writer will not impair or encumber or otherwise do anything to interfere with the granted rights.
- The writer should indemnify the producer for breaches of representations and warranties, misrepresentations, or damages resulting from the writer's breach of contract.

Credit

This clause specifies how the writer's credit is determined.

- If the producer is a signatory of WGA and the writer is a member of that union, the WGA will determine who gets writing credit and how they are credited. (See "WGA Credits," p. 117.)
- The producer should include a clause disclaiming liability for inadvertently making a mistake with the writer's credit. Typically, the remedy for credit error is a promise from the producer to correct the credits in future copies of the film.

No Obligation to Produce

Although the producer has the right to produce the film, they need to be sure that they are not *obligated* to produce the film. After all, the number of screenplays that are optioned far outnumber those that are actually made into movies

Publicity

The publicity clause gives the producer the right to use the writer's name and biography in connection with advertising, marketing, and publicizing the film.

- The producer needs to be able to use the writer's name, likeness, and approved biography in connection with the marketing of the film.
- Conversely, the producer will want to prohibit the writer from releasing any publicity about the motion picture without the producer's approval. You may want to point out to the writer that this means no unauthorized social media posting as well!

Remedies

The writer should waive any claim to injunctive relief arising out of a breach of the contract. Depending on the advice of counsel, producers may want any dispute to be settled through binding arbitration rather than through the courts.

♦♦♦♦♦

Law: Optioning and Selling the Screenplay

- Under US copyright law, all screenplay sales, assignments, and transfers *must* be in writing to effectively transfer the copyright.
- Both sides in the transaction need to be especially careful that everybody understands which rights are granted and which rights are reserved.
- What is being purchased is the copyright to the screenplay. A producer must make sure that all the screenplay's authors and contributors sign off on the deal.
- When you negotiate the exclusive right to buy (the option), you must also negotiate the sale (the purchase agreement).

Business Issues

Union rules may affect your negotiating range!

WGA member. If the writer is a member of the WGA and the producer is a signatory, many of the deal terms, such as minimums on how much a writer can be paid, the criteria for credits, and rights that will remain with the writer after they have sold the screenplay, will be controlled by the WGA Minimum Basic Agreement.

Non-WGA member. If the producer is not a WGA signatory, they will not be bound by the WGA rules and will be free to contract with a nonunion writer on whatever terms they mutually agree to. Even if the deal is not governed by the WGA, it may still be helpful to turn to the WGA provisions with respect to determining credit and other issues. Just because a non-WGA signatory producer uses the WGA MBA to determine credit, that doesn't mean that the rest of the deal is controlled by the WGA MBA.

Finances and Costs

Remember, the producer may need to negotiate several kinds of payments with the writer:

An option payment. This is for the option itself—often 10% of the purchase price of the script.

- *Option extension payments.* This is typically more money than the option payment itself.
- *The purchase price payment.* This is payment for the sale of the script, due when the option is exercised. The purchase price is usually broken down into:
  - *A fixed compensation payment.* This is the fee which is paid regardless of how much money the movie makes.

- *Contingent compensation payments.* These payments are based on a percentage of the money the movie makes. The writer is often granted 5% of the film's net profits. (Indie film deals may grant writers up to 10% because the fixed compensation paid may be lower.)
- *Other rights payments.* If the producer wants to exploit other rights, such as turning the movie into a television series or making a play from the screenplay, they may have to pay additional fees to the writer. If the production is governed by the WGA, the producer will definitely have to pay additional fees for these rights.

THE BOTTOM LINE: **The option agreement grants the producer the exclusive right to purchase the screenplay from the writer. The purchase agreement dictates the terms of the actual sale. The option and purchase agreements should be negotiated at the same time. Once they are signed by everybody, keep them together and treat them as one contract.**

Step by Step: The Screenplay Option Purchase

1. The producer should perform or commission a copyright search of the US Copyright Office to ensure that the producer has identified all the copyright owners. The producer should pay special attention to who owns the copyrights to any underlying works on which the script is based, such as a comic book or a novel. (See "Copyright Searches and Permissions," p. 159.)
2. If the script is based on another work, like a comic book, the producer will have to make sure that the writer has gotten—in writing—the right to turn that underlying work into a script for production. (See "Screenplay Adaptations," p. 142.)
3. If the copyright to the screenplay has not been registered, the producer should require that it be registered prior to the option/purchase agreement being executed.
4. The option/purchase agreement should be negotiated, written, and signed by all parties.
5. The producer should record the new additions to the chain of title. Remember, the chain of title is an unbroken record of the movie's ownership and is critical to selling a film. (See "Copyright Recordation, Assignments, and Transfers," p. 168.)
6. The producer should require the writer to execute a certificate of authorship. (See "Certificate of Authorship," p. 177.)
7. The option agreement may also be recorded with the Copyright Office.
8. When the script is sold, the writer should execute a short form copyright assignment, which is to be registered with the US Copyright Office.

THE SHOPPING AGREEMENT

Serving somewhat of a similar function and of increasing popularity in recent years is the shopping agreement. Like the option purchase agreement, the shopping agreement gives the producer the right to take the writer's script for a period of time and to try to interest a studio, actor, co-production company, or group of financiers to join the project. During this shopping period, the producer is "attached" to the film and remains attached if the film is produced as a result of the producer's efforts. Unlike an option purchase agreement, however, shopping agreements are often obtained for little or no money being paid to the writer for the right to shop around the script. So even though the producer obtains the exclusive right to set up a film project for a period of time, the writer is not well compensated (or compensated at all) for the loss of marketing opportunity during the period of time that the producer has exclusive shopping rights.

The upside for the writer (in a properly drafted shopping agreement) is that the writer retains the flexibility to negotiate their own sale price for the script as well as other aspects of their deal.

Shopping agreements typically deal with the following issues:

- The primary right is the right to offer the project to a studio or investor group.
- Unlike an option agreement, if there is interest in turning the property into a film, the writer typically negotiates their own purchase terms with that studio or financier group.
- Because the script purchase terms are usually undefined, producers rarely pay much money (if any) to the writer for the right to shop it.
- Shopping agreements usually contain attachments for the producer themselves so that they won't be cut out of the deal if the property owner sells the screenplay directly to the studio the producer lined up.
- Shopping agreements can be used for screenplays, stage play scripts, short stories, articles, comic books, novels, and virtually any kind of underlying property that can serve as the foundation for a film. A colleague of mine once negotiated a shopping agreement for a Tweet!

ATTACHMENT AGREEMENTS

When a producer is attached to project, it means that the project can't be made without them. At least, that's what producers want it to mean. In the United States, many producers use the terms "attachments" and "shopping agreements" synonymously. In a properly drafted shopping agreement, the producer's attachment ends when the term of the shopping agreement expires. There may be a "tail," or "sunset period" of six months to a year following the expiration of the term where a producer will still be attached to the project if it is set up with any of the people or entities the producer solicited and negotiated with during the term of the shopping agreement. Attachment language may also be used to tie performers, directors, writers, and other key personnel to a project in order to make it more attractive to a studio or group of investors.

"Shopping" and "Purchasing" Are Not the Same Thing

On the surface, the concept seems simple: in a shopping agreement, the producer gets the exclusive right to "shop" around the underlying work to investors and studios in the hopes of raising production funding. Once the funding is raised, the producer then purchases the audio-visual rights to the underlying work from the owner. If the movie is funded by a studio, the rights that the producer purchases from the owner of the underlying work may, in turn, be transferred to the studio.

However, the right to shop the property is not the same thing as the right to purchase a property. Thus, a producer who has negotiated only the right to shop a property to investors will still need to negotiate purchase terms with that property's owner. This can be very problematic for the producer who waits until the investors have agreed to finance the film before negotiating purchase terms with the screenplay's owner; in a scenario like that, the screenplay owner may have the leverage in determining the sale price of the script.

The converse is also true: if the producer has the right to shop a screenplay as well as to set the purchase price for that screenplay, they may be incentivized to pay the screenplay's owner very little for the script and will be able to take it out of circulation during the exclusive period during which the producer has the right to shop around. Depending upon the structure of the deal, this could mean that the screenplay's owner is beholden to the producer's ability to set up the project for several years before finally getting the rights back to offer to another producer.

To make matters worse, many producers use a hybrid of the option/purchase agreement and the shopping agreement without understanding which contract provisions are key and which ones are problematic.

Unlike option purchase agreements, which are fairly uniform in format, shopping agreements differ in their scope rather wildly from producer to producer and project to project. In my experience, many producers don't clearly distinguish between the function of an option agreement and a shopping agreement. The unstructured nature and relative informality of a shopping agreement can create a host of problems for the parties. For instance:

- Agreements which call themselves an "option agreement" yet don't contain any purchase terms for the underlying property.
- Agreements which call themselves a "shopping agreement" yet limit the writer's ability to negotiate the sale price of the underlying property.
- Agreements which call themselves an "attachment agreement" yet leave enough wiggle room for the producer to be replaced after they have introduced the writer to studio.
- Agreements which misidentify the underlying property owners, which purport to bind a party to an agreement even though they are not the proper underlying rights holder.

HIRING A SCREENWRITER

Often a writer will pitch an idea to a production company in the hopes that the production company will hire them to write the screenplay. (See "Idea Rights," p. 91.) Or a filmmaker will have an idea or own the rights to literary property and need to hire a writer to turn that idea or property into a screenplay. (See "Screenplay Adaptations," p. 142.)

At the outset, it is critical that the production company that hires the writer comply with all state and federal labor and employment laws. (See "Labor and Employment Law," p. 199; "Hiring Cast and Crew," p. 199.)

GOALS AND DEALS

For definitions and explanations of common contract clauses, see Appendix B, "The Clause Companion," p. 475.

The employment agreement that controls the relationship between the writer and the production company is called a *writer's services agreement.*

One of the most common, and most economical, ways to structure the employment arrangement is by creating a *step deal.* Like an option agreement, the step deal minimizes the production company's risk because the writer is hired and compensated in stages.

For example, the writer is first commissioned to create a treatment for which she is paid money, both when she starts writing the treatment and when she delivers the treatment to the production company. Once the production company has read the treatment during a *reading period*, the company may elect to have the writer try her hand at the first draft of the screenplay. However, on a non-WGA production, the production company is under no obligation to require the writer to continue working on the project. The production company can keep the treatment, pay the writer only for the treatment, and then turn around and hire another writer to develop the treatment into a screenplay.

Common payment and delivery stages for a step deal are:

1. Treatment.
2. Revision of treatment.
3. First draft of screenplay.
4. First revision of screenplay.
5. Second draft of screenplay.
6. Polish.

As always for most production service contracts, it is typical that the producer or production company will own copyright to the writer's work. (See "Work Made for Hire," p. 418). A work-for-hire deal is perfectly suited for this, although in California, deciding to hire a writer under a work-for-hire agreement may require the writer to be treated like an employee.

COMMONLY DEFINED TERMS IN A WRITER'S SERVICES AGREEMENT

Product form. The results of the particular stage being worked on by the writer. For example, treatments, rewrites, and drafts are all various product forms.

Delivery period. The time within which the writer must deliver each product form.

Reading period. The time within which the production company has to read and review the writer's delivered product form.

Option period. The time within which the production company must exercise its option on the writer's services, thereby obligating the writer to create the next step's product form.

Example: Wendy Writer has been hired by Nadir Pictures, LLC, to write the first draft of a screenplay based on the treatment she showed them during a pitch meeting. The contract calls for her to deliver the *product form*—which, in this case, is the first draft of the screenplay—within the *delivery period* of 12 weeks. Following that, Nadir will have a four-week *reading period* within which to review her screenplay, make notes, and decide whether to ask her to go on to the next step. Nadir's reading period is coupled with a four-week *option period* within which it must either tell Wendy that she's obligated to do a rewrite or let her off the hook.

MAJOR DEAL POINTS: WRITER'S SERVICES AGREEMENT

The Parties

- *Production company.* The production company is trying to hire the writer while minimizing the risk of paying for a complete screenplay before it has secured the money to make the movie. The form most favorable to the production company is the step deal.
- *Writer.* If the writer is being hired under a step deal, he will try to minimize the risk by negotiating a larger overall compensation package to offset the chance of being dismissed before the project's completion.

The writer may work for their own loan-out company, which would then be a party to the agreement. (See "Loan-Out Companies," p. 51.)

Engagement or Employment

This paragraph lays out the basis for the deal, which is that the production company is hiring the writer to perform writing services as specified in the agreement. If the writer is to be hired under a work-for-hire deal, it should specify that. If several writers are being hired, the agreement should specify that and define them as a *writing team.*

Writer's Services

This section details the specific services the production company is hiring the writer to perform.

- The steps and product forms are specified (e.g., writing a treatment and the first draft of a screenplay), along with the delivery periods within which the writer must deliver the product form. Typical delivery and reading periods:
  - First draft of a screenplay: 12–16 weeks.
  - Reading/option periods: 2–4 weeks.
  - First revision of the first draft: 6–8 weeks.
  - Second revision 6–8 weeks.
- *Option periods.* During the reading period, the production company usually has an option on the writer's services. If this option is exercised, the writer is obligated to write and deliver the next product form. Options usually run concurrently with reading periods. This section usually specifies that *time is of the essence*, meaning that even the slightest delay in delivery will result

in a breach of contract. (See Appendix B, "Breach of Contract," p. 496.) It is a good idea to specify that delivery must be made to a particular person in the production company.

- *Postponement of services.* The production company typically has the right to postpone the writer's services on any particular step for a period of up to two years. If such postponement occurs, the production company may ask the writer to resume writing on the condition that doing so does not conflict with any contractual obligations the writer may be under at that time.

Compensation

If the WGA MBA governs the contract, it will also dictate the minimum amount of compensation the writer must receive. Check the latest WGA schedule of minimums. There are several different ways a writer may be compensated:

- *Fixed compensation.* In a step deal, each product form is paid for separately. Usually, the writer gets some money at the commencement of the writing of a particular product form and the remainder on delivery of that particular product form.
- *Deferred compensation.* For low-budget pictures especially, production companies may want to put more of their actual cash into the production rather than into paying the salaries of the above-line personnel. As a result, the writer may be asked to defer some or all of their salary until the picture is produced, is released, and begins to make money. The writer should attempt to negotiate a higher salary if their salary is being deferred, because a deferred salary is an inherently risky proposition; after all, if something is deferred, it is not guaranteed. (See Appendix B, "Deferred Compensation," p. 478.)
- *Contingent compensation.* Writers are often granted a portion of the net profits from the picture, typically 2–5% of the film's net profits. (See "Net Profits," p. 66.)
- *Bonus compensation.* Writers often negotiate bonuses if the motion picture is produced because the number of scripts is far greater than the number of movies made from those scripts. The amount of the bonus will be greater if the writer is the only writer on the film, and it will be less if the writer shares screenplay credit with another writer. The bonus is usually paid on commencement of principal photography but subject to the writer's repayment to the production company if the writer's sole screenwriter credit status changes.
- *Additional payments.* If the motion picture is remade into another form, the writer typically gets paid for those forms as well:

  – *Sequel.* Fifty percent of the writer's fixed compensation.

  – *Remake.* Thirty-three percent of the writer's fixed compensation.

– *Television.* Rates differ depending on the length of the television program.

Accounting

If the writer is a net-profit participant or will receive any form of deferred or contingent compensation, this paragraph will delineate how often the writer may expect to receive accounting statements. This is coupled with the right to audit the production company, usually no more frequently than once a year.

Right of First Negotiation

Depending on the writer's leverage, they may request a right of first negotiation on any subsequent versions of the motion picture, such as remakes, sequels, and television shows. If this is agreed to, the production company should be given the power to revoke the writer's right of first negotiation if the writer is no longer actively engaged in writing screenplays for a living. (See Appendix B, "Right of First Negotiation," p. 492.)

Pay or Play

The production company has the right but not the obligation to use the writer's work, provided that the production company pays for the work.

Results and Proceeds

- All the results and proceeds of the writer's work must be assigned to the production company, including copyright, moral rights, rights and ideas in the screenplay, and any other creative and intellectual property right in and to the screenplay, its characters, and story.
- The production company may want to structure this deal as a work made for hire, with an alternate provision stating that if a court of competent jurisdiction finds that the work is not a work made for hire as that term is defined by US copyright law, then the writer assigns all copyright, title, and interest in and to the screenplay to the production company. California companies should be aware that contracting with a writer as a work for hire makes them a statutory employee. (See "Work Made for Hire," p. 418.)
- The writer should agree to execute any other documents necessary to convey the rights to the production company. This should be coupled with a power of attorney for the production company to execute documents on the writer's behalf if the writer fails to do so within a certain period of time.
- A *savings clause* allows certain provisions to survive the termination of a contract. The production company will need to keep the copyright in all the

writer's work that was produced and/or transferred under the agreement, even if the parties decide to cancel the contract.

- The writer should also agree to provide a certificate of authorship. (See "Certificate of Authorship," p. 177.)

Representations and Warranties

Representations and warranties are the promises the writer is making to the production company and are coupled with an indemnification clause stating that:

- The writer is the sole writer of the screenplay and that nothing in the script infringes or interferes with anyone else's rights.
- No other motion picture, dramatic, or other version of the script has been made or authorized.
- By selling the script, the writer will not be violating any third-party rights.
- The writer will not impair, encumber, or otherwise do anything to interfere with the granted rights.
- The writer should indemnify the production company against any claims arising from his or her breach of the representations and warranties.

Credits

- If the contract is governed by the WGA, so are the credit provisions. (See "WGA Credits," p. 117.) As mentioned earlier, it may be a good idea to have the WGA provisions govern credit, even if the production company is not a signatory of the WGA MBA.
- The producer should include a clause disclaiming liability for inadvertently making a mistake with the writer's credit. Typically, on non-WGA films the remedy for credit error is a promise from the producer to correct the credits in future copies of the film.

Publicity

The production company typically wants to restrict the writer's ability to give interviews about the script without the permission and control of the production company.

Net Profits

Like all profit participant contracts, the writer's services agreement should contain a rider that defines how the film's net profits will be calculated.

Remedies

The writer should waive any claim to injunctive relief arising out of a breach of the contract. Depending on the advice of counsel, producers may want any dispute to be settled through binding arbitration rather than through the courts. Keep in mind that if the writer is a member of the WGA, union rules will affect the parties' ability to change the remedies available to the writer.

♦♦♦♦♦

Step by Step: Hiring Writers

1. If your production company is considering working with a WGA writer, that company must become a WGA signatory. (See "The Writers Guild of America," p. 115.)
2. If the screenplay will be an adaptation of another work, permission to use that work must be obtained. (See "Screenplay Adaptations," p. 142.)
3. The production company must comply with the labor and employment laws when hiring any writer, regardless of whether they are in the WGA. (See "Federal and State Labor and Employment Laws: An Overview," p. 199.)
4. Negotiate the major deal points.
5. Make sure that product form and delivery stages are well understood by all parties.
6. The production company should set up a payroll schedule with its accountant.
7. Ensure that each product form is delivered to the same production company representative and that the delivery time and date are logged.
8. Pay close attention to delivery, reading, and option time periods.
9. Exercise the option at each stage by having a written notice sent to the writer and the writer's representatives (i.e., agents, lawyers, etc.).

SCREENPLAY ADAPTATIONS

A filmmaker might want to write or commission a script to be based on someone else's material (e.g., a book, comic book, graphic novel, article, or play). To do so, the filmmaker must negotiate with the author of that literary property (often called the *underlying literary property*) and buy or option the rights to turn that property first into a screenplay and then into a movie.

GOALS AND DEALS

For definitions and explanations of common contract clauses, see Appendix B, "The Clause Companion," p. 475.

In some respects, the *literary property acquisition agreement* is similar to the screenplay purchase agreement (see "Acquiring Screenplay Rights," p. 121). For instance, both contracts govern the acquisition of a property's copyright with the intention of developing it into a motion picture. However, rather than purchasing the rights to a preexisting screenplay, with a literary acquisition agreement, what is being bought and sold is the theatrical motion picture rights to a novel, comic book, or other literary property—which then will need to be written as a screenplay. Like a screenplay, these literary rights may also be optioned first rather than purchased outright.

MAJOR DEAL POINTS: THE LITERARY PROPERTY ACQUISITION AGREEMENT

The Parties

In this agreement, the owner of the literary property is conveying the motion picture and television rights to the producer.

- *Producer*. For the producer, acquiring the literary rights to a work is just the first step in preparing the screenplay. As a result, the producer does not want to be obligated to the owner of the underlying rights more than is necessary. It may be in the producer's best interest to negotiate an option. (See "Option Agreement," p. 124.) Additionally, the producer needs to make sure that they are dealing with all the owners of the underlying rights. Furthermore, the producer needs to be certain that they can acquire all the rights the need to effectively exploit the motion picture rights.
- *Owner*. The owner of a literary property, especially a literary property of proven worth, should only sell the motion picture rights to a producer who can actually bring the film to the big screen. To help ensure that the property will be made into a film, the owner should insist on a reversion clause, which would allow the owner to recapture the motion picture rights at a certain date if the producer has not been able to make the movie. (See Appendix B, "Reversion of Rights," p. 483.) Because the producer will want other rights in addition to the motion picture rights (such as merchandising, television, Internet, etc.) to make the property attractive to producers, the owner should be cautious about conveying away too many of the rights to other parties prior to negotiating a deal with the producer. The owner should pay particular attention to his or her own legal housekeeping. A motion picture producer will not acquire rights unless the owner can prove that he is the sole owner.

THE COMIC BOOK COPYRIGHT CONUNDRUM

Ownership of a literary property is not always obvious. For instance, if you want to adapt a published comic book into a film, you may think that the comic book creator is the right party to deal with. And, in fact, the comic creator may believe that they own the underlying copyright to the comic and are more than happy dealing with you. However, many comic book publishing companies take the audiovisual rights to the comics they publish—a fact that the comic book creator may not be aware of to the extent needed. Therefore, the proper party owning the audiovisual rights may be the comic book publishing company and not the comic book creator, or it may be both the comic book creator and the publishing company. The point is that for any underlying property that has been published, you should inquire as to the specific rights owned by the publishing company.

Rights Granted

The producer needs all the rights necessary to develop, produce, exploit, distribute, exhibit, publicize, and advertise the film adapted from the literary property that the producer is acquiring.

This section lays out the specific rights granted to the producer.

- *Motion picture rights.* At a minimum, the producer needs the exclusive right to make a motion picture from the property (obviously, if you're looking to produce a web series, those are the key rights). The producer needs to make sure that this right extends to all media in which that film will be exploited (such as theatrical release, television, video, Blu-ray, online media, and "any exhibition medium, now known or hereinafter developed").
- *Television rights.* The producer should also receive the right to televise the final film/video in all televised media (such as cable, satellite, free broadcast, pay-per-view, VOD, online distribution, etc.). Note: this is not the same thing as the right to make a television series from the screenplay if the key right you've acquired is the right to turn the screenplay into a motion picture. This is only the right to distribute an exhibit the motion picture in televised media.
- *Merchandising rights.* The producer is typically also granted the right to make T-shirts, action figures, and so forth from the characters and events in the script. The owner usually receives a portion of the money the producer receives from these sales.
- *Trademarks.* If the property has any trademarks associated with it, the right to use those trademarks in association with the exploitation of the granted rights must also be licensed to the producer.

- *Other rights* are subject to negotiation but frequently granted to the producer, such as the right to make derivative works (such as television shows, radio plays, sequels, remakes, video games, plays, and novelizations of up to 7,500 words for the purpose of advertising, publicity, and exploitation of the motion picture).

Copyright

This clause governs the mechanics of ownership and transfer of the screenplay, motion picture, and certain other aspects of the literary property's copyright.

- Unlike the screenplay option/purchase agreement, for an adaptation, the entire copyright is usually not transferred. For instance, if you are acquiring the rights to turn a comic book into a movie, you may only be acquiring the motion picture rights for one film but not the right to turn the comic book into a television series and almost certainly not the right to create comic books that would compete with the underlying property.
- It is critical that the producer perform a copyright search with the US Copyright Office to ensure that the acquired property is not owned by anybody other than the owner(s) or that it is not in the public domain. (See "Copyright Searches and Permissions," p. 159.) For any published work, make sure to investigate what rights the publisher has that are not subject to any deal you may strike with the writer.
- The literary property's copyright information should be listed in the agreement, including the property's title, registration number, and year of publication.
- The producer typically acquires the rights granted in perpetuity (forever). (But see Appendix A, "Termination of Transfer," p. 427.)
- The owner must promise to execute any additional documentation necessary to transfer the copyright to the production company.

Reserved Rights

- Reserved rights specify which rights the owner retains. These are the rights the producer does *not* get. The rights the owner keeps are the subject of negotiation. Often, the owner keeps:
  - Book and other publishing rights (the right to make an author-written sequel).
  - Radio rights.
  - Comic book rights.
  - Stage rights.
  - Online media rights (with the exception of the right to distribute the finished film over online platforms)

- The producer may ask for a *holdback period* for the reserved rights (often five to seven years). This means that for the holdback period, the owner *cannot* exploit those reserved rights that are subject to the holdback.
- Even though the rights are reserved by the owner, the producer will often ask for the *right of first negotiation/right of last refusal* for any sale or exploitation of the rights.

Right to Make Changes

The producer must have the unfettered right to adapt the literary property into a script and then into a motion picture as they see fit. If the property is well known, however, there may be some restrictions on what changes the producer can and cannot make. For example, if the producer were acquiring the right to turn a superhero comic book into a movie, the comic book publisher and/or the creator may impose limits to how much that hero's origin story may be changed.

Payment

This is where the purchase price is specified. Different rights (theatrical, television, etc.) are compensated at different rates.

- It is advisable to negotiate a *floor* (a minimum) and a *ceiling* (a maximum) to any monies being paid to the owner on a royalty basis.
- If the contract is not under the jurisdiction of the WGA, the purchase price is not regulated by the WGA MBA and will be what the parties themselves agree on, taking into consideration the nature of the literary work and the media in which it will be exploited.
- Rights transfer should be conditional on payment of the purchase price.
- Payment is usually due on the earlier of the exercise of the option or the first day of principal photography.

Rights Reversion

Often the owner will negotiate a return of the rights granted if they are not used within a certain period of time. The owner will usually want the rights to revert back to them if the film has not begun principal photography within five years from the date of the assignment of rights.

Right of First Negotiation/Right of Last Refusal

If the owner wants to sell or otherwise exploit any of the reserved rights, the producer often negotiates a right of first negotiation as well as a right of last refusal. (See Appendix B, "Right of First Negotiation," p. 492; "Right of Last Refusal," p. 493.)

Representations and Warranties

These are the promises the owner is making to the producer and are coupled with an indemnification clause. The owner must promise that:

- They are the sole owner of the literary property and nothing in the script infringes the rights of anybody else.
- Copyright registration is up to date and accurate.
- No other motion picture, dramatic, or other version of the script has been made or authorized.
- None of the granted rights are or have ever been granted to anyone else.
- By selling the literary property, the owner will not be violating any third-party rights.
- The owner will not impair, encumber, or otherwise do anything to interfere with the granted rights.

In addition, the owner should *indemnify* the producer for breaches of representations and warranties, misrepresentations, or damages resulting from the owner's breach of contract.

Credit

How the owner and producer determine credit obligations will be determined by the WGA MBA if the owner is a union member and the producer is a signatory.

The producer should include a clause disclaiming liability for inadvertently making a mistake with the owner's credit. Typically, the remedy for credit error is a promise from the producer to correct the credits in future copies of the film.

No Obligation to Produce

While the producer has the right to produce the film using the literary property, they need to be sure that they are not obligated to produce the film.

Publicity

The producer needs to be able to exploit the owner's name, likeness, biography, and so forth in connection with the marketing of the film. Conversely, the producer will want to prohibit the owner from releasing any publicity about the motion picture without the producer's approval.

Remedies

The owner should waive any claim to injunctive relief arising out of a breach of the contract. Depending on the advice of counsel, producers may want any dispute to be settled through binding arbitration rather than through the courts.

♦♦♦♦♦

Law: The Right Rights

One of the biggest business issues involved in literary acquisition agreements is making sure that you have *all* the rights you need to fully exploit the motion picture that you intend to create. You have to be extremely cautious and understand which rights are available, which rights are reserved by the owner, and which rights have been granted by the owner to other rights holders.

Remember, a producer typically acquires the following rights with regard to a particular literary property:

- The right to make motion pictures based on the property, in all media throughout the universe in perpetuity (obviously, the most critical right).
- The right to promote, publicize, advertise, distribute, and otherwise exploit any version of the literary property the producer is allowed to make.
- The right to televise the film.
- The right to create and market merchandise based on the film adaptation of the property.

THE ADVENTURES OF MAGGOT MAN

Penelope Producer wants to make a movie of her favorite comic book series, *The Adventures of Maggot Man*. She first contacts the comic book's publishing company, Carrion Publishing, Inc., and learns that they own all the rights (the copyrights, trademarks, and all other intellectual property rights) to the comic book series. In this regard, Penelope has been lucky; although it is often standard practice for the comic book publishing company to own the IP rights to its characters, this is not always the case.

Carrion Publishing, Inc., agrees to sell her the motion picture rights. If Penelope does not have the money to purchase these rights outright, she may structure the deal as an option/purchase.

While she is negotiating the agreement, she discovers that although the motion picture rights are available, the television distribution rights are not—they've recently been sold to a Japanese anime company. Furthermore, Carrion Publishing, Inc., is steadfast in retaining ownership of all publishing, video game, and merchandising rights. As a result, they will completely own all the revenue streams from action figures or future comic books.

This leaves Penelope with only the motion picture rights, significantly hampering her ability to fully exploit the property. Without the additional revenue streams of television, merchandising, and publishing, Penelope may be limited to monies from theatrical motion picture distribution, and the sale of Blu-ray discs. What looked like a good deal may now have to be reconsidered.

The Right Rights Holders

Prior to any literary acquisition deal, the producer must research and investigate the ownership of the copyright and other intellectual property rights to the literary property in question. (See "Copyright Searches and Permissions," p. 159.)

If any part of the literary property was created by writers or artists other than the owner, the owner's contracts with those artists and writers must be reviewed to ensure that the work was created as a work made for hire or that those rights were effectively assigned to the owner. (See "Work Made for Hire," p. 418.) If the owner can't prove their chain of title, the producer must demand that the owner obtain a written assignment of the writer's and artist's copyrights in the literary work prior to the deal moving forward. Problems here *could be fatal* to the producer's ability to own the copyright to the motion picture.

Step by Step: Screenplay Adaptations

Once the producer has decided to adapt the particular literary property, he or she should take the following steps, similar to those of a screenplay acquisition:

1. Identify the owner of the literary property. For novels, comic books, and other text-based works, the publishing company is the best place to start to get this information.
2. Cross-check the owner information with the search of the copyright office records. (See "Copyright Searches and Permissions," p. 159.)

3. Telephone or write the owner and discuss the possibility of acquiring the motion picture rights. Follow up your discussion with a certified letter that restates the main points of your conversation with the owner.
4. Assuming that you reach agreement on the main deal points, commission a copyright search report.
5. Negotiate and draft the literary property acquisition agreement. If your copyright search report turns up any other owners, this situation must be addressed before the contract is signed. If there are other owners, you must have their written approval to acquire the rights from them.
6. Execute the contract.
7. The owner should also execute a short form copyright assignment, which the producer should record in the copyright office. (See "Copyright Recordation, Assignments, and Transfers," p. 168.)
8. The producer should also prepare and have the author or owner execute a certificate of authorship. (See "Certificate of Authorship," p. 177.)

LIFE STORY RIGHTS

If the movie or project you're planning to shoot is based on someone's life story, you should obtain that person's *life story rights* through a *life rights consent agreement.*

Although no one has the exclusive right to tell his or her own life story, there is a veritable catalog of claims that a subject can file against the filmmaker who shoots an unauthorized biography, unflattering documentary, or fictionalized account of him or her. The frustrating thing is that film subjects who sue often lose their lawsuits, largely due to the protections afforded filmmakers by the First Amendment. That being said, the subjects can, and do, sue. The purpose of a life rights consent agreement is to get the subject's permission up front and to avoid lawsuits altogether.

Filmmakers need to be especially cautious when portraying subjects in a false light, attacking their reputations, or creating the appearance that the subjects have endorsed the movie when they haven't. Lawsuits stemming from these claims are not always won by the filmmakers. Furthermore, filmmakers should never feature a person in a television commercial or other advertising without their express written permission.

What Are Life Story Rights?

Actually, the term *life story right* is a bit of a misnomer. In reality, what you will be acquiring is a collection of rights and releases from liability. Typically, a life rights consent agreement grants to the filmmaker the following rights:

- The right to portray a particular person's life in whole or in part.
- The right to fictionalize or modify that person's life story.
- The right (and sometimes the obligation) to use pseudonyms for people and places portrayed in the life story.
- The copyright to or license to use any accounts of that person's life story (this may be limited by preexisting literary works, such as biographies, based on the life story).
- The life rights consent agreement should also include clauses, called *releases and waivers*, that say that the person granting the life rights (the *grantor*) will not sue the filmmaker for any of the following:
  - Libel and defamation. (See p. 449.)
  - Invasion of privacy. (See p. 443.)
  - Infringement of the right of publicity. (See p. 443.)
  - Copyright infringement. (See p. 429.)
  - Trademark infringement. (See p. 460.)
  - Intentional and negligent infliction of emotional distress.
  - Any other claim arising from the granted rights.

In addition to the previously listed causes of action, plaintiffs who have sued motion picture companies over life story issues have asserted claims for false advertising, false endorsement, commercial disparagement, and unjust enrichment. This is why it is critical for the producer to secure the release of "any claim or cause of action whatsoever arising from the use of the granted rights or portrayal of my likeness or life story."

Although it is true that the First Amendment may provide a solid foundation for defending against many of these claims, the point is to avoid the lawsuit altogether. Furthermore, your E&O insurance policy will probably demand a signed life rights consent agreement.

KRUSHER KRABB: ARMED AND DANGEROUS

Pedro the producer wants to shoot a biography of wrestling superstar Krusher Krabb, the only one-armed professional wrestler ever to be inducted into the Schenectady Wrestling Hall of Fame. Pedro first approaches Krusher for his life story rights but is turned down. He goes ahead with the movie anyway, excited to tell Krusher's uplifting triumph-over-adversity story. Trying to make his biography as compelling as possible, he decides to fictionalize a portion of Krusher's story.

In real life, Krusher lost his arm in a car accident; in Pedro's version, however, Krusher's limb is devoured by an alligator during a wrestling match at a gator farm. Because Krusher's 40-year marriage to his high school sweetheart is motion-picture monotony, Pedro creates a scene in which Krusher has an illicit affair with his trainer's wife—an event that never happened in real life.

Eager to contrast Krusher at his physical peak with the withered old man whom he has become, Pedro secretly photographs Krusher at home, struggling to bathe himself.

After screening the rough cut for his film for several licensing agents, Pedro strikes a deal with a toy manufacturing company to produce Krusher action figures.

Needless to say, Krusher is livid. He can sue Pedro for invasion of privacy (both false light and intrusion upon seclusion), libel, false endorsement, and misappropriation of the right of publicity.

What's Allowed in One State May Not Be Allowed in Another

What makes this area particularly tricky is that most of the rights involved in a life rights agreement are governed by state laws. And to make things even more complex, the laws differ from state to state. For instance, some states recognize a right of publicity; others don't.

To be on the safe side, you should obtain the broadest possible set of rights and releases from all people whose stories are depicted recognizably in the film.

It's CYA time here. If you don't, you could expose yourself to liability if you distribute your film in a state that gives the grantor rights that you have not received permission to use. For instance, depending on the state, if the subject is dead, certain rights may survive death. Therefore, the estate of the deceased may have to be negotiated with.

Even the Dead May Have Rights

Even though someone may be dead, his or her right of publicity may live on! The duration of rights of publicity varies from state to state. In California, it lasts for 70 years after your death, and although for a long time, New York did not recognize a postmortem right of publicity, it now protects the right of publicity up to 40 years after the deceased subject's death. When planning on telling a story about a dead person, filmmakers should seek permission from the *estate* of the deceased.

What Is an Estate?
An estate is not just a house in the country. The term also describes the property, assets, and rights left behind by a dead person. Rights of publicity, copyrights, and other intellectual property rights can be held by an estate. The person who manages the estate is the *executor* or an *administrator*.

If the consent cannot be obtained, the filmmaker should try to fictionalize that person's life story. Here the producer must use extreme caution—the life story must be so modified that the subject is not recognizable. This, of course, may leave the producer with a very different story from the one she had started out to tell.

THE BOTTOM LINE: **If you are filming someone's life story, have them sign a life rights consent agreement, change the events in the movie so that the story is no longer recognizable as theirs, or write the character out of the film altogether.**

GOALS AND DEALS

The filmmaker must make sure to negotiate and execute a life rights consent agreement with the appropriate party. Usually this is the person whose story the filmmaker wants to portray. However, there are some notable exceptions:

- If the subject of the story is dead, you might need to get the consent of his or her estate.
- Minors and legally incapacitated individuals will probably require the consent and signatures of their guardians.
- The filmmaker should get a life rights consent and release from every person who is portrayed in the film. In the Krusher Krabb example, this would mean getting releases from the wrestler's wife, his manager, and other real-life people who will be a part of the movie.
- If the motion picture is based on a preexisting literary work (e.g., a biography), the filmmaker may need to negotiate for the motion picture rights with the holder of the copyright of that book. (See "Screenplay Adaptations," p. 142.) Additionally, the filmmaker must verify that the book's copyright owner has already obtained a life rights consent from the subject and that such consent can be assigned to the filmmaker.

MAJOR DEAL POINTS: LIFE RIGHTS CONSENT AND RELEASE

The Parties

- *Producer.* It is critical that the producer negotiate the life rights consent *before* any other steps are taken on the film. If the producer waits until after the film is shot, the grantor can effectively hold the production hostage by refusing to sign the agreement unless a much higher price is paid. The producer should try to pay a flat fee to the grantor for the rights and releases contained in the agreement and should be very careful about giving any sort of approval over the story to the grantor.
- *Grantor.* The grantor is the person granting the life story rights in the *subject's* life. The grantor could be the same person as the subject of the biography; however, the grantor could also be the subject's parent, if the subject is a minor; her estate, if she's dead; or the business that owns the subject's life story rights. The grantor may want to consider whether he or she plans to turn the life story into a literary work, such as a book, separate and aside from the motion picture. If so, the right to authorize a book about the subject will have to be excluded from the grant of rights to the producer, because the producer will most likely want all the rights to a grantor's life story.

Rights Granted

This section of the agreement spells out the specific rights granted to the producer (also referred to as *assigned rights*). The producer will want the broadest grant of rights possible:

- The right to portray the subject's life in whole or in part.
- The right to fictionalize or modify the subject's life story.
- The right (and sometimes the obligation) to use pseudonyms for people and places portrayed in the subject's life story.
- The copyright and concept rights to any accounts of the subject's life story (this of course may be limited by any preexisting literary works based on the life story).
- Any other rights necessary to exploit the subject's life story.
- *Scope.* As a starting point for the negotiation, the producer should attempt to secure the rights throughout the universe, in perpetuity, in all media, whether now known or hereafter discovered, all methods of advertising, and merchandising. At a minimum, the producer needs the rights to make a movie and distribute it theatrically (theatrical rights), as well as the right to

distribute the finished product on television (network, cable, and OTT) and the right to make physical copies of the movie on Blu-ray, and "any exhibition medium, now known or hereinafter developed".

Reserved Rights

Reserved rights specify which rights the owner retains. These are the rights the producer does *not* get. As mentioned earlier, the producer should attempt to limit the reserved rights. However, the grantor may want to reserve the right to make a literary work, such as an autobiography, based on the subject's life story.

Releases

The producer should secure the following *releases* from the grantor. In other words, the subject is giving up the right to sue for any of the following:

- Libel and defamation.
- Invasion of privacy.
- Intentional and negligent infliction of emotional distress.
- Misappropriation of right of publicity.
- Copyright infringement.
- Trademark infringement.
- False endorsement.
- Any other claim arising from the granted rights.

Right to Make Changes

The producer should retain the unfettered right to change, modify, fictionalize, add, edit, rearrange, or otherwise add to or detract from the subject's life story—without the approval of the grantor. Obviously, this may be a hard sell given that most people want some control over how their own story is told. The producer should be wary about giving any control greater than a "consultation" right (which just means that the producer must consult with the grantor but does not have to incorporate the grantor's suggestions).

Representations and Warranties

The grantor must promise that they have the sole authority to grant the rights and releases in the agreement. The grantor must indemnify the producer, and anyone the producer has assigned the rights to, for a breach of that promise. As seen in other contracts, such representations and warranties often include promises that:

- The life story is true and accurate.
- The grantor is the sole owner of the life story, and nothing in the story infringes the rights of anyone else.
- Copyright registration in any literary property based on the life story is up to date and accurate.
- No other motion picture, dramatic, or other version of the life story has been made or authorized.
- None of the granted rights are or have ever been granted to anyone else.
- By selling the life story, the grantor will not be violating any third-party rights.
- The grantor will not impair, encumber, or otherwise do anything to interfere with the granted rights.
- The grantor should indemnify the producer for breaches of representations and warranties, misrepresentations, or damages resulting from the grantor's breach of contract.

Payment

Grantors are typically paid a flat fee for life story rights. The amount is largely based on how central the character is to the story. Fees may range from a few hundred dollars for a character who is ancillary to the story to thousands of dollars for a main or otherwise integral character. A famous personality or celebrity, especially one who has benefited from the commercial exploitation of his or her personality, will command a much higher price than someone who has not.

No Obligation to Produce

Although the producer has the right to produce the film about or featuring the subject, the producer is not obligated to produce the film.

Remedies

The grantor should waive any claim to injunctive relief arising out of a breach of the contract. Additionally, in all events, the grantor should be prohibited from rescinding the contract and recapturing the granted rights.

Credit

In addition to the person whose life story is being depicted, the movie should also credit the author of any source material (such as an autobiographical book) used to make the film that was based on the life story.

Unless your film is striving for complete accuracy of persons and events, the credit roll should contain a disclaimer, such as: "Certain characters, events, and dialogue in the motion picture in the film were created for the purpose of fictionalization."

♦♦♦♦♦

Business Issues

- You have better negotiating leverage if you secure the subject's life rights prior to production. The best practice is to secure the rights prior to writing a screenplay.
- Check your E&O insurance policy: when portraying actual people, a life rights consent and release is *almost always required* by distributors and by E&O insurance companies.

Step by Step: Life Story Rights

1. Make sure you get a life rights consent and releases from *everybody* whose lives will be portrayed in your movie.
2. If someone does not consent, try to write them out of the movie or change their character so substantially that they are not recognizable.
3. Include a disclaimer at the end of the motion picture.

10

CHAIN OF TITLE

Creating Links of Ownership

WHAT IS A CHAIN OF TITLE?

It's not enough to have a great screenplay. You also have to protect it by safeguarding its copyright. To care for your copyright, you must register it with the US Copyright Office, always display the proper copyright notice on all copies of the script and prints of the film, and maintain a clean *chain of title*.

The chain of title is the unbroken record of ownership of the copyright and other legal rights to the film property. You will need to prove the film's chain of title to distributors, financiers, unions, insurers, and a variety of other parties during the course of the life of a film.

DEV.

The following are key components in establishing and maintaining a clean chain of title for film property:

- Investigating the copyright to all source material used to make the script. (See "Copyright Searches and Permissions," p. 159.)
- Commissioning a screenplay clearance report to detect potential copyright ownership conflicts and problems. (See "Screenplay Clearance Report," p. 162.)
- Properly drafting and executing contracts which transfer copyright and other IP rights from the writer, screenwriter, or literary property owner to the production company.
- Registering the copyright in the script. (See "Copyright Registration," p. 164.)
- Obtaining a certificate of authorship from the writer. (See "Certificate of Authorship," p. 177.)
- Recording all copyright transfers and assignments with the US Copyright Office. (See "Copyright Recordation, Assignments, and Transfers," p. 168.)

***TIP:* Time is of the essence here. Do these steps before you go into production!**

COPYRIGHT SEARCHES AND PERMISSIONS

Frequently producers will need to find out copyright information concerning a particular work. For instance, you might want to make a movie from

DOI: 10.4324/9781003228479-14

somebody's copyrighted novel or use a copyrighted sculpture as art direction for a scene. Or you might need to provide an insurer, financier, or distributor with a copyright search report. In short, at some point (hopefully, early on) the producer or one of their staff will need to conduct or commission a copyright search. The process of researching a copyright and getting permission from the copyright's owners is called *clearing a copyright.*

Copyright searches are an art form all to themselves. All too often, an author's contact information is difficult to find and may require a good deal of diligent investigative work. Remember, just because you can't find out who the author is doesn't mean that you're off the hook and that you are excused from getting permission to use the work. Unknown authors still have rights, and you don't want to get the author's contact information for the first time from their lawyer's cease-and-desist letter. (See "Cease-and-Desist Letters and Lawsuits," p. 56.)

To clear a copyright:

- The producer needs to establish whether the particular work is still protected by copyright.
- If it is, the producer needs to get the contact information for that work's copyright owner so that he can attempt to negotiate a license to use that work.

There are four basic methods for researching the copyright to a work:

1. You can perform the research yourself.
2. You can hire a lawyer to perform the search.
3. You can commission the Copyright Office to perform a search.
4. You can use a professional copyright research company.

Often, your investigation will involve all these methods.

PUBLIC DOMAIN IN THE UNITED STATES MAY NOT BE PUBLIC DOMAIN IN OTHER COUNTRIES

If a work is *not* protected by copyright, it is in the *public domain.* This means that it can be used by anybody without seeking permission from the original author.

However, a work may be in the public domain in the United States yet still be protected by copyright law in other countries. This is because each country has its own laws regarding the scope and duration of copyright protection. Accordingly, a film that incorporates an unauthorized work that is in the public domain in the

United States but is still protected in another country may be considered an infringing work when it is distributed in that country without the permission of the copyright owner.

For more information on the public domain, see Appendix A, "Public Domain," p. 409.

Step by Step: Copyright Searches and Permissions

At some point in the filmmaking process, you will need to get permission to use somebody else's copyrighted work in your film. Unfortunately, finding a copyright owner can often be tricky. Here are some tips to help you locate a copyright owner and seek permission to use their work:

1. Get basic information about the work. To begin, you will need to get some fundamental information about the work itself:
   - *The year of publication.* If this is a book, this information will be found as part of the copyright notice. For example, "*Eight-Track Tape: A Herald of the Future* © 1975 Myopic Publishing, Inc.," means that this book was published in 1975. (See "Copyright Notice," p. 342.) Remember, if it is a work originally created and published in the United States before 1926, it is probably in the public domain, and you will not need permission from the author. (See "Copyright Duration," p. 406.)
   - *Author and publisher information.* For a book, this information will also be included next to, or as part of, the copyright notice. For sound recordings, the copyright symbol is ℗. The Copyright Office offers this advice: "Examine the disk, tape cartridge, or cassette in which the recorded sound is fixed, or the album cover, sleeve, or container in which the recording is sold."
2. Check out the public search portal of the Copyright Office website: www.copyright.gov/public-records/
   a. For works registered or renewed since 1978, search the Copyright Office website for free at https://cocatalog.loc.gov/cgi-bin/Pwebrecon.cgi?DB=local&PAGE=First
3. Pay the Copyright Office to search for you. If you can't find the information you need or if the work was registered prior to 1978, you might want to commission a search by the Copyright Office itself.[1] The Copyright Office charges an hourly rate and will provide you with an estimate of how long the search will take before it starts. You should be prepared to give the following information to the Copyright Office researchers:
   - The title of the work, with any possible variants.
   - The names of the authors, including possible pseudonyms.

- The name of the probable copyright owner, which may be that of the publisher or that of the producer.
- The approximate year when the work was published or registered.
- The type of work involved (book, play, musical composition, sound recording, photograph, etc.).
- For a work originally published as a part of a periodical or collection, the title of that publication and any other information, such as the volume or issue number, to help identify it.
- The registration number or any other copyright data.

4. Hire a professional search company. If all else fails, you can hire a professional copyright research company such as Clarivate[2] to conduct a full copyright search report. This may be the most expensive option, but given the fact that these companies search additional databases to the ones used by the Copyright Office, it is probably the most thorough option.
5. Use your production attorney to help you locate and secure permissions from the right parties.
6. Get permission *in writing* to use the work. Once you've identified the copyright owner, get permission to use the copyrighted work with a written copyright license signed by the rights holder.
   - For literary works. (See "Literary Property Acquisition Agreement," p. 143.)
   - For painting and sculptures. (See "Artwork License," p. 298.)
   - For music. (See "Music License Agreement," p. 320.)
   - For film clips. (See "Film Clip License Agreement," p. 335.)

Screenplay Clearance Report

Prior to production, you should have your entertainment attorney prepare a screenplay clearance report. Essentially, this report details potential legal problem areas in the screenplay. The report should combine the efforts of a copyright records search to identify conflicting copyright ownership and infringement issues with a comprehensive legal analysis to identify other intellectual property, defamation, and liability issues.

The report should alert you to the following legal issues, if present:

- *Libel and defamation.* (See "Libel and Defamation," p. 449.) Documentaries need to be particularly aware of libel and defamation claims. Any material that could affect somebody's reputation should be scrutinized. If the person being discussed or depicted is not a public figure such as a politician, extreme care should be used to ensure that all portrayals and discussions about that person are accurate and truthful. Ideally, anyone discussed or portrayed in the film should give their written consent. If you have E&O insurance, your insurance carrier will probably require written consent for all depicted individuals.

- *Invasion of privacy.* (See "The Right of Publicity and Other Privacy Rights" p. 443.) Does your film discuss private facts about people's lives? Remember, here the inquiry is focused on whether your script is prying into someone's personal life in an overly intrusive manner. For fictional films and programs, you should check all character names; you're better off having a character name that nobody in the real world shares or, conversely, that many people share. A character name shared by only a few people could help support an argument that your film is referring to that real individual, which is a prerequisite for a defamation or invasion-of-privacy lawsuit. For instance, from a legal perspective, John Smith and Xerxes Vander-Flärpenboot would be good legal choices for character names. The former name is common, the latter name unique.
- *Copyright.* (See "What Is a Copyright Infringement," p. 429.) Your attorney should flag any instances of copyright infringement. This is a two-part inquiry, which scrutinizes any copyrighted works referenced in the screenplay as well as the copyright to any works on which the screenplay is based.
- *Referenced copyright.* The first part of the inquiry focuses on any third-party copyrighted material directly referenced in the screenplay, such as song lyrics sung by a character or a scene in which two characters watch a copyrighted movie. In other words, references in the screenplay itself to other copyrighted works will need to be cleared and licensed. If these works cannot be cleared, they should be changed to noncopyrighted works or works commissioned by the production company as works for hire. If neither clearing the copyright nor changing the work is possible, the copyrighted work should be omitted from the film.
- *Underlying copyright and chain of title.* The second part of the inquiry analyzes the copyright in the screenplay itself, as distinguished from any copyrighted works *referenced* in the screenplay. Here the attorney will try to make sure that the structure, plot, scenes, characters, and dialogue originated with the screenwriter. If these elements are taken from another copyrighted work (e.g., a graphic novel, play, or book), the attorney will need to verify that the screenwriter had the right to create a derivative work based on that source and that the screenwriter has validly transferred that right to the production company. (See "Screenplay Adaptations," p. 142.) If the screenplay was written by two or more authors, the attorney should verify that all authors have conveyed their copyright interests to the production company. (See Appendix A, "Joint Authors and Joint Works," p. 415.)
- *Trademark infringement, tarnishment, and false endorsement.* In addition to ensuring that the screenplay doesn't depict any *copyrighted* works without permission, the production attorney should review all script references to

trademarked products and services. Like copyrights, unlicensed trademark use should be avoided. The attorney should be on the lookout for any use of trademarks or a celebrity's image:

- That might cast that trademarked product or service in a negative light, or
- That implies that the owners of the trademark endorsed the film (see "Trademarks on the Set," p. 300; also "False Endorsement," p. 464)

- *Potential legal problems in production.* The attorney should also bring to bear their general legal knowledge. If a scene involves extensive pyrotechnics, the attorney should make note that special permits will probably be needed. If the movie involves extensive use of child actors, the attorney should note that special child labor laws may restrict the shooting schedule. This portion of the review is often done in conjunction with script breakdown.
- *Conflicts with talent agreements.* Talent agreements often impose restrictions on the way an actor may be photographed. If partial nudity is required, make sure that there is a nudity rider in that actor's contract. For child actors, make sure that the parents give their signed consent to allow children to appear in scenes dealing with adult situations.
- *Conflicts with production services agreements.* If your company has been hired to make a program for a network or cablecaster (see "Production Services Agreement," p. 178), you need to make sure that nothing in your script violates that company's standards and practices guidelines. Furthermore, if you are planning on featuring specific products in your script, you will need to run that list of manufacturers by the network's marketing division to make sure that there are no conflicts with the network's current advertisers.

The screenplay clearance report should be completed well before shooting takes place, to give the production company enough time to secure the proper permissions or to make creative changes as needed.

COPYRIGHT REGISTRATION

Registration is the process of filing your copyright information with the government and gives you far greater protections over your copyright than if you don't register it. You should register the copyright to both your script and to your motion picture. You can hire a service to register the copyright for you, but it's actually a pretty simple process, so you may want to try to do it yourself. Registration consists of filling out and submitting an online copyright registration form along with a copy of the work you're registering as well as the correct registration fee. The ONLY place you can directly register your copyright is with the US Copyright Office (www.copyright.gov). Other places which offer the copyright registration service charge more money than the government does and then go ahead and register your copyright the same place as if you did it yourself.

And no, before you ask, a WGA registration is NOT the same thing as registering your copyright and doesn't offer any of the key protections copyright registration does.

WGA REGISTRATION VS. COPYRIGHT PROTECTION

A lot of writers believe WGA Screenplay Registration is the same thing as copyright registration. Noooo. Not by a long shot. ONLY copyright registration will allow you to sue for infringement, to collect statutory damages, to serve as constructive notice, list your production company as the registrant,[3] etc. I honestly don't know of any advantage a non-WGA member has in registering their script with the Guild over copyright registration. Register your copyright at www.copyright.gov and put the money you would have spent on the additional WGA registration back into your film.

Why Register the Work?

Although registration is no longer a requirement of copyright protection, it does provide the following HUGE benefits:

- Registration is usually required by distribution companies, E&O companies, and other third parties who may have an interest in maintaining and protecting the film property.
- Registration establishes a public record of the copyright claim.
- Before an infringement suit may be filed in court, registration is necessary for works of US origin.
- If registration is made before or within five years of publication, courts will start with the presumption that the copyright is valid and that all the facts stated in the certificate are correct.
- If registration is made within three months after publication of the work or prior to an infringement of the work, statutory damages and attorney's fees will be available to the copyright owner in court actions. Otherwise, only an award of actual damages and profits is available to the copyright owner. (See "Copyright Infringement," p. 429.)
- Registration allows the owner of the copyright to record the registration with the US Customs Service for protection against the importation of infringing copies.

DEPOSIT YOUR WORK—IT'S THE LAW!

Even if you don't want to *register* the copyright, it is a legal requirement that all copyrightable published works be *deposited* with the Copyright Office within three months of publication.[4] Failure to do so may expose you to a fine of $250 for each work, plus the retail price of the copies. And if you've repeatedly or intentionally refused to deposit the copies, an additional fine of $2,500 may be assessed against you.

This deposit requirement is fulfilled if the works are registered with the Copyright Office, so you might as well register the work while you're at it.

Online Copyright Registration

The Copyright Office has made registration easier than ever by moving it online. Although you can still print out a paper form (Form CO), fill it in, and mail it to the Copyright Office, it's so much easier to do everything from your browser, from filling in the form to uploading the video files and paying with a credit card. To register a motion picture, visit the website of the US Copyright Office at www.copyright.gov.

For a detailed, step-by-step explanation of how to register your copyright using the Copyright Office's online registration, see www.copyright.gov/registration/

What You Submit

To register the copyright to your script or movie, submit the following to the Copyright Office:[5]

1. A completed application form (preferably completed online).
2. A "best-edition" nonreturnable copy of your work. A best edition is the version that is the cleanest, most legible, and most complete. For more information on this requirement, see www.copyright.gov/circs/circ07b.pdf
3. For *unpublished* films, one copy of the motion picture, which can be uploaded digitally, size permitting.
4. For *published* films, two best edition copies of the movie, which must be sent in physically.
5. For screenplays, submit a copy of the script.
6. Check with the Copyright Office as to the particular file format you are submitting.

7. A description of the work itself—for example, a shooting script or synopsis of the film.
8. Payment (they take credit cards). As of this writing, it costs $45 for a standard registration of a non-work for hire by a single author, and $65 for other standard filings. Other prices apply when registering groups of works, contributions to periodicals, etc.[6]

You should receive a certificate of registration within a few months (sometimes as many as six months) after sending in your materials. No matter how long the Copyright Office takes to register your copyright, the date of registration will be the date on which the Copyright Office receives all your materials.

COPYRIGHT CONCEPTS

- *Work.* Under copyright law, the term *work* is used to describe scripts, movies, musical compositions, and any other copyrightable form of artistic expression. On the copyright registration form, the word *work* is used quite frequently to refer to the underlying copyrightable portion.
- *Publication.* "Publication of a motion picture takes place when one or more copies are distributed to the public by sale, rental, lease or lending, or when an offering is made to distribute copies to a group of persons (wholesalers, retailers, broadcasters, motion picture distributors, and the like) for purposes of further distribution or public performance."[7] For more, see Appendix A, "Copyright Law," p. 402.

THE COPYRIGHT NOTICE

Although it is no longer a requirement for copyright protection, it is advisable to include a copyright notice on all your copyrighted work. The proper format for the notice is ©, "Copyright," or "Copr.," followed by the year in which the work was first published, followed by the name of the copyright owner.

Example: *A Tomb with a View* © 2022 Zeus Pictures, Inc.

For motion picture or video, the copyright notice should be placed in one or more of the following places:[8]

- With or near the title.
- With the cast, credits, and similar information.

- At or immediately following the beginning of the work.
- At or immediately preceding the end of the work.

For the screenplay, it is customary to display the copyright notice prominently on the cover of the script.

For more information about copyright notice, see US Copyright Office Circular 3, "Copyright Notice," at www.copyright.gov/circs/circ03.pdf

COPYRIGHT RECORDATION, ASSIGNMENTS, AND TRANSFERS

Assignments and Transfers

Any contract or other document that transfers copyright ownership may be recorded at the Copyright Office. In other words, you should record writing agreements, options, literary property purchase agreements, copyright assignments, and contracts containing copyright assignment or licenses clauses. In fact, the Copyright Office will record any document "pertaining to a copyright."

Why Record?

Recording a contract or other document pertaining to copyright ownership has several effects:

- It establishes a public record of ownership by giving the world *constructive notice* of the new owner. Constructive notice means that once the copyright in a work is registered, everyone is presumed to know the ownership and other registration information on file with the Copyright Office—even if they have not, in fact, actually looked up the registration records.
- It determines *priority* of conflicting transfers (see following).
- It is necessary to prove a chain of title required by distributors, insurers, and other third parties.

Conflicting Transfers

It might be surprising to learn, but you could lose a copyright transferred to you if you don't record the transfer in time! If you fail to record the transferred copyright, and the original copyright owner transfers that same copyright to a third party who then records that second transfer, you could lose the copyright.[9]

BURNT BY TOAST

Wanda Writer has written a screenplay. Eager to strike a deal, she transfers the rights in her screenplay, *The Exciting World of Toast*, to Fly-by-Night Productions on July 1, 2020.

A week after Wanda signed the purchase agreement with Fly-by-Night Productions, Major Studio, Inc., approaches her to acquire the rights in her screenplay. Realizing that she has a much better deal with Major Studio, Inc., Wanda decides to transfer the rights to *The Exciting World of Toast* to Major Studio, Inc., even though she had assigned the same rights to Fly-by-Night Productions a week earlier. Major Studio, Inc., is unaware of the deal between Fly-by-Night Productions and Wanda. She signs a purchase agreement with Major Studio on July 15, 2020.

- If Fly-by-Night Productions records the assignment of copyright with the Copyright Office within one month after Wanda transfers her copyright to it (i.e., by August 1, 2020), Fly-by-Night Productions will own the rights to the screenplay.
- However, if Fly-by-Night Productions does not record the assignment of copyright by August 1, 2020, and Major Studio records its assignment of copyright first (for instance, on August 10), Major Studio will own the copyright to the screenplay, regardless of whether Fly-by-Night Productions records its assignment of copyright on August 11.

  No matter which production company gets the copyright to the script, the other (losing) production company cannot recover the screenplay copyright unless the winner is willing to sign it over.

Does the losing company have any cause for action? Yes, a breach-of-contract lawsuit against Wanda Writer. (See Appendix B, "Breach of Contract," p. 496.)

Short-Form Copyright Assignment

Keep in mind that recorded documents become publicly available, so any terms in a contract that is recorded will become known to anyone who views the recorded document. If you record the entire contract that contains the assignment clause, the entire world will also be able to read the contract clauses containing compensation, contact information, and other paragraphs that the parties might not want the public to access. For this reason, short-form assignments and transfers are often used rather than the longer contracts that justify the transfer.

Short-form assignments contain the minimum amount of information needed to effectuate the transfer of copyright. They are often executed concurrently with the longer contract that details the deal terms under which the assignment occurs (for instance, a literary acquisition agreement).

SAMPLE SHORT-FORM COPYRIGHT ASSIGNMENT

Date: ______

For one dollar in hand and other good and valuable consideration, the receipt and sufficiency of which is hereby acknowledged by all parties, the undersigned ______ (Assignor) does hereby assign and convey to ______ (Assignee), its successors, assigns, and licensees, the copyright to that [*motion picture, video, screenplay, etc.*] (the "Work"), currently titled: "______," and registered with the United States Copyright Office Registration #______. This assignment is perpetual in duration and applies to all derivative works of the Work and all copyrightable components which have comprised the Work.

Agreed to and Accepted by:

Assignee: ______ Assignor: ______

How to Record a Document

The Copyright Office does not determine the form of the documents to be recorded, so virtually any contract, from screenplay options to distribution agreements to director's services contracts, may be recorded.

A few basic requirements must be met. The document to be recorded must:

- Have original signatures of the parties who signed it (or proper certification of photocopy).
- Be complete by its own terms.
- Be legible.
- Be accompanied by the correct fee.[10]

COPYRIGHT CONCEPTS

The document must be *complete by its own terms*. That is, a document that contains a reference to any schedule, appendix, exhibit, addendum, or other material as being attached or made a part of it is recordable only if the attachment is also submitted for recordation with the document.[11]

For example, if you state in the assignment that the assignment is "subject to the terms and conditions of that option agreement entered into between the parties on December 3, 2019" that option agreement—or the short form version—had better be attached, or the assignment would be unrecordable.

See Copyright Circular 12 on the US Copyright website for more information at www.copyright.gov/circs/circ12.pdf

CERTIFICATE OF AUTHORSHIP

A *certificate of authorship* is a key document in the chain of title of a motion picture. This is a notarized statement by the writer identifying the author of the script. In the case of a work made for hire, the script's author is considered to be the production company. A certificate should be executed by all the script's authors.

THE CERTIFICATE OF AUTHORSHIP

"*I, [writer's name]* certify that I have written the attached screenplay as a work made for hire for *[production company's name]*, pursuant to that writer's services agreement, dated ______, between me and the aforementioned production company. Accordingly, I understand and agree that the production company shall be considered the author of the attached screenplay. If a court of competent jurisdiction determines that the screenplay was not created as a work made for hire, I hereby assign all copyright, title, and interest to that screenplay to the production company with full rights to assign said copyright in whatsoever manner the production company chooses. I waive any right to "*droit moral*," or other moral right, now known, or hereafter enacted. I understand and agree that as full owner of the copyright to the screenplay, the production company and its assigns, may make any modification or change whatsoever to the screenplay or its derivative works. I represent and warrant that nothing in the screenplay infringes upon any rights of third parties; the screenplay contains no defamatory material and does not infringe the privacy rights of any parties. All of the material not original with me which was used to create the screenplay was either provided to me by the production company or was in the public domain. I have the full right and power to execute this document, and nothing in the screenplay, or my services in connection with the creation of the screenplay does or shall infringe the rights of a third party."

Keep Your Records Clean

All the documents that affect your chain of title should be kept in a separate, well-organized binder. Presenting a financier, network, distribution company, insurer, or other co-production company with an easy-to-follow, comprehensive file goes a long way toward establishing your credibility as a trustworthy and reliable filmmaker.

NOTES

1 www.copyright.gov/circs/circ22.pdf

2 See https://clarivate.com/compumark/solutions/trademark-searching/title-copyright-entertainment-searches/ (Accessed November 11, 2021).

3 www.wgaeast.org/mo/script_registration/questions

4 See 17 U.S.C. 407 (2020).

5 Copyright Office Circular #45, "Copyright Registration for Motion Pictures, Including Video Recordings," www.copyright.gov/circs/circ45.pdf

6 See www.copyright.gov/about/fees.html (Accessed November 8, 2021).

7 Copyright Office Circular #45, "Copyright Registration for Motion Pictures, Including Video Recordings," www.copyright.gov/circs/circ45.pdf

8 US Copyright Office, Compendium of US Copyright Office Practices §2207.6 (3d ed. 2017).

9 17 U.S.C. § 205 (d) (2020) "(d) Priority between Conflicting Transfers.—As between two conflicting transfers, the one executed first prevails if it is recorded, in the manner required to give constructive notice under subsection (c), within one month after its execution in the United States or within two months after its execution outside the United States, or at any time before recordation in such manner of the later transfer. Otherwise, the later transfer prevails if recorded first in such manner, and if taken in good faith, for valuable consideration or on the basis of a binding promise to pay royalties, and without notice of the earlier transfer."

10 www.copyright.gov/about/fees.html

11 37 CFR § 201.4.

5

PRE-PRODUCTION

Once you've figured out which movie you're going to make and you've acquired all the rights to that film property, it's almost time to start staffing up and getting ready for the production. This section of the book provides information on:

- Negotiating a production services agreement. (See "Production Services Agreement," p. 178.)
- Starting an international co-production. (See "International Co-Productions," p. 185.)
- Negotiating a product placement or sponsorship agreement when you want to feature a product in your film and be compensated for it. (See "Product Placement & Sponsorship," p. 189.)
- A brief overview of employment and labor law. (See "Federal and State Labor and Employment Law," p. 199.)
- How to hire a producer. (See "The Producer," p. 213.)
- How to hire a director. (See "The Director," p. 214.)
- How to hire a crew member. (See "Crew Services Agreement," p. 233.)
- How to hire an actor. (See "Performer's Services Agreement," p. 256.)
- Dealing with the Screen Actors Guild—American Federation of Television and Radio Artists. (See "SAG-AFTRA," p. 243.)
- Getting a script to an actor and dealing with the agent. (See "How to Get a Script to a SAG-AFTRA Actor," p. 266.)

PRODUCTION SERVICES AGREEMENTS

If another company wants to hire your production company to produce a film or television show, you will first need to negotiate a *production services agreement* with them. (See "Production Services Agreement," p. 178.) This agreement lays out the budget and scope of the project, determines how your company will be paid, and dictates the precise technical and legal compliance standards of the program. For producers seeking international production partners, see "International Co-Productions," p. 185. The agreement may even dictate who you need to hire to write, direct, or star in your project.

PRODUCT PLACEMENT AND SPONSORSHIP

You might want to save money on props and set decoration by having manufacturers and advertisers supply you with their products in exchange for your promise to include their goods, trademarks, and/or services in your film. On bigger-budget films, movies with well-known actors, and programs with the potential to reach large audiences, manufacturers may also pay you a fee to feature their wares onscreen. (See "Product Placement," p. 189.) Or perhaps you have a popular YouTube channel and want to be sponsored on an ongoing basis by companies related to the subject matter of your programming. (See "The Sponsorship Deal," p. 194.) The time to start this process is in pre-production before the cameras start rolling.

Now it's time to cast actors, sign up a director (if it's not going to be you), and hire your crew.

HIRING CAST AND CREW

Hiring and managing employees and independent contractors is one of the trickier legal areas a filmmaker must face. This is because a whole host of laws apply to the employer/employee relationship. For instance:

- *Services contracts*. A *services contract* between the production company and the worker will govern the relationship of the parties and control issues such as the worker's duties, the worker's salary, the film credit the worker expects to receive, benefits for the worker (if any), and so on. Don't forget, a worker can be an employee or independent contractor, and the worker may have her own loan-out company, which is also a party to the services agreement. (See "Loan-Out Company," p. 51.)
- *Union collective bargaining agreements*. If the worker is a member of an entertainment union, such as Screen Actors Guild–American Federation of Television and Radio Artists (SAG-AFTRA), Writers Guild of America (WGA), or the International Alliance of Theatrical Stage Employees (IATSE), and the production company is a signatory of that union, the working relationship is governed by the rules of that entertainment union. That union's collective bargaining agreement will win out over any conflicting provisions in the services contract.
- *Federal and state labor and employment laws*. To complicate matters further, federal and state labor and employment laws will also trump the services agreement and impose limits and requirements on how a production company employer must deal with its employees.

11

PRODUCTION SERVICES AND CO-PRODUCTIONS

So far, we've explored those scenarios in which you're making a film or program on your dime or with investor money. Perhaps, Netflix, Hulu, or Amazon Studios has decided that it likes the movie idea you pitched to them and wants your production company to create it as well. Or, on a smaller scale, maybe an advertising agency wants to hire your production company to create a series of television commercials for YouTube ads for a local business.

In other words, this is a relationship where a larger media company pays your smaller production company to shoot and deliver to them the program according to detailed specifications. The production services agreement between the larger media company and your smaller production company controls both how the program will be produced and the technical and legal standards that govern its production.

NETWORKS, STUDIOS, TELEVISION MEDIA COMPANIES, AND OTHER BEASTS OF THE FIELD

In this day and age of global production, there are many kinds of entities that produce programming: traditional television media companies; OTT television companies like Netflix, Hulu, Amazon Prime; production arms of a distribution companies; broadcast divisions of motion picture companies, and so on. The lines between them are blurry and getting blurrier. For the sake of clarity in this chapter, I'll refer to the larger television media company that is commissioning a program from your production company as "the network"—even if it's a local advertising agency. I know this is not technically correct, but do you really want to read a chapter in which I'm constantly referring to "the commissioning entity" or the "supervising production entity"? "Network" it is. Even if, you know, it may not actually be a "network."

DOI: 10.4324/9781003228479-16

GETTING A NETWORK INTERESTED IN YOUR PROJECT

As a general rule, a network will only commission programming from a smaller production company if:

- You or your company has a track record in producing similar programming.
- You've worked with the network or one of its executives before.
- You have the exclusive rights to a key program element, such as life rights to the subject of a docudrama.

> ***Example:*** Your company, Pleonasm Motion Picture, Movie, and Film Productions, LLC, has an exclusive option on the life story rights of octogenarian demolition derby driver Maude "The Marauder."
>
> You pitch the Carnage Network on your idea of a one-hour documentary on the fender-bending grandma. Although the network might be able to do an unauthorized documentary on Maude "The Marauder," it really wants her cooperation for the interview segments in the one-hour documentary. Because it wants her, the network must deal with your company to get her participation.

Once you have the network's attention, you have to go in and pitch your program idea. Bringing a short trailer to the pitch meeting can help showcase both your concept as well as your ability to execute the program. Before you go in to pitch your idea, make sure you understand how to protect your rights. (See "Idea Rights," p. 91.) If the network likes your idea, thinks it can market or exhibit it, and thinks that your company can competently produce it, it is time to negotiate the production services agreement.

MAJOR DEAL POINTS: THE PRODUCTION SERVICES AGREEMENT

The Parties

The network may hire your production company directly to produce the program, or it might contract with a larger production company to supervise your company's production.

If you haven't done so already, you should form a limited liability entity, like an LLC or a corporation, and have your company (rather than you personally) be a party to the production services agreement. That way, if something goes wrong during the production and the network sues, it is your company's assets that will be on the line rather than your personal assets. (See "Setting Up the Production Company," p. 43.)

Engagement/Production Services

This paragraph outlines the specific duties required of the production company in producing the program. It typically contains:

- *The tentative title, subject matter, running time, and delivery date of the program.* Often, this section will reference a treatment or script that the production company has pitched to the network.
- *A reference to an attached schedule, budget, and production technical and legal specifications of the program.*
- *A key person clause* designating you or one of your production company's employees as the executive producer in charge of the production. (See "Clause Companion: Key Person," p. 480.) Note that this is usually a material provision. In other words, it is critical that this key person act as executive producer; no substitutions allowed! If they quit the project, you could find yourself in breach of contract. That's why you should make sure the key person is someone you know that you can rely on, such as someone you've worked with before. If you are working on other projects in addition to the one that is the subject of the production services agreement, make sure to stipulate that you may continue to work on those "outside projects" as long as it does not materially interfere with the work you're doing on the project covered by the production services agreement.

Rights

If the network is paying for the production, they will likely want ownership of the copyright and other intellectual property rights in the program. In the agreement, there will typically be a work-for-hire or rights assignment from your company to the network. (See Appendix B, "Rights Granted," p. 483.) If you own the underlying rights on which the program will be based, try to negotiate a grant only of the rights necessary to make the program at hand without giving away all rights to the property. In other words, if you are producing a one-hour documentary for basic cable, try to retain the theatrical film rights. However, be prepared for the network to laugh politely at this request and say "no."

Payment Schedule/Acquisition Price

This is the total production budget you will be given to make the program. If the network is paying for the entire production, your company will likely be offered a fixed budget to produce the program, out of which you will need to pay your own production company its fee. That may be the only money your company makes from the program, so make sure to protect your *production company fee* in the budget; many is the production company that ate into its own fee to pay for one more "perfect shot" that wasn't properly budgeted for. This is because the production company is responsible for all overages. In other words, if you run over budget, your production company must fund the difference. To counterbalance this risk, producers try to negotiate a provision allowing their companies to keep any monies left over (called *underages*) if they bring in the project under budget. Another variation is to split underages 50/50 with the network. You should be careful here; you don't want to give the impression that you will short-change the production in order to keep any underages.

- Often the largest payment, frequently as much as one half the budget or more, will be payable on execution of the agreement.
- The next payment, often a quarter of the budget, will be payable on delivery of the rough cut and production insurance binder. (See "Insurance Coverage," p. 59.)
- The final payment to your company will be withheld until the approval of all *deliverables, including* the *legal deliverables*. (See "Delivery Requirements," below.)

In addition to the fixed compensation of your production company fee, try to negotiate a contingent compensation provision if you have the leverage. For instance:

- If you are producing a one-hour documentary for a network, try to negotiate a residuals clause. For example, you may ask for your production company to receive a percentage of every home video (DVD, Blu-ray) sale.
- If you are producing a webisode series, try to negotiate a percentage of the advertising revenue received from online ads posted on the same webpage as the webisode.

Note: Many premium cable and OTT networks pay for their original content using a "cost-plus" model: the network essentially buys all the rights to the program, paying for the entire cost of production (e.g. 30%) and an additional percentage of the production costs to compensate the producers for future revenues from the licensing of their program (in essence, a "buyout"). This is entirely different from the old television network financial model of paying upwards of 60–70% of the production costs for a television series while allowing the producers to make money through syndication and other licensing arrangements (like derivative works and movies).

Production Specifications

Included as a separate schedule, this list of production requirements is what your production company must strictly adhere to in preparing the program. It includes sections on approvals, required elements, and legal and technical deliverables. It may also include a statement that the production must not be subject to any entertainment guild or union. Conversely, if it is a union production, the production specifications will often state which union contract should govern the production.

Smaller entities, like an advertising agency, may not always provide you with tech specs. Needless to say, it's much more difficult to deal with a commissioning party that doesn't understand the technical requirements they actually need, so be sure to suggest and include the technical specs in the contract so there's no confusion down the road. No one wants a 3 AM call from an angry client who told you to produce a 4K commercial but whose server can't handle the extra bandwidth.

Right of First Refusal

Suppose you suspect that the one-off production or webisode you've been hired to shoot may be a *backdoor pilot*—a way for the network to test the waters to see if there is enough audience interest in the show for them to sink more money into an actual series. If you have the leverage, ask for a right of first negotiation for your company to produce any future productions derived from the production that you're currently shooting. (See Appendix B, "Right of First Negotiation," p. 492.)

Approvals/Required Elements

Part of the production specs, this section will detail those elements over which the network will reserve the right of prior approval. It should also list the network executive in charge of giving that final approval (usually it's the network's executive producer or the executive in charge of production). *Be very careful here*: If the contract requires you to get network approval over an element, such as the choice of talent, you must make sure to get that approval prior to hiring that performer! Failure to do so may result in your having to buy that rejected performer out of his contract later *and* having to pay for the approved performer.

Networks will often require clearances or permissions for and reserve approval rights over the following:

- Above-the-line and below-the-line personnel. This is typically coupled with a requirement that all talent and above-the-line personnel grant the rights to use their names, likenesses, and biographies for marketing and promotional purposes for the program.
- All story outlines, treatments, scripts, and other materials.
- Photographs, titles, music, rough cut, final cut, and all credit obligations.
- Composer and music licensing agreements. Usually included is a minimum term for which licensed music must be acquired, as well as a list of media and territories for which the music must be licensed. Typically, the network requires a perpetual license throughout the universe, which is much more expensive than a license that is of limited duration and location. (See "Music Licensing," p. 315.)
- Any product placement agreements. Be sure to budget extra time for this; product placement agreements will almost always have to be cleared by the ad sales department of the television company to avoid sponsor conflicts.

Example: If the Buds n' Suds beer company has bought airtime to run its commercials during the broadcast of your cooking program, it may get upset and cancel future ad buys if your cooking show spends too much time singing the praises of another brand of beer.

- Any trademarks, copyrights, or other intellectual property-protected materials shown in the program, no matter how briefly.
- Permissions from all persons shown on camera.

With regard to permissions and clearances, it is important to keep in mind the difference between permissions *required by law* and those *required by your contract.*

Example: You may have filmed some people walking in the background on a city street as part of your B-roll footage for a documentary. Generally, people do not have a right of privacy over noncommercial uses of their images filmed while they are on a public street. As a result, you may not be required by statutory or case law to get a release from people incidentally shown on camera walking down the sidewalk, as long as you're careful not to defame them or use footage of them for *commercial purposes.* (See "Depiction Releases," p. 275.) However, your production services agreement will almost certainly have a *contractual* requirement that you obtain a written release from every person photographed and shown in the program.

From a practical standpoint, getting permission from everybody can be unwieldy. The solution? Get your production attorney involved. Have them put a call into the legal affairs attorney or the executive in charge of production at the network and negotiate a waiver of your appearance release requirement for a particular sequence. Failure to do so may result in you being noncompliant with your legal deliverable requirements and could delay your final payment.

Delivery Requirements

Be prepared to receive to a rather lengthy schedule of technical and legal delivery requirements that you must adhere to in creating your show. The *deliverables* are the finished program and other materials that the production company must deliver to the network to satisfy its producing obligations on the program; in a nutshell, it's the program; its components; and the contracts, releases, waivers, and other paperwork that give you the rights to the program. The list can be exhaustive and includes both technical deliverables (program masters, photographs, cue sheets, etc.) and legal materials (contracts, insurance binders, clearances, etc.).

This section specifies:

Technical deliverables:

- The length of the program, including where the commercial breaks must occur (this is called the network "clock").

- Specific media on which program, program elements, and soundtrack must be delivered. The network may require the production company to use only certain cameras or editing equipment. You must pay attention to the network's specified recording file formats, color space settings, file naming conventions, compression formats, and timecode settings. The network may even specify the manner in which you log all of this information, both on the set and in your deliverables.
- Soundtrack mixing requirements and cue sheets. Take this one seriously! Often when a show fails the network's quality control review, it is because of problems with the audio specs. Hold your audio studio contractually accountable for delivering the soundtrack in compliance with the network's requirements (which you will need to give your audio studio, of course).
- Specifications for promotional and marketing materials for the show. *Note:* Because networks advertise a program in advance of its broadcast, photos, video clips, and other program promotional materials usually must be delivered to the network earlier than the program itself. Be sure to stick closely to the exact technical specifications demanded by the television company. That being said, there may be a lot of boilerplate language here, requiring you to deliver such outdated items as 35-mm slides when a hi-res PNG or PSD file might just as easily do the trick. Be sure to look for, point out, and change any antiquated delivery requirements before you sign the contract.

Legal deliverables:

- You will have to deliver a legal binder containing all your talent and crew contracts, releases, permissions, and credit requirements.
- The program must be compliant with the network's *standards and practices* policies. Standards and Practices is the network department responsible for evaluating program content for obscenity, violence, and legal vulnerability. Unfortunately, many media companies fail to maintain written standards and practices policies, which can make it very hard for you to know what you're agreeing to under this clause. Try to obtain specifics; failing that, build in a notice-and-cure period where you have a chance to try to fix any problems before the network can declare that you are in breach of contract for failing to comply with its policies. (See Appendix B, "Default and Cure," p. 486.)
- Publicity restrictions and requirements. The production company is typically restrained from issuing any publicity without the prior written approval of the network. This means no posting about the project on social media!
- Network HR requirements. Your production company's executives may need to complete anti-harassment, anti-bias, health and safety, or other training to ensure your company's compliance with the network's policies.
- Construction, rigging, stunt risk assessment reports.
- Network accident, health and safety reporting forms.
- Network-approved accounting and tax forms.

It bears repeating: If you don't deliver everything as required by this section, your final payment will be withheld!

Representations and Warranties

The representations and warranties are statements of fact and promises that one party makes to another with the intention that the other party will rely on them. (See Appendix B, "Representations and Warranties," p. 482.) Representations and warranties are usually coupled with an indemnification clause requiring a party who has misrepresented something in the contract to pay the other party's damages that stem from that misrepresentation. Your company may be required to represent and warrant that:

- It has all the rights it is granting, and it will not infringe on any other rights holder in the making of the production.
- There is no libelous, defamatory, or obscene material in the program.
- It will be responsible for all royalties and reuse payments.
- It has not exhibited the program anywhere else (including festivals), and its first exhibition on the television company's channel is the program's premiere.
- There has been "no payola." Pursuant to federal regulations, the production company has not accepted any money, services, or other compensation in exchange for advertising goods or services in the program (unless it has prior approval from the network and the program discloses the sponsorship in the end credits).

Of course, your production services agreement will also contain other standard contract clauses such as such as notice, arbitration, jurisdiction, *force majeure*, etc.

PRACTICE TIPS

- *Alert the network to problems early on.* During the production, if you feel that you will have difficulty meeting a particular requirement, let the network know *as soon as possible*. You may be pleasantly surprised to find out how reasonable they can be. After all, they want to make the program, too. Remember, the production services agreement can be amended and changed many times during the course of creating your program. However, if you wait until delivering your program to let them know that, for example, you didn't get all the required clearances, your final payment will be withheld, and you may be faced with a breach-of-contract suit.
- *Best of knowledge and belief.* Try to modify the representations and warranties concerning intellectual property clearances so that they are to "the best of production company's knowledge and belief." Presumably, you do

not have the resources to ensure that the wall poster in the background of an interview scene is in the public domain throughout the world, or that the tastefully nude sculpture in front of the interview subject does not violate obscenity laws in Dubai. Accordingly, try to convince the network that while you will make a diligent effort to clear all materials, any promises as to whether or not they violate the laws of another country are only "to the best of your knowledge and belief."

- Try to limit your indemnification to payment of legal costs after any case has been lost and appeals exhausted. In other words, try to make sure you don't have to pay to defend bogus lawsuits. Make sure there is reciprocal indemnification!
- Build in a cure period for those breaches that can be cured.
- Whenever possible, try to avoid absolute obligations ("producer shall") and replace them with good-faith obligations ("producer shall use reasonable business efforts to").

INTERNATIONAL CO-PRODUCTIONS

US production companies are increasingly making movies and television shows with foreign investors and production companies, enabling them to better gain access to otherwise hard-to-secure locations and to take advantage of international financing, tax, and other production incentives offered by governments around the world.

The two main approaches that producers take are the pre-sale and the co-production.

- **Pre-sales**. A US producer may work with a foreign distribution company/financier and offer the distribution rights to the film (which has yet to be shot) in the foreign distributors' territory in exchange for production funding. The foreign distribution company/financier under this model will usually not finance the entire picture—if they did, they would own the entire copyright and it would be the distributor's film—and if they have contributed a large amount of money to the picture, the foreign distributor may also have certain creative approval over the script, casting, and above-the-line choices. More on distribution companies and presales can be found in Chapter 25.
- **Co-productions**. In this model, the US production company typically forms a *joint venture* (see "Joint Ventures," p. 47) with a foreign production company(s) and the two companies produce the film together. Both production companies may have a degree of ownership of the copyright in the resultant film, and the foreign co-production company will do most of the heavy lifting when it comes to organizing and facilitating the production in its home territory outside of the United States. Additionally, some countries—China, for instance—give greater access to its country's distribution market to films that were co-produced with Chinese production companies.

Producers contemplating international co-productions should make this decision before they reach out to investors to finance their films, since international financing and co-productions often require a producer to assign copyrights to the film, such as distribution rights, and rights to receive a portion of the films' proceeds. This can dilute investors' potential for return on their investment—something they would undoubtedly want to know before they invested money in the project.

Planning an International Co-Production

It's beyond the scope of this book to go into detail on all of the international co-production possibilities, so we will mostly just stick with laying out the areas you need to research.

WHICH COUNTRY?

Co-productions are best chosen when access to shooting locations in a co-producers' country is critical to your film. Even though virtually everything can be shot on a green screen if you have enough money for CGI, shooting on location can increase box office appeal. Would you rather see a film shot at the Great Wall of China or on a soundstage? And those of us who are from a particularly filmic area cringe when we see other locations doubling for it. I grew up in New York City and personally hate it when I see Vancouver doubling as NYC, especially when the characters refer to it as "The Big Apple";[1] I love Vancouver, but it just ain't New York, and it certainly doesn't look like NYC.

But aesthetic choices are not the biggest drivers of the country of choice for your co-producer. It more often comes down to what production incentives are offered by those other countries. In fact, that's a key reason so many US production companies co-produce with Canadian ones to shoot in Vancouver. It's cheaper because the Canadian production incentives help lower the cost of making the film. For an in-depth explanation of production incentives, see "Production Incentives," p. 77.

If you are considering an international co-production partner, you must know:

- All international film treaties to which the home country of the foreign co-producer is a member. Make sure you understand all intellectual property ownership requirements, both for the US production company as well as the foreign co-production company.
- The production incentives (like tax credits) offered by your co-producer's country. Just like production incentives in the United States (See "Film Tax Credits and Other Production Incentives," p. 77), your co-producer's country will almost certainly have requirements for the number of that country's citizens who must be included in the cast and crew and the above-the-line producing team.

- The immigration and visa requirements of your co-producer's country. Immigration law is highly specialized, and this is another one of those areas where you would do well to hire an experienced attorney familiar with your co-producer's country's immigration law. Many countries require work visas and limit the number of days noncitizens may work within their borders. Seriously, this is not something you can fudge. The last thing you want is for your cast and crew to be denied entry into the country where your shoot is scheduled.

China

China is a huge market for film distribution and is an essential part of every major movie release.[2] China has agreed to import at least 34 US films a year,[3] which means that for all practical purposes, indie filmmakers have very little chance to get their films shown in China if they are treated as "imported films." This restriction is sidestepped if the film is a co-production with the Chinese production company. As the Motion Picture Association Asia Pacific's "China—International Film Co-Production Handbook" explains:

> A Co-Produced Film is a film shot by a China-based film producer and a foreign producer that features joint investments (including funding, labor, and materials, joint filming, and joint sharing of both benefits and risks). Such films are subject to preferential policies that are typically applied to domestic Chinese films within the Chinese marketplace.[4]

As of the date this is written, China has 111 different culture industry funds that may be used by U.S.–Chinese co-productions.

Europe

The Council of Europe Convention on Cinematographic Co-Production (revised)[5] is a key film production treaty which lays out the legal and financial framework for working with co-producers from two or more European countries that are members to this treaty. One of the interesting things about the regulation is that it allows for US-based productions to benefit from the production incentives as long as the US company owns 30% or less of a co-production.

The advantages of working within this system are laid out in a very helpful—and free—publication by the European Audiovisual Observatory[6]

> If you are benefitting from a foreign tax or film incentive, make sure that you are meeting the spending requirements in that country.
>
> Victoria Jade Bennett, Esq.
> Jade IP Consulting

Checklist for International Co-Productions

- ▫ Find a foreign co-producer (this is a bit of a chicken/egg thing. The script calling for a location may determine what country before finding a co-producer or considering the tax incentives or cost. Talent may be attached before looking for a co-producer).
- ▫ Consult with an international entertainment attorney about tax and film incentives.
- ▫ Make and sign a co-production agreement with the foreign co-producer.
  - Check whether the two countries have a film treaty, as this could dictate certain aspects of the co-production agreement. The co-production agreement should be translated into a language that each party is proficient in.
- ▫ Check whether your cast and crew are permitted by their unions to film in the countries you've chosen.
- ▫ Consult with an immigration attorney about visa requirements in the countries you've chosen.
- ▫ If you are importing equipment, check for any customs requirements in the countries you've chosen.
- ▫ Make sure that your production is insured for an international production.
- ▫ Cast and crew will also need health insurance coverage in the countries in which you will be filming.
- ▫ If you are benefitting from a foreign tax or film incentive, make sure that you are meeting the spending requirements in that country.

NOTES

[1] Virtually no New Yorker uses the term "The Big Apple." We just call it "The City."

[2] Zhao, Shirley. "Hollywood Struggles for Fans in China's Growing Film Market." *Bloomberg.com*. https://www.bloomberg.com/news/articles/2021-02-15/hollywood-struggles-for-fans-in-china-s-growing-film-market (Accessed May 11, 2021).

[3] Ibid.

[4] MPA-APAC. China-International Film Co-Production Handbook. MPA-APAC, 2014. www.mpa-apac.org

[5] "Council of Europe Convention on Cinematographic Co-Production (Revised) Details of Treaty No.220." *Council of Europe*. www.coe.int/en/web/conventions/full-list/-/conventions/treaty/220 (Accessed May 12, 2021).

[6] Blázquez. Rep. *The Legal Framework for International Co-Productions*. European Audiovisual Observatory, 2018. https://rm.coe.int/iris-plus-2018-3-the-legal-framework-for-international-co-productions/168090369b

12

PRODUCT PLACEMENT AND SPONSORSHIP

Product placements can be a valuable source of production funding. Whether it's a sports car driven by a cinematic secret agent or the soda guzzled by television's latest "tween" idol, product placement plays an increasingly important role in the funding of television programs, motion pictures, and web series.

Or perhaps instead of needing a product to feature in your film, you want a company to sponsor your online video series by paying you money to regularly feature their products and logos in your programming, perhaps providing special discounts to your viewers. This ongoing relationship will typically require a sponsorship agreement, which may contain many of the specifics included in the product placement agreement.

WHAT IS PRODUCT PLACEMENT?

Product placement is the intentional inclusion of a brand name or product in a movie, TV program, web series, etc., for the purpose of increasing brand awareness.

Example: Pierre the producer is raising money for his film *The Girl with the Killer Knees*. He makes a deal with the Rubber Hose Stocking Company to include their stockings in a pivotal scene in the movie. In exchange for the company's logo to be featured prominently in the scene, the Rubber Hose Stocking Company provides a crate of stockings and pays $25,000 to Pierre's production company. The stocking package's inclusion in the film is a *product placement*.

PRODUCT PLACEMENT AGREEMENT

Let's turn first to the basics of a product placement deal.

The Parties

- *Production company*. The production company wants (1) to save money on props by getting products given to them by manufacturers; (2) to

DOI: 10.4324/9781003228479-17

receive money from manufacturers for including those products in the film; and (3) to retain the greatest amount of creative control over how, and whether, those products appear in the final edit.

- *Manufacturer/advertiser.* The manufacturer or advertiser wants to be sure the production company will (1) feature its products in the film, (2) do so in a manner that is consistent with the product's typical use, and (3) do so in a way that makes the product look attractive to potential consumers.

Placement Defined

Right off the bat, it's important to define what exactly is meant by *placement.* Will any depiction of the product satisfy the obligation? Must the product be featured in the scene, or is a brief glimpse in the background enough to satisfy the placement requirements? Producers may further want to limit the obligation to depict the product by medium and geographic territory (e.g., the product is only required to be shown on theatrically distributed versions of the movie in North America). The reason for this is that television broadcasters, in-flight movie regulations, and the laws of other countries may result in the distributor or exhibitor of the film editing out particular scenes, including those in which the product has been placed.

Payment

Is there a monetary payment or simply a donation of goods for use by the filmmakers? If inexpensive goods are being donated and there is no payment to the filmmaker, the filmmakers should be wary of agreeing to any absolute obligations to feature the products; a "good-faith attempt to depict the products" may be sufficient. After all, why tie your hands in production and the editing room for a crate of free soda?

If payment is being made in addition to the product being supplied, the fees can range from the tens of thousands to hundreds of thousands, depending on the extent to which the product is used in the film and the potential drawing power of the film itself.

The filmmaker may want the manufacturer to feature the film within a coordinated marketing campaign (think *E.T.* and Reese's Pieces). Of course, any marketing campaign featuring the film or characters from the film should also meet with the approval of the studio producing the film. Furthermore, if the film's performers will be featured in any commercial tie-in, they will need to have given their prior written permission (see below).

Failure to Place Products

What happens when the filmmaker fails to include the product in the film? Must the production company return any monies it has received from the manufacturer? The more money the production company was paid, the more likely the answer to this question will be "yes."

In addition to repayment, another solution to the problem of the omitted product placement is for the production company to offer a "redo" and feature the manufacturer's product in another program or motion picture. This is more common in a television series, where production companies produce more than one episode of a program.

Approvals/Manner of Depiction

The manufacturer wants to make sure that the product is shown in a flattering light. The producer, on the other hand, wants to make sure that she has as broad creative control as possible concerning the depiction of the product. This has real-world consequences: when a beloved character was shown dying of a heart attack while riding a Peloton exercise bike in the premier of the *Sex and the City* reboot, the company's stock fell sharply.[1] Understandably, creative control over a product's depiction is a highly negotiated area. This clause should spell out exactly how the product will be depicted in the picture. It's typical to reference a particular scene in the script, which should be attached as an exhibit to the agreement.

Manufacturers will often insist that their products not be featured in a manner that is inconsistent with the products' ordinary use, which begs the question: What happens when the director shows the product in a way that is objectionable to the manufacturer? Is the fee reduced? Does the matter go to binding arbitration? Does the manufacturer get to veto the product's inclusion in the film after the scene is shot? Producers are strongly cautioned to avoid giving manufacturers this sort of veto power (unless they want to shoot two versions of each scene, one with a product and one without).

***TIP:* A producer who wants to avoid overreaching control by the manufacturer may want to point out to them that the more control a manufacturer has, the more likely the film may be seen as an advertisement. If the film is an advertisement, it may be subject to increased regulations by the Federal Trade Commission (FTC) and the Federal Communications Commission (FCC) (if broadcast on television), such as stricter disclosure standards and manufacturer liability for inaccuracies in the way the product is described or represented.**

License of Intellectual Property Rights

To depict a brand, you need a license of that brand's intellectual property rights. This clause grants a nonexclusive license to the production company for the depiction of the trademark, trade dress, copyrights, and any other intellectual property rights in the brand that are necessary to effectuate the product placement.

The manufacturer should also be required to supply all necessary branding artwork, graphics files, mock-ups, etc.; *don't recreate a branded product or logo yourself!* If your art department makes a mistake in creating a mock-up of the product placement brand (wrong color label—oops!), you may be forced to pull that shot from the film.

If possible, the producer should secure a waiver from the manufacturer of any claims of trademark and copyright infringement, vicarious infringement, trademark dilution, and trademark tarnishment if the brand is depicted in the film consistent with the product placement agreement and the annexed script.

Representation and Warranty and Indemnity

The manufacturer will need to promise that it has the power to enter into the agreement and that it owns all the intellectual property rights (copyrights, trademarks, trade dress, and other rights in and to the products).

The producer will need to promise that the picture does not infringe any copyright, trademark, or other third-party right and that the producer has the authority to enter into this agreement.

Always coupled with the representations and warranties is an indemnification. Typically, this is a reciprocal indemnification. Many times, however, manufacturers want to be indemnified for any harm arising out of the production company's use of its product.

Insurance

The manufacturer will require that the production company name it as an additional insured in its general liability policy. Furthermore, the manufacturer may also require the production company to maintain certain policy limits and to insure high-ticket items such as vehicles.

RESTRICTED USES

Particularly with respect to potentially dangerous products, such as handguns and automobiles, the manufacturer may want to include a clause that requires that the producer only use the product in a very limited and specific manner and only with a licensed professional operating the product.

Publicity; Use of Performers

Manufacturers will often want to use, for their own advertising purposes, photographs, video footage, and other publicity materials featuring the film's performers using the products. Producers need to be aware that this will often raise issues with the performers themselves. Although most performers' services agreements have clauses allowing the producers to use an actor's likeness for publicity and promotion, that clause is typically restricted for publicity and promotion of the movie itself, not for unrelated products. Prior to agreeing to a manufacturer's use of publicity stills for its own advertising campaigns, a producer may need to negotiate with the particular actor or require that the manufacturer obtain the actor's permission directly. Typically, this involves paying the actor an additional fee for use of his likeness.

Example: Rex Raptor appears in a new action film, *Dino-mite*, which features a number of motorcycle chase sequences. Harley-Davidson, Inc., which lent several bikes for the film shoot, wants to use footage from the film in a new television commercial. Even though Rex has signed a performer's services agreement (see p. 256) for his role in the film, Harley-Davidson must still have his permission to use any film clip with him in it in their commercial. Of course, if Rex's performer's services agreement contained a provision allowing the production company to license *Dino-mite* film footage for commercial use unrelated to advertisements for the film itself, Harley-Davidson would only need to seek permission from the film company for the use of the footage.

Loss and Damage of Product

For consumables and inexpensive goods, manufacturers typically allow the producers to keep the products (although producers will have to pay any taxes on these). For more expensive products, such as automobiles, planes, expensive jewelry, etc., the production company typically assumes the risk of loss and responsibility for maintaining the products in good working order. In addition, the production company may be restricted in the manner in which it maintains or services the product (automobiles may be repaired only by authorized dealers, etc.)

Credit

This clause details how the manufacturer will be listed in the film's credits and should make clear that the production company has complete discretion over the look of the credits. As is true for all credit provisions, the production company should insert a clause in the contract that says that "inadvertent failure to accord the contracting party credit shall not be actionable." This clause should also require the injured party to waive the right to injunctive relief, leaving an obligation on the production company's part to correct the problem on all future prints as the only remedy for the production company's credit mistakes. The clause should further state that a mistake of this nature is not a breach of the product placement agreement.

Remedies

The right to injunctive relief should be waived by the manufacturer. Furthermore, no breach of the agreement by the production company should entitle the manufacturer to recapture any rights that he may have granted the production company.

THE SPONSORSHIP DEAL

Perhaps you have a YouTube channel dedicated to makeup tutorials. You attracted the eye of a new cosmetics company, Beauty Anna Beast Cosmetics, which wants to pay you a monthly stipend of $1,000 to use only their products in your videos. You had some email back and forth with the company's marketing department, and now it's time to put some kind of deal in place. Here are some of the key terms you need to negotiate:

Your Obligation to the Sponsor

This is a description of the promotional services you will be providing to the sponsor. It's probably in your best interest to keep it as general as possible, like "Filmmaker shall use reasonable efforts to promote sponsor's brand and products on the filmmaker's YouTube channel and other social media." If possible, try to give yourself as much leeway as you can to include other companies in your banner ads and in your social media posts—even those companies which compete with the sponsor's products and services. Sometimes that's not acceptable to the sponsor, and instead they want you to only use and promote their products exclusively. If that's the case, make sure to define exactly which products or product categories over which the sponsor requires exclusivity. And because exclusivity ties your hands from promoting other companies for sponsorship fee (or even at all), you may wish to use their request for exclusivity as a bargaining chip to ask for a larger sponsorship fee.

This section also often includes a requirement of how frequently you need to feature or promote their products, a description of what constitutes promotion (does merely using the product and mentioning the name count as promotion? Must you do an on-screen "plug"—like a brief commercial—of the product? How much influence does the sponsor have over the content of these plugs?). If you are required to post in accordance with the specific schedule, try only to promise to make "reasonable efforts" to do so. You don't want to be in breach of contract because the week you got married you didn't post a video. You'll also want to indicate that any technical failure—from Internet hosts, YouTube, or your own hard drive that has chosen this week to "brick" itself—does not constitute a breach of the agreement.

IP Licenses

The sponsor should grant you a license to use the trademarks, copyrights, and other IP rights in their packaging design for the purposes of you promoting their products or services. Furthermore, the sponsor should represent and warranty that they actually have all of those rights to grant you. Make sure the sponsor indemnifies you for any lawsuit you may be hit with involving the sponsor's intellectual property rights and for product liability just in case the sponsor's products or services injure one of your viewers and they sue you. You will likely also be required to grant the sponsor license to repost your videos and to use any trademarks and names associated with your channel in their marketing.

Sponsorship Fee

This is the compensation other promotional consideration you're getting in return. Sometimes it's actual cash being paid each month; sometimes it's services or goods being given to you for free that you would otherwise have to pay for.

Term

How long does this sponsorship relationship last? Once the term has ended, can the sponsor decide to renew the term on their own, or must both parties agree? Of course, other typical contract terms should be also included, such as choice of law, entire agreement, notice and cure, etc.

Federal Trade Commission (FTC) Requirements

Yay! You landed a sponsor. Now you just have to ensure that you comply with the Federal Trade Commission (FTC) truth in advertising and endorsement regulations for online influencers. It's not as onerous as it sounds: basically, you can only make truthful statements about products you are reviewing, and you must disclose if you have a financial, employment, personal, or family *relationship* with a brand that you are discussing (or if that brand is given you something of value to make the video).

Keys to FTC compliance:[2]

- You must disclose all financial, employment, personal, or family relationships with brands you discuss or which have given you something of value to make the video.
- You should use simple, clear, and un-confusing language in your disclaimers. It should be in the same language as the main language used in the rest of your video.

- You must disclose that relationship to your viewers in the video itself and not just in the description uploaded with the video.
- You can't talk about your experience with a product you haven't tried.
- If you're paid to talk about a product and thought it was terrible, you can't say it's terrific.
- You can't make up claims about a product that would require proof the advertiser doesn't have (e.g. scientific proof that a product can treat a health condition).[3]

Example: Marco reviews video editing software and has received a free copy of the new Edit-Done! program from the software company so that he may review it. Even if he reviews the software negatively, he must still disclose the fact that he was given a copy of the software for free to help with the review. As part of the description Marco fills out when he uploads the video, he writes: "Edit-Done! gave me software to review for this video." **Unfortunately, just indicating his relationship in the videos description is not enough. The disclosure needs to be in the video itself.** It's all about making sure a reasonable viewer perceives the disclosure. The best disclosures are both written and audiovisual—the reviewer making a brief mention of it. For instance, Marco could include a written disclaimer as an on-screen lower third when he starts talking about the project which reads: "Edit-Done! provided me with a review copy for this video." He should also mention it as part of his review.

Marco has used and liked other software programs from that company, but he just didn't have time this week to dive into the new software. He's not worried: given the stellar performance of their other programs, he sure this one is pretty good; furthermore, a few of his friends have used it and liked it. So Marco decides to give it a good review without trying it out. Marco has unknowingly violated one of the key aspects of FTC regulations: *in order to review a product, you must have actually used it.*

It can be very helpful to read through the FTC guidelines for social media influencers: www.ftc.gov/tips-advice/business-center/guidance/disclosures-101-social-media-influencers.

CONTRACTUAL RESTRICTIONS ON PRODUCT PLACEMENT, SPONSORSHIP, AND ENDORSEMENTS

As my father is fond of saying: "There is the law, and then there's real life." In other words, even if you comply with the letter of the law, there may be contractual and other forces that govern how, or if, you can place a product in your film or television program or show endorsements and testimonials. These forces include:

- *Standards and practices.* Networks and most cablecasters have a department that sets the standards for what can be shown on that particular broadcaster's network, usually referred to as *standards and practices*. Before producing any content for a network or cablecaster that has product placements or endorsements, be sure to check with this department to make sure that you comply with that particular network's regulations.
- *Conflicts between paid advertisers and product placement integrators.* Television networks make money by selling airtime to advertisers. This can create conflicts when a producer includes product placement for one branded product inside a program whose commercial airtime has been purchased by an advertiser of a competing brand. Producers are advised to clear any prospective product placements with the network sales department prior to accepting a product placement.
- *Talent veto.* Directors and actors, especially A-list talent, may refuse to work with product placement on principle. Furthermore, even those actors who agreed to work with placed products may demand additional fees on the grounds that they are appearing in a television commercial as well as television program or motion picture.

TIPS

- Before you take money from a sponsor, manufacturer, or advertiser in exchange for including that company's products in your program or film, you should discuss that placement with an experienced media lawyer.
- A bit of a reality check is in order: If your film does not feature a "bankable" star (many indie films don't), you will probably not receive paid product placements and may be lucky to receive free goods. Still, it doesn't hurt to contact a variety of companies, a press kit for your film at the ready, and see if anyone bites. One of the first film jobs I had in Hollywood involved my securing product placement goods for an indie film. It worked: We ended up with crates of blenders, beer, and powdered soup mix!
- Filmmakers often work with product placement agencies to help them match their productions with companies seeking to place their products in films. A great resource to help filmmakers find the right product placement agency is the Entertainment Resources and Marketing Association (ERMA): www.erma.org.

NOTES

[1] See www.cbsnews.com/news/peloton-stock-death-by-peloton-just-like-that-mr-big/ (Accessed December 10, 2021).
[2] www.ftc.gov/system/files/documents/plain-language/1001a-influencer-guide-508_1.pdf (Accessed April 20, 2021).
[3] www.ftc.gov/system/files/documents/plain-language/1001a-influencer-guide-508_1.pdf (Accessed April 20, 2021).

13

HIRING CAST AND CREW

FEDERAL AND STATE LABOR AND EMPLOYMENT LAWS: AN OVERVIEW

During pre-production, you will be hiring your cast and crew. This means that in addition to the service contracts you negotiate with them, you also *must* comply with state and federal employment laws.

Federal and state employment and labor laws govern discrimination, wages, workplace safety, child labor, immigration compliance, and workers' compensation/disability/unemployment insurance. Under these laws, an *employee* may be treated differently by the law than an *independent contractor.* These issues and more must be addressed during pre-production or the production may face delay, fines, or state and private legal action. An employer/producer must comply with these laws or demonstrate how they are exempt, but a producer may not ignore them. Before you staff up or cast your film, bring in your attorney and accountant to advise you.

This is only the beginning: in addition to state and federal labor laws, producers must contend with two other categories of law: union agreements (such as those with SAG-AFTRA, WGA, DGA, and the various technical unions for crewmembers) and private law, which typically takes the form of the service agreements your workers enter into with your production company. These three categories of law, federal and state labor protections, union requirements, and service agreements, all must work together as a seamless whole.

Finally, to the extent that any of these categories conflict with each other, such conflicts are typically resolved in the following order: a union requirement will supersede the conflicting requirement in a service agreement; federal and state labor protections will often supersede union regulations.

Example: Akira hires Leslie to star as the hipster leader of a doomsday cult in his new film: *Avocado Toast and the Apocalypse*. Leslie is a member of SAG-AFTRA so Akira's production company becomes a SAG-AFTRA signatory company, agreeing to work under that union's rules. Because this is Leslie's first gig, she agrees in her actor services agreement to perform for $20 a day for this low-budget feature. However, because that rate is well below SAG-AFTRA minimums for a low-budget feature, despite Leslie having agreed to receive only $20 a day, she must be paid at least the

DOI: 10.4324/9781003228479-18

SAG-AFTRA minimum. Furthermore, even if Leslie agrees to perform the climactic battle scene on a rickety catwalk above opened vats of toxic chemicals, federal OSHA laws certainly prohibit it, despite how many waivers she signed in her service agreement.

Hiring Employees: Layers of Law

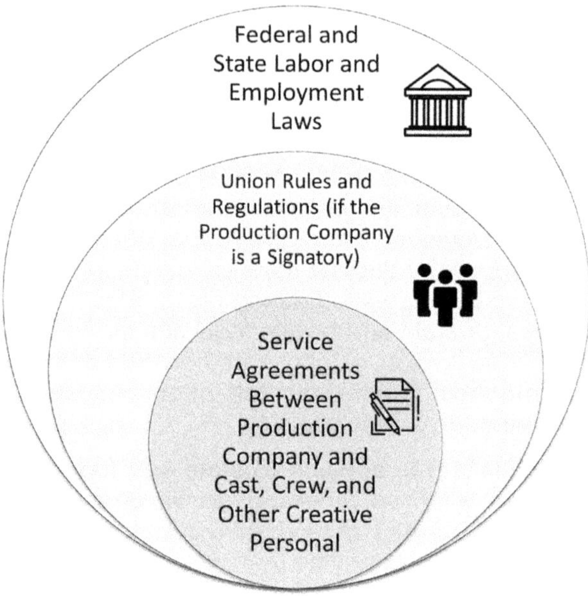

A PATCHWORK OF STATE AND FEDERAL LAWS

Each state has its own set of laws and requirements, which can differ quite radically from other states and even within a state. For instance, the determination of whether a worker is better classified as an independent contractor in California is largely controlled by A.B. 5; New York imposes state requirements as well as different classification requirements depending upon county (Nassau County, New York City, Suffolk County, and Westchester County each have slightly different employee classification systems).

This patchwork of law can be quite confusing to the producer who just wants to make a film but is suddenly faced with employees in California and New York.

On the federal level, the US government requires that employers comply with laws regarding wages, health and safety, family leave, and other key aspects of the employer/employee relationship. Some of these laws only apply if you're employing more than 50 people; however, given the size of a large film or TV shoot, these laws often apply to many productions. The following is just a small selection of worker protections under federal law that may apply to producers/production companies:

- ***Wages:***
  - The Fair Labor Standards Act (FLSA or Act) is administered by the Wage and Hour Division (WHD). The Act establishes standards for minimum wages, overtime pay, recordkeeping, and child labor.[1]
  - Wage garnishment.[2]
  - Child labor.[3]
  - Protections for disabled workers.[4]
- ***Safety and Health:***
  - Occupational Safety and Health (OSHA).[5]
  - Family and medical leave.[6]
- ***Work Authorization for Non-US Citizens***:
  - Immigration and Nationality Act of 1952, (INA) as amended.[7]
  - Visas: O-1B Visas for Individuals with an extraordinary ability in the arts or extraordinary achievement in motion picture or television industry; O-2: Individuals who will accompany an O-1 artist to assist in a specific event or performance.[8]

If you're an employer hiring an employee, there is also a lot of paperwork the law requires. Just a few of the documents you will need to deal with are:

- IRS Form SS-4. The form for the production company to apply for an employer identification number, allowing it to hire others.
- Form I-9. This is an immigration status form required by the US Bureau of Citizenship.
- IRS Form W-4/State W-4. These are federal and state tax withholding forms.
- W-2 Forms must be sent to the employee each year.
- New-Hire Reporting Form (state requirements differ).
- Workers' compensation insurance forms.

In many areas of labor and employment law, state law may demand more of the employer than the federal law's protections and requirements.

INDEPENDENT CONTRACTOR OR EMPLOYEE?

Whether a worker is classified as an employee or independent contractor has a huge impact on the working relationship, which forms you need to fill out, how much you must pay your workers, whether they get overtime, and other important distinctions.

Different sets of laws apply to each classification, and a production company has different responsibilities toward employees than it does toward independent contractors. Even the way the law treats a worker's ownership of the copyrightable contributions the worker produced on the movie differs between employees and independent contractors (see "Work for Hire," p. 418).

This distinction between independent contractor and employee is found at both the state and the federal level. Independent contractors, for example, do not have the same federal benefits as employees. However, the distinction between the two types of workers is not always clear, and courts and state agencies look at many factors when determining who is an employee or independent contractor.

There's no doubt about it—if the person you hire is an employee rather than an independent contractor, there's more law you need to pay attention to. How you hire and fire employees, the way you treat withholding taxes, and how much or how little you can pay employees are just some of the issues governed by federal and state employment law.

A PRODUCTION COMPANY'S DUTY TO EMPLOYEES

- *Federal regulations.* Employees have a host of federal laws to protect them. These laws govern:
  - Benefits.
  - Minimum wage and overtime.
  - Family and medical leave.
  - Health and safety in the workplace.
  - Discrimination.
- *Taxes.* Employers must withhold federal and state income taxes, Medicare, and Social Security from an employee's paycheck. Employers must also contribute to Social Security and Medicare for each employee. The employer must keep track of the employee's annual gross earnings and withholdings, reflected in a W-2, which must be sent to the employee.
- *Workers' compensation.* Employers must have workers' compensation insurance and possibly disability insurance when they have employees.
- *Unemployment.* Employers must make contributions to the state's unemployment insurance fund and pay federal unemployment taxes.

A PRODUCTION COMPANY'S DUTY TO INDEPENDENT CONTRACTORS

- *Federal regulations*. Independent contractors are treated as separate businesses. Overtime, minimum wage, and other laws may not apply.
- *Taxes*. Employers do not have to withhold anything from an independent contractor's check, nor do they have to send a W-2 form. If the independent contractor has been paid more than $600 in one year, the employer should send them a 1099-MISC Form with a copy to the IRS.
- *Workers' compensation*. Workers' compensation insurance is generally not required in dealing with independent contractors. To be on the safe side, the production company may want to confirm that an independent contractor has his own insurance to cover workplace injuries.
- *Unemployment*. There is usually no requirement to pay unemployment contributions or taxes for independent contractors.

As you can see, a production company has a lot more work on its hands if the worker is an employee and not an independent contractor. So why doesn't a production company simply hire independent contractors?

Many try to do just that. Unfortunately, whether a worker is an independent contractor or an employee—in other words, the worker's status—is not simply determined a matter of writing the words "independent contractor" on a contract.[9] To make matters worse, there are penalties for misclassifying a worker as an independent contractor if they should have been classified as an employee. To top it all off, a worker must be properly classified as either an employee or an independent contractor for *both* federal and state agencies.

Determining whether a worker is an employee or independent contractor in some states (I'm looking at you, California) has gotten increasingly more complex in the past few years. California recently enacted the A.B.5 employment legislation, effective as of 2020. It then amended the new statute with more legislation: A.B.2257. Just wait; it gets even more confusing, because you must analyze the worker's status under both state and federal law.

DETERMINING WORKER STATUS UNDER FEDERAL LAW

To determine a worker's status under federal law, the Internal Revenue Service (IRS) looks at three primary factors to determine whether a worker is an independent contractor or an employee:

- *Behavioral control*. If the production company has the right to direct and control how the worker accomplishes her job, the worker is most likely an employee. The more instructions a worker is given on how the work should be done, what steps the worker must perform, and what tools she must use, the more likely it is that the worker is an employee.

- *Financial control.* The more a worker has a financial stake in the business, shares in its profits and losses, or pays for supplies and materials without reimbursement, the more likely it is that a worker is an independent contractor.
- *Relationship of the parties.* How the worker and the employer perceive their relationship is also taken into account. Does a written contract specify that the worker is an independent contractor? If so, that tips the scales in favor of independent contractor status. Does the employer pay employee benefits? In that case, the worker is more likely to be an employee.

IRS RESOURCES

- For more on how the IRS determines a worker's status, see its brochure, "Contractor or Employee?" at www.irs.gov/pub/irs-pdf/p1779.pdf
- For information on an employer's tax responsibilities, see "Employer's Supplemental Tax Guide" at www.irs.gov/pub/irs-pdf/p15a.pdf

***TIP:* The IRS may be more likely to find that loan-out companies are independent contractors and their principals, the actors or crew members who run them, are not employees of the production company.**

In addition to the federal test for whether a worker is an independent contractor or an employee, the production company should also double-check the working relationship under the appropriate state law. Because, yes, it is possible to have a worker classified as an independent contractor under federal law but as an employee under state law. For reference, the law of two big moviemaking states, California, and New York, is provided below.

DETERMINING WORKER STATUS UNDER CALIFORNIA LAW

If you're shooting the film in California, the presumption is that any worker is an employee, and it's up to the hiring party—the producer production company—to prove otherwise. In fact, even if you don't own a production company based in California but use a California-based worker your company may be subject to this legislation.[10]

Treating a worker as an employee may be the simplest approach but not necessarily what a producer wants to hear. And furthermore, for a worker with their own business—like a videographer with a loan-out company—it may not be preferable either. In California, legislation has attempted to clarify this relationship . . . by introducing a complex and not easily understood series of exceptions to this "presumed employee" rule. Seriously, as of this writing, lawyers are still trying to parse the law on this one in California.

In California, certain workers (videographers, still photographers, professional performers, narrators, content creators, and several other creative professions) might be better classified as an independent contractor, rather than an employee, if all of the following are true:

1. If the worker has their own place of business.
2. The worker has the required business license or business tax registration.
3. The worker has the ability to set or negotiate their own rates for the services performed.
4. Outside of project completion dates and reasonable business hours, the worker has the ability to set their own hours.
5. The worker is customarily engaged in the same type of work performed under contract with another hiring entity or holds themselves out to other potential customers as available to perform the same type of work.
6. The individual customarily and regularly exercises discretion and independent judgment in the performance of the services.[11]

And even if your production company satisfies this test, as well all of the exceptions, the worker may *still* be found to be an employee if your company retains the right to control the manner and means by which the work is performed, not only the scope of the work itself.[12]

And if that isn't complex enough, under California law, any time you sign someone to a work-for-hire agreement, they are considered an employee and you must provide them with workers' compensation insurance.[13] Even issuing a worker an IRS Form 1099 rather than a W-2 does not automatically change an employee into an independent contractor.[14] Failure to insure them subjects your company to serious fines and possible criminal misdemeanor charges.[15]

THE BOTTOM LINE: The above is a simplified version of California's legislation—and perhaps even overly simplified. If you are utilizing California workers on your film, and you want them to be classified as independent contractors rather than employees, you should have a discussion with an attorney well-versed in California employment law.

DETERMINING WORKER STATUS UNDER NEW YORK LAW

In New York, as in California, the presumption is that a worker is an employee, but this presumption is rebuttable. New York takes a different approach from California to the common law tests of supervision, direction, and control.

The New York Department of Labor provides guidelines for determining worker status in the performing arts. The guidelines list "indicators of independence" that make a worker an independent contractor and "indicators of employment" that make a worker an employee. However, even though the presumption that a worker is an employee is rebuttable, the guidelines say "[i]n most film and theatrical production cases, performers would not be determined to be independent contractors."[16]

Let me stress that again: in New York, it's presumed that actors and other performers are employees of your production company. It's up to you to prove that they aren't, although in New York, it's possible to request a formal determination from the New York Department of Labor Liability and Determination Section whether any particular worker is an independent contractor or an employee.[17]

Under New York law, if the following factors are true of a worker, it indicates that they may be an *independent contractor* and **NOT** an employee:

- The worker has an established business (and you are hiring that business to provide their services).
- The worker advertises that business.
- The worker maintains a public listing of the business.
- The worker carries insurance typical of that business.
- The worker maintains a place of business and makes a significant investment in facilities, equipment, and supplies.
- The worker assumes the risk for profit or loss in providing services.
- The worker determines their own schedule and manner of work.
- The worker sets or negotiates their own pay rate.
- The worker provides services concurrently for other businesses, competitive or noncompetitive.
- The worker is free to refuse work offers.[18]

On the other side of the equation are the factors that, if true about the production company, indicate that the worker is an *employee* and NOT an independent contractor. The production company:

- Determines when, where, and how services will be performed.
- Directly supervises the job.

- Provides facilities, equipment, tools, and supplies.
- Directly supervises the services of the worker.
- Stipulates the hours of work.
- Requires exclusive services.
- Sets the rate of pay.
- Requires attendance at meetings and/or training sessions.
- Requires oral or written reports.
- Reserves the right to review and approve the work product.
- Requires prior permission for absences.
- Prohibits the worker from performing services for competitors.
- Reserves the right to end services on short notice.[19]

DON'T DISCRIMINATE

Discrimination in the workplace is strictly prohibited. If you use a worker's race, color, sex, age, disability, religion, or national origin as a basis on which to hire, fire, or demote someone, you are in violation of federal and state laws. If you harass or discriminate against someone in your hiring, firing, promotion, disciplinary practices, and treatment in the work environment because of those attributes, you are violating the law. Since the last edition of this book, the US Supreme Court has held that unless you are a religious organization, "employers are prohibited from firing employees on the basis of homosexuality or transgender status."[20]

WORKING WITH MINORS

As a rule, hiring and employing a child or minor is more regulated by federal and state law than hiring and employing an adult.

- Many states require an employer or production company to obtain special permits to employ children, and each child is required to obtain a permit to work.
- Children may also be restricted in the number of working hours according to their age.
- Some states, like New York and California, require that a portion of the child's income be deposited in a trust for the benefit of the child until he or she is 18 years old.
- Special state-regulated teachers may be required to be on set to help minors meet their educational requirements during a shoot.

A producer should consider whether an actual minor, someone under the age of 18, is required when an adult who can "play younger" would suffice. For more on working with child actors, see "Casting Minors," p. 269.

UNIONS

In addition to labor and employment laws, production companies may need to concern themselves with union laws and regulations. Many professionals in the entertainment industry are members of a union such as SAG-AFTRA, WGA, or IATSE. When you work with these unions, your contracts will need to comply with the applicable union's collective bargaining agreements and master bargaining agreements. These master contracts contain minimum salary, health and welfare contribution rates, grievance procedures, and regulations on how the member must be credited in the film. Employers/production companies are encouraged to seek guidance from the union signatory office of the union with jurisdiction over their type of production.

This book is written with the independent filmmaker in mind. Although it is true that the most experienced members of the film industry are members of an entertainment union, the typical independent filmmaker tends to avoid dealing with unions because of the perceived headache of paperwork, rules, and compliance that accompanies every union-regulated film production. So, given the availability of cheap, passionate film students and genuinely talented non-union professionals, many independent filmmakers will still choose to work with a nonunion crew. But if you're not going to work with a experienced union crew, at least make sure you work with an experienced crew. Your film may look better when it is shot by a professional camera operator rather than a film student.

There is one union, however, that you should consider working with, even if you decide to avoid all the others: the Screen Actors Guild. This is because casting a recognized "name" actor increases the likelihood that your film will be picked up by a distributor. (See "SAG-AFTRA," p. 243.)

SERVICES AGREEMENTS

In addition to contracts with the unions, a production company must also concern itself with its own contracts between itself and its workers (cast, crew, director, producer, etc.). The *services agreement* is the contract between the production company and the employee or independent contractor it's hiring. The terms of these contacts control the working relationship—except when they are superseded by union bargaining agreements or state and federal employment laws.

Negotiate your services agreements early in the pre-production stage. If a potential cast member knows your back is against the wall and you have to cast somebody for next week's shoot, you will have lost a good deal of leverage.

Checklist: Elements of a Services Agreement

In general, cast and crew services contracts will have clauses that deal with the following essential issues, many of which are defined in Appendix B, "The Clause Companion," p. 475:

- ☐ Duties of both the production company and the employee or independent contractor.
- ☐ Payment: amount, frequency, kind (fixed, contingent, deferred, bonus).
- ☐ Per diem.
- ☐ Term of service; days expected to work/be available.
- ☐ Travel and accommodations.
- ☐ Exclusivity.
- ☐ Releases: right of publicity, defamation.
- ☐ Work-for-hire/assignment of intellectual property rights.
- ☐ Union/nonunion status; if union, which union contract governs the agreement.
- ☐ Screen credit and other billing provisions.
- ☐ Force majeure.
- ☐ Suspension/termination.
- ☐ Approvals (if any) and their limitations.
- ☐ Limits on employee/independent contractor remedies, such as a "no injunction" provision, arbitration, duty to cure credit errors only on future prints, etc.
- ☐ Likeness and biography approvals.
- ☐ Notice and cure.
- ☐ Confidentiality and publicity restrictions.
- ☐ Representations and warranties that employee/independent contractor is free to enter into the contract and will not infringe any third-party IP rights.
- ☐ Restriction on the employee's/independent contractor's ability to hire others.
- ☐ Net profit definition and accounting rights (if the employee/independent contractor is a profit participant).

- Permission to pay monies to an agent/manager.
- Permission to withhold taxes.
- Permission to take out insurance covering the employee/independent contractor.
- Choice of law.
- Merger and integration of prior agreements and discussions.
- Inducement.

THE CONTRACT RIDER

A *rider* is a document attached to a contract, supplementing or amending it. Sometimes amending documents are labeled *exhibits*, but the meaning and effect are the same. In service contracts, riders can be used to list the duties an employee must perform or equipment the employee is supplying or to change an already existing contract by replacing preexisting language with newer, mutually agreed-upon terms and conditions.

NOTES

[1] Fair Labor Standards Act of 1938 (FLSA);(29 USC §201 et seq.; 29 CFR Parts 510 to 794) https://webapps.dol.gov/elaws/elg/minwage.htm (Accessed March 5, 2021).

[2] Title III, Consumer Credit Protection Act (CCPA); (15 USC §1671 et seq. (PDF); 29 CFR Part 870) https://webapps.dol.gov/elaws/elg/garnish.htm (Accessed March 5, 2021).

[3] Fair Labor Standards Act of 1938 (FLSA);(29 USC §201 et seq.; 29 CFR Parts 570 to 580) https://webapps.dol.gov/elaws/elg/childlbr.htm (Accessed March 5, 2021).

[4] Fair Labor Standards Act of 1938 (FLSA); (29 USC §201 et seq.; 29 CFR Parts 525) https://webapps.dol.gov/elaws/elg/flsa14c.htm (Accessed March 5, 2021).

[5] Occupational Safety and Health Act of 1970 (OSH Act); (29 USC §651 et seq.; 29 CFR Parts 1900 to 2400) https://webapps.dol.gov/elaws/elg/osha.htm

[6] Family and Medical Leave Act of 1993 (FMLA); (29 USC §2601 et seq.; 29 CFR Part 825) https://webapps.dol.gov/elaws/elg/fmla.htm (Accessed March 5, 2021).

[7] Immigration and Nationality Act of 1952, (INA) as amended. https://webapps.dol.gov/elaws/elg/aw.htm (Accessed March 5, 2021).

[8] www.uscis.gov/working-in-the-united-states/temporary-workers/o-1-visa-individuals-with-extraordinary-ability-or-achievement; www.uscis.gov/policy-manual/volume-2-part-m (Accessed March 5, 2021).

[9] *S. G. Borello & Sons, Inc., v. Dept. of Industrial Relations,* 48 Cal. 3d 341 (1989).

[10] "Legal Tests for Independent Contractor Classification Under California Law," Practical Law Practice Note w-022–3277 (Westlaw).

[11] Cal. Lab. Code Ann. § 2778.

[12] *S. G. Borello & Sons, Inc. v. Dept. of Indus. Rel.*, 769 P. 2d 399 (Cal. 1989).

[13] Cal. Lab. Code Ann. § 3351.5.

[14] *Toyota Motor Sales v. Superior Court,* 220 Cal. App. 3d 864, 877 (1990).

[15] Cal.Labor Code § 3700.5.

[16] See "Guidelines for Determining Worker Status Performing Artists." New York State Department of Labor. New York State Department of Labor, n.d. https://dol.ny.gov/system/files/documents/2021/02/ia318.17.pdf. (Accessed June 5, 2021).

[17] Id.

[18] "Independent Contractors." New York State Department of Labor. *New York State Department of Labor*. https://dol.ny.gov/system/files/documents/2021/05/ia318.14.pdf (Accessed June 15, 2021).

[19] "Independent Contractors." New York State Department of Labor. *New York State Department of Labor*. https://dol.ny.gov/system/files/documents/2021/05/ia318.14.pdf (Accessed June 15, 2021).

[20] *Bostock v. Clayton County, Georgia*, 140 S. Ct. 1731, 1753 (2020).

14

ABOVE THE LINE

Producers and Directors

As many filmmakers know, the terms "above-the-line" (ATL) and "below-the-line" (BTL) originate from the old Hollywood practice of dividing crewmembers into two categories on the film budget top sheet. Those with the most managerial and creative control were literally featured above an actual dividing line which separated them from the salaries and budgets of the other crewmembers, hence the name. ATL typically includes producers, directors, casting directors, well-known cinematographers, and principal cast. Depending upon the particular reduction, others may be featured above the line as well.

Since we've covered screenwriters in the prior chapter (see "Hiring a Screenwriter," p. 136), we're going to focus this chapter on engaging producers and directors. While their roles are very different, their services agreements are built using many of the same deal terms and are then modified to address the particularities of each job. In this chapter you'll find those overlapping deal points, along with key distinctions for each position. But first, let's talk about the individual roles.

THE PRODUCER

There are several kinds of producers, but all share a common element: they are responsible for the managerial, creative, logistical, administrative, and financial functions of the film. They are the first on the project and the last to "turn off the lights."

This book assumes that most people reading it will be the executive producers for their own independent films. However, there are different kinds of producers on a film—some of whom you may need to hire.

- An *executive producer* is at the top of the food chain. They are usually in charge of finding financing for the picture and making the top-level management decisions, such as which director or lead actor to hire. The executive producer often ends up with an ownership position in the film property.
- A *supervising producer* supervises one or more producers and facilitates their work, ultimately reporting to the executive producer.
- A *producer* supervises and controls the film project. They manage the project from the early stages of development and stay with the project until it

DOI: 10.4324/9781003228479-19

is in the can. Their duties range from hiring the cast and crew to overseeing the technical, logistical, and financial aspects of the production. If the executive producer is like a chairman of the board, the producer is like the CEO.

- A *line producer* is the day-to-day logistical manager on the film. They will hire the crew, organize and coordinate between the production office and the set, and handle the purse strings during production. Because line producers generally do not share in any ownership of the film property, filmmakers may be better off negotiating a deal with them that more closely resembles a crew services agreement. (See "Crew Services Agreement," p. 233.)
- An *associate producer* can mean anything and in fact is often a "giveaway title" handed out to entice name actors and financiers to sweeten the deal. Like a line producer, an associate producer usually does not own part of the film property, so a crew services agreement might be a better template to start the negotiation process. (See "Crew Services Agreement," p. 233.)

It is important to note that film and television often have different terms for the different kinds of producers and even producers that are unique to one medium or the other.

Furthermore, to get the project off the ground, a filmmaker might want to partner with other producers, such as a production company with studio facilities, a group of financiers, or a more experienced film producer. Accordingly, even on an independent film, a filmmaker may need to negotiate a *producer's services agreement* with a third party (not to be confused with a *production services agreement*, which is used when a network hires a production company to produce a show; see "Production Services Agreements," p. 178).

The core skills of a producer are organization, logistical thinking, managerial and financial expertise, and creative problem-solving. A good producer should have good "people skills" and be adept at negotiation and delegation, with the ability to pivot when needed to ensure the continuation of the production.

THE DIRECTOR

Like professional actors, professional directors have their own union, the Directors Guild of America (DGA; www.DGA.org).

Although many independent films are made with non-union directors, the DGA's definition of a director is instructional in that it outlines the expectation of every director—that is, to be involved in all of the creative aspects of a film's production. According to the DGA,

> The Director's professional function is unique, and requires his or her participation in all creative phases of the film-making process, including but not limited to all creative aspects of sound and picture. [. . .] The Director's function is to contribute to all of the creative elements of a film and to participate in molding and integrating them into one cohesive dramatic and aesthetic whole. [. . .] No one may direct, as the term direct is generally known in the motion picture industry, except the Director assigned to the picture.[1]

Not surprisingly, many of the battles fought between directors and the production companies that hire them involve issues of creative control, so special attention must be paid to that section of the agreement. Under DGA rules, a director must be allowed meaningful consultation with respect to most of the creative decisions of the film and the chance to deliver a "director's cut" of the film to the producer with final cutting authority.[2]

Several other key crew members fall within the directorial or producing departments and work closely with the director to facilitate the logistics of the shoot:

- *Unit Production Manager (UPM)*: the UPM's duties somewhat overlap with those of the assistant director and include prepping shooting schedule breakdowns; budgets; location scouting; production reports; securing releases; and overseeing the logistics of transportation, housing, and liaising with the local authorities.
- *First Assistant Director (1st AD)*: in addition to overlapping duties with the UPM, the 1st AD has a direct administrative role on set, directing background performers and otherwise supervising the cast and crew.
- *Second Assistant Director (2nd AD)*: the 2nd AD works directly for the 1st AD in the direct management of the production logistics on set.
- *Associate Director*: works on multi-camera productions, shot before a live audience, and helps the director plan and place the cameras.

MAJOR DEAL POINTS: ABOVE-THE-LINE SERVICES AGREEMENT

An ATL services agreement may be used to hire a producer or a director (with some key modifications to the clauses, depending upon the job, as indicated below). A separate contract should be prepared and tailored for each job, unless one individual is both a producer and director.

Note: Most of the agreements in this book are written from the producer or production company's point of view; however, the deal points for the following producer's services agreement are given from the point of view of a production company that wants to hire a producer. For definitions and explanations of common contract clauses, see Appendix B, "The Clause Companion," p. 475.

The Parties

- *Production company.* The production company will want to hire the producer or director while still maintaining final control over the rights, creative elements, and other management issues. The production company needs to be sure that the producer or director will deliver on time, on budget, and to spec. The production company also needs to be able to shift risk of loss and legal liability to the producer if these ATL crew members fail to meet those obligations through their own mismanagement.
- *Producer.* As the top level of management in the film's production, producers need to be sure they have all the funds and resources available to make the film that they are hired to make. It is not unusual for a producer to ask to verify production funding prior to executing their contract. Especially on independent features, a producer may ask that their salary be set aside in an escrow fund. Because negotiating is a large part of what producers do, a production company negotiating with a producer may find it one of the more intense negotiations of the shoot. Producers come in all shapes and sizes, from independent producers to other production companies offering technical services in exchange for a producing credit and a chance to add to their reels, résumés, and IMDB profiles; both the compensation as well as the engagement provisions need to be tailored to each situation.

- *Director.* The director wants to be sure the production company will not run out of money before the film is made. Like the producer, the director may require that the funding for the film and their salary be placed in an escrow account. The director might fight the hardest for creative control, wanting input over the script rewrites and casting and crew hiring decisions and demanding the chance to control the editing process of the first cut of the film and to direct reshoots. For DGA-governed shoots, many of these rights are granted to the director by default.

Is the director or producer working under a loan-out company? If so, the contract needs to be drafted accordingly. For instance, you will need to include clauses for *inducement* and *further assurances.* (See "Loan-Out Companies," p. 51.)

Conditions Precedent

Because producers and directors are hired for the long haul of the firm, a production company or ATL crew member will often want to make its obligations under the services agreement contingent on certain conditions; for instance, a producer's or director's engagement may often be contingent on the project having financing, In other words, if all the *conditions precedent* are not met, neither party is obligated to the other under the contract. (See Appendix B, "Conditions Precedent," p. 477.) Typical conditions precedent include:

- The receipt of financing from a particular entity.
- The engagement of a particular actor or director.
- A performer successfully passing a drug test prior to principal photography.
- Securing all the distribution agreements; this may not be necessary in the case of an independent film, where a distribution deal is often secured after the film is shot.

Engagement

- Describe the particular services the ATL crew member is obligated to perform for the production company. This paragraph should be written broadly, as in the following: "[Producer/Director] agrees to perform all services as are customarily rendered by [Producers/Directors] on a feature-length theatrical motion picture [or television program, webisode, etc.], additional services as specified in any rider attached hereto, and any other reasonable services which may be required by the production company during the term of the Agreement."
- A list, called a *rider*, should be attached at the end of the contract detailing the producer- or director-specific job duties that are not usually included under their job functions.
- This provision also contains the *term* of the agreement. The term provides the time periods during which the producer is obligated to provide their services to the production company. For DGA deals, a director must be exclusive to the film for not less than twenty-six (26) weeks.[3]
- ATL crew members with enough leverage may try to negotiate a "pay or play" deal in which they are paid regardless of whether the production company actually makes the film. (See Appendix B, "Pay or Play," p. 482.)
- The production company should also state that the [producer/director] services are "unique" and the loss of such services cannot be fully compensated by monetary damages. This may entitle the production company to injunctive relief against the producer, preventing them from working on another film, should the producer or director harm the production by quitting midstream.
- *Television cover shots*. Despite the fact that the producer is the top manager on a production, on set, the director, quite literally, calls the shots. As a result, the production company may want to include a television cover

shot clause that protects the company's interest in receiving a commercially viable film when the director's services are completed. The television cover shots clause requires the director to shoot additional shots of scenes that might be too sexual, violent, or otherwise inappropriate for television viewing. When the motion picture is aired over network television, the cover shots will take the place of the more graphic shots shown in the theatrically distributed version. Sometimes directors are averse to providing television cover shots, feeling that they damage the integrity of their work. However, because the production company's primary interest is in receiving revenue from as many different sources as possible, television cover shots are a necessity when it comes to sanitizing a PG-13, R, NC-17, or unrated film for network television.

- *Perquisites*. On studio films, directors get an office and administrative help. On low-budget films, this is infrequent at best. However, if such facilities are readily available, providing them to a director who has had to work at a reduced fee might be an acceptable concession on the part of the production company.

Reshoots, Automated Dialogue Replacement (ADR), and Post-Production Services

- In life two things are certain: death and taxes. If you're a filmmaker, two more categories get added to this list: reshoots and automated dialogue replacement (ADR). This clause ensures that the director will still perform services for ADR, reshoots, and other post-production services not directly related to the editing of the film. If these services are required after the term of the contract has expired, the director is usually obligated to provide those services as long as they are not contractually obligated to provide services to another party at that time. If they are, the director should be obligated to provide those services at their first availability thereafter.
- For post-production, the director may be compensated at a daily rate based on a formula derived from their weekly rate. Alternatively, and this is often the case on independent feature films, the director may not be paid at all for these additional post-production services. Either way, this clause should address whether compensation is due.

Exclusivity

Producers and directors may want to negotiate the ability to work on their own projects concurrently with your film; in other words, they want to be *non-exclusive* to your film project. This may be fine if it's writing another screenplay at night, but it could be problematic if it involves a producer shooting footage for their own film while on lunch break during your film's production.

Often, the producer's services are *nonexclusive* during development and post-production and *exclusive* during pre-production and principal photography. A director, however, will likely need to be engaged exclusively from pre-production through post-production.

However, depending on the needs of the film, the production company may need the producer to be either exclusive or *first-priority* during pre-production and post-production as well.

- To ensure that a producer's or director's other obligations don't conflict with their obligations to your film, be sure to:
  - Delineate those periods when the ATL crew member will be non-exclusive (e.g. development, pre-production, maybe post) vs. those periods when they will be exclusive (e.g. production, festival showings, etc.)
  - Require that even when the ATL crew member is non-exclusive to your production, their duties to your film should still be on a "first-priority" basis. This means that even though the producer may work on their own projects, they may do so only if it doesn't conflict with their work on your film.
- Exclusivity of directors:
  - *Writing and development services.* The director usually works hand in hand with the writer to prepare the script for production. Although the director's services are typically nonexclusive (but first priority) during this period, scripts in need of substantial rewrites may need the director's services on an exclusive basis.
  - *Casting and location scouting.* Like writing services, the director's casting and location scouting services tend to be on a nonexclusive (but first-priority) basis. Keep in mind that "nonexclusive" does not mean that the director can cancel appointments at will. If the director has committed to a casting session on a particular day, they are still obligated to make that scheduled session.
  - *Principal photography.* Obviously, the director's services must be exclusive during principal photography. It is often a good practice to have the director's services on an exclusive basis prior to the start of principal photography. For complex projects, such as feature films, this period of exclusivity can be as long as 12 weeks in advance of the start of production.
  - *Post-production.* The production company should secure the director's services on an exclusive basis during post-production, reshoots, ADR, and editing. If that's not possible, the director should, at a minimum, be on a first-priority basis.

– Because post-production invariably takes longer than anybody thinks it's going to, it is in the director's best interest to negotiate their termination-of-services date; this is the date beyond which they are no longer obligated to provide services on a first-priority or exclusive basis to the production company. Conversely, the production company will want to make sure that it has enough padding in the schedule to ensure that overages in post-production will not find the film without a director.

Option on Future Services

If the film is successful, the production company may want the option to hire the same producer or director again at a rate they lock in now (plus any negotiated salary increase for the next project). Similar in concept to optioning a screenplay, this clause is an option for the producer's or director's future services. They will usually require any future service obligations to be subject to their "professional availability." (See Appendix B, "Option on Future Services," p. 481.)

Costs and Expenses

Producers and directors should be reimbursed by the production company for all out-of-pocket expenses relating to the motion picture. However, to protect the production company, repayment of their expenses over a certain amount (e.g. $100) should require the production company's prior written approval.

Travel and Accommodations

Travel, accommodations, and *per diem* expenses should be negotiated and agreed on in advance.

Compensation

- Like other above-the-line personnel, producers and directors are often compensated in a variety of ways: fixed, deferred, and contingent compensation. Bonuses are sometimes given on independent films.
- Additionally, the producer's fees are often paid out in stages (this differs from a director's, actor's, or below-the-line crew member's fee, which is typically paid out on a weekly basis). If not paid weekly, producers often get paid as follows: first, on the completion of financing of the picture; second, on start of principal photography; third, on wrap of principal photography;

and fourth, on completion of the picture or completion of all the producer's services under the contract.

- The producer and director should agree to allow the production company to withhold taxes or other deductions required by law from their fees.

Fixed Compensation

The fixed compensation fee is usually considered *fixed compensation*. In other words, it is payable to the producer or director regardless of whether the film makes money. One method of calculating a producer's fee is to compute the fee as a percentage of the production budget. From 2% to 5% is customary, whereas the director's weekly salary on an indie film can range quite widely; a schedule of minimums for DGA-governed productions is based upon the actual budget.[4]

Fixed compensation fees are often paid in stages, similar to producer's and writer's fees. The stages can be as frequently or infrequently as the production company and the director agree (subject to the DGA agreement, if working with that union). Some common payment stages include:

- Approval of the budget.
- Weekly payments starting several weeks prior to the start of principal photography.
- Payments made weekly during the course of principal photography.
- A payment made when the director's cut is delivered.
- A final payment of the fixed compensation fee when the final cut is completed and accepted.

Keep in mind that these are all flexible stages, and the amounts paid during each stage can be the subject of negotiation.

Profit Participation

A producer or director may each receive anywhere between 5% and 10% of the film's net profits (or more for those who are well known). (See "Net Profits," p. 66.)

Accounting

If the producer or director is a net-profit participant or will receive any form of deferred or contingent compensation, this paragraph will delineate how often the producer may expect to receive accounting statements. This is coupled with the right to audit the production company, usually no more frequently than once a year.

Credit

For all above-the-line contracts, position in the credits is a heavily negotiated deal point. Producers and directors may expect to receive credits on a separate card.

- For all above-the-line contracts, position in the credits is a heavily negotiated deal point. Directors and executive producers may expect to receive credits on a separate card and a listing on IMDB.com as the film's director.
- Under the credit rules of the DGA:[5]
  - The only acceptable form for a director's credit is "Directed by," and only directors, assistant directors, directors of photography, and art directors may receive the word "director" in their credits.
  - A "Film by" credit (also known as a "possessory credit") may not be used on a director's first feature, unless that director also acquired the underlying literary property and helped develop it.
  - A director's credit(s) must appear on all ancillary materials associated with the product, like Blu-Ray discs, paid advertising, and publicity for the film where the film title is also mentioned.
- Even though the production company might not be a signatory to the DGA MBA, director's contracts often contain a billing provision that guarantees the director a "directed by" credit if a similarly situated director would receive the same credit on a production governed by the DGA MBA. The more heavily negotiated provisions of this clause include how large the director's credit is in relation to the title of the movie and whether the director's credit is required to appear on all paid advertising and promotional materials.

Other credit issues include:

- Whether their individual production company logos must also be shown in the credit roll.
- Whether the production company is obligated to include the producer's and director's credit in paid advertising and promotional materials. If the film is working with the DGA, the answer to this is "yes."
- This clause may also specify the order in which the credit must appear and how large the credit must be in relation to the other credits.

As is true for all credit provisions, the production company should insert a clause in the contract saying that "inadvertent failure to accord the contracting party credit shall not be actionable." This clause should also require the injured party to waive the right to injunctive relief, leaving an obligation on the production company's part to correct the problem on all future prints as the *only* remedy for the production company's credit mistakes. The clause should further state that a mistake of this nature is *not* a breach of the producer's or director's services agreement. The clause should make clear that the production company has complete discretion over the look of the credits.

Rights

The assignment of rights/work-made-for-hire provision is another standard clause in all motion picture or service contracts. In this paragraph, the producer or director must agree that all rights, proceeds, and results of their creative efforts are to be treated as a work made for hire. Any remaining rights not captured by the production company as a result of the work-made-for-hire clause should be assigned by the producer or director to the production company under the agreement. (See "Work Made for Hire," p. 418.)

Performance and Delivery Requirements

This section delineates the scope of the film or program itself and what the producer or director is responsible for delivering. It includes specifics on:

- The picture's rating (for instance, "The picture shall receive no greater than a PG-13 rating as that rating is accorded by the Motion Picture Association of America").
- Duration of the film.
- Delivery date.
- Delivery materials (also known as deliverables) are what physical materials the director is responsible for creating. This should include detailed technical specifications (for instance, "two master copies of the Film shall be delivered in 4K resolution with dialogue on a separate track").
- The requirement for TV cover shots.
- The need for the director and producer to stay within budget.

This is such a critical provision of the contract that production companies should insist on "strict performance" and "time is of the essence" with respect to a producer or director meeting the project requirements and deliverables deadlines. Producers or directors, on the other hand, may want to qualify this paragraph by making their compliance "to the best of their ability" and making deadlines "on or about" a certain date.

Publicity

The production company will want to control the publicity for the motion picture and thus require the right to use the producer's or director's name and likeness in any publicity, promotion, or marketing of the motion picture. Make sure to include language that allows the director's image to be used in the "making of" documentary or short clips that usually accompany the Blu-Ray version and online promotion. In the case of well-known directors, you should include an obligation for them to take part in any press junket for the film (at the production company's expense, which often includes day rate for the director).

***TIP:* Although it may be an unspoken "standard practice," if you are a producer or director, make sure to insert language in the agreement allowing you to include footage of the film in your reel or on your website, subject to the production company's approval. You should also require the production company to list you on IMDB.com**.

Confidentiality

Usually coupled with publicity provision are confidentiality obligations. Production companies need be able to restrain the producer or director from issuing publicity statements about the motion picture without the production company's prior written consent. Producers and directors take note: This means no blogging, Tweeting, Facebooking, etc. unless the production company approves it in advance.

If you are a producer or director:

- Carefully review the production company's definition of "confidential material" to make sure you understand what you can and cannot discuss.
- The production company may require the producer to ensure that all cast and crew sign NDAs. (See "Nondisclosure Agreements," p. 94.) Make sure to do so, but be careful about any language that requires that you indemnify the production company for breach of confidentiality by cast and crew.
- Put a time limit on this provision. Remember, lots of films never get finished, let alone distributed. You want to be sure you can talk about your project at some point!

Pay or Play

The production company and the producer or director should agree that there is no obligation on the part of the production company to produce and distribute the film (called a *no obligation* clause, naturally). The producer or director, however, may want the production company to pay their fees regardless of whether the film is actually produced. If the production company agrees to this clause, the producer's or director's compensation is *pay or play*. The pay-or-play clause obligates the production company to pay that employee a certain sum regardless of whether their services are actually used. Alternatively, for non-union shoots, the production company might counter a pay-or-play request with a "kill fee." (See Appendix B, "Pay or Play," p. 482; "Kill Fee," p. 480.) If the production is shooting with a DGA director, they must negotiate an additional fee in order to be able to refrain from using that director's services.

Representations and Warranties

The director and producer should be required to represent and warrant that:

- They are under no other obligations that would prevent them from performing their duties under their contracts. This clause typically contains an indemnity provision that obligates the director to indemnify the production company for any of their breaches of the representations and warranties or their other breaches of the agreement.
- Any material that they contribute to the production—writing, gags, *mise-en-scène*, and other creative elements—is original with them. This shifts liability to the director if the production company is sued as a result of the director adding unlicensed, copyright-protected material to the film.

Indemnification

A production company will typically require to be indemnified (to have their losses paid) by producers for damages arising from:

- IP infringement lawsuits stemming from the results and proceeds of the producer's or director's service.
- Breaches of contract by the producer or director.
- Conflicting contractual obligations of the producer or director.
- Falsehoods in the representations and warranties made by the producer or director.

> ***Example:*** In her producer's services agreement for *Green, Black, and Blue: Ultimate Vegan Martial Artists*, Fatima Filmmaker indemnifies her employer Potto Productions that the material she produces (her "results and proceeds") are original with her. However, she includes a clip of an old Jolly Green Giant commercial in the title credits and fails to get permission from the clip's owner, Giant Food Company. The Cable Channel, which broadcasts the show, and Potto Productions are both sued by the Green Giant Food Company for copyright and trademark infringement, false endorsement, and a host of other claims. Because of the indemnification clause, Fatima must pay the legal defense costs of both Potto Productions and the Cable Channel.

Final Say/Production Company Controls

This clause states bluntly that the production company has the final say with regard to creative, financial, artistic, managerial, and other matters on the motion picture. It should also list the production company executive in charge of giving that final say (usually the executive producer or the executive in charge of production).

This section may also detail those elements over which a production company will reserve the right for prior approval. Producers, be very careful here! If the contract requires you to get production company approval over an element, such as the choice of talent, make sure to get that approval prior to hiring that performer! Failure to do so may result in your having to pay for the damage, such as having to butt that rejected performer out of their contract and pay for the other "approved" performer.

Under the DGA agreement (which applies if you're working union with respect to the director), many of the director's rights vest if they've directed at least 90% of the film, and if a director has directed 100% of the film, they also have the right to direct additional scenes and retakes, subject to the director's professional availability.

Suspension/Termination

- This paragraph lays out the mechanism for resolving disputes. It typically describes events that would constitute *force majeure* (acts of God) and sets a time limit for how long a producer's or director's services may be suspended before the services are considered terminated.
- The production company should retain the right to terminate the producer's or director's services for any reason whatsoever, provided the production company pays the producer's fee up to the date of termination.

Morals Clause

With increasing frequency, film productions are being waylaid by bad behavior (actual or perceived) of principal cast and crew. Accordingly, a contract clause that got its start in the Golden Age of cinema has been once more returned to center stage: the morals clause. In the days of the Hollywood studio system, performer's contracts often included this clause, which attempted to regulate the actors' behavior on and off set by allowing termination by the studio for "immoral" acts. Being a communist or gay in those days was considered immoral, and failure to abide by the morals clause in their contracts would cost performers their jobs; during the anti-Communist scare of the early 1950s, it could cost them their careers. The morals clause fell out of favor somewhat and tended to be the first thing an actor's representative would strike from a contract.

In the last decade or so, the morals clause has experienced a resurgence in the wake of the #MeToo movement. It's a way for a production or studio to terminate a performer, director, or other crew member for bad acts like sexual harassment and substance abuse, which create a hazardous work environment for the other performers and crew members or expose the production or studio to bad publicity. A filmmaker's best bet is to include in the suspension and termination rights clause the right for the production company to suspend the actor's services on a particular film for specific acts, such as criminal or tortious behavior or being intoxicated. However, you may want to consider including a broader morals clause allowing the production to terminate the employee for:

- Slander and libel and other tortious behavior.
- Felonies and other criminal behavior.
- Specific problematic behavior (e.g. drug or alcohol use that interferes with work).
- Misogynistic, racist, homophobic, transphobic, and other intolerant acts and speech during production.
- Intolerant acts and speech, as above, which were posted on social media.
- Workplace/verbal abuse.
- Domestic violence and sexual abuse.
- Disparaging actions, speech, or conduct that is disparaging or injurious to the film project or the studio or production company's reputation or brand identity.

Needless to say, agents and managers will look to strike these clauses from the service agreements if they have the leverage to do so. At a minimum, you will need to negotiate:

- What acts allow for termination? Clearly defined definitions are a must.
- Is posting bigoted or harmful comments on social media treated in the same manner as an in-person act?
- If social media posts can trigger termination, does that include posts that are primarily political?
- When does the termination right vest: when the act is publicly known or when it occurs?
- Does notice and cure apply after the statement it is publicly known?
- What level of proof is required to determine the triggering acts occurred? Who decides? Are allegations enough? Is the determination arrived at only through arbitration or litigation?
- To what extent does indemnification by the terminated party apply?

A few important caveats before you start drafting a morals clause:

- Some states have anti-discrimination or off-duty conduct laws that prohibit an employer from firing an employee based on political affiliation or beliefs.
- The National Labor Relations Board may prohibit restrictions over employee speech that discusses hazardous work environments, management concerns, and wages.

Assignment

The production company always needs the right to assign the contract and the rights, results, and proceeds created under it. The producer and director should never have the right to assign or delegate their duties under the contract.

Remedies

As with all motion picture services agreements, the right to injunctive relief should be waived by the producer or director. Furthermore, no breach of the agreement by the production company should entitle the producer or director to recapture any rights that they may have granted the production company. When well drafted, this clause should leave the producer or director only with a right to recover money, if anything at all, from the breaching production company. You will also want to address such issues as whether to solve problems through arbitration or courts of law. (See Appendix B, "Arbitration," p. 484.) And while you're at it, just where will any adjudication or arbitration take place? (See Appendix B, "Choice of Law: Forum," p. 485.)

Further Documents

Here the producer or director should be obligated to execute any other documents necessary to further the intent of the contract. Examples include copyright assignment forms, workers' compensation claim forms, and so forth.

Inducement (If Dealing With a Loan-Out Company)

If the producer or director is working under a loan-out company, it is the loan-out company that will be a party to the contract. Furthermore, the contract should contain an inducement and further assurances clause. (See "Loan-Out Companies," p. 51.) If the production company is financing the film with production incentives like tax credits, you may need to include a provision in the agreement that:

1. Requires the loan-out company to register to do business and file a return in the production state.
2. Gives your production company the power of attorney to register the loan-out company to do business in the production state if the loan-out company fails to do so within a certain period of time (see "Production Incentives: Eligibility Requirements," p. 78).

Right of First Negotiation

The producer or director may want a right of first negotiation/first refusal for any sequels or derivative works arising out of the motion picture. Other variations of this clause include the right of last refusal. This is only given if the producer has a track record or has the leverage of being the initial rights holder.

Festivals and Premieres

The producer or director may want accommodations, tickets, and transportation to premieres of the motion picture and festivals that feature the film. However, the production company may get more bang for its buck by paying the costs of any of the film's well-known lead actors to attend these events than it does when it picks up the producer's tab. Accordingly, the production company may want to sharply define the festivals and premieres for which it will foot the producer's bill. And again, if working with the DGA, make sure to check the publicity tour requirements for directors in the basic agreement.

♦♦♦♦♦♦

LAW

Producers and directors, like other employees, will be protected by federal and state labor laws. However, they may be treated as an independent contractor if they are working through their own loan-out companies (see "Loan-Out Companies," p. 51).

BUSINESS ISSUES

Try to Cap the Producer's Fixed Compensation Fee

Production companies may want to cap the maximum fee a producer is entitled to. For instance, if a low-budget film shooting on a budget of $500,000 has agreed to pay its producer 2% of the budget, the producer is entitled to $10,000. However, if the production company is able to secure several well-known actors, raising the budget to $5 million, the producer would be entitled to a fee of $100,000. Understandably, the production company may not want hand over $100,000 to a relatively unknown producer simply because the film has had the good fortune of attracting name talent. Accordingly, the production company may want to cap the producer's fee at a specific sum, say $50,000, regardless of how high the budget goes. This cap is often referred to as a *ceiling*.

The producer, however, may make the counterargument that attracting name performers and other personnel may be due to their efforts as a producer, and thus the producer should be entitled to a fee based purely on the percentage alone, without a cap. In fact, the producer may want to guard against the possibility of the production budget diminishing by negotiating a *floor* for himself. A floor is a fixed sum that sets the lower limit of the producer's fee.

Without a floor, in the previous example, if the producer's fee is 2% and the production budget suddenly drops to $250,000, the producer would be entitled to only a $5,000 producer's fee. The producer should try to guard against this contingency by negotiating a floor of, say, $8,000 as a producer's fee. If the production company agrees, the producer knows that no matter how low the production budget drops, they will receive a fee of at least $8,000.

Net Profits

Like all profit participant contracts, the producer's services agreement should contain a rider that defines the film's net profits. (See "Net Profits," p. 66.)

STEP BY STEP: HIRING A PRODUCER

From the production company's point of view:

- Try to select a producer with experience in film contract negotiation. However, the more experienced the producer is, the more you will have to pay them.
- Make sure everyone understands exactly what *duties* are expected of the
  - *Producer*. Will the producer negotiate contracts? Select and hire crew? Organize the shoot? Depending on the size of the production, the producer's role may be spread among several crew members. Make sure to define the producer's specific duties in the producer's services agreement.
  - *Director*. Is the director responsible for shooting the entire movie, or will there be individual production units with their own unit directors? How involved will the director be in the development phase? Will they be doing their own script rewrite? Will they be going on location scouts?
- Define what is expected of the producer and director during each phase of production. Does the production company need the director full time during pre-production? Will the producer manage the post-production process? How active a role will the producer play during the hunt for a distributor? All these issues should be defined in the services agreement.
- Define what rights to the film property the producer will receive (if any). Normally no one except the production company should receive rights to the film property (although many people may receive royalties from the exploitation of the film property). However, a producer who initially owns

the film may want to retain an ownership position in the copyright to the film. If this is the case, make sure the production company retains the sole authority to decide how and when the film property is exploited.

- Negotiate, draft, and execute the appropriate services agreement.
- During pre-production, make sure one production company executive is responsible for supervising the producer. Keep in mind that in this scenario, it is the production company that is the boss.

STEP BY STEP: HIRING A DIRECTOR

1. Review the director's reel and résumé. Double-check the director's credits with www.imdb.com.
2. When interviewing the director, find out what experience they have had with other production companies. Try to get a sense of how the director dealt with creative control issues with those companies.
3. Ask the director to provide production company references. When you contact their references, ask whether the director's films were delivered on budget and whether there were any creative control issues.
4. Negotiate and execute the director's services agreement.

NOTES

[1] Article 7, §7–101, *DIRECTORS GUILD OF AMERICA, INC. BASIC AGREEMENT OF 2017*, (www.dga.org/-/media/E912CA508ACF4446BA1C0DEB1B49ED89.pdf).

[2] See 7–505 Preparation of Director's Cut, *DIRECTORS GUILD OF AMERICA, INC. BASIC AGREEMENT OF 2017.*

[3] See 5–101 Term Contract Defined, *DIRECTORS GUILD OF AMERICA, INC. BASIC AGREEMENT OF 2017.*

[4] Section 3–100 Minimum Salaries, *DIRECTORS GUILD OF AMERICA, INC. BASIC AGREEMENT OF 2017.*

[5] See www.dga.org/The-Guild/Departments/Credits.aspx (Accessed November 20, 2021).

15

BELOW THE LINE

Crew Services Agreements

In contrast to the above-the-line contracts, below-the-line contracts tend not to be as heavily negotiated. Accordingly, many production companies tend to work with deal memos rather than long-form contracts when hiring crew members. This approach has the advantage of simplicity—a fill-in-the-blank approach favored by time-strapped producers.

The downside is that many deals are not as "one size fits all" as producers would like to believe. For instance, a cinematographer who is hired on the condition that they come with their own camera requires additional provisions in their contract concerning insurance and equipment damage, as opposed to a gaffer who will be working with the equipment supplied them by the production company. The best way to deal with these contracts is to handle them the same way all your contracts should be handled: by sending them to the production attorney for their review prior to execution.

UNION OR NONUNION CREW?

As mentioned before, many indie films are shot with nonunion crews. However, shooting with a union crew has its advantages. For instance, a union crew member may be more experienced than their nonunion counterpart. The two main theatrical unions for crew members are:

- IATSE. The International Alliance of Theatrical Stage Employees, Moving Picture Technicians, Artists and Allied Crafts of the United States, Its Territories and Canada (www.iatse-intl.org). This union represents nearly everyone who is not an actor, director, or choreographer. This includes camera operators, electricians, wardrobe, animators, Teamsters, sound recordists, grips, carpenters, and so forth. Different kinds of crew members may be in different local unions.[1] For instance, IATSE Local 44 represents Special Effects and Prop Shop workers.[2]
- NABET-CWA. The National Association of Broadcast Employees and Technicians-Communications Workers of America (www. nabetcwa.org). It represents crew members working in broadcasting, distributing, telecasting, recording, cable, video, sound recording, and related industries.

DOI: 10.4324/9781003228479-20

The downside of working with a union crew is that the production company has another set of rules and regulations to adhere to the union rules themselves, and in contrast to the world of studio film-making, many indie directors act as their own cinematographers, making the decision to use a union crew a murkier one. Unlike name actors, who are always union members, having a union gaffer associated with the film will not increase your chances of landing a distributor except insofar as your film may be better lit as a result of that union member's expertise.

***TIP:* It is important to note that just because you are working with SAG-AFTRA actors, you are not required to work with a union crew. However, union or not, you are still required to comply with federal and state labor laws.**

GOALS AND DEALS

For definitions and explanations of common contract clauses, see Appendix B, "The Clause Companion," p. 475.

Crew services agreements tend to be shorter than above-the-line agreements. They often contain only two parts:

1. A "fill-in-the-blanks" deal memo, often a single sheet, that details the deal points of that particular crew member's deal: salary, position in the crew, contact information, other terms.
2. A longer "standard terms" rider that provides the (usually) non-negotiated terms and conditions of the contract; this rider is used for every crew member's contract.

Because many independent films are shot with a nonunion crew, the following deal points are for a nonunion contract.

MAJOR DEAL POINTS: CREW'S SERVICES AGREEMENT

The Parties

- *Production company.* Because the production company will be hiring many crew members, it wants a contract it can use over and over with a minimum amount of redrafting and negotiation. If you need a crew member to perform duties additional to those customarily performed by such a person, make sure to detail the exact services the crew member will be providing.

- ***Example:*** If you just write "camera operator," most crew members would not assume that the job also includes picking up the rest of the crew in the production van every morning.

- *Crew.* Crew members will want definitive work and pay schedules. If they are to supply their own equipment (e.g., cameras, trucks, lighting), they will want a rental fee in addition to their services fee, and they will want their equipment to be protected by the production company's insurance policy.

Here, as in other services agreements, the production company must be aware of exactly whom it is contracting with. Is it a loan-out company or an individual? The drafting of the contract, and whether an inducement and further assurances are required, will be affected by each consideration. (See "Loan-Out Companies," p. 51.) Most crew members are hired as individuals, although cinematographers and other crew members who supply their own equipment often work though loan-out companies.

Legally, the safest route is to treat the crew member as an employee rather than an independent contractor. However, if you are dealing with a loan-out company, you are probably dealing with an independent contractor rather than an employee.

Make sure to get full contact information, including Social Security numbers for individuals and federal ID numbers for companies. These will be necessary for handling payroll and other taxes. Also include contact information for the crew member's attorney or agent if they have one.

Engagement

- This paragraph describes the particular services that the crew member is obligated to perform for the production company. The clause is usually drafted fairly broadly, as in the following: "Crew member agrees to perform all services as are customarily rendered by [insert position, e.g., "grips," "gaffers," etc.] on a feature-length theatrical motion picture, plus additional services as specified in any rider attached hereto."
- Any additional services that the crew member is required to perform should be attached to the agreement in a separate rider. You may need the crew member to pick up equipment and drop it off again when the shoot wraps. You may also need the crew member to be responsible for purchasing materials necessary to do their job. For example, you may need the gaffer to be responsible for buying lighting gels and tape, an art director may be needed to pick up building supplies and props, and so on. All of this detail should be included in the rider.

- This provision also contains the *term* of the agreement: the time periods during which the crew member is obligated to provide their services to the production company. If the start date cannot be determined at the time the contract is executed, the production company may want to include a range during which they can designate a start date.
- The production company should also state that the crew member's services are "unique and the loss of such services cannot be fully compensated by monetary damages." This may entitle the production company to injunctive relief against the crew member, preventing them from working on another film, should the crew member harm the production by quitting midstream.

Exclusivity

Often, the crew member's services are nonexclusive during development, pre-production, and post-production and exclusive during principal photography. However, depending on the needs of the film, the production company may need the crew member to be either exclusive or first priority during pre-production and post-production as well. A crew member whose daily services were required during pre-production or post-production should probably be exclusive for these periods as well.

Costs and Expenses

Crew members should be reimbursed by the production company for all out-of-pocket expenses relating to the motion picture. However, to protect the production company, repayment of crew member's expenses over a certain amount (e.g., $100) should require the production company's prior written approval. The crew member should also be prohibited from hiring others without the prior written approval of the production company.

CREW MEMBER GEAR

If the crew member is supplying their own equipment (camera rigs, lighting, etc.), the contract should state that the crew member is solely responsible for the upkeep, maintenance, and safety of their own gear. The production company should check with its insurance company to determine to what extent the crew member's equipment is covered under the production company's policies.

Travel and Accommodations

Travel, accommodations, and *per diem* expenses should be negotiated and agreed on in advance.

Compensation

- Typically, crew members receive only fixed or deferred compensation, or some combination of the two kinds of compensation, but not a portion of the film's net profits. (See Appendix B, "Compensation," p. 476.)
- There is typically no guarantee that all the deferred compensation will be paid out to the crew member, because the film may not make any money at all. Accordingly, if a large percentage of a crew member's fee is deferred, that crew member may feel entitled to a higher overall salary to offset the risk of not recouping their fee. (See Appendix B, "Deferred Compensation," p. 478.)
- The crew member should agree to allow the production company to withhold taxes or other deductions required by federal and state laws from the crew member's fee.

Credit

- As is true for all credit provisions, the production company should insert a clause in the contract that says that "inadvertent failure to accord the contracting party credit shall not be actionable." This clause should also require the injured party to waive the right to injunctive relief, leaving an obligation on the production company's part to correct the problem on all future prints and copies as the only remedy for the production company's credit mistakes. The clause should further state that a mistake of this nature is not a breach of the crew member services agreement. The clause should make clear that the production company has complete discretion over the look of the credits.
- The production company should agree to list the crew member's appropriate credit on IMDB.com.

Rights

The assignment of the rights/work-made-for-hire provision is another standard clause in all motion picture or service contracts. In this paragraph, the crew member must agree that all rights (like copyrights), proceeds, and results of their creative efforts are owned by the production company, typically as a work made for hire (with an alternate copyright assignment provision). California productions engaging independent contractor crew members may want to have copyrights assigned to them to avoid having to treat independent contractors like employees. (See "Work Made for Hire," p. 418.)

Publicity

The production company will want to control the publicity for the motion picture and thus be able to restrain the crew member from posting pictures and statements about the motion picture on social media without the production company's prior written consent. The production company will also require the right to use the crew member's name and likeness in any publicity, promotion, or marketing of the motion picture. Make sure to include language that allows the crew member's image to be used in any "making of" documentary for the film.

Representations and Warranties

- The crew member is typically required to represent and warrant that they are under no other obligations that would prevent them from performing their duties under this contract. This clause typically contains an indemnity provision that obligates the crew member to indemnify the production company for any breaches of the representations and warranties or other breaches of the agreement.
- The crew member should also warrant that any material that they contribute to the production—writing, props, scenery, wardrobe, gags, *mise-en-scène*, and other creative elements—are original with them. This shifts liability to the crew member if the production company is sued as a result of the crew member adding unlicensed copyright-protected material to the film.

Suspension/Termination

- This paragraph lays out the mechanism for resolving disputes. It typically describes events that would constitute *force majeure* (acts of God) and sets a time limit for how long a crew member's services may be suspended before the services are considered terminated.
- The production company should retain the right to terminate the crew member's services for any reason whatsoever, provided that the production company pay the crew member's fee up to the date of termination.

Assignment

The production company always has the right to assign the contract and the rights, results, and proceeds created under it. The crew member should never have the right to assign or delegate their duties under the contract.

Remedies

Like all motion picture services agreements, the right to injunctive relief should be waived by the crew member. Furthermore, no breach of the agreement by the production company should entitle the crew member to recapture any rights that they may have granted to the production company. When well drafted, this clause should leave the crew member only with a right to recover money, if anything at all, from the breaching production company. You will also want to address such issues as whether to solve problems through arbitration or courts of law. (See Appendix B, "Arbitration," p. 484.) And while you're at it, just where will any adjudication or arbitration take place? (See Appendix B, "Choice of Law: Forum," p. 485.)

Further Documents

Here the crew member should be obligated to execute any other documents necessary to further the intent of the contract. Examples include copyright assignment forms, workers' compensation claim forms, and so forth.

Inducement (If Dealing With a Loan-Out Company)

If the crew member is working under a loan-out company, it is the loan-out company that will be a party to the contract. Furthermore, the contract should contain an inducement and further assurances clause. (See "Loan-Out Companies," p. 51.) If the production company is financing the film with production incentives like tax credits, you may need to include a provision in the agreement:

- Requiring the loan-out company to register to do business and file a return in the production state, and
- Giving your production company the power of attorney to register the loan-out company to do business in the production state if the loan-out company fails to do so within a certain period of time. (See "Production Incentives: Eligibility Requirements," p. 78.)

LAW

- Crew members, like other workers, will be protected by federal and state labor laws. However, the crew members may be treated as independent contractors if they are working through their own companies, such as a loan-out company. (See "Federal and State Labor and Employment Law: An Overview," p. 199.)
- If you are certain that the crew member is an independent contractor and not an employee, you should include a clause in the crew services agreement stating that the parties understand that the crew member shall be treated as an independent contractor. However, keep in mind that a court

will look at the actual work relationship to determine the crew member's status rather than determining status based solely on what the parties agreed in the contract.

BUSINESS ISSUES

As part of the crew member's perks, it is typical to give them a copy of the finished film on Blu-ray or other physical format and to allow them the right to incorporate portions of the film into their reel.

NOTES

[1] A good list of IATSE Local Unions can be found here: www.csatf.org/about/union-guild-directory/

[2] You can see a list of all of the IATSE Local 44 craft descriptions here: https://local44.org/Joining-Local-44/craft-descriptions

16

PERFORMERS

The choice of performers is critical to a narrative film's success. The majority of the time, the lead performers are the single most important elements in making your film. Actors' performances breathe life into a film, and their fame gives a film its marketing power.

An actor's creative contributions begin before they are even cast. Watching performers audition can expose the weaknesses in a role and may underscore the need for a script rewrite. Casting directors are often a great investment and can help you get access to performers you might not otherwise be able to reach.

Because performers realize the power they have over a film project, negotiating the performer's services agreement can be a nail-biting experience. Virtually every recognizable performer has a team of agents, managers, and attorneys ready to protect the actor's interests and negotiate the best deal they can for their client. Negotiating the actor's contracts is one area in which you may want to lean heavily on your entertainment attorney or an experienced executive producer.

The *performer's services agreement* is the contract between the production company and the performer.

PRE-
PROD.

- If the production company wants to use actors to secure film financing but is not yet ready to bind them to a full performer's services agreement, it will need to use a letter of intent. (See "Letters of Intent," p. 241.)
- If the production company wants to hire professional actors, it will also need to deal with the Screen Actors Guild–American Federation of Television and Radio Artists and comply with Guild rules. (See "SAG-AFTRA," p. 243.)
- If your production company is using non-SAG-AFTRA actors only, you can skip the SAG-AFTRA section and jump right into the performer's services agreement deal points. (See "Major Deal Points: Performer's Services Agreement," p. 256.)

LETTERS OF INTENT

Hands down, the thing that is most likely to get your film sold is having a known actor or actress as your lead. Your brother—your film's major investor—may be a wonderful actor, but unless he has had a recurring role in a television series or at least a supporting role in a feature film, he will not help you sell your movie.

DOI: 10.4324/9781003228479-21

Sure, there are exceptions to this rule; for instance, if your film is a documentary, the only union performer you might want to consider would be the providing the voiceover. Many international films are shot with local nonunion talent as well. And if your end goal is to create a YouTube or TikTok channel, it's the dynamic personalities of non-actors which drive people to subscribe.

But if your intent is to create a narrative film or television show with an eye towards landing a distributor or attracting a television network or studio, you should be thinking about professional performers. For studios and networks to feel confident enough to put their resources behind the marketing and selling of your film, they need to believe there is a reasonable chance for a return on their investment. Featuring a known actor or actress in a film's advertising and on the Netflix, Hulu, or Amazon Prime thumbnail increases the likelihood that the film will be seen and thus increases the appeal of your project to distributors, networks, and studios.

However, as one might guess, the more well-known a performer is, the more "bankable" they are and the less likely they will be to obligate themselves to a film that has no financing. In fact, as a practical matter, most theatrical agents will want to know whether the film is financed prior to showing your script to their clients.

However, assuming that you can get a known actor to read your script and like it, how do you get her to agree to be in a film that doesn't have financing? As you can see, it's "chicken-and-egg time" (or "Catch-22," depending on where you fall on the avian reproductive–military logic scale of metaphor preferences). (See "How to Get a Script to a SAG-AFTRA Actor," p. 266.)

One potential solution is to get the performer to agree to let you use her name to secure financing for the film without obligating her to shoot your film if you can't raise the money. This is where a *letter of intent* (LOI) comes in handy. An LOI is a letter from the performer that shows their interest in appearing in your film and includes some of the main deal points to be agreed on. Like many entertainment industry contracts, letters of intent come in many different "flavors," some more binding than others. Many LOIs are just "agreements to agree," which is not the same thing as a legally enforceable contract.

Some financiers, especially those used to the seat-of-the-pants world of independent low-budget filmmaking, will accept an LOI that states little more than the fact that the actor has read the script, likes it, and is interested in portraying a specific role once contingent on:

1. Financing being secured.
2. The performer's availability.
3. Material contract terms being negotiated and agreed on in a performer's agreement. (See "Performer's Services Agreement," p. 256.)

Such letters of intent are far cry from a binding contract that obligates the actor to perform in your film. However, such an LOI from a bankable performer may be enough to convince your financiers that that performer is interested enough to be in your film if the investors will just put the money behind it.

PERFORMERS

SHORT-FORM PERFORMER'S LETTER OF INTENT

[PERFORMER'S AGENT'S CONTACT INFORMATION]

[PERFORMER'S NAME]

[DATE]

Thank you so much for your interest in our film, tentatively titled [INSERT NAME OF FILM] (the "Film"). As we've discussed, this letter serves to confirm that your client [INSERT PERFORMER'S NAME] has reviewed our script, is familiar with the Film project, and is interested in performing in the Film in the role of [INSERT PERFORMER'S ROLE], subject to [INSERT PERFORMER'S NAME]'s professional availability and an agreement between all parties on financial and other material terms.

[INSERT PERFORMER'S NAME] hereby grants to the producers of the Film the right to use this letter of intent in seeking financing for the Film, and the right to use [INSERT PERFORMER'S NAME] name and likeness for project development purposes in conjunction with the Film, for a period not to exceed [ONE YEAR] from the date of this letter.

If this letter reflects your and your client's understanding, please have your client sign below, and return an original signed copy to me.

We look forward to the possibility of working together on [INSERT NAME OF FILM].

Best regards,

____

[PRODUCER'S SIGNATURE]

____

[PERFORMER'S NAME]

It is important to note that the more money that is being raised and the more sophisticated the financier, the less likely it will be that a nonbinding short-form LOI alone will satisfy the financier's requirements.

WORKING WITH SAG-AFTRA

If you want to work with a professional actor, you will also need to work and comply with the rules of SAG-AFTRA.

What Is SAG-AFTRA?

The Screen Actors Guild-American Federation of Television and Radio Artists is a labor union for professional film and television actors. Production companies that want to work with actors who are SAG-AFTRA members must become *signatories* of the SAG-AFTRA Codified Basic Agreement (Basic Agreement). This means that the production companies must sign a contract with SAG-AFTRA in which they agree to abide by SAG-AFTRA's rules and regulations with respect to the SAG-AFTRA actors they employ.

Among other things, the basic agreement dictates the minimum requirements for:

- An actor's payment and other forms of compensation.
- The hours the actor is required to work.
- Pension and health contributions.
- Overtime.
- Consecutive employment.
- Working conditions.

SAG-AFTRA Contract Terms Will Supersede Conflicting Production Company Contracts

Once a production company is a SAG-AFTRA signatory, the SAG-AFTRA Basic Agreement, like other union agreements, will overrule any contrary provisions in the contract between the production company and an actor.

Example: Electric Space Pickle Productions, LLC, has just become a SAG-AFTRA signatory and is producing a film for $500,000 under SAG-AFTRA's "Moderate Low Budget Film" contract. The Modified Low-Budget agreement requires that actors be paid a minimum of $361 a day, plus pension and health payments. Because the producers want to pour most of the funds into special effects, everybody has agreed to take a salary cut. The production company drafts Actor's Services Contracts giving the SAG-AFTRA actors only $100 per day, no health and pension payments, which the actors begrudgingly sign. Unfortunately for the production company, the SAG-AFTRA Modified Low-Budget agreement supersedes the production company's contracts. Therefore, even though the actors agreed to $100 a day with no P&H contributions, they must still be paid the $361 a day plus P&H specified in the SAG-AFTRA agreement.

A Low-Budget Contract for Every Film

SAG-AFTRA has made an effort to accommodate filmmakers of all budgetary levels. Whether you're making a $1,000 short film, a YouTube series, a $2.5 million low-budget film, or a half-billion-dollar Hollywood blockbuster, SAG-AFTRA has a contract for you.

In general, the lower your budget, the less you have to pay your SAG-AFTRA actor. However, there are restrictions on how your film may be exhibited, depending on the level of contract you've used to engage your actors. If a film is distributed in a manner that exceeds the SAG-AFTRA contract limitations, the filmmakers may have to pay additional fees.

The following list highlights a few major deal points of SAG-AFTRA's contracts for low budget independent filmmakers. Filmmakers are advised to request both more detailed summaries as well as the contracts themselves from the SAG-AFTRA.

The SAG-AFTRA low-budget contracts change from time to time. As this book is being written, the following are the current SAG-AFTRA contracts available:[1]

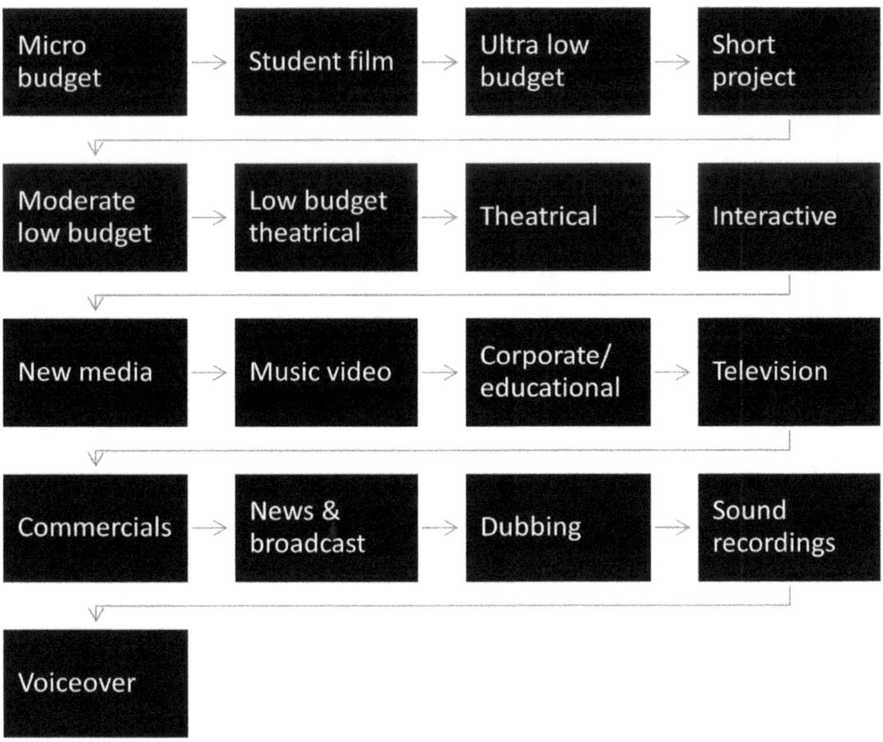

A BRIEF SUMMARY OF THE SAG-AFTRA CONTRACTS OFTEN USED BY INDIE FILMMAKERS

Name	Max Budget; Shooting Days; Running Time	Requirements	Prohibitions	Exhibition	Actor Rate
Micro-Budget	▪ $20K or less per picture or per episode	▪ Live action only (unscripted or scripted) ▪ Must be shot in United States ▪ Producer must obtain a "Micro-Budget Project Agreement Acknowledgement" from each performer and background actor	FILM CAN'T BE ▪ Animation ▪ Branded/influencer content ▪ Commercials ▪ Corporate or educational videos ▪ Music videos ▪ Audio-only content, including audiobooks, podcasts, and radio plays ▪ Video games ▪ News/broadcast ▪ Projects including any nudity or simulated sex ▪ Projects including any hazardous stunts ▪ Projects where the producer has received any cwompensation in exchange for the right to distribute or exhibit it	▪ Film festivals ▪ Free-to-the-consumer new media (AVOD) ▪ Required screenings for Academy Award consideration ▪ Public access TV ▪ For demo purposes ▪ In the classroom (student producers)	▪ Most terms will be subject to negotiation between producer and performer ▪ Producer must still comply with workers' compensation and minimum wages

Student Film	$35K/20 days total/35 min.	▪ The producer must be a student enrolled in a filmmaking or television class in an accredited educational institution. The student (producer) must own the project	▪ Performer can't be exclusive during production	▪ Film festivals ▪ Classroom ▪ Required screenings for Academy Award consideration ▪ Use as a visual résumé	▪ Rate: > $125 per day ▪ OT: 1.5× for the first 9–12 hours; 2× OT thereafter ▪ P&H ▪ Travel costs
Short Project	$50K/30 days principal/40 min.	▪ Shot entirely in the United States	▪ Animated projects, music videos, corporate or education videos, video games, television or new media series, or student films ▪ Performer can't be exclusive during production	▪ Film festivals ▪ Classroom ▪ Required screenings for Academy Award Consideration ▪ Use as a visual résumé	▪ Rate: > $206 day player ▪ OT: 1.5× for the first 9–12 hours; 2× OT thereafter ▪ P&H: 20% performers ▪ Travel costs
Ultra-Low	$300K	▪ Shot entirely in the United States	▪ Producer may not use any digital scanning techniques to create digital reproductions of any performer in connection with the project without SAG-AFTRA's consent	▪ Film festivals ▪ Classroom ▪ Required screenings for Academy Award consideration ▪ Use as a visual résumé	▪ Rate: > $206 day player or 35% of the day rate from the Basic Agreement current at the time of performance if greater

(Continued)

PRE-PROD.

Continued

Name	Max Budget; Shooting Days; Running Time	Requirements	Prohibitions	Exhibition	Actor Rate
				▪ Unpaid on one public access television channel for not more than ten exhibitions within one year from the first run date	▪ OT: 1.5× for the first 9–12 hours; 12+ payable at no less than double the Moderate Low Budget Project ▪ P&H: 20% performers ▪ Travel costs ▪ Residuals for other uses
Moderate Low	$700K	▪ Qualifying for the Diversity-in-Casting Incentive increases total production cost maximum to $950,000 ▪ Qualifying for the Background Actor Incentive increases total production cost maximum by $112,000	▪ Animation ▪ Branded/influencer content ▪ Commercials ▪ Corporate or educational videos ▪ Music videos ▪ Audio-only content, including audiobooks, podcasts, and radio plays ▪ Video games ▪ News/broadcast	▪ Film festivals ▪ Required screenings for Academy Award consideration ▪ Use as a visual résumé ▪ Unpaid on one public access television channel for not more than ten exhibitions within	▪ Rate: > $361 day player or 20% of the day rate from the Basic Agreement current at the time of performance if greater ▪ OT: 1.5× for the first 9–12 hours; 12+ payable

				one year from the first run date	at no less than double the Moderate Low Budget rate ▪ P&H: 20% performers ▪ Travel costs ▪ Residuals for other uses
Low	$2M	▪ Qualifying for the Diversity-in-Casting Incentive increases total production cost maximum to $3,000,000		▪ Bona fide initial theatrical release of the picture is required ▪ Initial release into any non-theatrical market will require "step-up" payments to performers equivalent to the Basic Agreement unless, after three (3) yearsfrom the end of principal photography, the	▪ Rate: > $670 day player or 65% of the day rate from the Basic Agreement current at the time of performance if greater ▪ OT: 1.5× for the first 9–12 hours; 12+ hours payable at no less than double the Low Budget rate ▪ P&H: 20% performers ▪ Travel costs

(Continued)

Continued

Name	Max Budget; Shooting Days; Running Time	Requirements	Prohibitions	Exhibition	Actor Rate
				picture fails to get a theatrical release	▪ Residuals for other uses
New Media	[see note in rates]	Only for programs designed for exhibition on the Internet, through mobile devices, or other tech now known or hereafter devised	Motion pictures, videogames, commercials, media covered by other SAG-AFTRA agreements	▪ Only for programs designed for exhibition on the Internet, through mobile devices, or other tech now known or hereafter devised ▪ Programs that are initially released in other media pay step-ups per that basic contract	▪ Budgets of 50K–250K Rate: > $125 ▪ Budgets of 250K–700K Rate: > $335 ▪ Budgets of 700K–1M Rate: > $630 ▪ Budgets of >1M Rate: per TV agreement ▪ P&H: 17% performers ▪ Residuals: Initial compensation applies to first 26 weeks ofresiduals; 3.6% distributor's gross thereafter

Using SAG-AFTRA's Diversity in Casting[2] incentive, filmmakers may raise the budget thresholds and still shoot under a lower-budget SAG-AFTRA agreement if they diversify their casting as follows:

A minimum of 50% total speaking roles and 50% total days of employment are cast with performers who are:

- Women.
- Seniors 60 or older.
- Performers with disabilities, or
- People of color (for at least 20% of total employment days).

IMPORTANT: The SAG-AFTRA contracts change more frequently than this book is updated. Stay current and double-check the status of these contracts on both:

- **www.sagaftra.org**
- **www.sagindie.org**

SAG-AFTRA TERMS DEFINED

Consecutive Employment

The SAG-AFTRA MBA requires that producers pay actors for *consecutive employment.* This means that actors must be compensated for days in between those days when they were directly involved in the shoot.

Example: If an actor is supposed to work on Tuesday and Thursday, you must pay him or her for Wednesday as well. However, all the low-budget SAG-AFTRA agreements have done away with this rule. As a result, if an actor is working under a low-budget agreement and is scheduled for Tuesday and Thursday, these are the only two days for which they get paid—unless, of course, the producer has agreed to pay consecutive employment in the performer's services agreement. *Remember, SAG-AFTRA only sets the minimum requirements for an actor's services agreement and does not prohibit actors or their representatives from negotiating better deals than those required by the union.*

Residuals

Residuals are additional payments required to be paid to union performers when the film is licensed in ancillary markets such as broadcast television, cable, home video, and SVOD but not theatrical distribution.[3] When the production company becomes a SAG-AFTRA signatory, it agrees to make residual payments for the film's actors and to ensure that the film's distributors sign an *assumption agreement.* The assumption agreement is a contract with the distributor (or a clause in the distribution agreement itself) in which the distributor agrees to pay the residuals directly to SAG-AFTRA.

Example: Pariah Pictures has shot its film *The Adventures of Millard Fillmore* under the SAG-AFTRA ultra-low-budget agreement. The film is shown on free television, and 3.6% of the distributor's gross receipts are owed to the SAG-AFTRA actors. Because of Pariah Pictures' assumption agreement with Dusty Distribution, Inc., Dusty pays 3.6% of its gross receipts to SAG-AFTRA, which disburses the monies directly to the actors.

Becoming a Signatory

To become a signatory with SAG-AFTRA, you will need to provide them with a good deal of legal documentation—much of which, if you've been following along in this book, you should have by now. SAG-AFTRA requires that you submit the following forms *at least one month prior* to working with SAG-AFTRA actors. You will need to start the process by downloading, filling out, and submitting to SAG-AFTRA a *preliminary theatrical information sheet*, available on its website at www.sagindie.org/resources/contract-downloads/.

Once the information sheet has been reviewed, you will be assigned a SAG-AFTRA representative, who will be your contact with the Guild.

For SAG-AFTRA to approve your production company's eligibility to work with its members, depending on the contract applicable to your film, you may be asked to give the union the following:

- A copy of the completed copyright registration form. (See "Copyright Registration," p. 164.)
- A copy of the US Copyright Office receipt, which shows that the office has received the completed form.
- All chain-of-title documents relating to the copyright in the screenplay and the picture. (See "Chain of Title," p. 159.)
- A copy of the script.
- A copy of the shooting schedule.
- A detailed film budget.

- Financial structure documents. These are the legal documents pertaining to the formation of your business. Examples include partnership agreements, articles of incorporation, articles of organization and operating agreements, business certificates, and fictitious name statements. (See "Setting Up the Production Company," p. 43.)
- A company authorization form.
- SAG-AFTRA Agreement for Independent Producers of Theatrical Motion Pictures.
- SAG-AFTRA Agreement for the SAG-AFTRA contract you are shooting under.
- SAG-AFTRA Producers Pension Plan Adherence Letter.
- SAG-AFTRA Television/Theatrical Production Checklist.
- Complete pre-production cast list (and Diversity in Casting Form, if applicable).
- Financial assurances. SAG-AFTRA may also require assurances that your production company has the money it needs to make the film. SAG-AFTRA may require:
  - A security deposit.
  - A first-position *security interest* in the film. A security interest is similar to a mortgage on a house: If you default in your mortgage payments, the bank can sell your house to repay your loan. With SAG-AFTRA's security interest, if you default on your payment obligations to the SAG-AFTRA actors, SAG-AFTRA can seize your film and sell it to pay your debts to your actors.

SAG-AFTRA Compliance

PAPERWORK

Your duties to SAG-AFTRA don't end with the signatory process. During production (and to a lesser extent during post-production and distribution), you will have a LOT of forms to fill out and rules with which you must comply. Delegate to a member of the producer's team the task of making sure the production company is complying with all SAG-AFTRA's rules and regulations. This "SAG-AFTRA compliance producer" should pay special attention to rules regarding:

- Weekly payroll reporting and delivery of checks to the Union.
- Weekly pension and health payments to the Union.
- Daily Production Time Report Form recording of production schedule and overtime.

- Working conditions for the performers.
- Minors.
- Meals.
- Transportation.
- Nudity.
- Exhibition restrictions.
- Any other item required under the contract with SAG-AFTRA.

NUDITY AND ROLES REQUIRING SIMULATED SEX

Hollywood history is littered with the horrible practices of some producers holding "casting couch" and "Ogling Auditions." SAG-AFTRA takes sexual harassment and sexual exploitation of its members very seriously and has very stringent rules in this area designed to ensure that performers are not exploited and do not feel pressured or coerced into performing nude or in sexual scenes they are uncomfortable with.

- If you are a SAG-AFTRA signatory, you must let actors know *before* they audition for the role that nudity is required. You cannot ask the actors to audition nude, but you may ask them (for the last audition only) to wear "modesty garments" (G-strings, thongs, genital "socks," pasties, etc.).
- All performers who appear in nude scenes must agree in writing to do so in a rider that outline the parameters of nudity or simulated sex. The right to use a double in place of the actor must also be agreed to in writing beforehand.
- A performer may withdraw their written consent—and they don't need to do it in writing—at any time prior to the camera rolling. If consent is withdrawn, the producer can use a double (even a digital CGI double), but only if those terms were included in the nudity rider.
- In shooting nude or sexual scenes, it is critical that the set be closed to all nonessential personnel, no personal recordings made, and cover-up garments provided to the performers for in between takes.
- More information here: www.sagaftra.org/files/sa_documents/SAG-AFTRA_quickguide_intimscenes_F2.pdf.

PRODUCER'S TIP: When shooting a nude scene, the key is to make the performers feel as comfortable as possible. A good practice is to collect all cellphones prior to shooting. Make sure the temperature is warm enough for the actors to feel comfortable in the buff. This may mean space heaters and a sweaty crew, but the actor's performances will be the better for it. See that blankets and robes are always handy. Talk to the crew beforehand to make sure that there are absolutely no off-color or bawdy remarks. Not only should the crew be on its best behavior, but they should also be as silent as possible. The more crew members blend into the background, keeping chatter to a minimum, the less vulnerable and exposed the actors will feel. Above all, the only people who should be on the set are those necessary for taking the shot. There should be nobody standing around who does not have a job to do—absolutely no gawkers and no still photographs without the prior written permission of the actors. Unless you want to lose an actor's trust and have SAG-AFTRA come down on you hard, avoid turning your set into a peep show.

SAG-AFTRA Cautionary Notes

Remember: SAG-AFTRA Sets the *Minimum* Contract Requirements Only

If the production company is a SAG-AFTRA signatory and is using SAG-AFTRA actors, the terms of the union's contracts will set the *lower* threshold of elements such as compensation, working conditions, and the like. Actors and their agents, of course, will try to negotiate higher salaries than those required under these union contracts. *Be very careful here!* It is easy for budgets to spiral out of control when it comes to an actor's compensation.

- On one hand, a name actor is, without a doubt, the most important element in selling a motion picture to a distribution company and therefore is worth the time and expense it takes to negotiate a deal with which all parties feel comfortable.
- On the other hand, if you have several name actors of approximately the same industry recognition value, you simply cannot increase the salary of one without dealing with the demands of the others. This is why low-budget films featuring a cast of several name performers frequently pay only the SAG-AFTRA minimum and not a penny more. Remember, despite your best efforts, you will not be able to keep salaries a secret. Do not pay one actor more than another similarly situated actor unless you want a disgruntled performer on your hands. (See Appendix B, "Most Favored Nations," p. 479.)
- Remember: a production company that is a signatory with SAG-AFTRA is *required* to abide by all of SAG-AFTRA's rules. Anything in your contracts contrary to SAG-AFTRA's agreements will be superseded by SAG-AFTRA's agreements.
- SAG-AFTRA may require production companies to post a bond to secure the actors' payroll (which can be up to 40% of the budgeted payroll).
- Once the company is a signatory and is working with SAG-AFTRA actors, you may be limited in your ability to use nonunion actors. If you're shooting

a film under the student, short, or ultra-low-budget contracts, you may use both SAG-AFTRA and non-SAG-AFTRA actors. However, if you are shooting under the modified low-budget and low-budget agreements, all your actors may need to be SAG-AFTRA members or become members shortly after being hired.

- After you've signed up with SAG-AFTRA, you will have continuing payroll and reporting paperwork during production as well. It's a good idea to dedicate a producer to deal with this often-overwhelming aspect of working with the Union.

For more information on SAG-AFTRA contracts and policies for independent producers, see www.sagindie.org.

***TIP:* Start your SAG-AFTRA signatory application processes as early as possible (at least four weeks prior to shooting). You need to be a signatory before you can sign a SAG-AFTRA actor to a deal.**

THE PERFORMER'S SERVICES AGREEMENT

Goals and Deals

You should always hire your performers with a written performance services agreement, regardless of whether you're working with SAG-AFTRA or shooting a nonunion film.

For union films, even though you will be asked to provide the actors with a SAG-AFTRA contract applicable to the particular budget level of your film, you should also provide each actor with their own services contract from the production company. "Ugh, two contracts!" I know, I know. Here's why: the SAG-AFTRA contract probably doesn't go into every aspect of the performer's contract needed by a production company. Keep in mind that any conflicting deal points between the two contracts will be decided in favor of the SAG-AFTRA contract. For definitions and explanations of common contract clauses, see Appendix B, "The Clause Companion," p. 475.

Very often a *performer's services agreement* will come in two parts: a brief (two pages or so) *deal memo* coupled with a much longer "Terms and Conditions" section. You can hold in the SAG-AFTRA agreement as an attachment to your contract if you like,

The deal memo proper contains key compensation and engagement terms applicable to that particular actor's deal. The "Terms and Conditions" section is designed to apply to the deals of *all* the actors in the film.

MAJOR DEAL POINTS: PERFORMER'S SERVICES AGREEMENT

The Parties

- **The Production Company—**This needs to be the company that signed the union signatory agreements if it's a union production. And if you don't have a company already, make sure to form one before hiring anybody. Seriously, there are so many areas of filmmaking that can expose a producer to litigation risk that you really should have a business structure that limits your personal liability. (See "Setting Up the Production Company," p. 43).
- **The Performer or the Performer's Loan-Out Company—**You are either contracting with the performer themselves or with a company they have set up to provide their services, called a loan-out company. (See "Loan-Out Companies," p. 51). The drafting of the agreement for a loan-out company is significantly different than the agreement for an actor in their individual capacity, so make sure you get this information before you start drafting a contract or you will have a lot of rewriting to do. Make sure to get the proper spelling of the performer's professional and legal names, their contact information, and both the performer's Social Security number and their company's federal tax ID number, if they have a loan-out company. Get contact information for the performer's attorney or agent, if the actor has one.

Engagement

- *Role*. Specify the particular role(s) that the actor will be playing, along with the category of role (principal, background, choreographer, other).
- *SAG-AFTRA agreement*. If this is a *union* agreement, this paragraph should specify under which union contract the film is being shot (e.g. SAG-AFTRA's Ultra-Low Budget Agreement).
- *Services*. These should be described as "all services as are customarily rendered by actors on a feature-length theatrical motion picture, including appearing in any 'making-of' or 'behind-the-scenes' documentaries, plus additional services as specified in any rider attached hereto." If this is a nonunion shoot requiring everybody, even actors, to perform more than just the customary duties of their job, these additional services should be spelled out in a detailed rider attached to the contract. For actors on a non-union shoot, this might include transporting themselves and other actors to the set, selecting and purchasing their own wardrobe, and so forth. SAG-AFTRA considers all performers working for a film employees of the production company.

- *Location.* The location of all principal photography is usually specified. This is important, especially for SAG-AFTRA agreements, which have different rules regarding consecutive employment, travel, and other accommodations, based on the particular geographic zone in which the shoot occurs.
- *Unique services.* The production company may want to say that "the performer's services are of a unique nature, the loss of which cannot be fully compensated by monetary damages." If the performer breaches the contract with the production company, then starts work for a third party, the producer can use the "unique services" language and try to get an injunction preventing the performer from working for the third party. Unfortunately, an injunction can't compel a performer or other employee to work with your production company. It can only prevent them from working with another party during the term of your performer's services agreement with that actor.

Availability Dates

This section details all the dates for which an actor must be available to the production company and whether they will be exclusive to the production company during that time period; this should also include pre-production, production, post-production, and publicity and promotional activities.

- *Exclusivity.* Whenever possible, performer should be exclusive to you during the production if they are in main or supporting roles. Even on those days where they're not exclusive, you may want to make your production their "first priority."
- Keep in mind, however, that some SAG-AFTRA contracts (e.g. student and short film) actually prohibit the performer from being exclusive during production. However, this does not mean that they can decide to flake. Once they've committed to perform on set on a certain day, they will be in breach of contract if they fail to show up.
- *Define the start date.* This is the first day for which the actor will get paid.
- *Pre-production.* This is the number of days or dates for which the actor must be available for wardrobe fitting, rehearsal, makeup, and so on. These dates are typically nonconsecutive and often are nonexclusive to the production company. If the pre-production dates are to be nonexclusive, the production company should require that they have first priority on the actor's time for those dates.
- *Production.* These are the dates for which the actor must be available to the production for shooting. It is typical to list all consecutive days and weeks of employment and to make an actor's services exclusive to the

production company on those days or weeks on which the actor is performing in the movie.

- *Post-production.* Number of days or dates for which the actor must be available for looping, reshoots, etc.
- *Reshoot tip.* Often dates for post-production activities have not yet been scheduled when the actor's agreement is being negotiated and signed. In those instances, it is common practice to put the number of days, rather than the date, for which an actor must be available for these activities. Keep in mind, however, that when a specific date is not negotiated, performers usually condition their availability to the production company on whether they have prior contractual commitments that keep them from performing for the production company on a particular date. If this is the case, contract language should specify that it is the actor's obligation to provide services at the earliest possible date thereafter.
- *Publicity.* Number of days or dates for which the actor must be available for photo sessions, interviews, and other publicity or promotional activities.
- *Free days.* Days beyond the production dates for which the performer will be available for reshoots and the like. Compensation should be negotiated for these days as well.

Compensation

- *Fixed compensation.* This is the rate at which the actor will be paid regardless of whether the movie makes money. It is typically coupled with the pay-or-play provision, which requires the production company to pay the actor even if the actor's services are not used. If you are a SAG-AFTRA signatory company working with SAG-AFTRA actors, the particular SAG-AFTRA contract under which your production is being shot will dictate the minimum amount you can pay your performers.
- *Contingent compensation:*
  - *Deferred compensation.* SAG-AFTRA agreements impact whether an actor can defer their salary. (See Appendix B, "Deferred Compensation," p. 478.)
  - *Profit participation.* An actor might get a portion of the film's net profits. For longer contracts, the film's net profit definition is often included in the contracts of all contingent compensation participants. (See "Net Profits," p. 66.)
  - *Reuse/residuals.* These are fees payable to a performer when the motion picture is televised, broadcast, or the like. Union contracts will set the minimum rate for these as well. On a nonunion production, companies often have the actors waive these fees.

- *Favored nations.* Most principal cast members will insist on favored-nations treatment for their compensation and any definition affecting compensation. (See Appendix B, "Favored Nations," p. 479.)
- *Merchandising.* Although the right to manufacture merchandise from an actor's likeness is typically granted to the production company, the performer will want to receive a portion of the proceeds from the merchandise. One formula is to grant the performer 5% of whatever the producer receives from the license of merchandising rights. This fee should be reduced if other actors share the same merchandise property. For example, for a T-shirt deal that features a picture of several cast members, the percentage each actor receives should be reduced according to the number of actors featured on the shirt, so that they all share in the 5% compensation to be paid to the actor, as well as a proportionate increase in compensation for any other actors who have a favored-nations provision regarding compensation perks.
- *Agent fee.* Actors and agents will often try to negotiate to have the production company, rather than the actor, pay the agent's 10% commission. If this is agreed to, producers need to understand that this effectively means a 10% increase in salary.
- *Permission to pay the agency.* Agents usually require that their actor clients have their salaries paid directly to the agency. The agency then takes its commission and passes the remainder on to the actor. If this is the arrangement for your performer, the performer's services agreement must contain a clause giving the production company the right to pay the salary to the agency as opposed to the actor.

SAG-AFTRA Pension and Health Payments

SAG-AFTRA agreements require the producer to make pension and health contributions to SAG-AFTRA directly for covered performers (20% for principal performers and 19.5% for background). These contributions are based on a percentage of the actor's salary and need to be tendered to the union weekly along with the SAG-AFTRA Pension & Health Report of Contributions form.

Perquisites

Perks are fringe benefits not counted as part of the salary.

- *Per diem.* This is a daily allowance that is supposed to compensate the actor for meals, incidental transportation, and other expenses the performer incurs as a result of being away from home. Be wary of agents here—especially when an actor has agreed to work below their quote, an agent may attempt to recapture money for the actor by increasing the actor's *per diem.*

Credit

- It should come as no surprise that credit is one of the more hotly negotiated provisions of the contract. In addition to the position that the credit occupies with respect to the other actors' credits, other negotiable credit terms are whether the credit must appear in all paid advertising, posters, publicity, and so forth.
- It is common for lead actors to negotiate a favored-nations clause with respect to the size, placement, priority, duration, and prominence of their credit in the film itself as well as those forms of advertising and marketing which their names must appear.
- As with all credit provisions, the producer should contract for as much discretion as possible in creating the look of the credits and any other matter with respect to the credits for which the performer has not been given approval rights.
- As is true for all credit provisions, the production company should insert a clause in the contract that says that "inadvertent failure to accord the contracting party credit shall not be actionable." This clause should also require the injured party to waive the right to injunctive relief, leaving an obligation on the production company's part to correct the problem on all future prints as the only remedy for the production company's credit mistakes. The clause should further state that a mistake of this nature is not a breach of the performer's services agreement.

Rights Granted; Results and Proceeds

This section lays out the specific rights granted ("assigned") to the producer. This should always be structured as a work-made-for-hire provision. That way, initial ownership by the production company in the performer's work on the film is automatic. (See Appendix A, "Work Made for Hire," p. 418.). Make sure to define the film as including behind-the-scenes footage.

The producer needs the broadest grant of rights possible:

- The copyright in the performer's work on the film.
- A waiver of *moral rights* and *droit moral*. (See Appendix A, "Moral Rights," p. 457.)
- A grant of the right of publicity to exploit the actor's likeness for merchandising and other tie-ups. (See Appendix A, "Right of Publicity," p. 443.)
- The right to use doubles for the performer and to dub the performer's voice.
- The production company needs the perpetual right to be able to use the actor's name and likeness in connection with the publicity and promotion of the film.

Approval

Principal performers often require certain approval rights over elements of the film's promotion, merchandise, and publicity, such as poster images or publicity stills, used to promote the film.

- The production company should never give absolute approval rights to the performer; instead, the performer should be obligated to approve no less than 50% of all the images submitted to them for approval (and perhaps 75% if the performer is in the picture with somebody else).
- This stipulation should be coupled with a time limit within which the performer must approve or reject the stills or likenesses. If the performer does not reject the likenesses within such time period, the clause should state that the production company may assume that the performer's approval has been granted.

Right to Withhold

The production company needs the right to withhold monies for tax purposes as well as to pay a performer's agents and managers directly.

No Obligation to Produce

Although the production company has the right to produce the film, it needs to be sure that it is not *obligated* to produce the film.

Suspension and Termination Rights

It's no secret that sometimes actors can go off the deep end during a production. This clause allows the production company to terminate its relationship with the performer, subject only to payment of monies earned to date, if certain triggering events occur. For a more in depth discussion, see "Morals Clause," p. 226 & 490.

Reasons to suspend or terminate often include:

- A performer who is either unable or unwilling to show up for production.
- A drastic change in that performer's appearance.
- Unprofessional or illegal behavior.
- *Force majeure* (act of God), like earthquakes, wars, and pandemics.

This paragraph typically gives the producer the right to suspend or terminate the performer's contract at the discretion of the producer. If the contract is *terminated*, it means that neither the producer nor the performer have further obligations with respect to the other. If the contract is *suspended*, the performer is put on hold until the performer corrects the problem. During the suspension period, the performer may not work for other people.

Representations and Warranties; Indemnification

The performer typically promises the production company that:

- The performer is free to enter into this contract with the production company and that they have no prior commitments or legal obligations that would prevent them from performing her duties under the contract.
- Any material that the performer contributes is original with them (e.g. lines of dialogue that they improvise in the film are original with them).
- They have no health conditions that would undermine their ability to perform their services. The performer should also grant the production company the right to take out insurance on the performer, naming the production company as a beneficiary.
- The performer should indemnify the production company for breach of these warranties.

Remedies

The performer should waive any claim to injunctive relief arising out of the production company's breach of the contract. Additionally, in all events, the performer should be prohibited from rescinding the contract and recapturing any of the granted rights.

Publicity

- The producer needs to be able to exploit the performer's name, likeness, biography, and so forth in connection with the marketing of the film. They may also want the right to engage the performer to engage in publicity for the film, such as a press junket.
- Conversely, the producer will want to prohibit the performer from releasing any publicity or social media posts about the motion picture without the producer's approval.

Accounting

If the performer is a net-profit participant or will receive any form of deferred or contingent compensation, this paragraph will delineate how often the performer may expect to receive accounting statements. This is coupled with the right to audit the production company, usually no more frequently than once a year.

Assignment

The production company needs the right to assign this contract and all the rights under it. At the same time, the production company needs to prohibit the performer from being able to assign the contract.

Inducement

If the actor is providing services on behalf of a loan-out company, it is the loan-out company that will be a party to the contract. Furthermore, the contract should contain an inducement and further assurances clause. (See "Loan-Out Companies," p. 51.) If the production company is financing the film with production incentives such as tax credits, you may need to include a provision in the agreement:

- Requiring the loan-out company to register to do business and file a return in the production state, and
- Giving your production company the power of attorney to register the loan-out company to do business in the production state if the loan-out company fails to do so within a certain period of time. (See "Production Incentives: Eligibility Requirements," p. 78.)

◆◆◆◆◆

LAW

Like all services contracts, the actor/production company's relationship is also controlled by federal and state employment and labor laws.

In working with any children for any length of time, child labor laws must be complied with. (See "Casting Minors," p. 269.)

BUSINESS ISSUES

Perks

Perks are fringe benefits not counted as part of salary. What you gain in keeping down an actor's compensation you may lose when it comes to negotiating the perquisites. It is not uncommon for an actor to agree to defer a good portion of their salary while steadfastly insisting on first-class airfare and five-star hotel accommodations.

Frequently requested perks include the following:

- First-class airfare.
- Five-star hotel accommodations.
- Flying the actor's family to the shooting location and providing them with accommodations.
- An on-set nanny for the actor's child.
- Invitations to, airfare to, and accommodations at film festivals.
- A dressing room.
- The right to keep wardrobe.
- Copies of the finished film for their reels.

Although you may be tempted to give these perks to your lead actor, keep in mind that if you do, you may be obligated to provide the same perks to any other actor with a favored-nations clause regarding perks. (See Appendix B, "Favored Nations," p. 479.)

Option on Future Services

If the production company is making a television series or a movie with sequel potential, it may want to obtain an *option* on the performer's future services. (See Appendix B, "Option on Future Services," p. 481.) Performers, on the other hand, might not want an option on their future acting services; they want the greatest freedom possible, especially the right to renegotiate their quotes with the production company.

Net Profits Definition

If the actor is a profit participant, the performer's services agreement should contain a rider defining how the production company will compute the film's net profits. (See "Net Profits," p. 66.)

The Morals Clause

As we've seen in the chapter on above-the-line agreements, the morals clause allows the production or studio to terminate a performer, director, or other crew member for specific behaviors, like sexual harassment or substance abuse, which create a hazardous work environment for the other performers and crew members or expose the production or studio to bad publicity. In drafting this clause, you must be specific as to which behaviors will trigger the production company's suspension or termination rights. For more detail on this clause, see "Morals Clause," p. 226 & 490.

HOW TO GET A SCRIPT TO A SAG-AFTRA ACTOR

Find the Actor's Agent

The best way to locate a particular SAG-AFTRA actor is through their agent. If an actor is represented by an agent, pitch the project first to the agent; never talk business directly with the actor. Agents are very protective of their actors. Nothing gets under an agent's skin more than feeling like a production company is going behind his back and negotiating directly with the performer.

But how do you find out which actor is represented by which agent? If you're working with a casting director, don't worry about it—that's part of her job. But if you're trying to get a script to an actor by yourself, here again SAG-AFTRA comes to the rescue. The SAG-AFTRA "Actors to Locate" service provides contact information for SAG-AFTRA members' agents.

> You can reach the Screen Actors Guild "Actors to Locate" service by filling out the form at www.sagaftra.org/locate-performer.

Pitch the Movie to the Agent

Once you've located the agent, your next step is to figure out how to best pitch the project to them. If the agent thinks the project is a good fit for the actor, they will then set up a meeting or audition with that performer.

Some points to consider in constructing your pitch to the agent:

- First and foremost, trot out your strongest elements first. Is your screenplay based on a well-known book? Has the writer or the director ever won an award for their work? Are other well-known actors already attached to the project?
- Actors are always looking for good scripts, especially those with complex lead characters. Movie actors often get typecast; this is especially true for television actors. You could make headway in attaching a known actor to your movie by offering them a chance to play against type.
- Actors are always eager to work with other well-known actors they have not worked with before. Once you've secured your first actor, others may be easier to entice.
- When television programs wrap their production each year, the actors go on hiatus. Many of them spend this time acting in independent film

projects. Try to schedule your production accordingly. It also helps if you're shooting your film someplace an actor might enjoy; the Adirondack Mountains in the autumn coupled with an offer to fly out your lead actor's family may be just the thing to clinch the deal.

- It can be extremely helpful to have your script submitted by a casting agent or your attorney.

CAUTION! I have never found the "sympathy pitch" to be very successful. Don't try to win over an agent by explaining to them that without their client, you can't make the movie. It's a bad ploy because:

1. It shows that you're desperate, which completely destroys your leverage if and when it comes time to negotiate with the agent, and
2. It destroys any credibility you might have built up with the agent. No agent will want to attach their client to a production unless they know that the production will be made or, at the very least, that the client will be paid in full.
3. Most agents representing well-known performers will not consider an indie project that isn't fully funded and, even then, will likely require that you put the performer's salary into an escrow account to ensure that no matter what happens with the rest of the film, their client will be paid (and the agent will get their commission).

Casting Directors

Hiring an experienced casting director might seem like a luxury on a low-budget independent film. However, it can mean the difference between hiring a known actor and casting a lead whose only experience is community theater. Casting directors add credibility to a project; it signals to the actor's agent that you are professional. *It cannot be stressed strongly enough: until you have built a reputation in the film industry, you'll have to constantly fight against the presumption that you will not be able to get a professional film in the can.* Casting directors go a long way toward alleviating an agent's concerns about your inexperience and free up the producer and director, requiring their presence only at the final stages of the auditions.

You can locate casting directors by contacting the Casting Society of America: www.castingsociety.com.

Auditions

You should be aware that the more famous an actor is, the less likely it is they will want to audition for you. They might meet with you to discuss the script, but they might not even do that until they are actually *offered* the role in your film. One possibly apocryphal story illustrates this point: When multiple Oscar winner Shelley Winters was being considered for a certain movie role, she was asked to audition for the part. She sat down with the producer, looked him in the eye, pulled out her Oscars, and plopped the statuettes on the table between them, saying, "Audition? Some people think I can act."

Negotiating the Deal

Once you've gotten an actor's attention, it's time to negotiate the deal. Here again is where casting agents can come in handy: they will be familiar with the actor's current *quote* (the salary range the actor has received for their last few films).

You will want to have an experienced negotiator help you with this part. The negotiator who is experienced in performer's services agreements can help you navigate the rough waters of actors' agents and managers. Here are a few tips:

- *Show restraint.* It is far too easy to "give away the farm" during your first few negotiations. For instance, one contract clause most agents will insist on for a principal actor is a favored-nations clause, which obligates the producer to ensure that no one has a better deal than that actor. Favored-nations clauses typically come into play when it comes to compensation and credit provisions. If you grant a favored-nations clause to a supporting actor with regard to their compensation, make sure you qualify that by indicating it is favored nations with respect to other supporting actors—after all, you don't want to end up paying a supporting actor the same as your highest-paid lead (unless the supporting actor is the most famous performer in the cast).
- *Be wary of the "two bites of the apple" ploy.* You negotiate with an actor's agent, giving ground to close the deal. Just when you think you're done, the agent shifts you over to another agent or the attorney for the agency to continue the negotiations. This is often a business necessity from the agency's point of view. After all, the agent may have painted the deal in large brushstrokes, and it's the agency's attorney's job to provide the fine details. There is a danger for the production company, however, that goes beyond mere exhaustion. Sometimes the second agent or attorney will try to backpedal, removing some of the deal points the first agent conceded to while leaving your concessions on the table. To counter this tactic, point out that the deal points were already agreed to and

they form the basis for concessions on your part. If they can backpedal, so can you.

- *Walk-away point.* Before you start the negotiation process, make sure you have a walk-away threshold with regard to compensation. This is the point at which you will walk away from the deal, no matter how much you love the actor, because you simply can't afford to hire them. Make sure that this figure includes all the fixed costs, perks, and other expenses associated with hiring that particular actor (don't forget your SAG-AFTRA P&H payments!). *It cannot be stressed strongly enough:* It is very important to leave the bargaining table if the deal exceeds your walk-away threshold.

  For one, the other side may be seeing how far they can push. When you walk away, that sets your limits. They may respond by lowering their quote to keep the deal. Be flexible; there may be some in-kind services and perks you can give them that won't break your bank but may enable you to trade them against higher fixed compensation costs.

  If you continue to hash out a deal with a performer once he has exceeded your threshold, you may not have enough resources to pay other necessary performers.

- *Start early.* Make sure to start your negotiations early so that your back is not up against a wall. It will absolutely destroy any leverage you have if a performer's agent realizes that you don't have time to look for another performer should this deal fall through.

CASTING MINORS

What if you want to cast kids in your movie? And by kids, I mean minors—anybody under the age of 18 in the United States. First of all, I'll save you the burden of reading this section: don't hire minors. It really is a pain requiring a lot of paperwork in coordination with their parents. Hire an 18-year-old actor who looks a few years younger. Of course, an 18-year-old actor is not going to be able to substitute for a 5-year-old, but maybe your film can be rewritten?

Okay, if you're still reading this you're not convinced. Or maybe your film really and truly needs child actors. In all seriousness, I actually think working with child actors can be the right choice for number of reasons: there is a verisimilitude to somebody playing their own age, child actors are often less self-conscious than adult actors, and child actors tend to be less "ego-driven" than their adult counterparts.

But . . . from both a legal and logistical perspective, they can be a huge headache. They can't work the long hours an adult can, they require special permits and trust accounts, and depending upon the nature and length of the shoot, they may even require teachers to be on set. Let's take a look at the requirements for California.

CALIFORNIA CHILD LABOR LAW

- In California, a producer who wants to hire a minor to act in a film must first obtain from the Division of Labor Standards Enforcement a Permit to Employ Minors in the Entertainment Industry (PEMEI) or file an Application for Permission to Employ Minors in the Entertainment Industry and be granted one.[4] Start the process here: www.dir.ca.gov/dlse/Entertainment-Permit-to-Employ-Minors.htm.
  - You MUST have workers compensation insurance to work with child actors in California.
- The parent or guardian must apply for an Entertainment Work Permit (DLSE form 275) (EWP) by completing an Application for Permission to Work in the Entertainment Industry. Parents/guardians/theatrical agents should start that process here: www.dir.ca.gov/dlse/Entertainment-Work-Permit.htm.

Work Hours for Minors in California

As a general rule, "[m]inors in the entertainment industry may not work more than eight hours a day or more than 48 hours in a week and may only work between the hours of 5 a.m. and 10 p.m. or to 12:30 a.m. on days preceding a non-school day."[5] Variables such as hours they are allowed to work, whether a school teacher is necessary on set, how long they can be on set, and even how many footcandles of light infants can be exposed to are all highly regulated. For a complete chart of these factors, see the California Division of Labor Standards Enforcement chart: www.dir.ca.gov/dlse/minorssummarycharts.pdf.

Violations of the child labor laws can result in civil penalties of up to $1,000 for each and every violation, and "criminal penalties and criminal violations of child labor laws are misdemeanors punishable by fines ranging up to $10,000 or by confinement in the county jail for periods up to 6 months or both fine and imprisonment."[6] For a violation of California's child labor laws, "[t]he employer, never the minor, is liable for child labor violations."[7]

Mandatory Trust Fund

In addition to the aforementioned restrictions and requirements, a parent or guardian and every employer must comply with the Coogan Law, named for the actor Jackie Coogan. Coogan was a child performer who shot to stardom in 1921 at the age of seven, staring opposite Charlie Chaplin in *The Kid*. He had earned $4 million by the age of 13. However, in 1935, when he demanded his money from his mother and stepfather (who had been his manager), they refused. He filed suit, and the court held that under California law he had no right to the money he earned as a minor. Because of the notoriety of this case, California passed the Child Actor's Bill in 1939 to protect a child performer's income for his future use. The law, which became known as the Coogan Law, has been amended several times since 1939. Jackie Coogan later went on to play Uncle Fester in the television show *The Addams Family*.

The law applies to all minor actors[8] and to any contract in which a minor and

> a person agrees to purchase, or otherwise secure, sell, lease, license, or otherwise dispose of literary, musical, or dramatic properties, or use of a person's likeness, voice recording, performance, or story of or incidents in his or her life, either tangible or intangible, or any rights therein for use in motion pictures, television, the production of sound recordings in any format now known or hereafter devised, the legitimate or living stage, or otherwise in the entertainment field.[9]

The current California law requires that 15% of a minor's gross income be put into a trust in California,[10] called a Coogan Trust Account, that is established no later than seven business days after the contract is signed by the parties.[11] The trustee is the parent or guardian who is entitled to physical custody of the minor, but a court may appoint a trustee if needed.

There are many more requirements to complying with California's Coogan Trust Laws. Make sure you comply with all of them, as the penalties are severe!

Avoiding Disaffirmance of a Minor's Contract

Most states have laws that allow a person to get out of contracts that they made when they were a minor (called *disaffirming* a contract). This can be extremely problematic for filmmakers who find that the contracts they have with their minor performers are no longer valid. In California, however, if an entertainment contract is approved by Superior Court, it cannot be disaffirmed.[12]

Any party can seek court approval, and the approval extends "to the whole contract and all of its terms and provisions, including, but not limited to, any optional or conditional provisions contained in the contract for extension, prolongation or termination of the term of the contract."[13]

STEP BY STEP: HIRING ACTORS

- First, decide whether your film will have SAG-AFTRA performers. If you decide to shoot a union production, you need to become a signatory. (See "Becoming a Signatory," p. 252.)
- SAG-AFTRA regulations and labor laws must be complied with. Assign a producer, ideally two producers, the task of ensuring that the production

company complies with SAG-AFTRA and labor laws both on the set as well as off. (See "SAG-AFTRA," p. 243; "Labor and Employment Laws," p. 199.)

- Engage a casting agent to help select performers and provide initial contact with agents.
- If you are not using a casting director, locate the performer's agent and deal with them first. Do not initiate contact with a represented actor directly with an offer for the project.
- When negotiating the deal with the actor's representative, make sure to have a walk-away threshold. (See "Negotiating the Deal," p. 268.)
- If you are dealing with child actors:
  - You will need their parent or legal guardian's signature on all contracts.
  - You will need special work permits from the state government allowing you to hire minors as performers.
  - You may want to get their contracts approved by the appropriate state court so that they cannot disaffirm their contracts when they become adults.
  - Additionally, the child's parents will need to set up a trust fund for the child's salary in accordance with that state's version of the Coogan laws.
  - You may need to hire a teacher to be on set.

NOTES

[1] www.sagaftra.org/contracts-industry-resources (Accessed March 25, 2021).
[2] www.sagaftra.org/diversity-casting-incentive-information
[3] www.sagaftra.org/contracts-industry-resources/financial-assurances/residuals-reserves
[4] "CALIFORNIA CHILD LABOR LAWS." Information on Minors and Employment. Department of Industrial Relations Division of Labor Standards Enforcement. www.dir.ca.gov/dlse/ChildLaborLawPamphlet.pdf (Accessed June 15, 2021).
[5] Id. at 40.
[6] "CALIFORNIA CHILD LABOR LAWS." Information on Minors and Employment. *Department of Industrial Relations Division of Labor Standards Enforcement.* www.dir.ca.gov/dlse/ChildLaborLawPamphlet.pdf (Accessed June 15, 2021).
[7] Id.
[8] "[i]ncludes, but is not limited to, services as an actor, actress, dancer, musician, comedian, singer, stuntperson, voice-over artist, or other performer or entertainer, or as a songwriter, musical producer or arranger, writer, director, producer, production executive, choreographer, composer, conductor, or designer." CFC §6750(a).
[9] Cal. Fam. Code Ann. § 6750 (West).
[10] Cal. Fam. Code Ann. § 6752 (West).
[11] Cal. Fam. Code Ann. § 6753 (West).
[12] CFC §6751(a) (West).
[13] Id.

6

PRODUCTION

QUIET ON THE SET!

Okay, now it's almost time to roll camera. But wait! There are still some legal issues you will have to take care of first. Ideally, many of these issues will be addressed during pre-production rather than waiting for the first day of principal photography.

This section will help you:

- Identify when you need a release from an extra. (See "Depiction Releases," p. 275.)
- Recognize trespass and other potential property claims. (See "Why You Need a Location Release," p. 283.)
- Negotiate a location agreement. (See "Major Deal Points: Location Agreement," p. 287.)
- Know when you need a shooting permit. (See "Shooting Permits," p. 285.)
- Keep your art direction from infringing somebody's copyrights. (See "On-Set IP Infringement," p. 293.)
- Understand the fair use of copyrights. (See Appendix A, "Fair Use," p. 433.)
- Negotiate an artwork license. (See "Artwork License," p. 298.)
- Learn about problems relating to shooting trademarks. (See "Trademarks on the Set," p. 300.)
- Negotiate a trademark license. (See "Trademark Clearance Letter," p. 304.)

STAGES OF PHOTOGRAPHY

- *Principal photography* is what most people think of when they think of a film shoot. It is the time when the cameras roll, capturing the filmed dialogue sequences. It is the heart of the shoot itself.
- *Second-unit photography*, by contrast, consists of that photography done by a second camera crew that films scenes that do not include the main performers. Examples of second unit photography include establishing shots, backgrounds, crowd scenes, and footage for computer animation.
- *Pick-up shots* are shots or scenes shot after the completion of principal photography. The need for a pick-up shot is established when a scene couldn't be shot during principal photography—for instance, due to bad weather or, as is often the case, when the director is in the editing room, cursing at themselves for not having the *one* shot they need to make the sequence or movie perfect.

17

EXTRAS AND DEPICTION RELEASES

Extras and background performers are almost always needed in feature films to provide a sense of reality. In fact, one of the marks of an amateur film is seeing actors performing in empty streets. Even worse are scenes in which actors perform in crowded streets while pedestrians steal glances at the camera, wondering what's going on.

To avoid these problems, you will want to hire *extras*, also known as *background performers*. If you are a SAG-AFTRA signatory, you will have to comply with the SAG-AFTRA background performer rules that govern your particular contract. (See "SAG-AFTRA," p. 243.)

Whether you are a guerrilla filmmaker filming your actors in a crowded city street or an independent producer who films all her scenes on a locked-down, tightly controlled set, you will need to worry about securing releases for your extras.

***THE BOTTOM LINE:* As a general rule, if a person is identifiable in a scene, you need to consider getting a depiction release before including them in your film.**

DEPICTION RELEASES

PROD.

Although there is generally a very limited right to privacy on public streets, there are several legal claims producers need to concern themselves with, namely misappropriation of the right of publicity, defamation, and invasion of privacy.

- *Right of publicity*. The right of publicity protects a person's rights to commercial exploitation of his or her likeness (e.g., voice, image, catchphrases). This generally isn't an issue in feature films, but producers shooting television commercials—a form of commercial exploitation—will require signed releases. (See Appendix A, "Right of Publicity," p. 443.)
- *Defamation*. Defamation and libel suits arise when a person who is distinguishable on camera claims that they were portrayed in a false manner harmful to their reputation. (See Appendix A, "Libel and Defamation," p. 449.)

  Example: Even newsmakers are not exempt from defamation lawsuits. In a news story on prostitution, ABC News producers shot footage featuring

DOI: 10.4324/9781003228479-23

close ups of a black woman walking down the street as the voice-over commented on the number of black prostitutes who cruise for white johns. The woman featured was not a prostitute but an ordinary pedestrian, unaware that she was being photographed for the story. When she sued for defamation, the court held that she had made a case for defamation.[1]

- *Invasion of privacy.* "Hidden camera" documentaries need to be especially cautious here. While you may have a First Amendment right to photograph somebody, you generally don't have the right to intrude where a person has a reasonable expectation of privacy or to expose their private affairs in a way that is objectionable to a reasonable person. (See Appendix A, "The Right of Publicity and Other Privacy Rights," p. 443.) Privacy law does differ widely from state to state. In NY, an ABC television crew was found not liable for invasion of privacy for filming a man dying in a hospital without his or his family's permission, nor did the court see the film crew's actions as sufficiently outrageous to support the claim for intentional infliction of emotional distress, although they did allow the family of the deceased to sue the hospital and treating physician for breach of physician-patient confidentiality.[2]

A depiction release is the best solution to these situations. Even those of you shooting in New York shouldn't put too much faith in its lax privacy laws, because depiction releases are often required by errors and omissions (E&O) insurance carriers.

Note: In keeping with industry practice, the following depiction release is structured as though the person being filmed were writing a letter to the producer. It uses the pronouns *I* for the person being filmed and *you* for the producer.

DEPICTION RELEASE

For the sum of $ ____[*the producer should pay someone something—i.e., $5.00*] and other good and valuable consideration received, and as full and complete payment for all rights and

releases granted hereunder, I hereby grant to ____PRODUCTION

COMPANY, LLC (hereinafter "Producer" or "you" or "your"), and its assigns and licenses the ownership and any and all rights to use any and all of the depictions you have taken of me, including photographs, voice recordings, video footage, film footage, likenesses, sobriquets, contained in any interviews, performances, "behind the scenes" footage, or any other recording of me, whether that depiction is recorded in film, video, audio, or still photography, or any other medium, now known or hereafter developed (the Depiction).

I give up any and all rights to the Depiction and assign them to you. These rights include, but are not limited to, copyright, trademark, rights of publicity, rights of privacy, and moral rights. You may copyright the Depiction in your name. You may use my name in connection with the Depiction.

I hereby waive, release, and discharge any claims I may have for libel, defamation, misappropriation of right of publicity, invasion of privacy, intentional or negligent infliction of emotional distress, or any other claim I may have resulting from your use of the Depiction.

The rights I grant to you in the Depiction are perpetual and irrevocable and may be transferred by you to any other party at your discretion. Coupled with your ownership of the Depiction, I grant you the rights to sell, display, perform, distribute, publish, republish, commercially exploit, use in advertising, promotion, and to create derivative works from the Depiction and any work which embodies it.

You have complete discretion to edit or otherwise modify any work in which the Depiction appears and to use the Depiction in any manner or for any purpose whatsoever without any further remuneration to me.

I shall indemnify you and hold you harmless from any claims or actions arising from any misrepresentations I have made in this release. I hereby release you, your agents, and your assigns from any claims resulting from any injuries I may sustain while my Depiction is being taken.

You are not obligated to use the Depiction or to exploit any of the rights I have granted. All rights conveyed inure to the benefit of you and your assigns.

I am of full legal age and capacity and fully understand the rights I am assigning or waiving. I am freely and voluntarily entering into this Agreement, and have read and understood each and every provision, as set forth herein. I agree that any interpretation of this Agreement shall not be construed against a party by virtue of its having drafted the terms and conditions hereunder. This is the entire agreement between me and the Producer. In entering into this agreement, I have not relied on any statements by the Producer or anyone else regarding the nature of the film, its content, or how I will ultimately be depicted.

This release shall be interpreted according to the laws of the State of [insert your state here].

Name and Contact information: [insert the contact information of the person being filmed]

Signature ____

[The person being filmed should sign the release]

Depiction Release: Child

For a child, the depiction release will require the signature of a parent or legal guardian. Additionally, the parent should agree as follows.

> Parent/Guardian acknowledges that he/she has read, understood, and agrees to all of the terms, conditions, grants, and waivers contained in the release. Parent/Guardian understands that the production company is relying on the rights and releases conveyed under this document, the loss of which by the production company cannot readily be compensated through the awarding of monetary damages. The Parent/Guardian represents, warrants, and guarantees that neither they, nor the child, will disaffirm this release any time, whether as a minor or as an adult.

Under the law, minors may be able to *disaffirm* a contract, that is, to void their obligations under a contract. Although the preceding parent/guardian clause may not provide iron-clad protection against the release being disaffirmed by the child, it should obligate the parent/guardian to avoid encouraging or helping the child disaffirm the release. To provide greater protection against a minor being able to disaffirm any production contract, you may want to have that contract ratified by a court. (See "Casting Minors" p. 269.)

Notice Release

What if you're filming in a crowded restaurant, concert hall, or other large public venue and obtaining signed releases from all the potential background performers is not possible? You may want to post a sign, known as a *notice release*. Although this might not be as effective as a signed release, it could afford some protection.

A notice release should be posted outside the entrance to the location and contain the following information.

> **ATTENTION**
>
> You are about to enter an area in which [*name of production company*] is filming a motion picture [*or television program, video, etc.*]. Accordingly, your voice and/or likeness may be captured on

film. By entering this area you are consenting to be filmed by us. Furthermore, you agree that we shall own in perpetuity and without reservation any and all rights to the footage shot here today. We may use this footage for any purpose whatsoever, including, but not limited to, theatrical, television, promotional, and advertising use without any further compensation to you. Furthermore, you waive any claims you may have arising out of or use of this footage, or any depictions of you contained within. You understand that we are relying on your consent to these terms.

If You Do Not Agree to These Terms, Please Do Not Enter.

If you do not agree to these terms you may proceed to:

[*Provide alternative directions for those who wish to enter the venue but not be photographed. For example, those who do not consent should be directed to another area of a stadium where the cameras will not be focused.*]

TIP: **Signs like this one should be posted near all entrances! Shoot some footage of the crowd walking past the sign to establish that the sign has been posted in an open and obvious position. Try to get footage of people reading the sign as they enter.**

CAUTION: NO FRAUD OR MISREPRESENTATIONS ALLOWED!

Many courts will try to view the depiction release in a light most favorable to the person whose depiction you are using. If your subject can persuasively argue that they were misled as to how you would use the footage or that you have defrauded him into signing the release, the court may void your release. If you are planning to use the depiction in a way that a subject might object to, make sure to include language in the release that describes that use.

Example: "Production Company may use your depiction in any manner, including as a background in a violent satanic music video."

THE *BORAT* DEFENSE

The producers of the movie *Borat* were sued (several different times, actually) by the unwitting subjects of the mockumentary. In one case, Michael Psenicska, a driving instructor from Maryland, had agreed to give a driving lesson to Sacha Baron Cohen, a.k.a. fake Kazakhstani journalist Borat, for what Mr. Psenicska thought was a "documentary about the integration of foreign people into the American way of life."

Mr. Psenicska signed a depiction release and was promptly subjected to a hair-raising car ride by Borat, in which the actor cursed at other drivers and pretended to drive drunk. When the film was released, Mr. Psenicska sued for fraud, unjust enrichment, and infliction of emotional distress. At the heart of his complaint was that the depiction release was invalid because he had been told that this was a documentary and not a parody; in short, he contended, he was *defrauded* into signing the release because he relied on the producers' statements regarding the kind of film it was.

The Court thought otherwise, pointing to specific language in the depiction release that disclaimed reliance on "any promises or statements made by anyone about the nature of the Film or the identity of any other Participants or persons involved in the Film."[3] Nor did the release contain any written statements that the film was in fact a documentary about a foreigner's travels in the United States.

The Court held that where a plaintiff "has in the plainest language announced and stipulated that it is not relying on any representations as to the very matter as to which it now claims it was defrauded," the disclaimer "destroys the allegations in plaintiff's complaint that the agreement was executed in reliance upon these contrary oral representations."

Sacha Baron Cohen won the lawsuit. As Borat might say: "*Very nice!*"

***BOTTOM LINE:* Always include language in your depiction release that specifically states that the subject is not relying on any statements or representations by the film crew on the nature of the film or how he or she will be depicted.**

Filming people without their permission

If you film, photograph, record, or otherwise depict people without their permission, you could be making yourself or the production company vulnerable to lawsuits. Review the situations that follow to help determine your risk.

You used footage or recordings of the subject that you did not create or own. Possible claim: Copyright infringement (p. 429)	• Fair use • De Minimis • Parody • Criticism • Commentary
You are using somebody's name or likeness which they use as a trademark. *Possible claim*: trademark infringement, false endorsement, tarnishment (p. 460)	• Fair use of trademark • Informational use • Criticism • Parody • Comparative advertising
You are using someone's image or likeness for commercial or advertising purposes. *Possible claim*: violation of right of publicity (p. 443)	• Noncommercial use (documentaries, film, news) • De Minimis use • Incidental use
Your false portrayal of the subject might damage their reputation. Possible claim: defamation (p. 449)	• Truth • Privileged communication • "Actual malice" required for public figures • Opinion • "Gross irresponsibility" test for matters of public concern
You filmed or recorded the subject where they had a reasonable expectation of privacy. *Possible claims*: intrusion upon seclusion (p. 446)	• Filmed in a public space • Filming or disclosures not intrusive to a reasonable person

NOTES

[1] *Clark v. ABC*, 684 F.2d 1208 (6th Cir. 1982).

[2] *Chanko v. Am. Broad. Companies Inc.*, 49 N.E.3d 1171, 1179 (N.Y. 2016).

[3] *Psenicska v. Twentieth Cent. Fox Film Corp.*, 409 Fed. Appx. 368, 370 (2d Cir. 2009) (unpublished).

18

LOCATIONS

WHERE ARE YOU SHOOTING?

Once you've scouted and chosen your locations, you need to ensure that you have the legal right to shoot there. If you are shooting on public property, you may need a *shooting permit*. If you are shooting on private property, you should have a *location release*. Depending on the location, you may also need a shooting permit to shoot on private property.

Special locations, such as military bases, federal buildings, airports, and cruise ships, will probably require more than just the simple permit issued by a city.

WHY YOU NEED A LOCATION RELEASE

If you shoot on somebody's private property without their permission, you may expose your production to criminal penalties and civil liability for *trespass, trespass to chattels, invasion of privacy*, and *nuisance*. A location release is a contract between you and the property owner or other authorized party that gives you the right to enter that property and shoot your film. In addition to preventing lawsuits, a location release is also an enforceable contract that gives you a right to shoot in a location at a particular time. Nothing is worse than showing up to a location with a cast and crew only to find that the owner has now changed their mind about allowing you to shoot on their property.

If you shoot on someone's property without a location release, you could be sued for the following:

- Trespass to land.
- Trespass to chattels.
- Invasion of privacy.
- Nuisance.

Trespass to Land

Most people know that if you enter the property of another person without permission, you are trespassing. However, you don't need to set foot on somebody's property to be liable for trespassing; any physical intrusion on

DOI: 10.4324/9781003228479-24

the land of another will do. This means that if you place your light stand on somebody's property, park a truck in their driveway, or plug a cord into their electrical outlet, you are trespassing unless you have that person's permission to do so.

Trespassing also occurs when your rights to be on somebody's property have expired. So, if you have a location release that allows you to shoot in a warehouse on Saturday, you'll technically be trespassing if you or your equipment are still there on Sunday. This is why you want to leave ample room in your location releases to allow you to leave equipment that needs to be set up or wrapped out.

Watch out for the following:

- You don't even need to touch the land to commit trespass! A boom microphone or crane that never touches the ground but that nonetheless crosses a property line would expose you to a claim of trespass.
- The fact that you didn't know the property was owned by somebody else will not relieve you from liability. Mistake is no defense to a claim of trespass; if you intended to enter the property, you're trespassing unless you have the owner's permission.
- Just because a shop or restaurant is open to the public does not mean it is public property for the purposes of filmmaking. The business has opened its doors and granted an implied license for customers to enter the property for purposes of shopping, not for the purposes of production companies who want to shoot a film there. You'll still need to secure the store's permission to shoot your film on the premises.

Trespass to Chattels

Chattel is the legal term for physical property, as distinguished from *real property*, the legal term for land and the houses on it. *Trespass to chattels* occurs when you interfere with somebody's right of possession to their physical property. For instance, if you interfere with somebody's car, bicycle, television set, computer, and so forth, you may be liable for trespass to chattels. The point here is that a gaffer who, without the owner's permission, clamps a light to the roof of a parked car, scratching the paint, is exposing the production to liability for trespass to chattels.

To claim trespass to chattels, the plaintiff has to establish that you interfered with the property owner's right of possession and you caused some sort of damage. However, depriving the owner of use in the chattel may amount to sufficient damage. So, in the case of the car, because the gaffer rigged the light to the top of the car, the owner could not use the car until the light was removed, and thus his or her ownership rights have been violated and trespass to chattels has probably occurred.

Privacy Law

Photographing people on private property when they have a reasonable expectation of privacy may violate their rights. For a detailed discussion of privacy rights, see Appendix A, "The Right of Publicity and Other Privacy Rights" (p. 443).

Nuisance

A nuisance results when a filmmaker creates a substantial, unreasonable interference with the *use* and *enjoyment* of somebody's private property. Nuisance very often comes into play when a filmmaker shoots in a residential neighborhood in the middle of the night. The production company's bright lights, smoke machines, generators, and loudspeakers may create a nuisance. Note that if you are planning to use equipment like this, a location release for the particular lot on which you're filming might not be enough. You might need to secure the permission of the neighbors as well.

GETTING PERMISSION TO USE A LOCATION

Shooting Permits

A shooting permit is permission from the city or municipality to shoot on public or private property within that jurisdiction. Many filmmakers believe that they only need to worry about shooting permits if they are filming on public property, such as streets or parks. In actuality, some jurisdictions require filmmakers to secure permits and pay filing fees even if they plan only to shoot on private property within the municipality!

The key is to check with the city clerk's office in the city or municipality in which you will be shooting several weeks prior to the shoot. Expect to pay a fee for a shooting permit. Some cities charge upward of $500 a day!

Shooting Permit Requirements

Although the requirements for issuing a shooting permit differ from city to city, filmmakers are often required to provide some or all of the following:

- *A completed application.* This must be signed by an authorized representative of the production company.
- *A certificate of insurance.* You will probably be required to add the municipality as an additional insured on your policy. An additional insured, you may remember, is a person, company, or municipality whose interests will also be protected by your insurance policy. In the case of shooting permits, the city will be added as an additional insured to your general liability policy

so that if it is sued by someone injured by your film production, the city will be covered by your insurance policy. (See "Insurance," p. 59.)

- *Fees.* Remember, film shoots are a source of revenue for many municipalities; therefore, expect to pay for the right to film within a municipality's borders. Common fees include:
  - *Application fee.* A nonrefundable fee for processing the application.
  - *Filming fee.* A daily or weekly fee for the right to film within the municipality.
  - *Bond check.* This is sort of like a security deposit on an apartment; it is money the city can use if you damage its property. Assuming you haven't caused any damage or caused the city other expenses, your check should be returned several weeks after filming is completed.
  - *Garbage removal fees.*
  - *Fees to hire off-duty police officers.*
- *Letters of intent and notification* to be distributed to the neighbors near the filming location.
- *Notarized letter of indemnification* stating that your production company will indemnify and otherwise hold harmless the municipality for any damages to property or injuries incurred by your production company.
- *Parking list.* A list of all the trucks, generators, vans, crew cars, and any other mobile equipment to be parked on the city streets.
- *Shooting* schedule.

WARNING: **If you do not obtain a permit and choose instead to shoot guerrilla style, you may be looking at substantial penalties, both civil and criminal, as well as jail time, depending on the jurisdiction. Additionally, many municipalities require you to have a shooting permit as well as a police escort if you are going to be using proper weapons or performers in police uniforms.**

Local Rules

In addition to securing a permit for a shoot, municipalities may also have special rules that apply to the film shoot itself. You can find this out from the office that issues the permit. Such rules typically govern:

- "Blackout hours"—times when no shooting may take place.
- You may not be able to park catering trucks or "honey wagons" (portable bathrooms) near restaurants.
- Noise.
- The requirement of having local police on the set.
- Garbage and waste.

- Lighting (you may need to provide blackout material for residents' windows when doing a night shoot).
- Treatment of electrical cables.
- Treatment of pedestrians and local traffic.
- Truck height and weight limits for streets and bridges.

THE LOCATION AGREEMENT

For definitions and explanations of common contract clauses, see Appendix B, "The Clause Companion," p. 475.

A *location agreement* is a contract that grants the production company the permission to shoot on *private* property.

For the contract to be valid, the production company needs the signature of the property owner or the owner's authorized representative. In securing permission to shoot in a commercial establishment, make sure to get the permission of the owner or supervising manager. A clerk, waiter, or other nonmanagerial employee usually does not have the power to sign contracts for a company or property owner. In fact, many businesses do not even allow their managers to enter into contracts on behalf of the company. The safest route is to secure the permission of both the owner of the building and the owner of the business.

MAJOR DEAL POINTS: LOCATION AGREEMENT

Parties

- *Production company.* The production company wants to be able to shoot unhindered in a particular location. It will need time to load and set up equipment, the right and the time for the art directors to change the location, and time to remove equipment and to restore the property to its original state.
- *Grantor.* The person or company granting the rights in the location release is called the *grantor.* It is usually the property or business owner. Make sure to get the full legal name of the grantor if it is a business. Do not assume that the manager of a business has the power to grant the location release.

Right to Depict Location

- The grantor must grant the production company the right to depict the location in the motion picture and in stills, audio, video, and nonphotographic licenses, in "any and all media whether now known or hereafter developed, for any purpose whatsoever."

- For commercial establishments, these rights must include the right to depict any trademarks or *trade dress* owned or licensed by the business that occupies the location. Trade dress is a particular and distinctive way a store is decorated when such decoration functions as a trademark.

The grantor must also grant the following rights:

- The right to alter the appearance of the location (any physical alterations should be subject to the filmmaker's obligation to return the property to its original condition on completion of the shooting).
- The right to juxtapose scenes filmed in other locations with the location that is subject to the release so as to create the appearance of a seamless whole.
- The right to use the name of the location.
- The right to bring personnel and equipment onto the location and to leave the equipment there.
- The grantor must agree that the production company is not obligated to use any of the footage in the final film, nor will the production company be obligated to depict the location in any particular matter.

Right of Access to Location

This is the paragraph that protects filmmakers against trespass charges. Filmmakers must be careful to specify not only the days and hours on which they want to film but also the amount of time and start and stop dates needed for loading and setting up equipment and set dressing and wrapping out the same.

Releases

- The grantor must release the production company and its employees from any claims of libel, invasion of privacy, trespass, trademark and trade dress infringement, copyright infringement, nuisance, trespass to chattels, right of publicity, or violation of any other right that may be implicated in the normal course of filming on location.
- The grantor must agree to waive any equitable relief, such as injunctions, against the production company and look solely to monetary damages for any remedy.

Period During Which Location Access Is Granted

- It is often helpful to avoid being too specific as to the timeframe for equipment removal. The filmmakers should use the phrase "on or about [*time frame*]" to give them the flexibility to be a little late or a little early.

- Write something like: "The production company will use reasonable efforts to remove all of its equipment from the Property on or about 9:00 A.M., Friday the 13th, 2023."
- If, instead, you write: "The production company will remove all its equipment from the Property at 9:00 A.M., Friday the 13th, 2023," the production assistant who shows up to remove the equipment at 9:15, 15 minutes late, may be denied access, and the presence of your equipment on the property may expose your production company to a claim of trespass.
- Include a statement that should the timeframes change, the terms of the location agreement shall apply to the new times as well.

Payment Terms

- This is usually structured as a flat one-time fee.
- Include a statement that the grantor did not pay the production company any fee to be featured in the film. This is often referred to as a *no kickbacks provision*.

Indemnification

- The production company should indemnify the grantor against damage or lawsuits that arise out of the production company's use of the location (except for breaches of the grantor's warranties).
- The grantor should indemnify the production company against the grantor's breaches of the warranty of authority. A *warranty of authority* is a promise by the grantor that they have the power to grant the location release. If the person granting the location release does not, in fact, have the power to grant the release, this clause holds that false grantor accountable for any of the production company's losses that result from the grantor's misrepresentations of their authority to grant the release.

Insurance

Grantors typically require that they be named as an additional insured on the production company's insurance policy.

Credit Provisions

The grantor's credit preferences should be indicated; however, any credit should be at the production company's sole discretion. Producer should include a clause disclaiming liability for inadvertently making a mistake with the grantor's credit and preventing the grantor from seeking an injunction.

Remedies

The grantor should waive any claim to injunctive relief arising out of either a breach of the contract or destruction of the property. Depending on the advice of counsel, producers may want any dispute to be settled through binding arbitration rather than through the courts.

♦♦♦♦♦♦

Safety on the Set

Not only do you need the right to shoot in a location, but you must make sure that it is safe for your cast and crew. Set safety protocols has been brought into sharp focus in recent years as a result of the global COVID-19 pandemic. And while guerrilla filmmakers unfortunately often play fast and loose with safety issues, if you are under contract with a studio or network, or working with union cast or crew, you must adhere to their safety requirements. You should have the unit production manager, producer, and ideally a production safety expert ensuring compliance with all safety protocols.

Netflix, for instance, requires production companies to complete required safety forms, a sample of which includes:[1]

- Production Safety Compliance Report.
- Construction & Rigging Safety Compliance Report.
- Location Risk Assessment.
- Incident/Accident Investigation Report.
- Stunt Risk Assessment.
- Personal Protective Equipment (PPE) Hazard Assessment.
- Emergency Action Plan.
- Risk Assessment.

Performing a location risk assessment is a best practice even if not required by a studio, union, or insurance carrier. Assign a producer to ascertain the following:

- Whether there are safety hazards known by the owner or manager of the location.
- Identifying fire extinguishers and emergency exits.
- Whether during the shoot the location is open to individuals not associated with your shoot or the location ownership and management.
- Making sure all locations have an identified liaison who is aware of the scope of your shoot and is easily contacted in case of emergency.
- Ensuring that all location security is aware of the production company's presence and expected activities.

Stunts, Pyrotechnics, Weapons, and Performers in Police Uniforms

Any time you're dealing with these items, you must ensure that you are in compliance with all shooting permit municipal regulations. New York City, for instance, has a fairly filmmaker-friendly policy when it comes to shooting on city streets. However, the minute you bring out a prop gun or have an actor in police uniform, you must have a police presence. Most municipalities will require you to clear all pyrotechnics with their local fire department, which in turn will usually require your production to engage a certified pyrotechnics specialist. And on all SAG-AFTRA productions, if you are planning on having stunts, whether scripted or not, you must engage the services of a stunt coordinator who meets the union's "Stunt Coordinator Minimum General Standards."

You should hire an experienced firearms safety coordinator if you are planning on using firearms on a set (to be clear: live rounds should NEVER be permitted on set). There are strict protocols which must be followed: they should be the only ones handing the gun to the actor and retrieving it when done. They should check the weapon multiple times during the day and always before it is handed to the performer for use. And when not in actual use on set, all firearms should be kept under lock and key. As this book goes to press, we see the tragic results of what happens when those protocols are not followed.

Pandemic Protocols

During the COVID-19 pandemic, SAG-AFTRA enacted several requirements to deal with the pandemic, such as implementing a "COVID-19 Zone System," which governed frequency of performer testing; restricting the use of COVID-19 liability waivers; establishing quarantine sanitization holding areas for performers to wait while not on set; and requiring producers to guarantee sick days for affected performers.

TIPS

- The property owner is first and foremost worried about having the property damaged and having their business disrupted; as a result, the production company should be prepared to do a lot of handholding with the property owner, constantly providing reassurances that nothing will go wrong.
- The production company should arrange the shoot so as to minimize the amount of interference the shoot will cause to the owner's business or life. If the location is a private home, the production company may have to pay for the family to stay in a nice hotel for several days.

- The property owner should be added as an additional insured to the production company's insurance policies. Even though your insurance company should pay claims stemming from location damage, it doesn't hurt to have some petty cash on hand to pay the grantor for minor damages.
- When shooting exteriors, it is often helpful to have some petty cash on hand to pay people to be quiet. Knowing how disruptive noise can be to a film shoot, some unscrupulously opportunistic people will actually stand on public property and yell, mow their lawns, or otherwise try to throw off a shoot in the hopes of getting some hush money. Unfortunately, it's often quicker to hand them a couple of bucks than to try to charge them with being a public nuisance.

NOTE

[1] https://partnerhelp.netflixstudios.com/hc/en-us/categories/4403386233747-Production-Safety (Accessed June 3, 2022).

19

ON-SET IP INFRINGEMENT

When the director yells "Action!," what the camera captures can spark lawsuits. All it takes is one suddenly inspired art director to place an uncleared Warhol print on the wall of the hero's apartment or the Coca-Cola logo on the mirror the drug-addicted villain uses to cut his cocaine. Unless the producer has the permission of all the respective copyright and trademark owners, photography can lead to infringement.

Copyrighted materials appear everywhere: posters, sculptures, product labels, makeup designs, even the tinny music playing over the radio held by an extra. All these materials should be *cleared* for use. Indeed, copyright is the bane of the conscientious art director. Don't fall into the trap of thinking that just because you have a valid location release from a homeowner that you also have the right to photograph any of the copyrighted materials in his or her home. The homeowner may no more have the right to authorize the photography of the Warhol print than the art director does.

BE CAREFUL THAT YOUR INSPIRATION IS NOT INFRINGEMENT

In a scene in the film *12 Monkeys*, Bruce Willis's character spends a few minutes being interrogated while being restrained in a futuristic chair. The design of the chair was inspired by a drawing of a chair, titled *Neomechanical Tower (Upper) Chamber*, by the artist Lebbeus Woods. The film's director, Terry Gilliam, discussed the drawing with his production designer, and the film's chair was constructed without Mr. Wood's permission being obtained.

When Mr. Woods sued,[1] the court found that substantial portions of his drawing were copied; in other words, unless the copying was excused, it would constitute infringement. Universal tried to argue that because the chair appeared in less than five minutes of the 130-minute film, the copying was *de minimis*—in other words, insignificant. (See Appendix A, "*De Minimis* Taking," p. 440.) The court disagreed with Universal and granted Mr. Woods motion for a preliminary injunction enjoining Universal from "distributing, exhibiting, performing or copying those portions of the motion picture

PROD.

DOI: 10.4324/9781003228479-25

entitled *12 Monkeys* which reproduce his copyrighted drawing, or any portion of it." The movie company settled the suit and paid a license fee to Mr. Woods.[2]

Filmmakers must worry about more than artwork on the set. Trademarks can also cause problems. It's a sign of the breadth of the global economy that some trademarks, such as Coca-Cola or the Nike "swoosh," are among the most recognized symbols in the world. With a trademark's fame comes tremendous legal power to control its use. Unauthorized trademark use can often bring the unwelcome attention of the trademark owner's lawyer—especially when the trademarked goods are shown in a bad light. Famous trademarks may be *tarnished* if they are placed in a vulgar or slanderous context, and the trademark owner can sue. (See "Trademarks on the Set," p. 300.)

CLEARANCES

Clearance is the process of:

1. Determining which trademarks and copyright-protected artwork and music used in a film require the rights owner's permission before it can be used, and then
2. Obtaining permission to use that trademark or copyright, and
3. If you can't get permission, or think you have a fair use defense, explaining to a contracting party (like a publisher) or an insurance carrier (like an E&O insurer) why permissions aren't necessary.

PROD.

When a film or video is "cleared," all the necessary intellectual property rights associated with the film or video—the copyrights, trademarks, and rights of publicity—have been granted or analyzed to determine that permissions are not needed. Consequently, the film or video work may be distributed and shown to the public without undue fear of costly IP infringement suits. However, clearances can be time consuming. IP law controls virtually every aspect of a film—the soundtrack, the screenplay, an actor's appearance, a corporate logo, stock footage—everything. The best tactic is to know what clearances are needed before production starts and to work with a staff trained in securing the proper permissions. (See "Copyright Searches and Permissions," p. 159; Appendix A, "A Filmmaker's Guide to Intellectual Property Law," p. 401.)

Caution: Artwork and Logos Ahead

The following items can cause problems if featured in a scene without first clearing their trademarks and copyrights:

- Paintings.
- Posters.
- Sculptures and sculptural reproductions.
- Books and magazines.
- Product labels.
- Websites.
- Social media posts.
- YouTube, TikTok, and other social media videos.
- T-shirt logos and designs.
- Dolls, action figures, and other toys.
- Location background music.
- Halloween masks.
- Television or video clips that play over an on-screen television.
- Video games.
- Street performances.
- Billboards.
- Storefront signs.
- Trademarks used in a manner that tarnishes their image.

COPYRIGHTS ON THE SET

Watch out for props and set dressing. Remember, mere ownership of a particular copy of a work of art does not give you any copyright rights to it. Even though you bought a poster, sculpture, painting, prop, and so forth, you still need to get the permission of the owner of the copyright to use that item.

If you are unable to get permission to use a particular piece of art, you may be better off removing it from the scene. If that's not possible, make sure, at a minimum, that the artwork is not featured in the scene, and if it's depicted at all, such depiction should be fleeting and incidental.

Of course, you may be able to defend a copyright infringement lawsuit on the grounds that your use constituted *fair use* under copyright law. However, as a practical matter, relying on fair use is a pretty costly choice. People assert a fair use defense after they've already been sued and have had to pay a lawyer to defend them. That being said, what exactly is fair use of a copyright?

Fair Use of a Copyright

Fair use is a defense to copyright infringement. It allows the taking of some part of a copyrighted work without the need to secure the author's permission. Examples of fair use include news reporting, criticism, comment, teaching (including multiple copies for classroom use), parody, scholarship, or research.

In general, a court is more likely to find fair use when the use has been *transformative*. To determine whether the use is transformative, the court will ask: Does this new work add anything to the original or recast it in a different light? Or, instead, does it merely copy and compete in the same marketplace as the original?

How Do Courts Decide If a Use Is Fair Use?

The federal copyright statute says that courts must give weight to the following four factors in determining fair use under copyright law:[3]

1. "The purpose and character of the use, including whether such use is of a commercial nature or is for nonprofit educational purposes;
2. The nature of the copyrighted work;
3. The amount and substantiality of the portion used in relation to the copyrighted work as a whole; and
4. The effect of the use upon the potential market for or value of the copyrighted work."

Unfortunately for the producer, it is up to the court to decide—after the fact—whether the taking was excused because of the fair use doctrine. This means that the filmmaker has already been dragged into court by the copyright holder, something clearances are designed to avoid altogether.

Documentary filmmakers may have a bit of an advantage over narrative filmmakers when it comes to fair use. In general, a copyrighted work that just happens to appear fleetingly in the background of a scene in a documentary should not cause infringement.

> ***Example:*** Penelope Producer is shooting an interview with Dr. Matheus Liebeenhög, world's foremost authority on dryer lint, for her documentary *Dust Bunnies and Their Furry Friends*. On a side table behind the good doctor is a small, copyrighted sculpture, which is partially obscured by his elbow. If she were sued for infringement by the sculpture's copyright owner, a court would probably side with Penelope. However, Penelope was still sued for infringement, and even though she won, she may have to pay court costs and attorney's fees. The better practice would have been to move the sculpture or use something in the public domain.

One helpful resource for evaluating whether your use of an unlicensed copyrighted work in a documentary is fair use is the *Documentary Filmmakers' Statement of Best Practices in Fair Use*, created by American University's

Center for Social Media (AUCSM).[4] AUCSM has also created a helpful website[5] to help artists negotiate the often-rough waters of fair use.

For a more in depth look of copyright and fair use, including some helpful examples, see Appendix A, "Fair Use," p. 433.

Fair Use in Copyright

Fair use is a defense to copyright infringement. It allows the taking of some part of the copyrighted work without the need to first secure the author's permission. *Caution: only a court can tell you (after you've been sued) whether your unpermitted use was fair use.* When you defend a copyright infringement lawsuit with a fair use defense, the court will analyze what you did by asking the following four questions and balancing the answers.

What did you do with the copyrighted work you took?	
For fair use	**Against fair use**
✓ You made a documentary or news program ✓ You used it for education ✓ You used it for parody or social criticism ✓ You substantially transformed the original work	✗ You made a TV commercial ✗ You used it to replace work you could have made yourself ✗ You featured the work in a narrative film that did not parody or comment upon the work you took
What kind of copyrighted work did you take?	
For fair use	**Against fair use**
✓ News ✓ A compilation of facts or data ✓ A scholarly to technical work	✗ The work was fiction, narrative film, or an expressive work ✗ Copyrighted paintings, sculptures, graphic arts ✗ Copyrighted stories, poems, novels ✗ Copyrighted musical compositions or recordings
How much of the copyrighted work did you take? How important was the portion you took to the rest of the work?	
For fair use	**Against fair use**
✓ You took a small portion ✓ Your use was fleeting or incidental ✓ The portion you took was not critical to the overall meaning of the copyrighted work	✗ You took a large portion of the work ✗ You used the work in your film for a substantial amount of time ✗ You took the "heart" of the copyrighted work ✗ You featured the copyrighted work prominently in a scene
How did your taking affect the value or market for the work?	
For fair use	**Against fair use**
✓ The work has limited economic value ✓ The work is not usually licensed or resold ✓ You used it for parody or social criticism ✓ Your work does not directly compete with the work you took	✗ The original work's owner lost potential or actual licensing revenue ✗ Your infringing work directly competes with the original work

Other factors

Acting in good faith. Give proper attribution; make sure to display the copyright notice of any work you take. Keep in mind, however, that giving proper attribution will not automatically entitle you to fair use. The court still must ensure that the answers to the preceding questions favor you as well.

Transformative use. A court will be more likely to consider your use fair use if you can show that you "transformed" the copyrighted work you took. A transformative use is one that adds something new to the original work, recasts it in a different light, giving it a new meaning or message.

Architectural Copyright

Architecture is a special case under copyright law. Even though architecture is protected by copyright, an exception to the law allows you to photograph buildings that are located in or visible from a public place without first securing the permission of the copyright owner.[6] However, there is an exception to this exception . . . stay with me here . . . special local and state rules may protect local landmark buildings, requiring you to obtain permission.[7] If you routinely shoot in a particular geographic area, it might be helpful for your attorney to compile a list of any local, state, or historic landmarks that your camera crew should avoid.

The Artwork License

If you really need to include a particular work of art in your film and you can't hire an art director to create a satisfactory original work as a work made for hire, try obtaining an *artwork license*. This license grants the production company the right to use the art in all versions of the motion picture.

For definitions and explanations of common contract clauses, see Appendix B, "The Clause Companion," p. 475.

MAJOR DEAL POINTS: ARTWORK LICENSE

The Parties

- *Production company*. The production company wants to be able to use a work of art in its motion picture.
- *Grantor*. The person or company that owns the rights to the artwork. It could be the artist, the artist's estate, or any party to whom the artist has assigned the copyright to the art. If the artist is well known, the production company will probably not be able to get the right to reproduce and sell the art itself, apart from its depiction in the motion picture.

Representations and Warranties: Authorized Person

In addition to the usual representations and warranties, the grantor, in this case the copyright holder, must represent and warrant that they are either the legal owner of the copyright to the artwork or someone with the power to authorize licenses of the work (such as an attorney for the legal department of a corporation that owns the work).

Title and Description of Film

Provide the title of the film, but make sure it is described as "tentatively titled."

Description of the Artwork

The artwork itself must be described. Be careful here. There are often several versions of a piece of art. The production company will only have permission to use those versions specifically listed in the artwork license agreement.

Grant of Rights

This section lays out the grant of rights from the grantor to the producer. The grantor must license the following rights to the production company:

- The right to use the artwork in the motion picture, in whatever forms that motion picture takes (i.e., film, video, streaming, etc.). This is usually phrased as "in any and all media, whether now known or hereafter devised."
- The right to make copies of the film containing the artwork.
- The right to exploit and distribute that film any way the producer sees fit.
- The right to use the artwork in advertising promotional materials.
- All rights should be of perpetual duration and irrevocable.
- The rights are usually nonexclusive, meaning that other production companies can license the same artwork for their films. If the producer requires the rights to be exclusive, the licensing fee will be much greater.

Compensation

- A licensing fee should be negotiated, and some amount, even if it's only a few dollars, should be paid. Nonexclusive licenses are cheaper than exclusive licenses.
- The producer should try to negotiate the license fee as a one-time flat fee, with no residuals or other contingent payments to be paid.

Credit and Copyright

- The manner in which the copyright owner and artist is credited should be specified. The production company often retains the right not to credit the artwork owner at all. In addition to credit, the production company may be obligated to place the owner's copyright notice and information in the credits.
- As with all credit provisions, the producer should contract for as much discretion as possible in creating the look of the credits and any other matter with respect to the credits for which the copyright owner has not been given approval rights.
- As is true for all credit provisions, the production company should insert a clause in the contract that says that "inadvertent failure to accord the

contracting party credit shall not be actionable." This clause should also require the injured party to waive the right to injunctive relief, leaving an obligation on the production company's part to correct the problem on all future prints as the *only* remedy for the production company's credit mistakes. The clause should further state that a mistake of this nature is *not* a breach of the artwork license agreement.

Waivers

- The grantor must waive any right to inspect the film or approve of the matter in which the artwork is depicted.
- The grantor must waive any copyright claim to the film itself.
- The grantor must waive any and all moral rights, rights under the Visual Artists Rights Act, trademark rights, or other related rights with respect to the artwork's use in the film.

Remedies

The artist should waive any claim to injunctive relief arising out of a breach of the contract. Depending on the advice of counsel, producers may want any dispute to be settled through binding arbitration rather than through the courts.

TRADEMARKS ON THE SET

When most people think of a trademark, they think of logos for products (Coke®, Nike®, McDonalds®) or services (Club Med®, SuperCuts®, Amazon.com®). This is fairly accurate, since trademarks and service marks are used: (1) to identify and distinguish a trademark owner's goods and services from those sold by others and (2) to identify for consumers the source of those goods and services.

Trademarks are found on product labels, billboards, and clothing insignias. But trademarks can also be sounds, such as the NBC three-tone network chime. Trademark rights can also protect a particular and distinctive way a store is decorated, called *trade dress* (think the design of every Starbucks® or McDonald's® you've ever visited).

In general, there are broader fair use and free speech rights concerning trademarks than there are for copyrights. The essence of trademark infringement is that the consumer *might be confused* as to the source of the goods or service being marked.

> ***Example:*** If you sell a bag of nacho cheese chips and call it "Dolitos," the Frito-Lay company, makers of Doritos® brand tortilla chips, will probably

win if they sue you for trademark infringement. Your brand name is confusingly similar to theirs, and consumers may be confused as to just who is manufacturing the bag of chips in their powdered-cheese-stained hands.

False Endorsement

Filmmakers get into trouble when it appears as though a trademark owner or celebrity endorsed, approved, or sponsored the film, a claim known as *false endorsement*.[8]

Example: In the 1999 Steve Martin/Eddie Murphy film *Bowfinger*, Martin's character, Bowfinger, secretly follows and films a famous actor, Ramsey, played by Murphy. Bowfinger makes a film by editing together the surreptitiously obtained shots of Ramsey, along with shots starring an actor who looks like Ramsey. The result is *Chubby Rain*, a movie in which Ramsey appears to have starred. If this had been real life and not "reel" life, Ramsey could sue Bowfinger for *false endorsement* (as well as invasion of privacy and a few other claims) because *Chubby Rain* creates the illusion that Ramsey intentionally starred in the film and, therefore, endorsed it.

Filmmakers who feature celebrity "look-alikes" in their work should display a prominent disclaimer that boldly and explicitly states that the actual celebrity did not endorse the film or the products and services being advertised.[9] Even the unlicensed use of a celebrity's *voice* can raise the issue of false endorsement, as the makers of the video game "Madden 06" found out when they used the voice of football announcer John Facenda in their game without first securing his permission.[10]

Using the name of a real person in a film's title is generally permitted as long as there is an artistic relationship between the movie's content and the film's title.[11] The title, however, should not be explicitly misleading.

Example: A Fellini film about two aging dancers, nicknamed *Fred and Ginger* after famous hoofers Fred Astaire and Ginger Rogers, did not falsely imply that Ginger Rogers had endorsed the film.[12]

Be very careful if you are using a celebrity impersonator in a commercial or other advertisement! As one court reasoned: "a celebrity whose endorsement of a product is implied through the imitation of a distinctive attribute of the celebrity's identity has standing to sue for false endorsement."[13]

NAKED EXCEPT FOR A LAWSUIT

Times Square in New York features neon lights, Broadway shows, and a nude singing cowboy. He's naked except for a hat, boots, underwear, strategically placed guitar and a trademark registration for the same. The Naked Cowboy®, a.k.a. performer Robert Burck, a famous New York City street performer, sued candymaker Mars, Inc., for misappropriation of his right of publicity (in New York, a privacy law claim) and trademark infringement. The candymaker and its advertising agency had created an advertising campaign featuring a blue M&M candy dressed up as the Naked Cowboy, placing the ads on electronic billboards in Times Square and inside its Times Square candy store. Burck sued, and Mars, Inc., filed a motion to dismiss the suit.

Burck lost on his right of publicity claim. Even though the New York statutes make it a misdemeanor to use "for advertising purposes, or for the purposes of trade, the name, portrait or picture of any living person without having first obtained the written consent of such person,"[14] the court held that the scantily clad blue M&M was neither a portrait nor recognizable likeness of Burck. Furthermore, it pointed out, "merely evoking certain aspects of another's character or role" does not violate New York's right of privacy law.[15] In "look-alike" cases, the Court reasoned, although "any recognizable likeness, not just an actual photograph, may qualify as a 'portrait or picture,' that likeness must be a 'close and purposeful resemblance to reality' of the actual person."

Although the right of publicity claim fizzled, the court allowed Burck to continue with a *false endorsement* claim, appropriate when a person (or company) falsely implies the endorsement of a product or service by a person.[16]

To prove a false endorsement claim,[17] you have to show that the defendant (1) in commerce, (2) made a false or misleading representation of fact, (3) in connection with goods or services, (4) that is likely to cause consumer confusion as to the origin, sponsorship, or approval of the goods or services.[18]

Even though Mars, Inc., asserted a parody defense, the court ruled that whether the "naked" M&M was a protected parody was a question for a later proceeding. M&Ms may melt in the mouth, but this false endorsement claim survived a motion to dismiss.

Informational Use of a Trademark Is Permitted

If you are using a trademark to describe or depict the goods or services of the trademark owner, generally your use is *informational* and you don't need permission from the trademark owner.[19]

Example: Max Mogul is shooting a documentary about soft drinks and wants to feature a montage of the changing shape of the Coca-Cola bottle throughout the 20th century. Even though both the name Coca-Cola® and the shape of the bottle itself are registered trademarks of the

Coca-Cola Company, it is unlikely that Max needs to seek the company's permission, since his use is informational.

Courts understand that: "[T]he appearance of products bearing well-known trademarks in cinema and television is a common phenomenon."[20] However, note again that it is a court that will make this determination—after the trademark owner has sued you and brought you into court.

Tarnishment

Unlicensed use of famous trademarks can get filmmakers into trouble when the trademark is depicted in a vulgar or disparaging context. In such an instance, the trademark owners can sue for *tarnishment*. To be tarnished, a trademark must be both famous and cast in an unflattering or unseemly light. One such case arose when the Dallas Cowboys Cheerleaders successfully sued the makers of the adult film *Debbie Does Dallas* for using the cheerleaders' trademarked uniforms in the context of a pornographic movie.

However, not every negative reference to a trademarked good must be cleared by the good's manufacturer. Trademark law must yield to the First Amendment, and thus using trademarks to convey information, news, or for comparative advertising is usually permitted. For example, the makers of Caterpillar® brand bulldozers sued Disney when their machines appeared in the film *George of the Jungle 2* and were described as "deleterious dozers" and "maniacal machinery."[21] The court sided with Disney, and the case settled. The point here for independent filmmakers to remember is not just that Disney won but that they got sued in the first place.

Parody

Parody is another defense to the claim of trademark infringement, false endorsement, and tarnishment. To be successful, a parody by its very nature must conjure up the appearance of the original trademark. The key here is to:

- Avoid confusing that audience. Make the parody different enough so that an average person would know that it is not looking at the trademark itself.
- Use the parody to poke fun at the original trademark rather than just using it for humorous effect.

SPA'AM: A TRADEMARK PARODY IN ACTION

Jim Henson Productions successfully asserted a parody defense when they were sued for trademark infringement by Hormel Foods over a character from *Muppet Treasure Island*. Henson created a wild boar character named "Spa'am," and was promptly sued by Hormel, makers of SPAM® brand luncheon meat.

The court pointed out that a successful parody must evoke the original to be effective: "A parody must convey two simultaneous—and contradictory—messages: that it is the original, but also that it is not the original and is instead a parody. To the extent that it does only the former but not the latter, it is not only a poor parody but also vulnerable under the trademark law." As the court stated: "No one likes to be the butt of a joke, not even a trademark. But the requirement of trademark law is that a likely confusion of source, sponsorship or affiliation must be proven, which is not the same thing as a 'right' not to be made fun of."[22]

Keep in mind that just because you might have the fair use right to use a trademark, many trademark designs are also protected by copyright, and you might not necessarily have the right to use the copyrighted material that embodies that trademark.

Example: Spider-Man is protected by both trademark and copyright. You might have the right to use the Spider-Man trademark in a documentary on comic books, but you would not automatically have the right to reproduce pages from an entire comic book in your film, since these are also protected by copyright.

Trademark Clearance Letter

If you plan on featuring a trademark or logo prominently within a scene, the best practice is to get permission from the trademark owners. The best way to do that is with a *trademark clearance letter.*

It is common practice to first contact the trademark's owners and to explain your needs. You might need to send them your script or the scene from the film that contains their mark. Once the trademark's owners have agreed to let you use their trademark in your film, follow up your telephone conversation or e-mail with a letter of agreement. This very simple release is often drafted in the form of a letter *from* the trademark owner *to* the production company granting the nonexclusive right to use the trademark in the film.

TRADEMARK CLEARANCE LETTER

Dear [*Production Company Name*]:

We, [*Trademark Owner Name*], are the owners of the trademark(s) [list the trademarks; you may need to attach them to the letter. If they are federally registered trademarks, include the registration numbers as well] (the "Trademarks"). You have requested our permission to include the trademarks in your feature film, currently titled [*insert movie title*] (the "Film").

For good and valuable consideration, the sufficiency of which is hereby acknowledged, we hereby grant you the irrevocable, perpetual, nonexclusive rights to use the Trademark(s) in any manner you so choose, in your sole discretion in connection with the Film. These rights include, but are not limited to, the right to photograph, videotape, create film depictions of, refer to in dialogue, and to otherwise use the Trademark(s) in your Film, in any advertising, promotional, and marketing materials related to the Film, in any and all media, manner of exhibition, reproduction, transmission, or display now known or hereafter invented in perpetuity throughout the universe. The rights granted herein are fully assignable and transferable to your licensees, assigns, and successors.

We hereby warrant and represent that we are the owners of the above-referenced Trademark(s) and that we have the power to grant the license in rights herein. We agree to indemnify you for any breach of these representations or warranties and against all claims, expenses, damages, arising from our breach of this agreement.

Sincerely, ____

[*Trademark Owner*]

WAYS TO AVOID ON-SET INFRINGEMENT

GET PERMISSION.
Contact the owner of the artwork in question and negotiate a license to use the work (Artwork License, p. 298). If you are planning to feature a trademark prominently, try to get the trademark owners' written permission. (Trademark Clearance Letter, p. 304.)

COMMISSION.
If a particular piece of art is going to be crucial to your film, you may want to commission the artwork from an artist. Make sure that you have a written contract with the artist that gives you the right to use the work as a work for hire or license. (Work Made for Hire, p. 418)

NO FALSE ENDORSEMENT.
Don't imply the trademark owner or the celebrity endorsed or sponsored the film when they haven't. (False Endorsement, p. 464.)

PROP RENTAL HOUSES.
Most prop rental houses rent items that have already been cleared for use. Make sure they represent and warrant that in their rental agreement with you. (Representations and Warranties, p. 482).

PUBLIC DOMAIN WORK.
Artwork in which the copyright has expired is always a safe bet. (Copyright Duration, p. 406.) Artwork and imagery that is prepared by the federal government is also in the public domain. (Public Domain, p. 409.)

FAIR USE.
If you're going to rely on fair use, make sure that your defense is a good one and scores favorably in the fair use factors (Fair Use, p. 433).

E&O AND OTHER CONTRACTUAL OBLIGATIONS

As we've seen, a production requires several different types of insurance. The key to protecting against IP infringement lies in a producer's errors and omissions (E&O) insurance.

A good E&O will typically cover you for claims arising from: IP infringement, invasion of privacy, defamation, infliction of emotional distress, and other causes of action related to people and IP depicted on screen. However, in order to be covered, you will have to answer questions like:

1. Is the name or likeness of any living person used or is any living person portrayed and have you obtained their permission?
2. Have you obtained permission from the estate of any deceased persons whose names appear in the film?
3. Have all of the IP rights in third-party materials been cleared for use?

Your first thought might be: "If I had all those permissions, why would I need your insurance?" But believe it or not, even missing permissions, you may still get coverage. The trick is to keep the insurance company informed by having your lawyer write to them and argue why permission wasn't needed in the cases you failed to obtain it. Hopefully the E&O company will agree with your attorney, grant you a waiver for that instance, and bind your coverage.

Example: Let's say you will be featuring the Coke logo and bottle—both famous registered trademarks—in your documentary about the soft drink industry. Regardless of the fact that your use of the logo is probably informational (thus, not infringing), if your E&O policy states that you must get a release for all identifiable trademarks, *you need to do so or get a waiver from them stating that you don't need a release.* Remember: You need this insurance, and the surest way to get a claim denied by an insurance company is to fail to comply with the policy requirements.

Similarly, if you are under a production services agreement to deliver a film or television program to a broadcaster, studio, or other commissioning party, you will be bound by those contractual obligations as well. (See "Production Services Agreements," p. 178.) It is standard practice for studios and broadcasters to require filmmakers to clear *all* copyright and trademark-protected materials.

So once more, you should turn to your attorney for guidance and hire them to write an opinion letter to the insurance company or studio explaining why your use of the material is not likely to trigger a successful lawsuit. I've done this successfully for numerous clients and trained law students how to do this as well. And I will say that insurance companies tend to be more receptive to arguments that are persuasively backed up by case and statutory law, which is why this really is a task for an attorney. The opinion letter in some cases, can be quite extensive—one documentary client required an opinion letter 98 pages long and brimming with case law! Often these opinion letters are accepted; sometimes they're not. Again, the most secure practice is to get permission if at all possible.

NOTES

[1] *Woods v. Universal,* 920 F. Supp. 62 (SDNY 1996).
[2] www.benedict.com/visual/monkeys/monkeys (Accessed May 3, 2021).
[3] 17 U.S.C. § 107 (2021).
[4] https://cmsimpact.org/code/documentary-filmmakers-statement-of-best-practices-in-fair-use/ (Accessed May 4, 2021).
[5] www.centerforsocialmedia.org/resources/fair_use/ (Accessed May 4, 2021).
[6] 17 U.S.C. § 120 (2021)."Scope of exclusive rights in architectural works: (a) Pictorial representations permitted. The copyright in an architectural work that has been constructed does not include the right to prevent the making, distributing, or public display of pictures, paintings, photographs, or other pictorial representations of the work, if the building in which the work is embodied is located in or ordinarily visible from a public place."
[7] See 17 U.S.C. §301(b)(4) (2021).
[8] "15 U.S. Code § 1125—False designations of origin, false descriptions, and dilution forbidden."
[9] *Allen v. National Video, Inc.*, 610 F. Supp. 612, 627, 226 U.S.P.Q. 483 (S.D.N.Y. 1985).
[10] *Facenda v. NFL Films*, 542 F.3d 1007 (3rd Cir Pa. 2008).
[11] *Rogers v. Grimaldi*, 875 F.2d 994, 10 U.S.P.Q.2d 1825 (2d Cir. 1989).
[12] *Id.*
[13] *Waits v. Frito-Lay, Inc.,* 978 F.2d 1093, 23 U.S.P.Q.2d 1721, 1733 (9th Cir. 1992).
[14] N.Y. Civ. Rights Law §§ 50–51 (McKinney 1992).
[15] *Burck v. Mars, Inc.,* 571 F.Supp.2d 446, 452 (2008).
[16] 15 U.S.C. § 1125(a)(1).
[17] Under the Lanham Act (15 U.S.C.).
[18] *Warner Bros. Entm't Inc. v. Ideal World Direct*, 516 F.Supp.2d 261, 268 (S.D.N.Y. 2007).
[19] See 15 U.S.C. §1115(b)(4) (2021).
[20] *Caterpillar Inc. v. Walt Disney Co.,* 287 F. Supp.2d 913, 922 (C.D. Ill. 2003).
[21] *Caterpillar Inc. v. Walt Disney Co.,* 287 F. Supp.2d 913 (C.D. Ill. 2003).
[22] *Hormel Foods Corp. v. Jim Henson Productions, Inc.,* No. 95 Civ. 5473, slip op. at 4, 1995 WL 567369 (S.D.N.Y. Sept. 22, 1995).

7

POST-PRODUCTION

FIXING IT IN POST

It is said that a film is made three times: once when it is written, once when it is shot, and once when it is edited.

If a producer runs into legal problems during principal photography, it is usually as a result of the frenzied pace of production. By contrast, legal problems that arise during post-production usually occur as a result of fatigue. Exhausted after a shoot, producers are still hard at work trying to schedule reshoots, secure music licenses, and line up distribution companies to view screener tapes. Furthermore, money is usually tight during post-production, and producers often find themselves having to secure additional funds to complete a film.

The most important thing a producer can do is to slow down and make sure that all the legal issues are being dealt with. Above all, don't abandon your lawyer at this point!

Some of the legal issues a producer will encounter during post-production include:

- Hiring an editor, post-production supervisor, music supervisor, post-production artists, and technicians. (See "Post-Production Staff," p. 311.)
- Understanding special issues relating to music copyright. (See "Music Copyright," p. 315.)
- Licensing a prerecorded song. (See "Using Prerecorded Music," p. 315.)
- Rerecording a song. (See "Rerecording an Existing Song," p. 318.)
- Commissioning music. (See "Commissioned Music," p. 330.)
- Using stock footage. (See "Stock Footage Companies," p. 336.)
- Obtaining film clips from a movie studio. (See "Movie Studio Footage," p. 336–337.)

TIP: **It is often extremely helpful to hire a post-production supervisor to help deal with many of these issues. (See "Crew Services Agreement," p. 233.)**

20

POST-PRODUCTION STAFF

During post-production, you will be working with an entirely new crew: editors, composers, post-production supervisors, music supervisors, VFX artists, animators, color graders, Foley artists, sound engineers, and laboratory technicians, just to name a few.

Some of these artists will be hired directly by the production company, but some will be providing services while in the employ of either their own or other companies.

HIRING POST-PRODUCTION ARTISTS AND TECHNICIANS DIRECTLY

If you are hiring these artists directly or through their loan-out companies, you can create an agreement using the crew member deal points shown earlier in this book. (See "Crew Services Agreements," p. 233.) For composers, you'll want to use a separate agreement based on the deal points as outlined later in this section. (See "Commissioned Music," p. 330.)

As always, if the production company is employing these artists, you need to comply with all labor and employment laws. (See "Labor and Employment Law," p. 199.)

POST.

ARTISTS AND TECHNICIANS PROVIDED BY POST-PRODUCTION FACILITIES

If you are using an editor, engineer, animator, or other artist provided by a post-production facility, you may be presented with one of their "standard contracts." Read it before you sign it! At a *minimum*, these production facilities contracts *must* contain the following provisions:

- *Work for hire/assignment of rights*. The artist and the company they work for must agree that the copyrights and other rights to the artist's contributions shall be entirely owned by the production company. *The contract*

DOI: 10.4324/9781003228479-27

must contain a work-made-for-hire/assignment clause! Remember: For copyrights to transfer from nonemployees to the production company, you must have a written agreement stating that the work is a work made for hire—and that agreement must be signed by the contractor. (See "Work Made for Hire," p. 418.)

- *Scope of work, deliverables, delivery date.* Make sure that you clearly define the file formats and other technical deliverables expected from each post-production crewmember. Pay special attention to the particulars of any production services agreement you may have with a network, studio, or other third party to whom you have to deliver your film or program. (See "Production Services Agreements," p. 178.) In this same vein, make sure that your post-production crew is delivering their work to you well in advance of any deadlines you may have with distributors, networks, studios, etc. To emphasize the importance of timely delivery, you may want to include the phrase "Timely delivery in accordance with this contract is of the essence, and failure to do so shall be considered a material breach."
- *Representations and warranties/indemnity.* The artist and the company they work for must agree that all contributions by the artist will originate with the artist or are in the public domain. This should be coupled with an indemnity provision creating an obligation for the artist's company to indemnify the production company for any breaches of the representations and warranties or other breaches of the agreement (such as "timely delivery," above). This shifts liability to the artist or their company if the production company is sued as a result of the artist adding uncleared copyright-protected material to the film or failing to deliver on time. (See Appendix B, "Representations and Warranties," p. 482; "Indemnification," p. 488.)
- *Remember:* If the contract does not have these clauses, you might not be protected—and you might not have the rights you need to distribute your film!

CAUTION!

- *Assignment of copyright.* Some post-production companies, especially startups, have been known to bury within their contracts copyright assignment clauses that assign a portion of the film's copyright to the post-production company! Although it is not unusual for a post-production company to provide services to a production company in exchange for a portion of the film's revenues, the ownership of the copyright should remain with the production company.

- *Liens.* Many post-production contracts contain clauses allowing the post-production house to have a *lien* on the film and other materials used in post-production. A lien is a creditor's interest in property, like a security interest, similar to a mortgage on a house: If you fail to pay your mortgage payments, the bank can seize your house and sell it to pay the debt that is owed. If a post-production company has a lien on your film, it can seize your film and sell it to pay any debts you owe it. Try to negotiate a waiver of the lien in exchange for the production company providing the post-production company with a cash security deposit.

21

MUSIC

In general, there are three ways music is acquired for film:

- Pre-existing musical recordings are licensed for use in the picture.
- A pre-existing musical composition is rerecorded and used in the picture.
- Music is composed especially for the picture.

Many films use a combination of these three methods.

MUSIC LICENSING

Using Pre-Recorded Music

Music licensing is one of the trickiest areas of entertainment law. For pre-recorded songs, the work of seeking permissions is doubled. This is because there are actually *two* kinds of copyrights to every piece of recorded music, and licenses need to be obtained from each copyright owner. You need to secure the permissions from:

- The party who owns the copyright to the *musical composition.*
- The party who owns the rights to the *recording* of the composition that you plan to use.

Music Copyright

The two copyrights contained in every piece of recorded music are (1) a copyright in the *musical composition* and (2) a separate copyright in the *recording* itself.

- A copyright in the musical composition.
  - The musical composition, also referred to as the *musical work* under copyright law, is the combination of music and lyrics (if there are any). The copyright protects those notes and words that you would see transcribed into sheet music.
  - This musical composition copyright is typically owned by one or more music publishing companies or the music publishing company and the songwriter.

DOI: 10.4324/9781003228479-28

- *Example:* The song composition "Lump," written by the band The Presidents of the United States of America, is owned, respectively, by David M. Dederer Publishing, EMI April Music Inc., Flying Rabbi, Raw Poo Music, and Universal Polygram International.

- A copyright in the recording itself.
  - The sound recording of a musical composition is protected by its own copyright, usually owned by the record company. You can find this information by looking at the copyright owner information contained in the phonographic copyright notice—the "P in a circle." NOTE: Copyright in sound recordings have potentially different terms than other works. (See Appendix A: "Copyright Duration," p. 406)

  Example: The recording of the song "Lump" used in the music video of the same name is owned by Sony Music Entertainment, Inc.

Rights Required and the Licenses That Grant Them

To use a piece of pre-recorded music in your film, you will need several different kinds of rights, and consequently, you will need to negotiate and acquire several different types of licenses that grant you those rights. The licenses you need are the following:

1. *Synchronization license.* A synchronization license is needed from the *music publisher.* This license allows the producer to use the musical composition in an audio-visual work.
2. *Master use license.* A master use license is needed from the *recording company.* This license allows the producer to use the particular recording in the film.
3. *Performance license.* A performance license is needed from the *publishing company.* This license allows the producer to show the film containing the composition to the public via broadcast, cable, and satellite television. If the film will be transmitted digitally over the Internet, a performance license may be needed from the *recording company* as well.
   - In the United States, you do not need a performance license to show your film in movie theaters. Furthermore, most television entities have blanket licenses, which cover the performance rights of songs. Despite this, you should still secure performance rights for your film because your film may be distributed internationally, and performance rights requirements differ from country to country. Furthermore, you may show your film in other public venues that do not have blanket license agreements (trade shows, business conventions, in-store advertisements, etc.).
4. *Videogram license.* A videogram license is needed from the *music publisher.* This license allows the producer to make and sell physical goods containing the composition and recording, like Blu-ray copies of the film.

What Music Rights do you Need for a Pre-Recorded Song?

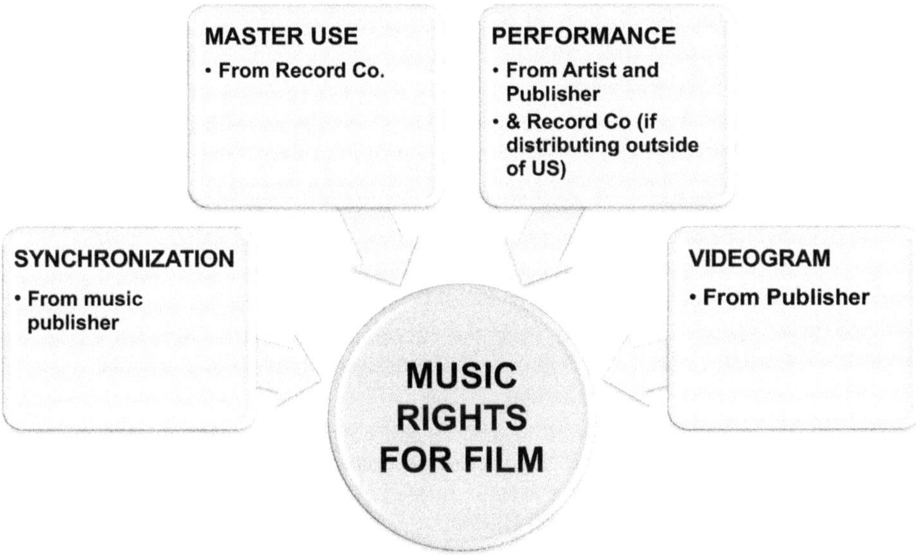

Locating the Correct Music Publisher for a Particular Song

To find the music publisher of a particular song, conduct a search with the *performance rights societies.*

Performance rights societies are organizations that monitor music use on radio, on TV, and in nightclubs. They collect royalties for public performances from these entities to pay to the music publishers (not to the record companies). The main performing rights societies are:

- The American Society of Composers, Artists, and Publishers (ASCAP; www.ascap.com)
- Broadcast Music, Inc. (BMI; www.bmi.com)
- SESAC (www.sesac.com)

When a performing rights society collects money for a certain song, it pays half the money to the writers of that song and half the money to the song's publishers. These royalty payments are referred to as the *writer's share* and the *publisher's share*, respectively.

MUSIC LICENSING IN ACTION

Fred wants to use a song in his film *Life Sucks*, written by Greg Grubb and published by Dirtz Publishing, LLC, an ASCAP-affiliated publishing company. The recording of the song that Fred wants to use is by the Grubz, off of their 1994 album, *Eat the Dirt*. The record company that owns the copyright to this song's recording is Dark Dayz Records, Inc.

Fred knows he will want to sell DVDs of his film after it has been shown in theaters.

Fred will need:

1. A *synchronization license* from the music publisher, Dirtz Publishing, LLC, which allows the producer to use the musical composition in an audiovisual work.
2. A *master use license* from the recording company, Dark Dayz Records, Inc., which allows the producer to use the particular Grubz recording in the film.
3. A *performance license* from both the publishing company, Dirtz Publishing, LLC, and the record company, Dark Dayz Records, Inc., if the film will be shown in public, over the Internet, or theatrically outside the United States.
4. A *videogram license* from the publishing company, Dirtz Publishing, LLC, which allows the producer to make and sell physical copies of the film (like Blu-ray discs) that contains the publisher's composition.

***THE BOTTOM LINE:* There are two copyrights in every musical recording. To be able to put one prerecorded song on your film's soundtrack, you must secure several types of licenses from several different parties.**

Rerecording an Existing Song

Instead of licensing a preexisting recording of a song, filmmakers often choose to have an existing song composition rerecorded. This can save money by eliminating licensing fees to the record company.

It does not, however, eliminate licensing fees to the publishing company, and it adds the cost of rerecording the song (musicians, technicians, studio time, etc.) to the budget. Furthermore, if musicians are hired to rerecord the song, the producer must take care to engage them under contracts stating that the work they do is a work made for hire. You might want to add up all the costs of rerecording a song and compare them to the cost of licensing a song before you decide to go one way or the other.

For rerecorded songs, the producer will still have to get permission from the music publishing company and will still need to negotiate and obtain the following:

- A synchronization license.
- A performance license.
- A videogram license.

CAUTION! IMITATION IS THE SINCEREST FORM OF INFRINGEMENT

Sound-alike recordings. Suppose you want to use a popular song in your movie, but you don't want to pay for the rights to use the recording. You decide to rerecord the song, and you tell your singer to sound as much like the original singer as possible. Believe it or not, this can land you in legal hot water. Sound-alike recordings may violate a singer's right of publicity and give rise to claims of false endorsement.

Example: Singer Tom Waits successfully sued the Frito-Lay company when it broadcast a commercial jingle for its SalsaRio Doritos corn chips that featured a sound-alike singer—a performer who had spent years imitating Waits's distinctive gravelly voice in a cover band.[1] (See "Right of Publicity," p. 443, and "False Endorsement," p. 464.)

Sampling. For those who want to create their own compositions by sampling (taking snippets of other people's recordings): Think twice before sampling without a license. One Sixth Circuit court indicated that even small musical samples (three notes long!) needed to be cleared. According to that court, sampling was per se (automatic) infringement—and that the *de minimis* exception to copyright infringement did not apply to sampling. (See Appendix A, "*De Minimis* Taking," p. 440.) As the court put it: "Get a license or do not sample."[2] However, other federal circuits disagree with this reasoning holding "that the 'de minimis' exception applies to infringement actions concerning copyrighted sound recordings, just as it applies to all other copyright infringement actions."[3]

GOALS AND DEALS

You will need to deal with several parties in securing the rights to a piece of music by approaching each with a licensing request letter in which you explain:

- The potential use for the song in your film (both placement and context. Whether the music is in the end credits or used under montage in the film itself will impact the licensing fee).
- How much of the song you want to use.
- The amount of time you're seeking the license for.
- The potential avenues of distribution for your film.
- A request to discuss licensing fees and terms.

Each music licensing agreement should be drafted differently, depending on which rights are being licensed and from whom. For prerecorded songs, you will be approaching both the music publishers and the record companies. If you plan on recording your own version of a song, you only need to approach the music publisher.

Most licensors have their own standard agreements that they prefer to use. Remember, just because something is a "standard agreement" doesn't mean that it is not negotiable.

Before negotiating the rights to a licensing agreement, keep in mind your exact needs. If you are releasing your movie straight to video, you probably do not need to pay for theatrical release rights; if you're shooting a television commercial that has a shelf life of one year, you probably do not need to pay for the music rights in perpetuity. The less you need, the less it will cost you.

For definitions and explanations of common contract clauses, see Appendix B, "The Clause Companion," p. 475.

MAJOR DEAL POINTS: MUSIC LICENSING AGREEMENT

The Parties

Production company. The work of the production company is doubled, and it may need to negotiate and execute two separate license agreements from two or more parties. Make sure you are asking the correct party for the correct license.

Music publisher. You will always need to secure the license to use the musical composition from the publisher. In one contract from the publisher, obtain the following licenses: synchronization, performance, and videogram licenses.

Record company. If you need to use a particular recording of a musical composition, you will need to negotiate with the record company for the following licenses: master use and international performance licenses.

Grant of License(s)

Unless you have a pressing reason that your film should be the only one entitled to use the song, all you need is a nonexclusive license.

- The *synchronization license*, obtained from the publisher, is the right to use the composition in synchronization or in time-relation with the motion picture in all its forms.
- The *performance license*, obtained from the publisher, is the right to publicly perform the composition in relation to the motion picture in all its forms.
- The *master use license*, obtained from the record company, is the right to use a particular recording of the composition in relation to the motion picture in all its forms.
- The *videogram license*, obtained from the publisher, is the right to reproduce in video form and sell the composition as matched to the motion picture in all its forms.

Use

- You will likely need to explain to the license for how you plan to use the composition or recording in your film. Be prepared to give them information on:
  - Where and how the music will appear—opening or closing credits? In the body the film itself? Advertisements for the movie?
  - The duration of the music clip you plan to use—the entire song? Only portion?
- Keep in mind that the licensing price tends to increase when the song is used as a opening or closing credit piece or advertisements and if the movie itself is based upon the title or plot of the song.

Term

For feature films, it's of course best if you have a perpetual licensing term, although that can get very expensive. To save money, you may want to license the song for shorter period of time (e.g. 10 years), with your option to renew the song license for a specific price when the term expires.

Territory

- For feature films, try to define the territory as "the world" or "the universe."
- For television commercials, you may be able to reduce the cost of the license fee by restricting the territory to domestic television.

Media

- When negotiating the language of the license, try to define your motion picture as broadly as possible—for instance: "The Motion Picture, in all its forms, in every media and method of distribution now known or hereafter invented."
- Even for feature films, make sure your licenses cover all distribution media for that film (broadcast TV, cable TV, OTT TV, streaming, satellite, in-flight movie, closed-circuit, Blu-ray, and downloads).

License Fee

- Be aware that music licensing can be very expensive. It is not unusual for popular recorded songs to be licensed for tens of thousands of dollars.
- Try to negotiate a flat fee and avoid having to pay any royalties or other contingent compensation.
- Keep in mind that both record companies and publishing companies of popular songs may want their fee to be on a most favored nations basis with respect to other songs in your film. As you may have done with your performers, make sure to heavily qualify this request: for example, "most favored nations with respect to diegetic songs in the film." (See "Most Favored Nations," p. 479.)
- If SAG-AFTRA, the American Federation of Musicians (AFM), or the American Federation of Television and Radio Artists (AFTRA) has jurisdiction over the movie, reuse payments may have to be made to the musicians and vocalists on the recording.

Modifications to the Composition/Recording

- If you intend to modify or change the composition or recording, you must have the rights holder's permission to do so.
- At the very least, you will need the rights to edit the recording or the composition for time—shortening or lengthening it to fit your shots.

Representations and Warranties

- The licensor must represent and warrant that it is the sole holder of the rights being licensed and/or have the power to enter into this agreement on behalf of the sole rights owners.
- The licensor must indemnify the producer for any breach of the representations and warranties.

Credit

- As is true for all credit provisions, the production company should insert a clause in the contract that says that "inadvertent failure to accord the contracting party credit shall not be actionable." This clause should also require the injured party to waive the right to injunctive relief, leaving an obligation on the production company's part to correct the problem on all future prints as the only remedy for the production company's credit mistakes. The clause should further state that a mistake of this nature is not a breach of the agreement.
- The clause should make clear that the production company has complete discretion over the look of the credits.

♦♦♦♦♦

STEP BY STEP: PRERECORDED MUSIC LICENSING

1. Find out who the rights holders are.
   - The CD label will probably list both the record company and the publishing company.
   - For more detailed contact information on the music publisher, use one of the performance rights societies' databases. ASCAP's "ACE" title search feature is very helpful for locating music publishers. See www.ascap.com/ace.
2. Once you've located the correct music publisher and the record company, review their websites and look for information on their licensing department. Very often your preliminary questions about whom to contact, what kinds of rights they can grant, how long the licensing process takes, and so on are answered on the website.
3. Contact the rights holders. Prior to writing a letter, it is often preferable to put in a preliminary phone call to the licensing department to explain your needs.
   - Be prepared to tell them how the song will be used. For instance, they might want to know what scene the music will accompany and the duration of the song in the movie.
   - If you license any other songs for your movie, you may want to let the rights holder know. It shows that you have been trusted by other licensors.
   - Negotiate the deal points discussed previously.
   - Offer to provide a licensing agreement in letter form, drawn up for their signature. However, be prepared for them to send you their "standard contract."

4. Send the person you spoke to a letter restating the deal terms that you've discussed. If the licensing manager has agreed to your providing the agreement, your letter can be drafted as a contract, with the signature block for all parties at the bottom.

Securing music licenses takes a lot of work. If you have the budget, consider working with an attorney who handles music licensing or a music permissions and licensing service. For a fee, these services will investigate the availability of your chosen music and negotiate the appropriate licenses.

STOCK AND ROYALTY-FREE MUSIC

Rather than dealing with the headache and cost of licensing music from publishers and recording companies, many producers choose to purchase stock and royalty-free music. Although technically the producers are still licensing this music, the procedure is far less involved.

Stock and royalty-free music is music designed especially to be used in connection with audiovisual programs. Most stock music companies also license sound effects. Many companies offer a one-time fee purchase whereby a producer pays for a particular track one time and then can use it in perpetuity. Usually, these companies have websites that allow you to demo certain tracks and buy them over the Internet. For background tracks, the variety and volume of available royalty-free music makes this a very attractive option for producers on a budget.

A new development in the area of music scoring marries the advantages of royalty-free music with the customization of a personal composer. A handful of emerging AI software packages create soundtracks that are customized to your movie. These programs work in conjunction with your computer video editing program. Some even analyze the duration of your video track and create a piece of music tailored to your film. Licensing is usually a one-time fee, but producers will need to make sure that they are paying for the *commercial* license if they plan on selling the film that contains the royalty-free music.

***TIP:* With royalty-free music, licensing costs are usually handled as a one-time fee. However, producers will need to make sure that they are paying for the *commercial* license if they plan on selling the film that contains the royalty-free music.**

COMMISSIONED MUSIC

Sometimes a filmmaker needs a soundtrack or song composed especially for their movie, so this music is commissioned from a composer.

Independent producers typically work with composers who own their own recording studios. Thanks to the proliferation of computer-based music composition, recording, and editing software, finding a composer with a studio should not be that hard. From a legal perspective, a composer/studio owner makes things easy as well: instead of dealing with two contracts—one for a composer's services, the other for studio facilities—you can handle the issues in a single contract.

THE AMERICAN FEDERATION OF MUSICIANS (AFM)

Just like cast and crew, musicians have their own union: the American Federation of Musicians (www.afm.org). Just like SAG-AFRA members, musicians belonging to AFM can only work for companies that comply with their union's guidelines. If you are not willing to deal with the regulations, rights, and residuals terms of AFM, you must make sure that your contract with your composer specifically states that the production company is *not a signatory* to any AFM agreements and will not be obligated under the terms of the AFM contracts. As extra protection, the composer agreement should limit the composer's ability to hire musicians without the production company's prior written approval.

For definitions and explanations of common contract clauses, see Appendix B, "The Clause Companion," p. 475.

MAJOR DEAL POINTS: COMPOSER'S SERVICES AGREEMENT

If you are hiring a composer with his or her own equipment and recording studio, you will need to negotiate a *composer's services agreement*.

In working with the composer, the ownership of the rights to the soundtrack is a key issue. Producers should structure the deal as a work made for hire, with rights to both the recording and to the composition vesting initially in the production company. This will avoid issues of controlling the exploitation of the publisher's share of the copyright. It is almost always better to pay a little bit more money to the composer in exchange for ownership of all of the rights.

The Parties

- ***Production company***. The production company is seeking an all-in-one composer/recording studio. In addition to the actual physical recorded soundtrack master, the production company should try to obtain all the copyrights to the materials produced by the composer. Here, as in other services agreements, the production company must be aware of exactly whom they are contracting with. Is it a loan-out company or an individual? The drafting of the contract, and whether an inducement and further assurances are required, will be affected by each consideration. (See "Loan-Out Companies," p. 51.) Along with the contact information, remember to get Social Security numbers for individuals and federal ID numbers for companies. These will be necessary in handling payroll and other taxes.

- ***Composer***. The composer might want to retain a copyright interest in the composition. Keep in mind that it is fairly standard for production companies to require the entire copyright interest be assigned to them. However, if the composer is allowed to retain any copyright interests, the production company should negotiate—up front—the royalty fees for future licenses. These license royalty fees, such as synchronization, mechanical, and performance licenses, are typically split 50/50 with the other copyright owner of the composition—in this case, the production company. Additionally, the composer will want royalties from record sales and music publishing.

Engagement/Services

This paragraph describes the particular services the composer is obligated to perform for the production company. It is usually drafted fairly broadly, such as: "Composer shall write, score, compose, conduct, record, produce, mix, complete, and deliver to the producer the final instrumental composition and master for and to the feature film tentatively titled [name of picture], for use in the Motion Picture, as hereafter defined."

- The term "Master" should be defined as the recording of the soundtrack.
- The term "Composition" should be defined as the written musical work and accompanying lyrics (if any) for the soundtrack.
- The composer should be obligated to comply with all the directions and reasonable requests of the director.

Composers with their own studios are often hired as independent contractors rather than employees. If you are certain that the composer is an independent contractor and not an employee, you should include a clause in the contract stating that the parties understand that the composer shall be treated as an independent contractor. However, keep in mind that in determining whether a composer is an employee or an independent contractor, both the courts and the IRS will focus on the actual work relationship rather than what the parties agreed in the contract. (See "Labor and Employment Law," p. 199.)

Term

The *term* should be defined as starting on commencement of the composer's services, which is usually a predetermined date, such as the date of contract execution. The term continues until the composer's services are completed to the production company's satisfaction.

The composer will want to know when he or she can start scoring the picture. The date the film is delivered to the composer for scoring is called the *start date*. If the start date cannot be determined at the time the contract is executed, the production company should include a range during which they can designate a start date.

Deliverables

- The exact form, media, and format of the finished soundtrack should be specified and defined as the *deliverables*.
- The *delivery date* (as distinguished from the term) is the date that the deliverables are due.
- Payment of any final fees should be conditioned on the production company's acceptance and approval of the deliverables. However, mere receipt of the deliverables should not count as "acceptance"; only a written notice that the deliverables have been accepted and approved by the production company should suffice.

Approval

The production company needs to build in approval stages, allowing them to periodically review and approve the composer's work. All approval over the deliverables, the composition, and the master should rest entirely with the production company. Furthermore, payment should be contingent on approval of each stage by the production company.

Nonunion Status

If the production company is not an AFM or other music union signatory, it should state that in the contract and require that none of the recordings be made under union contracts.

Costs and Expenses

Who pays for the tape stock, studio musician fees, and equipment rentals? If these costs are not figured into a flat fee for the composer, they need to be itemized here. Costs should be capped, and any expenses over a certain amount should require prior written authorization from the production company.

Composer's Equipment

If the composer is supplying their own equipment (computer, microphones, mixers, musical instruments, etc.), the contract should state that the composer is solely responsible for the upkeep, maintenance, and safety of their own gear. This provision notwithstanding, the production company should check with its insurance company to determine to what extent it is covered for damage to composer equipment.

Compensation

- On independent films, composers are typically paid a flat fee. Like directors and producers, composers are often paid in several stages: commencement, production company's review of soundtrack, and on approval and acceptance following delivery of the soundtrack.
- If the composer retains a copyright interest, you will have to include provisions for how royalties and residuals will be computed and paid to the composer. As mentioned earlier, it is in the production company's best interests to take the entire copyright for itself.

Credit

As is true for all credit provisions, the production company should insert a clause in the contract that says that "inadvertent failure to accord the contracting party credit shall not be actionable." This clause should also require the injured party to waive the right to injunctive relief, leaving an obligation on the production company's part to correct the problem on all future prints as the *only* remedy for the production company's credit mistakes. The clause should further state that a mistake of this nature is *not* a breach of the composer's services agreement.

The clause should make clear that the production company has complete discretion over the look of the credits.

Rights

- From the production company's standpoint, they may want to hire the composer on a work-made-for-hire basis. A well-written assignment of rights/

work-for-hire provision is another standard clause in all motion picture or service contracts. In this paragraph, the composer must agree that all rights, proceeds, and results of their creative efforts in both the composition and the master are agreed to be treated as a work made for hire. Any remaining rights that are not captured by the production company as a result of the work-made-for-hire clause should be assigned by the composer to the production company under the agreement. (See "Work Made for Hire," p. 418.). All transferred rights should be perpetual in duration and irrevocable and survive any termination of the agreement.

  - If the composer is allowed to retain any portion of the copyright, the production company may want these reserved rights to be subject to a holdback provision. This would require the composer to refrain from exploiting their reserved rights for a period of time. (See Appendix B, "Holdback Provisions," p. 480.)

- The composer will likely want to retain the copyright to the compositions for themselves. If that is the case, production companies at a minimum need to make sure that it has an exclusive license to use the music in the movie and all of its derivatives. This leaves composer with the rights to anything the producer doesn't negotiate for, like potentially the soundtrack album rights. And the composer will have a right of reversion from copyright's termination of transfer in 35 years from when the license in the music was granted. (See "Termination of Transfer," p. 427.) However, an exclusive license is often much cheaper than hiring a composer as a work for hire.

Publicity

The production company will want to control the publicity for the motion picture and thus be able to restrain the composer from issuing publicity statements about the motion picture without the production company's prior written consent. The production company will also require the right to use the composer's name and likeness in any publicity, promotion, or marketing of the motion picture. Make sure to include language that allows the composer's image to be used in the "making of" documentary.

Hiring Others/Purchases

If the production company authorizes the composer to hire other musicians or singers, these other artists must also be bound by written and signed contracts stating that their contributions are works made for hire, similar to the provision in the composer's agreement. The production company should either provide these contracts, or, if the composer is supplying the contracts, the production company attorney should review them prior to their execution.

Representations and Warranties

- The composer must promise that they are under no other obligations that would prevent them from performing their obligations under this contract. This clause typically contains an indemnity provision that obligates the composer to hold harmless and indemnify the production company for any breaches of the representations and warranties or other breaches of the agreement. (See "Indemnification," p. 488.)
- The composer must also warrant that any material that they contribute to the production—samples, melodies, harmonies, and so forth—are original with the composer or are in the public domain. This shifts liability to the composer if the production company is sued as a result of the composer adding uncleared copyright-protected material to the film.

Errors and Omissions (E&O) Insurance

You should check your E&O policy to determine whether there are any special requirements for composers and add your composer as an additional insured. (See "Insurance," p. 59.)

Assignment

The production company always has the right to assign the contract and the rights, results, and proceeds created under it. The composer *never* has the rights to assign and delegate their duties under the contract.

Remedies

Like all motion picture services agreements, the right to injunctive relief should be waived by the composer.

Furthermore, no breach of the agreement by the production company should entitle the composer to recapture any rights that they may have granted the production company. If well drafted, this clause should leave the composer only with a right to recover money, if anything at all, from the production company.

Further Documents

Here the composer should be obligated to execute any other documents necessary to further the intent of the contract. Examples include copyright assignment forms, workers' compensation claim forms, certificates of authorship, and so forth.

INDUCEMENT (IF DEALING WITH A LOAN-OUT COMPANY)

If the composer is working under a loan-out company, it is the loan-out company that will be a party to the contract. Furthermore, the contract should contain an inducement and further assurances clause. (See "Inducement," p. 489.)

♦♦♦♦♦

LAW

- Composers may be treated as independent contractors if they are working through their own company, such as a loan-out company. (See p. 51; "Federal and State Labor and Employment Laws," p. 199.)
- You should have the composer complete a certificate of authorship (COA), similar to the one completed by a screenwriter. (See "Certificate of Authorship," p. 177.)
- *Fair use* (see "Fair Use," p. 433). Don't forget, fair use applies to musical copyrights as well. *Expelled* was a feature documentary that addressed the debate between proponents of intelligent design and the scientific theory of evolution. Its filmmakers included a sequence contrasting marching soldiers and other symbols of dictatorship with a 15-second sound recording of John Lennon singing: "Nothing to kill or die for/And no religion too," from his most famous song, "Imagine." The intended effect was to show "the naïveté of John Lennon's views on a world without religion."[4] The film's producers used the music clip without permission from the song's owners. When Mr. Lennon's widow, Yoko Ono, and other owners of his song sued for copyright infringement, the filmmakers defended, in part, on the grounds that their criticism of the Lennon song and the fact that they used so little of it should be excused as fair use. The court agreed with the defendants:

  > Defendants' use of "Imagine" is transformative because their purpose is to criticize the song's message. Moreover, the amount and substantiality of the portion used is reasonable in light of defendants' purpose. Although "Imagine," as a creative work, is at the core of copyright protection, and defendants' use of the song is at least partially commercial in nature, [finding fair use is likely] given that defendants' use is transformative.[5]

Business Issues

- If the composer, in addition to composing the soundtrack, is also performing and recording it, the technological specifications should be decided in advance. The format and delivery date of the soundtrack materials should also be determined in advance.

- If the composer is working with other musicians, they should be under contracts either provided or reviewed by the production company's attorneys. Remember, if the production company is not working under a musician's union contract, it will need to make sure that the musicians the composer uses are not members of that union.
- Distributors, and exhibitors (e.g. television channels, OTT companies) will require you to provide them with a "cue sheet." This is a list of all of the music in your film, the timecode where it appears, and the pertinent licensing contact information for all of the music rights holders.

Cue Sheets

Okay, so you got the rights to the music in your film. Good thing, too, because proving up those permissions is an obligatory step when dealing with broadcasts and exhibitors. You will not be allowed to put your film on television if you can't supply the broadcaster with a "Cue Sheet," essentially a list of music used, whom it's licensed from, and where it occurs in your film. It's used by performance rights organizations to keep track of what royalties are owed their members.

A properly drafted cue sheet will have the following information:

- Production company information.
- Series/film title.
- Episode title.
- Episode number.
- Air date.
- Show length.
- Song/cue title.
- Music length.
- Music usage.
- Composer.
- Publisher.
- Performing rights society.
- Timing.

BMI provides helpful cue sheet templates, which can be found here: www.bmi.com/creators/detail/what_is_a_cue_sheet.

Music Supervisors

One of the easiest ways to deal with all of your music issues is to hire a music supervisor:[6] a post-production professional whose primary job is to secure all of the music needed in the film.

Music supervisors must be adept at:

1. Devising realistic budgets for music licensing.
2. Drafting request letters to music publishing and record companies seeking music licensing possibilities.
3. Negotiating and securing music licensing agreements with music publishers and record companies.
4. Negotiating in securing the services of composers.
5. Ensuring that all of the music deliverables meet the project's technical requirements.
6. Filling out cue sheets.

For post-production hiring practices, See "Post-Production Staff," p. 311.

NOTES

1 *Waits v. Frito Lay,* 978 F. 2d 1093 (9th Cir. 1992).

2 *Bridgeport Music, Inc. v. Dimension Films,* 410 F.3d 792, 801 (6th Cir. 2005).

3 *VMG Salsoul, LLC v. Ciccone*, 824 F.3d 871, 874 (9th Cir. 2016).

4 *Lennon v. Premise Media Corp.*, 556 F. Supp. 2d 310, 323 (S.D.N.Y. 2008).

5 *Lennon v. Premise Media Corp.*, 556 F. Supp. 2d 310, 323 (S.D.N.Y. 2008).

6 For more on music supervisors, see www.guildofmusicsupervisors.com/ (accessed November 29, 2021).

22

FILM CLIPS AND STOCK FOOTAGE

Using stock footage or clips from other movies is a common practice. For instance:

- Documentarians may want to use a film clip from an old movie to illustrate a particular time period or natural phenomenon.
- For establishing shots, filmmakers may find it cheaper to use another film's footage of the Eiffel Tower rather than flying to Paris to shoot it themselves (although going to France would be more fun).
- A scene in which characters watch television or a movie will require the filmmakers to either use clips or create the onscreen programming themselves.

Depending on the kind of footage a filmmaker needs, there are three categories of sources filmmakers tend to turn to:

- A stock footage company.
- A studio or other rights holder of a film.
- The National Archives.

Filmmakers should first identify the length and type of clip they need and then contact the appropriate party to obtain permission to use it.

OWNING A COPY OF THE FILM IS NOT THE SAME AS OWNING THE COPYRIGHT TO THE FILM

Filmmakers must keep in mind that, just like music, copyright protected film clips must be licensed before they can be incorporated into a movie. The mere ownership of a *copy* of a movie does not grant any rights to the *copyright* of that movie. If you own a Blu-ray disc, you merely have the right to watch that film. You do not have the right to create another movie with it.

We've seen how relying on fair use is problematic. (See "On-Set IP Infringement," p. 293; Appendix A, "Fair Use," p. 433.) The solution? Our old friend the license agreement. (See "Film Clip License," p. 337.)

DOI: 10.4324/9781003228479-29

STOCK FOOTAGE COMPANIES

Stock footage companies are in the business of licensing clips to production companies. In addition to providing the right licenses and footage, they will also help you search for a good clip for your production. Their fees are based on:

- The length of the clip.
- The filmmaker's final exhibition and distribution media.
- The duration of the license.
- The geographic territories in which the film that incorporates their clips will be shown.

Note: Duplication costs (like laboratory fees for film) are often additional.

These companies will supply their own license agreements and are generally reluctant to change them. When you license stock footage, make sure that the stock footage company is representing and warranting that it has all the rights needed to enable it to license the clip to you. (See Appendix B, "Representations and Warranties," p. 482.) Further, make sure that you're being indemnified by them for any breach of these representations and warranties. (See Appendix B, "Indemnification," p. 488.) If you are licensing footage from a website, be sure to read the fine print: you'd be surprised at just how many stock footage companies will license footage even though they haven't cleared the rights to use any of the people and products in the film clip they are licensing!

MOVIE STUDIO FOOTAGE

Unlike stock footage houses, movie studios might not be as amenable to licensing clips of their films to independent producers. Furthermore, the studio might not have all the rights you need to license. For instance, if the film was based on a pre-existing literary property, such as a stage play, novel, or comic book, the studio might have obtained the rights to exploit that literary property within that motion picture only. In other words, it might not have the right to license clips from that movie for use as stock footage.

If any professional actors appear in the footage, you should contact SAG-AFTRA to determine whether residual payments need to be paid to the performers. The production company might also need to secure the written permission of recognizable performers who appear in the film. (See "Right of Publicity," p. 443.)

BE WARY OF "QUITCLAIM" LICENSES

A *quitclaim* is a statement by the studio that it is not promising to the filmmaker that it has all the rights to convey. All that is being granted to the filmmaker are any rights that the studio has, along with the promise that the studio won't sue for copyright infringement if the clip is used according to the film-clip licensing agreement. In other words, it is expressly *not* promising that the filmmaker won't be sued by any other rights holder who may have a legal stake in the footage.

Example: Frodo Filmmaker licenses the rights to a film clip from *Bayonne or Bust* from Big Studio, Inc., under a quitclaim license agreement. Frodo uses the footage in his film and is promptly sued by Paola Playwright, the owner of the play on which the movie *Bayonne or Bust* was based. Paola's contract with Big Studio specified that clips from the movie version of her film could not be relicensed for inclusion in another film. Because Frodo's license came with a quitclaim, Frodo can't sue Big Studio, Inc., for a breach of a representation.

For definitions and explanations of common contract clauses, see Appendix B, "The Clause Companion," p. 475.

MAJOR DEAL POINTS: THE FILM CLIP LICENSE AGREEMENT

The rights holder, typically a studio, will issue a nonexclusive license to the filmmaker for the rights to use a particular film clip in the filmmaker's movie.

The Parties

- *Production company*. The production company should seek the broadest possible grant of rights in perpetuity. Additionally, the production company should ask for assurances from the studio/rights holder that all of the rights needed to use the clip are being granted.
- *Studio/rights holder*. The studio or rights holder may attempt to limit its liability by *quitclaiming* any warranties (see earlier). It may also require certain restrictions over the way the film clip is used.

Grant of License/Rights

- The license will almost always be nonexclusive.
- As is true for any license, the *territory*, *duration*, *media*, and *fee* will be specified, as will a description of the particular clip. The fee should be a

one-time flat fee. These requirements are often detailed in a separate exhibit or rider.

- The studio/rights holder may also require the filmmaker to provide a script and assurances that the clip will be used only in the manner depicted by the screenplay. Because the studio/rights holder may be bound by its own contractual restrictions regarding the footage, it may specify that the clip may not be used in commercials or in a derogatory manner and that the filmmaker may not edit or change the clip in any way other than editing it for time.
- The studio/rights holder will explicitly reserve for itself any rights not granted under the agreement. This means that the filmmaker may not reuse the clip for other purposes, such as inclusion in a sequel.

Copy of Finished Film

The studio/rights holder will often require the filmmaker to send it a copy of the filmmaker's finished film.

Representations and Warranties

The filmmaker should seek representations and warranties from the studio/rights holder that all rights in the clip have been cleared. Conversely, the studio/rights holder may want to quitclaim any rights.

Guild Payments, Permissions, and Music Licenses

- As a condition for the grant, the studio/rights holder may require the filmmaker to obtain permissions from performers, directors, writers, and music rights holders whose work appears in the film clip. The filmmaker may be required to pay any union-mandated residuals to musicians and performers—even if the filmmaker is not a union signatory. (See "SAG-AFTRA," p. 243.)
- The studio/rights holder will usually require copies of these permissions to be delivered to it.

Credit

- As is true for all credit provisions, the production company should try to insert a clause in the contract that says that "inadvertent failure to accord the contracting party credit shall not be actionable." This clause should also require the injured party to waive the right to injunctive relief, leaving an obligation on the production company's part to correct the problem on all future prints as the *only* remedy for the production company's credit mistakes. The clause should further state that a mistake of this nature is *not* a breach of the agreement.

- The studio/rights holder may not agree to letting the production company have complete discretion over how the clip is credited. Be prepared to give a little on the wording of your credit clause.

Copyright Notice

The studio/rights holder will require that its copyright notice be placed on the film. This does not transfer the copyright in the filmmaker's work, but it will serve to protect the copyright in the clip itself, reserving it for the studio/rights holder.

Remedies

- The studio/rights holder may insist on an equitable relief clause, giving it the right to seek an injunction against the filmmaker for breaches of the license agreement. (See Appendix B, "No Injunction," p. 490.) The filmmaker, on the other hand, should try to eliminate any equitable remedies, leaving the studio/rights holder's only remedy the right to sue for money damages.
- The studio/rights holder will probably want an automatic termination provision, which cancels the license for any breach of the agreement. The filmmaker, on the other hand, should attempt to negotiate a cure provision, creating a mechanism for remedying any default before it becomes a breach of the agreement.

THE NATIONAL ARCHIVES

The National Archives and Records Administration (NARA) in Washington, D.C., has a huge selection of public domain footage produced by the US government. Most of this material is copyright free, does not require a license agreement, and can be obtained for little more than the cost of laboratory and other duplication fees. Because the US government may hold material that is protected by copyright, you still need to check whether any particular asset you use is copyrighted. NARA does ask that material used be credited as follows: "Courtesy: National Archives and Records Administration."

For details on how to obtain copies of public domain films from the National Archives, see www.archives.gov/research/alic/reference.

For a great selection of newsreels, see: www.archives.gov/research/motion-pictures/newsreels.

STEP BY STEP: FILM CLIPS

1. Locate the copyright holder of the film clip you want to use. (See "Copyright Searches and Permissions," p. 159.)
2. Contact the copyright holder and negotiate a film clip license agreement.
3. Secure the necessary permissions from the other rights holders (performers, directors, musicians, etc.) included in the clip.
4. Provide copies of these permissions to the film clip's copyright holder.
5. When you edit the clip into your film, make sure that you are using it in a manner consistent with the license you have been granted.
6. In your credit roll, make sure that the copyright holder's credit provisions are strictly adhered to. For NARA footage, include: "Courtesy: National Archives and Records Administration."
7. When you distribute, exhibit, and/or broadcast your film, make sure it is consistent with the license provisions in the film clip license agreement.

23

CREDITS AND COPYRIGHT NOTICE

Your edit is complete, the soundtrack is amazing, and now you're ready to celebrate. . .

Wait! Stop! You have one more critical step: double-checking your credit roll. This issue is important enough to have given it its own chapter. That's because at the end of the edit, you're likely exhausted and just want this darn thing to be done. That's the perfect recipe for dropping details. And believe me, the credits are not something you want to mess up: you undoubtedly have made promises to hundreds of people and entities regarding the how, where, and when their credits will be included in the film and advertising.

> ***CAUTION!*** **Be very careful here! Make sure to check your credit roll to ensure that it conforms to the credit clauses in all your contracts. If you have used union writers, actors, or crew, make sure that your credits conform to all union requirements.**

- Double-check the credit clauses in every agreement, especially:
  - Performers.
  - Above- and below-the-line crew agreements.
  - All associated production companies and co-producers.
  - All government agencies and film commissions which provided film incentives.
  - Trademark and copyright licenses.
  - Music licenses.
  - Location releases.
  - Special effects and other post-production agreements.
  - Distribution agreements.
- If you are a WGA signatory company working with a WGA writer, you will need to submit your proposed writing credits to the WGA for approval. (See "WGA Credits," p. 117.)

DOI: 10.4324/9781003228479-30

- Keep in mind that you may have "favored nations" credit obligations, such as:
  - Making sure that one actor's name is displayed as big as or as prominently as another actor's name. (See "Favored Nations," p. 479.).
  - Make sure that your advertising and promotional material also complies with these requirements.
- You should register the copyright of your finished film before it goes over to the distributor and certainly before you publicly distribute it. In your copyright registration, make sure you reference the copyright number you received when you registered your screenplay. See "Copyright Registration," p. 164.

COPYRIGHT NOTICE AND DISCLAIMER

In addition, your credits should always feature a copyright notice and trademark and libel disclaimer that says something similar to this:

> Copyright © [*YEAR*] [*NAME OF PRODUCTION COMPANY*]. All Rights Reserved. This motion picture is protected under the laws of the United States and other countries. Any unauthorized duplication, distribution, or exhibition is strictly prohibited and may result in both civil and criminal penalties. All product and company names are trademarks ™ or registered ® trademarks of their respective holders. Use of these marks does not imply any affiliation with or endorsement by them. The persons, characters, and events depicted in this film are fictitious. Any similarity to actual persons, living or dead, is purely coincidental.

8

DISTRIBUTION

SELLING YOUR FILM

Distribution is the act of licensing the film to exhibitors, broadcasters, and other parties in exchange for a fee or participation in the film's revenues. Distributors put films in movie theaters, on television networks, on Netflix and Hulu, and on Blu-Ray discs sold at big box stores. But distribution is also the process of putting your film on YouTube, Amazon Prime, or even your own website. In short, distribution is the economic engine for filmmakers, because without distribution, your film will not make money.

Of course, even with a distribution deal, a film might not make money, but if the distribution company does its job, at least the film will be seen by prospective licensees and buyers. These licensees and buyers range from theatrical exhibitors, network television broadcasters, and cable casters to "over-the-top" television companies like Netflix, Hulu, and Amazon Prime.

Not all good films are picked up by distribution companies, and some filmmakers would rather become their own distributor. Such "DIY" distributors may pay theaters to show their films, put them online with iTunes or Amazon, or launch their own YouTube channel.

This section will explore:

- How to get ready to distribute. (See "Preparing for Distribution," p. 345.)
- How to prepare film festival submissions. (See "Prepping for Festival Submission," p. 349.)
- How to "work" a film market or festival to land a distributor. (See "Attending a Film Festival," p. 350; "If You Snooze, You Lose; if You Schmooze, You Win," p. 351.)
- The role of a distribution company. (See "What Distributors Do," p. 355.)
- How the money gets from the audience's pocket into yours. (See "The Money Pipeline," p. 358.)
- Common varieties of traditional distribution deals. (See "Types of Traditional Distribution Deals," p. 356.)
- How to negotiate a distribution deal. (See "Distribution Rights Acquisition Agreement," p. 362.)
- How to put your film in a theater without a distributor. (See "DIY Distribution," p. 273.)
- How to work with content aggregators to get your film on iTunes, Netflix, and other OTT platforms. (See "Content Aggregation and Over-the-Top Television," p. 379.)
- How to make money from putting your film on YouTube. (See "Making Money From YouTube," p. 387.)
- How to navigate copyright issues on YouTube. (See "YouTube and Copyright Takedowns," p. 393.)

24

PREPARING FOR DISTRIBUTION

Unless you want to make movies that are seen by only friends and family—in which case I'm not sure why you're reading this book—you need to get a solid grasp of the distribution and exhibition processes. In fact, if you're planning on making money from your movies, you really should understand this process before you even begin development.

In the broadest possible sense, distribution is the process of getting your film into the hands of exhibitors, who, in turn, will show the film to viewers. Making money from distribution, exhibition, and merchandising your film is called "exploiting your film." It is probably the one time an artist actually *wants* to be exploited.

So much has changed in this area since the first edition of the book was written: new methods of self-distribution have risen to prominence, while others have faded away. The most important change—indeed, an actual paradigm shift—has occurred as a result of widespread accessibility to digital filmmaking tools coupled with Internet-based distribution and exhibition portals like YouTube, Netflix, Hulu, and Amazon, bolstered by the seemingly endless array of social media apps to drive marketing and promotion.

For the first time in history, we are living in an age where anybody can make a feature film as long as they have a cell phone, computer, and Internet connection. It's both liberating and daunting because the only barrier to making and distributing your film is your own inertia.

In this section, we will walk through traditional methods of distribution involving film distributors. We will also spend a lot of time talking about the newer do-it-yourself (DIY) methods of film distribution and exhibition, from renting a movie theater to creating an online channel and beyond.

The hurdles you will face range from the Byzantine notice and takedown procedures of YouTube to the federal laws regarding sponsorship, head-spinning accounting provisions in distribution agreements, and the sheer amount of time and energy you must spend to even have a shot at breaking even financially. It's no exaggeration to say that this part of the filmmaking process often lasts several times longer than making the film itself. But the biggest "boss battle" you will face will be against the slacker demon of your own indolence. When faced with the incessant slog of writing social media posts to hype your film, battling yet another YouTube takedown over

DOI: 10.4324/9781003228479-32

background music you barely noticed, or weathering the seemingly endless unsuccessful attempts to land a distributor, it's all too tempting to push it aside and start a new project. After all, most of us would rather be on the set actually shooting our film than figuring out yet another way to tell our Patreon supporters why we need even *more* money to enter yet another film festival in the hopes of landing a distributor that *might* be able to get us onto Netflix.

LEGAL ISSUES IN DISTRIBUTION

Have I scared you off yet? If not, and you are the kind of filmmaker who's shouting back at the book, "Bring it on!" then let's get started.

You know you have a great film; now it's time to prove that it's a commercially viable film. And that means it needs to be more than just creative and entertaining—it also has to be a project that isn't going to get a distributor and an exhibitor sued. Even if you're going to put it on YouTube yourself, you need to be sure you won't get hit with a takedown notice shortly after upload.

And even beyond the lawsuits that can be triggered by infringed copyrights, defamation, and uncredited performers, the marketing and promotion of your film must also be compliant with the law. And when your film makes money—one can hope—you need to ensure that all of your obligations to SAG-AFTRA performers are met, such as residual payments, and your net profit participants and crewmembers have deferred their pay or are being compensated correctly.

First the good news: if you've been following along with the book so far, you should have a solid understanding of what you need to do. And many of the same tricks that you've learned already—such as copyright licensing—apply in much the same way when it comes to marketing and promotional materials.

However, we're not quite done with legal issues. Not by a long shot. So, let's take a 10,000-foot view of the legal issues in distribution and exhibition to get the lay of the land.

As your film is being finalized in post-production, you should start putting together a distribution game plan—a business plan, if you will—which will outline the steps you need to take in trying to land a distributor for your film. Even if you're planning to go straight to YouTube and not submit the film to festivals or producers' agents, you should outline the steps, schedule, and costs of how you're going to promote your project. Film festivals cost money to enter and, if you do get accepted, even more money to travel to the festival itself. Marketing materials may have to be made, from websites and trailers to handouts and business cards. Yes, I know, most promotion is done online, but distributors attend screenings at festivals to see which films they want to acquire, and having a printed one sheet with a picture of your film, names of the cast, and URL to find more information can be a very effective marketing tool.

If you are fortunate enough to attract a distributor to your film, you really should put aside money to hire a lawyer to negotiate your distribution agreement. Seriously. If you haven't negotiated a distribution agreement before, an experienced attorney can make the difference between getting paid and being sued.

"FINAL PRE-FLIGHT CHECK" TO LAUNCH

Prepping your film for distribution involves a host of technical areas, from making sure audio tracks are split correctly, cue sheets and credit info are accurate, color grading has been performed, etc. Now add to that the marketing materials you have to create to attract a distributor and the legal "pre-flight check" you need to go through. Whew! But since this is a legal guide, I'm going to leave the myriad tech and creative details to you and just dive into the legal aspects of what comes next.

Before you offer your film to a distributor, submit it to a film festival, or even host excerpts on YouTube, you need to double-check a few areas to make sure you've buttoned down any major legal risks, such as:

- **The screenplay and underlying work.** If you have written the film by yourself and not based it on any other property, this may be an easy step. If not, ensure that you have written agreements with all other authors clearly transferring to you the right to make and distribute the film. If you have based your film on another property, like a comic book, novel, short story, etc., make sure that the work you base it on is in the public domain or you have written permission from the copyright owner. Some distributors may require you to have a title search report, proof of copyright registration, and all key chain of title documents.
- **The film itself**. Make sure that you have written and signed agreements with all creative personnel clearly transferring the copyright to you and that all of your performers have signed written agreements in which they've given you permission to use their name and likeness in marketing and promotional efforts. Double-check that you are compliant with SAG-AFTRA rules. Make sure that any music you used is fully licensed and cue sheets have been prepared. The same goes for any third-party material that you use, like film clips, photographs, prominently displayed artwork, etc. Verify that your screen credits are accurate and comply with any specific obligations as to priority and other requirements, especially with respect to performers. And if you haven't done so already: register the copyright to your film!

- **Production company**. Make sure that your production company accounting is in order, especially with respect to any projects involving investors or production incentives, like tax credits. You may want to bind your E&O policy at this stage. Review any unmet payment obligations, such as cast and crew salaries, license agreements, etc.
- **Marketing materials**. You will need to create websites, flyers, trailers, and maybe even promotional giveaways before going to film festivals to try to land a distributor (See below). Make sure you have all written agreements with any graphic artists, web designers, and other creatives to help you with this part of the process. It shouldn't come as a surprise that you will need to ensure that you own the copyright to everything that they create by having them sign written agreements. And you also need to make sure that those artisans only include in your marketing materials their own work, work that is in the public domain, or work for which they have the ability to grant commercial rights to use to your production company. If none of this sounds familiar, you may want to reread the sections of the book dealing with hiring crew (See "Hiring Cast and Crew," p. 199), especially those provisions dealing with copyright, representations and warranties, and indemnification. It's a very similar contract to the one you would need those artists to sign if they worked on the film itself, but shifted into the media of marketing materials. It is especially critical that you make sure these artists don't infringe any IP rights, because marketing and advertising materials typically constitute "commercial use," which is an element against you in any copyright fair use defense you may have (See "Fair Use of Copyright," p. 433).

FILM FESTIVALS, MARKETS, AND MEETING DISTRIBUTORS

But before we can worry about negotiating a distribution agreement, we need to get a distribution company interested in our film. As anyone who has tried to land an agent can tell you, this can be an uphill battle. Fortunately, the Internet has made the process of connecting filmmakers and distributors more streamlined. Not easier, mind you—you still have the hard work of convincing a distributor to pick up your film—but there are now many more tools to facilitate this connection.

A solid route to getting your film in front of a distributor is submitting it to film *festivals* . . . and hopefully wining a category. It really does help to be able to add to your marketing materials that little olive branch-bracketed "I won this film festival" logo. However, it is the film *markets* where the commerce of film really gets going, because these yearly conventions are the beating heart of the distribution trade. Film buyers, exhibitors, producers' representatives, and filmmakers all converge for the business of buying and selling media. Fortunately, film festivals are often attached to film markets (but not always).

A SELECTION OF KEY FILM MARKETS AROUND THE WORLD

American Film Market (AFM)	https://americanfilmmarket.com/
BANFF	https://banffmediafestival.playbackonline.ca/2022/
CineMart	https://iffr.com/en
European Film Market (EFM)	https://www.efm-berlinale.de/en/home/homepage.html
Hong Kong International Film & TV Market (FILMART)	https://event.hktdc.com/fair/hkfilmart-en/Hong-Kong-International-Film---TV-Market--FILMART-/
Hot Docs	www.hotdocs.ca
Marche du Film	www.marchedufilm.com
MIPCOM	www.mipcom.com
MIPTV	www.miptv.com
TIFFCOM	https://tiffcom.jp/en

Prepping for Festival Submission

One of the best ways to enter film festivals is through the popular website filmfreeway.com, the eponymous cinema superhighway for festival submissions. Create an account, check out film festival submission requirements, enter, upload, and pay your entry fee all in one place. Just have a screenplay and not a finished film? Filmfreeway.com will guide you to all screenplay contests you can afford to enter. A great way to research new festivals and to compare notes with other filmmakers is also through the popular film education and social media website Stage32.com (full disclosure, I've taught a few online courses for them).

Note something important here: you must pay to play. Virtually every contest and festival requires you to pay an entry fee. Furthermore, many festivals and contests prohibit filmmakers from entering other festivals concurrently to theirs. Since submission costs can quickly add up, as can submission exclusivity restrictions, you need to plan out a festival submission strategy before you toss your hat in the festival ring. Some factors to consider are:

- How well known is the festival in the film industry? Does it typically get news coverage?
- Do a little Googling and find out if distributors regularly attend and whether you can find any films that were bought at the festival.
- What is the cost of entry to the festival? Can you afford to go there in person if you are accepted? Hint: it is critical to be there if you want to make contacts.

- Are the festival rewards prestigious? Do they offer money, scholarships, partnerships, etc.?
- Can you enter the festival and others at the same time? If your film has won other festivals, can you still enter the festival you're researching?

Submission Materials

Most festivals will require you to submit a combination of

- Project information.
- Production company information.
- Credit information.
- Synopsis of your film.
- Cast and crew list; SAG-AFTRA restrictions
- Project technical specifications.
- Other festivals to which the film was submitted and awards won.
- Media files: video of your film and promo photographs.

Attending a Film Festival

If you are accepted into a prestigious festival, you should go. Winning an award there is an excellent opportunity for PR through awards ceremonies, media interviews, and awards parties. One of the most important aspects of going to a film festival is it gives you the chance to network with agents, distributors, financiers, and other producers.

When you go to a film festival or market, make sure you have the following:

- A website for your film. One of the pages should be an online press kit (with a downloadable PDF of the same). Your press kit should have:
  - A synopsis of the film.
  - A video of your film or trailer.
  - Film script.
  - Publicity photos.
  - One sheet.
  - Bios of key above-the-line personnel.
  - A diversity statement if your film has a diverse cast.
  - List of any awards your film has won to date.
- A Vimeo or other only-video portal account with a link to a private screener of your film.

- Business cards with your contact info, your film's website, and a link to your film.
- You may want to invest in fun branded promotional materials (T-shirts, Frisbees, stickers, pins, etc. with your film's logo, catchphrase, or iconic image).

At the festival, you will want to try to network with distributors, sales agents, producers' representatives, other filmmakers, financiers, press, and enthusiastic fans.

Go to as many parties and events as you can. Film is a collaborative art, and you will get further if you support other filmmakers (even those competing with you)—if you go to their screenings, they and their fans will come to yours.

A SHORT GUIDE TO KEY PLAYERS IN FILM DISTRIBUTION

Distributor (also called a **buyer**)—a distributor's job is to take the film and license it to exhibitors, like television stations, movie theaters, OTT companies (Netflix, Hulu, Amazon, etc.), and others who show your film to the audience.

Producer of marketing and distribution (PMD)—a type of film producer who comes onto the project to help develop the distribution and marketing strategy.

Producer's representative (producer's rep)—producer's representatives typically act as intermediaries between the film's producer and distributors or buyers. Many distributors prefer dealing with producer's reps because of their familiarity with the current film market.

Sales agent—another link in the chain connecting film producers with distributors. Sales agents are typically extremely versatile in separating out rights and offering them in different territories.

Content aggregator—a content aggregator is a type of sales rep who specializes in bringing content to OTT platforms like Hulu, Netflix, iTunes, etc.

If You Snooze, You Lose; if You Schmooze, You Win

To "schmooze" someone is not just to talk with them, but it also combines the connotations of "networking," "socializing," and perhaps a bit of "currying favor." Not just chatting but fraternizing with an eye to business. It is an art form whose greatest masters populate the film industry. Schmoozing really comes into play when you're at cocktail parties and other social gatherings. In other words, this is not the time to walk up to somebody with a drink in their hand and start pitching them before you get to know them a little bit. It's impossible to teach the subtleties that separate "schmoozing," from "sucking up to," but I'll try to share a few tips and tricks that I find helpful:

- **Common Interests—"People like those like them"**: as every single "how to succeed in business"-style book will tell you, business is about people. Hardly profound, I know. But rather than trying to use silly tricks like repeating somebody's name three times in the conversation to show that you're engaged, try something a little more natural: engage them first as a person, try to find some commonality between you that doesn't just have to do with film, and work from there. Point being, if you view a conversation at a party as only a means to an end—that end being trying to solicit a business deal—people may find it off-putting in a semi-social setting like a film festival party. Literally try to spend a few minutes getting to know the person and having a good time with them before you bring up business. Obviously, if a distributor comes up to a party at SXSW, hands you their card and says "I want to talk you about your film," don't shift the subject and start telling them about all the good barbecue joints in Austin, Texas.
- **Numbers Game—"Know your market"**: distributors, agents, and financiers all have one thing in common: in order to be good at what they do, they know the economics of the film marketplace. The converse is also true: they may take you less seriously if you don't. That means before you talk with any of these people, you should have a really good understanding of how well films in your genre are doing at the box office and what makes your film different and more marketable than your competitors and be ready with reasonable estimates for how much it might cost to bring your film to market.
- **Appeal to Emotion—"How does your film touch them?"**: In a sense, this is the flip side of the "numbers game." Once the conversation has naturally and organically turned to your film, look for a way to set up the emotional appeal of your movie. If you directed a drama whose central emotive core is the heart-wrenching journey your protagonist goes through after divorce, look for a few ways to personify that emotion. Don't start with: "my character goes through an emotional journey after heartbreaking divorce." That's fine for a synopsis, perhaps, but it lacks emotional bite. In other words, think like a director again. Perhaps even reference a song that has the emotion you want. So, for your heartbreaking divorce drama, you might want to say something like, "the morning his wife leaves him, the cold reality of the breakup still hasn't hit our hero. He gets up, makes enough coffee for two; when he realizes his mistake, he drinks all the coffee because he knows how much his wife hated it when he wasted food."[1]
- **You Are a Marketing Tool—"Why YOU must tell the story"**: not only must the story be emotionally compelling, but you must be the right person

tell the story. What is it about your personal history that make your particular vision the one audiences will be most interested in? Are you telling the story of an underrepresented group of people of which you are a member? Does your work or life experience give you a particular authentic insight into your narrative? Remember, you're not just selling your film, you're selling yourself as the right filmmaker to have made your film. Even if you have no direct experiences linking you to the story you told—which, if you do, is the best hook—perhaps what excited you the most was the chance to tell the story in a unique and artistic way. Perhaps you wanted to tell a spy thriller by using the reality TV techniques popularized by early 2000s workplace comedies like *The Office* or *Parks and Recreation*. Do not beat yourself up here or fall into the imposter syndrome trap of thinking that you made a boring film compared everybody else. Your film would not have been accepted into the film festival in the first place if it didn't have anything to offer. Be confident that you and your film have something unique.

- **Reciprocity—"Be the resource"**: psychological testing has shown that people feel a social obligation to reciprocate when somebody does a favor for them. Here's how you can bring this into play: let's say you're talking to an agent who tells you that she's just started taking kickboxing classes and she's interested in learning more about it. In other words, something having nothing to do with the film industry. Now if you know something about kickboxing, this is a great opening for you. Offer to send her links to a very helpful kickboxing websites, perhaps a YouTube channel that you particularly like that teaches kickboxing techniques, or maybe the title of a book on the history of kickboxing that you've read. The key here is that you are happy to go a little bit out of your way to be a resource. The fact that it's not about the film industry or getting your film distributed is even better. Once you get the agent's card and send them the kickboxing information you told them about, they are likely to be much more amenable to considering your film pitch.
- **Be Shiny—"Style/uniqueness/charisma/experience counts"**: boy, do I get the stink eye sometimes when I teach this one in film schools. But I honestly believe that it is too important to leave out. Style matters in the film industry. Let me pause—I don't mean being good-looking, or even "stylish"—although those things obviously help in the real world. No, what I mean is developing an interesting style that people can identify with you and that fits your personality. If you're not the sort of person who wears suits, for goodness's sake, don't throw on a three-piece suit just to try to look cool. But it can help tremendously if there is something interesting and catchy about the way you present yourself. I've been to many Hollywood parties where people in expensive Armani suits are quite engaged by a motorcycle jacket-wearing director. If wardrobe is not your thing, you may want to get some counsel from a performer friend. Looking casual is fine; looking dirty or sloppy is not—unless you've already made it. Whatever your

style is, consider it like a trademark—people will start to associate it with you and remember you as the person with a rainbow Mohawk and "normcore" khakis. A little "peacocking" will get you a long way.

After the Festival

Even if you make a great connection with a distributor, agent, or financier, you may not be doing any negotiating with them at the festival itself (as opposed to a film market). Just get their business card and make sure to follow up quickly after the festival is over—many distributors go from festival to market several times a year, and you want to reach out to those with whom you have connected before they are on to their next port of call.

And honestly, not landing a traditional distributor is no longer the death of your film it once might've been. You can always rent a movie theater yourself (see "DIY Theatrical Distribution," p. 373) or put it online in the myriad ways available to filmmakers (see "Putting your Film Online," p. 379).

But let's be optimistic and say you've caught the eye of a distributor and now you're ready to talk about getting your film distributed by them. Now it's time to turn the page and learn a little bit about traditional distribution deals.

NOTE

[1] That particular wistful emotional beat is drawn from the Mountain Goats' song "Woke Up New." Good songs are often wonderful places to look for emotional hooks.

THEATRICAL DISTRIBUTION

WHAT FILM DISTRIBUTORS DO

Distributors "exploit" a film by licensing it in a variety of markets to exhibitors who will show it to their audiences, which could include TV viewers, theatergoers, OTT binge watchers, and old-school DVD collectors. Depending on the deal the production company negotiates, the distributor or its agents—called subdistributors—may license the film for exhibition, broadcast, or sale in the following markets:

- Theatrical: movie theatres.
- Free television: broadcast television, as opposed to cable.
- Pay television: cable, satellite, pay-per-view, on-demand.
- Over-the-top television: programming exhibited via online portals and their downloads, such as Netflix, Hulu, Amazon Prime, etc.
- Mobile devices: through Google play, the iTunes Store, etc.
- Home video: sales of the film via Blu-ray or DVD.
- Commercial video: distribution of Blu-ray or videocassettes for public exhibition.
- Airline: in-flight movies.
- Ships: public exhibition aboard ships.
- Hotel/hospitality: hotel and motel closed-circuit television.
- Educational: distribution via cable, closed circuit, or satellite for school exhibition.
- Military: exhibition on military bases.

In addition to placing films with exhibitors, distributors may also want to rep the underlying property rights in a film (although many filmmakers want to hold onto those rights or have them represented by more specialized agents in certain areas). In addition to the right to distribute the film, distributors may also want to help license the following rights in the finished film:

- Television series rights.
- Sequels/prequels/"in-universe" derivatives.

DOI: 10.4324/9781003228479-33

- Merchandising: toys, clothing, games, role-playing games, etc.
- Videogames.
- Amusement park attractions.
- Legitimate theater: plays and musicals.
- Soundtracks.
- Books and comic books.

To do these deals, distributors attend film and television markets (e.g. MIPCOM, American Film Market, European Film Market, etc.) where they promote the films in their catalog with an eye towards licensing them to the exhibitors who attend. In fact, promotion, advertising, and marketing is a big part of what the distributor does for film. They will typically create movie posters, television commercials, and localized versions of the film for the markets in which they're placed. But not every distributor has contacts in every territory where the films will be shown, so many work with *subdistributors* who are specialists in a particular region (e.g. Oceania, North Africa, Latin America, etc.).

As you might imagine, both distributors and subdistributors need to be compensated, and the expenses for promotion, marketing, prints, localization, editing and graphics, postage, and virtually every other expense that can be directly tied to the promotion and marketing of your film are typically deducted from the money that the film makes. Not surprisingly, understanding how and when your production company will be paid is a big part of evaluating whether a particular distribution deal will work for you.

TYPES OF TRADITIONAL DISTRIBUTION DEALS

There are several common types of traditional distribution deals (DIY distribution is discussed in the next chapter):

- *Production-financing/distribution agreement* (also known as a *PF/D agreement*). Here a distributor with a studio division (or a production studio with a distribution division) is the primary source of production funding. The distributor/studio usually steps in after the producer has presented it with an already developed and packaged project. Because the distributor/studio company is putting up the funds, it almost always retains all rights in the film.
- *Negative pickup agreement*. This is similar to the PF/D agreement in that the distributor's money is enabling the production to be funded; however, in this scenario, the distributor does not advance the money. Instead, the distributor agrees to pay the production costs and expenses if the film meets certain delivery requirements. This contractual guarantee from the distributor is used by the producer to secure a loan from a bank or group

of investors. And because the lender wants to make sure that the film will be made no matter what, the lender will almost always insist upon a *completion guarantee*. When a completion guarantor is brought on board, the project runs the risk of being produced and directed by somebody else if there's a cost overrun.

- *Pre-sale*. This is a limited distribution agreement in which the distributor promises to pay the production company (upon delivery of the film) for the right to distribute the film in a certain territory. It's not typically offered to first-time producers without a track record.
- *Distribution rights acquisition agreement*. In this scenario, the producer comes to the distributor with an already finished film, and the distributor advances the money to market, distribute, and exploit the film. The distribution rights acquisition agreement is, hands down, the most common type of deal available to independent producers without a prior track record; the distributor is not being asked to fund the film, merely to distribute it. Because the distributor's risk is lower than it would be under a negative pickup or PF/D deal (see earlier point), a distributor may be more likely to give a new producer a chance. After all, the distributor can look at the film itself to see whether it is marketable.

There are several ways a producer is typically paid under the distribution rights acquisition agreement. The payment model the producer ends up with is a subject of negotiation with the distributor:

1. *Royalty deal*. The distributor absorbs all marketing, promotion, and distribution expenses and any advances paid to the producer; it then pays the producer a royalty. For example, if the distributor is only acquiring Blu-ray rights, it would pay the producer a royalty on the wholesale price (perhaps 15–25%) of each Blu-ray it sells to the retailer or video rental company. This deal can benefit the producer if the costs to bring the film to market are high because a producer receives some money regardless of the distributor's expenses; the downside is that if the film is an indie success, the producer is still only getting a 25% royalty.
2. *50/50 net deal*. The distributor receives money from the film's exploitation; deducts any advances paid to the producer, marketing, promotion, and distribution expenses; and splits the rest with the producer 50/50. With this deal, the filmmaker gets more money if the film is a hit—50% of the proceeds after expenses. The flip side is that distributor's expenses can take a big bite out of the proceeds of a film with lackluster sales.
3. *Distribution fee*. Here the distributor receives money from the film's exploitation, deducts a distribution fee (perhaps 35%), then deducts any advances paid to the producer, marketing, promotion, and distribution expenses. The remainder is given to the producer. For details on this popular financial model, see "How Does the Money Get From a Movie Theater to the Producer?" p. 358.

THE THEATRICAL DISTRIBUTION MONEY PIPELINE

DISTRIBUTION FINANCIAL TERMS

- *Distributor's gross rentals.* The money received by the distributor for renting the film to theatrical exhibitors for movie house exhibition.
- *Distributor's gross receipts/distributor revenue.* Collectively, all the monies the distributor receives through film rentals, television licensing, Blu-ray sales, and any other income stream related to the film property.
- *Distributor's fee/distribution fee.* The fee a distributor charges for its services. This is typically a percentage of the distributor's gross receipts before expenses are deducted.
- *Distribution expenses.* Costs a distributor incurs for distributing the film property. It typically includes marketing, prints, advertising, promotional, and other costs.
- *Subdistributor fee.* A fee charged by a subdistributor hired by the main distributor to exploit the film property, usually in foreign markets.
- *Prints and ads (P&A).* The costs of making copies of the film to distribute to the exhibitors plus the costs of advertising the film.
- *Film's net profits/producer's gross.* The monies remaining after the distributor has taken its fee and has been repaid its expenses. This money is then paid directly to the production company and is usually the level from which the investors and net profit participants draw their payments. (See also "Net Profits," p. 66.)
- *Negative cost.* The cost of actually getting the finished film in the can (but not the advertising, prints, or marketing expenses).
- *Production company's net profits.* Any money that is left over from the film's net profits after the production company has paid investors and net profit participants, deferred salaries, costs of producing and promotion the film, and other costs of doing business.

HOW DOES THE MONEY GET FROM A MOVIE THEATER TO THE PRODUCER?

Let's say that a distributor wants to put your movie in theaters. How does the money from ticket sales get from the audience's wallets into yours? As you may imagine, it all depends on the kind of deal that you've been offered. So, let's assume that you have a theatrical distribution rights acquisition deal in which the distributor is taking a fee (see earlier discussion), and let's follow the money.

Movie Audience

1. *Moviegoer* pays for ticket. A theater's ticket sales from a particular movie are its *box office receipts*; the total ticket sales of a movie become the *box office gross.*

Movie Theater (Exhibitor) Takes Its Cut

2. *Exhibitors* (movie theaters) first deduct an agreed-upon amount, called the *house nut*, from their box office receipts to cover their overhead. The balance after the house nut is deducted is called the *exhibitor's net.* During the first week or two of the movie's run, the distributor may get as much as 90% of the exhibitor's net. Each successive week of the movie's run, the distributor's share is reduced, and the exhibitor's share is increased. Over the run of the film, the distributor may receive between 25% and 65% of the exhibitor's net, with the average being close to 43%. The distributor's share of the exhibitor's net is called the *distributor's rentals.* It is important to note that any money from concessions—candy, popcorn, soda—is kept by the exhibitor and not shared with the distributor.

   The monies actually given to the distributor may be lower than the contractually obligated amount due to *settlement transactions*, which are negotiated reductions in the monies paid to the distributor. Settlement transactions are based on a number of factors, including the film's box office performance, how many other films by the distributor are being shown by that exhibitor, and cooperative advertising obligations between the exhibitor and the distributor.

Distributor Takes Its Cut

3. The money that the distributor receives from the exhibitors is called the *gross rentals.* This sum, plus other sums from the exploitation of other rights (television, video, cable, etc.) granted under the distribution contract, make up the *distributor's gross receipts.*
4. The distributor may exclude from its definition of gross receipts items such as advances to the producer and monies not collected (*distributor exclusions*). The gross receipts minus the exclusions become the *distributor's adjusted gross receipts* (although the distributor may still call it the *distributor's gross receipts*).

5. The distributor takes its *distribution fee*, typically between 20% and 40% of the *distributor's adjusted gross receipts*.
6. *Subdistribution fees* are then deducted, especially in foreign markets. *Watch out here*—make sure that your distribution company doesn't charge you for its full distribution fee in a market where you are paying a subdistribution fee.
7. *Distributor's expenses* are then deducted, such as the following:
   - *Direct distribution expenses*. All costs associated with the advertising, exploitation, marketing, and distribution of the film. Some of the biggest expenses are:
     - Prints.
     - Advertising and publicity.
   - Any money advanced by the distributor to pay for the film's deliverables.

***CAUTION!:* The distributor may try to include expenses for overhead. Overhead is the distributor's cost of doing business not directly attributable to your film, such as rent, insurance, salaries, and so on.**

8. *Union residuals* are paid if the distributor has signed an assumption agreement. *Note:* If the production company is a SAG-AFTRA signatory, it must have the distribution company sign an *assumption agreement*. (See "Assumption Agreement," p. 252.)
9. *Other costs*. Depending on the deal, other costs will be deducted at different stages:
   - Taxes.
   - Interest.
   - Collection costs.
   - Distributers may also want to deduct anticipated expenses. Try to cap this or eliminate it altogether.

Production Company Is Paid

10. *Remainder* is passed on to the production company, along with the remainder from the other revenue streams from all distributors and licensees, and becomes the *producer's gross*, a.k.a. the film's net profits. (See "Net Profits," p. 66.)

Production Company Pays

11. The order in which the production company pays the following is defined by the "waterfall" provision in the financing documents with the film's financiers.

- Creditors are typically repaid first. Remember, these are not investors but people to whom you have an absolute obligation to repay regardless of whether the film makes money.
- The film financiers are paid near the top, plus their "premium"—the profit they make for their investment in the film—this is usually 10–20% of the amount that they invested and perhaps 50% of the film's future profits after the breakeven point.
- SAG-AFTRA. However, if the distribution company did not sign an assumption agreement, or if there is no distribution company, the production company may have to pay SAG-AFTRA *residuals* per its union agreements (unless they have been paid by the distributor).
- The *negative cost* of the film (i.e., the costs of producing the film), if the producer or production company were the only financiers.
- *Deferred salaries*. (See Appendix B, "Deferred Compensation," p. 478.)
- The production company's *profit participants* (e.g. writers, actors, director, etc.) are paid. (See "Net Profits," p. 66.)
- *Overhead* and other costs of doing business.
- Any monies remaining become the *production company's net profits*.

Keep in mind that this revenue map only emphasizes monies coming in from one distributor's theatrical exploitation. Ideally, the production company will have additional revenues from other markets, such as home video, television broadcast, merchandising, and the like.

Theatrical Distribution Money Pipeline

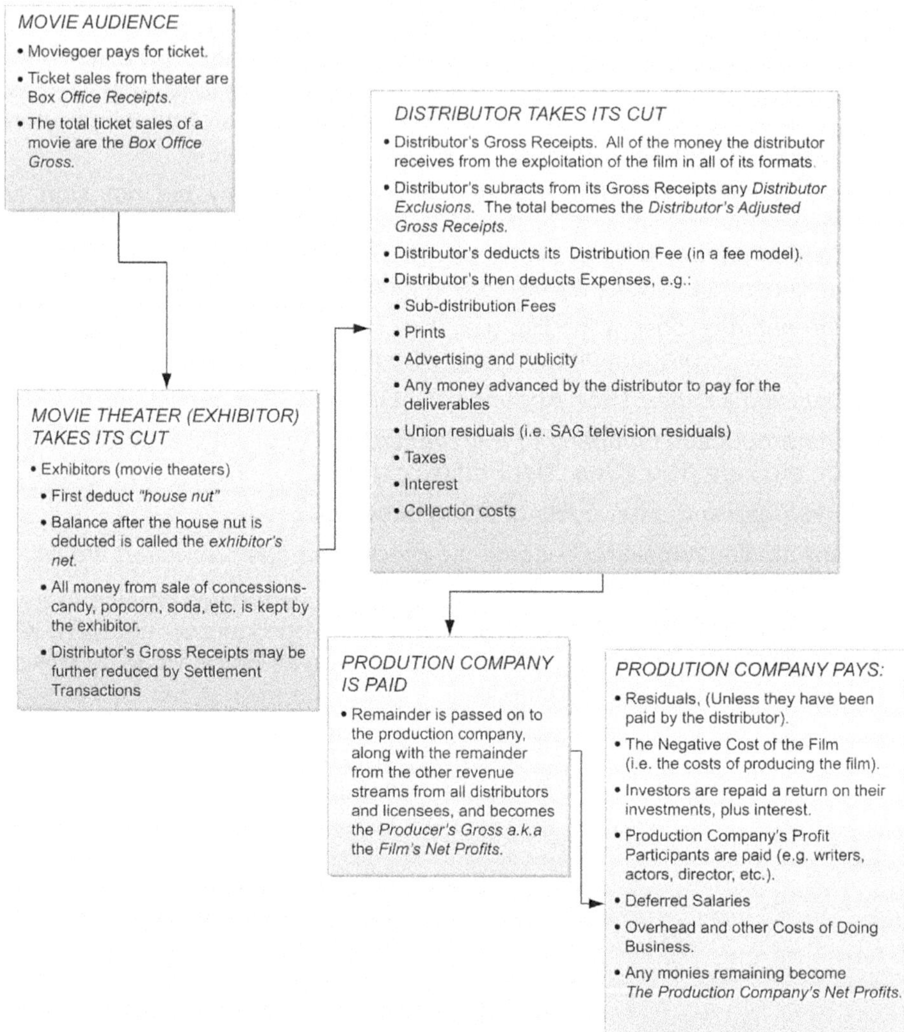

DISTR.

DISTRIBUTION RIGHTS ACQUISITION AGREEMENT (DISTRIBUTOR'S FEE DEAL)

Goals and Deals

The distribution agreement may be the single most important document to a producer trying to make money from their film. This is the document that controls how the film makes money.

The distribution agreement controls the grant of the distribution rights and specifies the places, duration, and scope of this copyright license. The agreement's terms control key aspects of how the film is exploited, for starters:

- When, where, in what media, and for how long a distributor has the license to distribute the film.
- How and when a producer gets paid.
- What rights the producer can still license to others.

For definitions and explanations of common contract clauses, see Appendix B, "The Clause Companion," p. 475.

MAJOR DEAL POINTS: DISTRIBUTION AGREEMENT

The distribution agreement is the contract governing the relationship between the distributor, who exploits the film, and the production company, which created the film. The following pages outline a distribution agreement where the distributor is taking a *fee*.

The Parties

- *Production company*. The production company is seeking a distributor with the ability to license the film effectively in certain territories. All distributors have their strengths and weaknesses: for instance, many distributors are better at exploiting domestic rights than international rights. It may be in a producer's best interest to split the rights among several distributors, each exploiting the property in its own individual territory.
- *Distributor*. The distributor, on the other hand, will probably want to acquire as many rights as it can from the production company. After all, it figures that if it doesn't have the contacts to distribute the property in one market, it can always bring in a subdistributor who can. Additionally, the distributor may be able to offset losses from one market against gains in another, a practice known as *cross-collateralization*.

Rights Granted

- **Rights granted**. This clause defines specific rights being granted to the distributor. It typically grants the right to distribute, exhibit, market, exploit, advertise, publicize, and manufacture copies of the film.
- **Media and markets**. Also included here are media and markets with respect to which the distributor can distribute the film. (See "What Traditional Film Distributors Do," p. 355.)

- **Advertising rights**. The distributor needs the right to create trailers, commercials, and other promotional materials.
- **Regionalization**. The distributor needs the right to edit the film to meet with the censorship laws of a particular country or to dub the film into another language. However, any editing rights provision should be carefully worded to avoid giving the distributor any right to edit the picture solely for creative reasons.

Reserved Rights

The rights not granted to the distributor should be reserved to the producer. Such rights often include:

- Print publication.
- Merchandising.
- Radio and stage.

Exclusivity

- The distributor will typically insist on being the exclusive distributor of the film with respect to the rights granted within the specified territories for the specified term.
- Sometimes Internet, VOD, PPV, streaming video, and similar distribution methods will be granted on a nonexclusive basis.

Term

- The *term* is the length of time that the distributor will have the rights granted to it.
- Distributors will want a "perpetual" term. However, it is to the production company's advantage to avoid having the film locked up with a distributor that might not be performing well. The production company should try to obtain a limited initial term of two to three years, during which time the distributor must meet certain financial thresholds in terms of gross receipts from the exploitation of the film. If these thresholds are not met, the production company should be given the right to cancel the contract. If the threshold is met, the distributor should be given an option to renew the distribution contract for a longer period of time—for instance, ten years.
- *Be careful of rights being granted beyond the term of the distribution agreement.* For instance, if the distributor has the power to subdistribute and sell the rights, the filmmaker can be bound by a contract that exceeds the term of the original distribution agreement. This happens if, toward the

end of the term of the distribution contract with the production company, the distributor enters into an agreement with a subdistributor. This new subdistributor agreement might have a new term that extends beyond the term of the original agreement between the distributor and the production company.

- Production companies may want to limit the ability of the distributor to enter into an agreement like this by capping the term of such a subdistribution agreement so that it cannot extend more than five to seven years beyond the term of the original agreement between the production company and the distributor.

Territories

- The *territory* is the geographic area within which the distributor may exploit the film.
- It is not uncommon for one distributor to handle domestic distribution and another to handle international distribution (called a *split rights deal*). Split rights deals actually help producers; splitting up the territories prevents a single distributor from cross-collateralizing between a poorly performing domestic market and a lucrative foreign market. Even distributors who insist on capturing both domestic and international distribution rights usually work with subdistributors who distribute the film in other markets.
- Producers may want to try to set territorial minimums for the distributor. The effect of these minimums is to require the distributor to seek a producer's written approval prior to accepting a deal that would bring in less than the agreed-on territorial minimum.

Advertising and Promotion

- If pushed, distributors may agree to consult with the production company regarding key art in the ad campaign and marketing strategy for the film, but they will usually insist on having final approval.
- The production company should reserve the right to approve (rather than consult on) the performers' bios, performer's pictures, and appearance of the credits in all paid ads and should in turn obligate the distributor to comply with all of the production's written credit, likeness, and promotional requirements with its writers, performers, crew, and licensors.

Allocation of Proceeds

This paragraph can be lengthy; it sets out who and what gets paid before the producer receives their share. (See "The Money Pipeline," p. 358.)

- Typically, the *gross receipts* represent all the monies taken by the distributor for the exploitation of a particular film.
- The distributor then computes its *distribution fee* based on a percentage of the distributor's adjusted gross receipts. This fee typically ranges from 20% to 40%.
- After the distributor computes its fee, it recoups its marketing and promotional expenses, advances to the producer, and interest. (See the following section, "Distributor's Recoupable Expenses.") The producer should insist on a fairly detailed list of recoupable expenses, coupled with financial caps on certain expenses.
- The remaining money then becomes the *producer's gross*, which, from the investor's and net profit participant's point of view, is the film's net profits.

Distributor's Recoupable Expenses

These are the expenses the distributor is allowed to recoup prior to distributing the producer's gross. Typical recoupable expenses include:

- Advertising and promotional expenses, such as preparing posters, trailers, one-sheets, commercials, and so forth.
- Expenses for taking the film-to-film markets for its first year.
- Prints, Blu-ray, and other manufacturing expenses directly related to producing copies of the film.

Be *very* careful here! When structuring the deal:

- Provide a minimum and maximum the distributor can spend on ads and promotions.
- Make sure to cap the distributor's expenses for going to markets so that your film does not end up paying for more than its fair share of the distributor's market costs.
- Limit all the distributor's expenses to actual, verifiable, third-party "out-of-pocket" expenses.

Advance

The filmmaker should push very hard for any advance; this may be the only money a production company actually sees. As a result, the production company should be wary of giving away any rights without first receiving a nonrefundable advance from the distributor.

Distributor's Right to Package Film Property

- The distribution company will probably want the right to package the film with other films, thus offering a sort of bulk discount to exhibitors. The production company should try to make sure that in a package sale, the distributor can license the film for no less than a prespecified minimum.

- Make sure that in any package deal, the amount of money allocated to your film is specified in writing and is computed according to a reasonable formula.

Credit

- The distributor will negotiate the language and placement of its own credit.
- The distributor must be obligated to adhere to all credit provisions in the producer's contract with third parties, such as actors, directors, musicians, and so forth.

Default

- Prior to termination, the injured party is usually obligated to serve notice of default to the defaulting party, giving the defaulting party a reasonable time with which to cure the problem (e.g., 30 days).
- The production company should insist that if the distributor defaults on the contract and does not cure the default, the contract may be terminated by the production company and all rights under the contract will then revert back to the production company. The production company would then be free to seek out another distributor.

Notice

This paragraph is fairly straightforward and lists the parties and representatives, such as attorneys and agents, to whom notice must be delivered.

Audit Rights

- The audit is typically conducted at the production company's or its profit participants' expense unless the audit uncovers a discrepancy of 5% or more, in which case the distribution company or its profit participants should have to pay for the audit.
- The production company usually only has the right to audit once a year and may be required to give 30 days' notice of an audit.

Production Company's Representations and Warranties

The production company usually promises that:

- The production company owns a valid copyright to the film and nothing in the film infringes any intellectual property or other rights of third parties.

- The production company will safeguard its copyrights and other rights needed to exploit and license the film property.
- The production company is responsible for and has secured all rights, licenses, and permissions to any music contained in the film property. The distributor will make it the production company's obligation to pay any music-licensing royalties and other fees.
- The film has not been previously distributed or exhibited in the territory, with the exception of film festivals.
- The production company will promise to pay for all production costs, including deferred payments, residuals, and royalties.
- The production company is under no other obligations that would prevent it from performing its obligations under this contract.
- This clause typically contains an indemnity provision that obligates the production company to indemnify the distribution company for any breaches of the representations and warranties or other breaches of the agreement. (See Appendix B, "Indemnification," p. 488.)

The Distribution Company's Representations and Warranties

The distribution company should promise that:

- It is not on the verge of bankruptcy and can pay all its bills.
- There are no lawsuits or pending claims that would interfere with the distribution company distributing the film property and performing its duties under the contract.
- All work done on the marketing and advertising campaign will be done as a work made for hire.
- Because the distributor is able to recoup the costs of producing these materials, the production company should try to negotiate a provision that states the marketing and ad materials become the property of the production company at the expiration of the term of the distribution agreement.
- That it will comply with all credit, likeness approval, photographic, and biographic obligations for which the production is obligated, provided that the production company has provided the distribution company with copies of those provisions.
- The distribution company will use its best efforts to exploit, promote, and distribute the film property.
- This paragraph should contain an indemnity provision that obligates the distribution company to indemnify the production company for any breaches of the representations and warranties or other breaches of the agreement.

Deliverables

- The exact date of delivery of the film and other materials to the distribution company is the *delivery date*.
- The *deliverables* are the film and other materials that the production company must deliver to the distributor. The list can be exhaustive and includes both physical and legal materials. Make sure there's enough money in the budget to pay for all the deliverables the distribution company will require.

The deliverables usually are separated into two categories:

- *Physical deliverables*. These are items related to the manufacture of copies of the film and its publicity and exploitation. The distributor will need all the elements to make copies of the film, television commercials, trailers, posters, censored versions of the film, and so forth. Such physical deliverables often include:
  - The completed film's negative.
  - The film soundtrack, with dialogue on a separate track from the other audio.
  - Music and effects track.
  - If shooting actual film: access to the original film negative and interpositive and internegative prints.
  - Video masters with separated tracks.
  - Photographs.
  - Music cue sheets.
  - Title sheets.
  - Medium-specific copies, including versions for broadcast television and in-flight movies.
  - Copies of the film's script.
- *Legal and business deliverables*. These are items that prove the producer has both the ownership of the film and the rights necessary to exploit it. Legal and business deliverables often include:
  - Copyright title search reports.
  - All cast and crew contracts.
  - Separate credit requirements.
  - All copyright and trademark licenses and clearances.
  - Laboratory access letters.
  - All publicity restrictions.
  - Music licenses and composer agreements.

- Copyright chain of title materials.
- E&O policy listing the distributor as an additional insured.

Assignment

The production company must always have the right to assign the proceeds it receives from the distributor. The distributor should not be able to assign the contract without the production company's prior written permission.

Errors and Omissions Insurance

If the production company has E&O insurance, the distribution company will want to be added as an additional insured.

♦♦♦♦♦

LAW: COPYRIGHT ISSUES

The distributor might want to investigate your film's chain of title pretty thoroughly. Be prepared to supply the following:

- All contracts pertaining to the film property. These include screenplay agreements, literary rights acquisition agreements, life rights consents, and assignments of all the copyrights in and to the film property to the production company. (See "The Film Property," p. 25.)
- All service contracts of creative personnel, especially performers, writers, directors, and musicians. The key here is that all these contracts should contain adequate work-made-for-hire provisions. (See "Work Made for Hire," p. 418.) In addition to copyright, these contracts should also grant to the production company all the other necessary rights, such as rights of publicity, waiver of defamation claims, and so forth, needed to exploit the film.
- Proof of copyright registrations and recordation of assignments. (See "Copyright Registration," p. 164.)
- Credits will be checked to make sure that they comply with the production company's contractual obligations.
- Financing documents and documents creating a security interest in the film.

Under copyright law, the owner of a copyrighted work has the exclusive right to distribute that work. Without a copyright license from the film's owner, distribution of the film is copyright infringement. In the distribution agreement, the copyright owner grants to the distributor the exclusive right to distribute and exploit the film. Because a distribution agreement is a document that "pertains to a copyright," it may be registered with the US Copyright Office. (See "Copyright Recordation, Assignments and Transfers," p. 168.) Recording all transfers and licenses of copyright ownership preserves a clean chain of title. (See "Chain of Title," p. 159; Copyright Circular 12 on the US Copyright website for more information: www.copyright.gov/circs/circ12.pdf.)

Lab Access Letter

If you are actually shooting film, the distributor will also require permission from the production company to deal directly with the film laboratory or video duplication house responsible for producing copies of the film. This is usually done in the form of a *laboratory access letter* in which the production company grants to the distributor the right to access the copies and to order more on account.

***CAUTION!* THIS IS WHY YOU NEED CLEARANCES**

A distributor needs to know that it has very little chance of being sued when it sells the film to exhibitors and broadcasters. Accordingly, permissions and clearances are a central component of the producer/distributor agreement. As part of every distribution contract, the producer must represent and warrant to the distributor that all the intellectual property rights in the film or video have been cleared and that there are no pending or anticipated legal claims created by the film or video. (See "Copyright Searches and Permissions," p. 159.) The producer also indemnifies the distributor for any misrepresentations of the representations and warranties. (See Appendix B, "Indemnification," p. 488; "Representations and Warranties," p. 482.)

As a result, if the distributor is sued for IP infringement, the distributor now has the right to look to the producer of the allegedly infringing film or video to cover any money damages and costs that arise from such lawsuits.

Example: One scene in Max Mogul's film was shot inside a museum's sculpture garden. Unfortunately, Max never secured copyright licenses to photograph all the sculptures. Now both he and his distributor are hit with a copyright infringement lawsuit from an irate artist. Because of his distribution contract, Max must cover *both* his own and the distributor's legal costs of defending against the suit.

Assumption Agreement

If your production company is a SAG-AFTRA signatory (see "SAG-AFTRA," p. 243), you are required by the terms of your signatory agreement to ensure that a distributor sign an *assumption agreement*. In this agreement, the distributor assumes the obligations of paying performer residuals directly to SAG-AFTRA. A signed copy of the assumption agreement must then be delivered to SAG-AFTRA.

BUSINESS ISSUES: DISTRIBUTOR'S EXPENSES

Because distributors may deduct their expenses prior to paying the production company, the expenses that a distributor may be allowed to deduct should be carefully defined. Care should be taken to expressly limit the distribution company's ability to include any overhead within the recoupable expenses. When negotiating with the distributor, you should argue that because the distributor is taking a distribution fee, it is from that fee the distributor should pay for its ordinary costs of doing business. Only verifiable out-of-pocket expenses should be deducted.

Reread Your Talent Agreements

Before the film is publicized, exploited, or distributed, it pays to read your talent agreements. (See "Performer's Services Agreement," p. 256.) Double-check your agreements for:

- *Any publicity restrictions or likeness approvals* you may have given to the talent. Movie posters can create big problems if they are created without attention to a performer's likeness approval clause.
- *Credit and billing obligations*. Find out which performer's names must appear in paid advertising, how large the names need to be, in what order they must appear, and so on.
- *Publicity obligations*. Work with performer's agents in arranging screening and publicity events.

Film's Net Profits

The producer's gross receipts from the distributor may be the same thing as the film's net profits as far as your investors and net profit participants are concerned. When you negotiate an investor's or net profit participant's contract, be sure to define the film's net profits as monies actually received from the distributor(s) for the exploitation of the film, pursuant to the distribution agreement with the respective distributors. It follows, then, that investors and other net profit participants might want to include clauses in their contracts allowing them to examine the distributor's accounting records for the film.

DIY THEATRICAL DISTRIBUTION

If you can't land a theatrical distributor, you can still get your movie into a theater. Although it can be the most expensive form of do-it-yourself distribution, there is nothing like sitting down in that red-cushioned seat, bucket of popcorn on your lap, and watching your film flicker to life on the silver screen. *Now* it's a movie! But theatrical distribution has additional benefits beyond greasy popcorn and self-gratification:

- Until the COVID-19 pandemic hit in 2020, theatrical distribution in Los Angeles was a requirement for a film to be considered for Academy Awards nomination: "Current Academy Awards rules (under Rule Two, Eligibility) require that a film be shown in a commercial motion picture theater in Los Angeles County for a theatrical qualifying run of at least seven consecutive days, during which period screenings must occur at least three times daily."[1] When the pandemic receded, other big cities were added to the list of qualifying locations (the City of New York; the Bay Area; Chicago, Illinois; Miami, Florida; and Atlanta, Georgia), but theatrical distribution was still on the requirements list.
- When you exhibit your film in a major city, you are more likely to interest other theaters in showing your film and distributors in selling it.
- A film with a theatrical run (not just a premiere) is eligible to be included in the Internet Movie Database (IMDB.com).

Booking a Theater

There are generally two ways a DIY-distributed film makes it to a theater: via a *film booker* or via the filmmaker herself.

- *Film bookers* (*a.k.a. movie booking agents*). Although they are technically agents, film bookers can be thought of as theatrical distributors for hire. You pay them a monthly fee (or a fee based on theaters booked), and they try to interest theaters in showing your film. Bookers can be expensive, with fees of thousands of dollars per month. Their contracts often require the filmmaker to utilize their services for a contractually specified minimum number of months. However, bookers have solid relationships with theaters and theater chains and can often place films when a filmmaker has struck out. Keep in mind that, like theatrical agents, bookers serve a "gatekeeper" function and often have to be convinced that your film will bring in an audience before they will work with you.

When the theater is interested in your film, the film booker negotiates the *theatrical exhibition agreement* with that theater, hopefully trying to get you the highest percentage of the box office revenue she can. The film booker negotiates the *commitment*—the number of weeks the theater is obligated to show your film. Theaters often require the option of extending the commitment of a film that performs well and the ability to cancel a run due to poor performance; a skilled film booker will know how to negotiate and set limits to both of these options. Finally, once the film is booked and the contract negotiated, the booker oversees the task of getting the physical film into theaters for exhibition.

- *Self-booking.* If you can't afford a booker, you may try to keep the DIY theme going and book theaters by yourself. Without connections from a distributor, sales agent, or booker, this can be difficult, although it helps if your film has won awards at film festivals, is about an extremely topical subject, or features a well-known actor.

  Basically, there are two kinds of deals you can expect to work out with an interested theater:

  - *Percentage of the box office. This* is the deal you probably want: The theater pays you a percentage of the ticket sales (usually between 25% and 65%) for your film during its run. If you're a filmmaker who has yet to establish a core following, be prepared for the theater to ask for a *minimum guarantee* against your percentage. In other words, if your film does not make at least the minimum guaranteed amount from ticket sales, you are responsible for paying the minimum amount to the theater.

    Example: Drago's new film, *The Way of the Wimpy Warrior*, has been booked for a one-week run at Spooler Cinema. The theatrical exhibition agreement specifies a minimum guarantee against the box office of $7,000. Unfortunately, the film's lackluster performance has generated only $6,500 in box office receipts by the end of the week. Instead of making money from the run, Drago now owes the theater $500 ($7,000 – $6,500 = $500)!

    You will also have some expenses: generally, theaters will require the distribution company (you, in this scenario) to spend at least a contractually specified amount of money on local adverting (print ads, television commercials, radio spots). Additionally, they may require that you hire a PR firm to help bring your film to the attention of film reviewers.

  - *Four wall.* Also known as "rent-a-theater" distribution, because you do just that: You rent the four walls of the theater and pretty much everything between them. For one fee, you hire the theater, the projectionist, the ticket taker, and so on. Unlike a percentage of the box office deal, you get to keep all the ticket sales (and you can charge as much as you want for those tickets). The catch is that you need to pay the rental fee for showing your film, and that fee can range from $10,000 to $20,000 per week in larger metropolitan areas.

Example: Drago decides to gamble with *The Way of the Wimpy Warrior* by placing it in a major metropolitan theater under a "four wall" agreement. Now he's paying the theater up front—$10,000 for the week. To maximize his chances for success, he's done a lot of advanced advertising and promotion, secured a favorable review in a local paper, and given his cast and crew enough time to send e-mail blasts to all their friends and family. His promotion has paid off: The film pulls in a lucky $13,000. Unlike last time, now he gets to keep all this money. Drago has made $3,000 ($13,000 – $10,000 = $3,000). Even better, the theater management is so impressed with the movie's success that they decide to book it for the next three weeks under a percentage of the box office agreement.

THE FOUR-WALL AGREEMENT

Parties

The company that owns the movie theater will be one party to the contract. The producer or the production company will be the other.

Engagement

This section lays out the fact that the relationship is a "four-wall" relationship (in other words, you're renting the theater). It also specifies the specific dates on which the movie will be shown. A typical movie run is one week; make sure to specify how many times that film must be run within a week. Also include the minimum number of runs per day your movie must have. Typically, you will get to specify the movie times when your movie will be shown. You may also want to specify the format in which the film is to be shown (make sure the theater can handle the media your movie is on), as well as the particular screening room, if the movie theater houses more than one.

Services

Be as detailed as you can about the specific services the theater will provide you, including the provision of managers, ushers, cashiers, cleaning crew, and, of course, the projectionist. The exhibitor should also agree to set your film up for advanced ticket purchases online. If you plan to do a Q&A session afterward, you should specify that the theater will remain open during that time.

Four-Wall Fee

This is the amount of money that you will have to pay the theater. Make sure you understand all of the costs involved. Typically, the theater sets the rental fee, which includes the staff salaries, cleanup fees, utilities, and so on. In other words, you should be paying a flat fee for the week that your film is shown there. Confirm that no concession stand costs are being charged to you, since the typical four-wall arrangement allows the theater to keep all the money made on concessions.

Box-Office Receipts/Income

This section specifies that you get to keep all the money from your movie's ticket sales (a.k.a. box office receipts). *Be careful here:* If the movie theater includes a provision in which they take a portion of the box-office proceeds, then it is not a four-wall agreement but rather a very bad percentage of the box-office deal. Be sure to include a deadline by which you must receive the box-office proceeds. Many theaters ask producers to wait 30 days before they get the money from the ticket sales. Try to negotiate immediate and complete payment upon conclusion of the movie's run; that way, when the film leaves, so do you and your money. Ask for an accounting provision to be included in the contract as well so that you can double-check that the theater has given you all the money that you are due. (See Appendix B, "Audit and Accounting Provision," p. 485.)

Publicity and Advertising

The theater should agree to place your movie posters and lobby cards (which you will need to supply) in its theater, place your movie title on the marquee, and run your movie's ad in the entertainment section of the local newspaper, along with the other movies it's showing. You should also try to get the theater to agree to show your movie trailer before its other films in advance of your movie's exhibition dates.

Shipping Costs

The producer always pays for the costs of shipping the film to and from the theater.

Rights and Permissions

The producer grants the theater the right to exhibit the film during the engagement period as well as the rights to advertise and promote the film in the theater's newspaper advertisements.

Representations and Warranties

The producer typically promises that the film is a certain running time, that nothing in the film will infringe any rights, is obscene or libelous, and that the filmmaker has secured all rights and permissions necessary for the theater to exhibit the film. The theater company should promise that the theater will be clean and operable and that it complies with all safety codes. (See Appendix B, "Representations and Warranties," p. 482.) Both sides should indemnify each other for any damages they cause to each other. (See Appendix B, "Indemnification," p. 488.)

Four-Wall Tips and Tricks

- Use a well-established theater. Part of what will draw your crowd is the reputation of the movie house.
- Know what film formats the theater supports. The last thing you need is to lose a day of your movie's run while they transfer your film into another format they support and charge you for the transfer.
- Make sure you are aware of all the costs. When you're four-walling, you shouldn't have to pay additional fees for a projectionist, ticket seller, or usher. These should all be included.
- Four-walling a film used to be the sign of a potentially bad film—the rationale being that if a film couldn't attract a distributor, it wouldn't attract an audience. This perception has started to change: As more and more people are making movies, the sheer number of films on the market means that many good films aren't able to attract theatrical distributors. Although four-walling your film no longer has the stigma it once did, it's usually not something you want to advertise. The public doesn't need to know that you are renting the theater; they just need to know what your film is about and when they can see it.
- If you are going to incur the expense of four-walling, you must put in the money to promote it. What good is having a rented theater if you can't fill the seats with interested patrons? One of the most important things you can do is get your film reviewed. Hold a press screening early or send links to your film to local film critics, along with a digital press kit.

NOTE

[1] www.oscars.org/news/awards-rules-and-campaign-regulations-approved-93rd-oscarsr (Accessed June 2, 2021).

PUTTING YOUR FILM ONLINE

ONLINE EVERY TIME

Even if you go with the traditional distributor, your film will undoubtedly end up online at some point whether it's distributed through an OTT platform like Netflix, streamed on YouTube, or on a paid download from Amazon.com or your own website.

Content Aggregation and Over-the-Top Television

Most filmmakers would like to get their movies on to over-the-top television platforms like Netflix, Hulu, Amazon Prime, and iTunes. However, most OTT platforms won't take your film—that is, not directly. These services have become so popular, and so inundated with independent films, that they require films be submitted via a *content aggregator*. Content aggregators are a specialized form of distributor that act as both sales agents and content gatekeepers for larger distribution outlets.

Here's how that works: You submit your film to a content aggregator. Then, for a fee, the aggregator submits your film to an OTT site.

CONTENT AGGREGATOR

A content aggregator is a distributor and/or exhibitor who specializes in new media technologies such as streaming video, VOD, pay-per-view, and mobile downloads. The aggregator gathers media content, such as your film, and offers it for sale or license through a variety of exhibition platforms. Some aggregators are also exhibitors; some merely distribute to exhibitors. Aggregators usually have relationships with popular online video portals, such as iTunes and Netflix, and may be the only way to get your film on such sites. As a result, working with an aggregator is like working with a distributor in that the relationship requires the filmmaker to pay careful attention to the exclusive rights she is granting, in what markets, and for how long.

DOI: 10.4324/9781003228479-34

Some content aggregators work for a percentage of your film's licensing fees; some companies charge a flat fee to submit your film to OTT companies and let you keep all the licensing fees.

THE CONTENT AGGREGATOR DEAL

Fee

Is the aggregator paid a flat fee or a portion of your film's licensing proceeds? If it's a flat fee, make sure that a majority or all of it is refundable if the aggregator cannot place your film on iTunes or Netflix. If the aggregator is paid from your film's proceeds, make sure the aggregator's payment comes from only those companies or territories in which the aggregator actually handled the licensing. In other words, the aggregator should not be entitled to a portion of your theatrical box-office receipts. Make sure you understand all the additional costs and expenses the aggregator plans to charge. For instance, some aggregators charge a setup fee to convert your film into the proper format for online distribution.

Grant of Rights/Territories

The only rights that you should grant to the aggregator are:

- The rights to distribute your film on OTT and video-on-demand services on which you and the aggregator agree.
- The right to advertise and promote your video to potential exhibitors, as noted previously.

Reservation of Rights

You should reserve the right to distribute your film in *all* other media and manners. Unless a content aggregator has strong relationships with merchandisers, you should not give it the right to enter into merchandising deals on your behalf. You may also want to reserve the right to distribute the film yourself—for instance on your own website or through Amazon.com.

Term

When starting off with a content aggregator, try to limit the term to one year or 18 months. You might want to place further restrictions by requiring that they secure a deal with OTT providers you specify within the first six months; if they don't, the contract becomes voidable by you.

Power of Attorney

A content aggregator will ask for the authority to negotiate and enter into agreements with distributors/exhibitors on your behalf. Producers who have some familiarity with licensing their films should require prior approval over the deals the aggregator negotiates.

Exclusivity

Be prepared for the aggregator to require that it be the exclusive online distributor for your film. If you are paying the aggregator a flat fee, it is acting more like a service provider than a distributor, and you might not want to give it such exclusivity. Aggregators working on a percentage of the license fee basis are taking a greater risk and thus have a better argument for being your exclusive online distributor. However, if you grant exclusivity, you might want to include some restrictions, such as the following:

- Limiting the duration of the exclusive relationship.
- Limiting the media or outlets over which the aggregator has exclusivity. For instance, you might grant the aggregator the right to be the exclusive distributor with respect to iTunes and Netflix, but you retain the right to sell downloads of your movie from Amazon.com.
- Requiring certain benchmarks to be achieved prior to exclusivity kicking in. For instance, the content aggregator must place your film with iTunes and Netflix to get exclusivity over your film's distribution on either site.

No Assignment

You want to make sure you know who has the rights to license your film and that they will be in business to do so; accordingly, you should limit the aggregator's ability to assign the rights to distribute your film to third parties. After all, mayflies live longer than some online businesses.

Accounting

The aggregator should be required to send you periodic accounting statements as well as grant you access to its books for an audit no less frequently than once per year.

Representations and Warranties/Indemnification

If you've been following the discussions in this book since the beginning of your project, you should be familiar with this clause. In short, you're promising that you have all the rights required for the film to be distributed without anyone having to worry that they will be sued for copyright infringement, defamation, trademark tarnishment, or the like. Furthermore, you're promising to pay the aggregators' and the exhibitors' damages should they get sued because of your film's content. (See Appendix B, "Representations and Warranties," p. 482; "Indemnification," p. 488.)

Amazon Prime

Amazon Prime Video Direct is one of the few OTT sites that a producer can submit to directly without the need of a content aggregator (although they can certainly help). But when I say "submit" to Amazon Prime, I mean just that—there's no guarantee that it will be accepted by Amazon Prime. They reserve the right to accept your film and even take it down at their discretion. They often have a very high standard: expecting only professionally produced TV shows and movies. And as of this writing, they no longer take nonfiction (documentaries) and short-form content.

Producers uploading their video stand to gain 50% of the net revenues from films that Amazon subscribers buy or rent.

If your film is provided free to Amazon Prime subscribers, how much you will receive is dependent upon the region where it is shown. In the United States, per hour of viewing, producers may earn anywhere between $0.01 and $0.12. That's the downside. The upside is that the license you grant them is nonexclusive.

In order to submit to Amazon Prime, you must:

- Set up an account.
- Create a profile.
- Link your bank account.
- Submit tax information.
- Ensure that your video assets comply with their standards (including captioning and graphics).

Because of the ever-changing nature of this service, I won't go into too much detail here on all the technical and account creation requirements. Go directly to their website for more information: https://videodirect.amazon.com/home/landing.

Netflix

Netflix requires you to submit your film to them through either a content aggregator or other distributor, producer's rep, or sales agent. In the past several years Netflix has increased the amount of money it is pouring into its own original programming in comparison to how much is paying for licensed films. In 2019, it had roughly $14.7 billion of licensed content on its site;[1] by 2020, the cost had risen to $17.3 billion.[2] Netflix original content deals are often structured as a buyout, with Netflix paying production costs, plus a premium (often 30% of production costs),[3] in exchange for most (or all) worldwide rights. For more information on negotiating a production services agreement or a co-production agreement, see "Production Services and Co-Productions," p. 177.

If you've already made your film, you will want to have it mastered and finished at one of the Netflix Preferred Fulfillment Partners (NPFPs).[4] Because Netflix has extremely exacting standards, NPFPs are a kind of technical gatekeeper for Netflix. They work closely with content aggregators to handle localization, dubbing, and audio descriptions and put together the digital cinema package (DCP)—the files needed to allow you to show a digital film in the movie theater.

Once your film meets the Netflix tech specs, you need to make sure you work with a content aggregator, distributor, attorney, producer, or agent that has a pre-existing relationship with Netflix. Netflix does not accept unsolicited material.

YouTube

With over 500 hours of video content uploaded every single minute, YouTube is the largest audiovisual content distributor/exhibitor in history. The social and political impact of YouTube cannot be overstated and has fundamentally reshaped journalism, television and movie production, and politics. YouTube's strength is allowing virtually anybody to create their own channels and post their own content. As a result, it has the power to both inform and misinform, depending upon the popularity of the creator. Because of this potential for disruption, a number of countries have temporarily or intermittently blocked the site, and some have blocked it permanently.[5]

For filmmakers, YouTube offers the chance to offer their work to the largest audience in the world. But that in itself can be both a blessing and a curse. It's hard to make money off of YouTube, and it can be just as hard to build an audience who will sit through your longform film when there are countless videos of makeup tutorials, dancing cats, and videogame playthroughs vying for the same eyeballs. Additionally, if you post your work for free on YouTube, many distributors will not want to pay you for the distribution rights.

If you have sunk a considerable amount of cash into your film—whether your own or your investors' money—you may want to look to YouTube only as a means of promoting and marketing your film. Post a few trailers and behind-the-scenes clips to drive the audience into the theaters or one of the many over-the-top television platforms, like Netflix, Hulu, or Amazon Prime, where your movie is actually hosted for a fee.

That doesn't mean that YouTube isn't a value to filmmakers. Quite the opposite: YouTube itself is changing the way film and TV are being created, with new types of content emerging initially on the site and then percolating out to the traditional media platforms. Many contemporary filmmakers start building their "brand" on YouTube by creating regular content, growing their subscriber base, and then using that momentum to land lucrative film and television deals. Other filmmakers, having exhausted their attempts to land traditional distribution deals, have placed their films on YouTube (sometimes in serialized format) and increased their viewership logarithmically. Still others have found a successful niche solely as YouTube content creators with no desire to pivot to Hollywood where they would have to sacrifice their creative vision on the altar of focus groups and risk-averse studio executives.

Building a YouTube Channel

The key to growing an audience on YouTube is in the creation of a channel: a curated section of the site containing only those videos you upload, which can be marketed and promoted like a mini-television network. And if it becomes successful enough, you will even be paid for allowing advertisers to put commercials on your channel and have access to other revenue streams (see "Making Money from YouTube," p. 387).

There are channels for every type of content you can imagine (and depending upon your age, probably content that you never imagined would be popular). Currently some of the most popular genres on YouTube are:

- Product reviews and "un-boxing" videos.
- Comedy skits.
- Makeup and beauty.
- How-to guides (especially digital tech).
- Gaming tutorials and gaming playthroughs.
- VLOGS.
- Food and cocktail recipes.
- Educational content.
- Music and music videos.
- Q&A videos.
- Livestreams.
- Movie reviews.

- Short-form documentaries.
- Short films.
- News and journalism.
- Lifestyle.
- Infotainment.
- ASMR.
- Travelogues.

You may notice in the list above that feature films aren't represented. Short films are, but only just barely. That's not to say that you couldn't put your film on YouTube; it's just that right now, moviegoers don't primarily view indie films on YouTube. That's not to say that this won't change (I believe it will). YouTube genres shift quite rapidly: were I writing this section five or six years ago, I might've included cat videos in the list. To be sure, they're still there, but they don't lead the YouTube vanguard.

To start a channel, you must agree to YouTube's terms and services and post content.[6] Super simple, right?

Sure, from a technical standpoint. But there are legal pitfalls, and this is a law book, after all. So, let's look at a few areas you should take care of before you create your channel and start uploading content.

YouTube Terms of Service

To create a channel, you must sign up for a YouTube account. And to do that, you must agree to the YouTube Terms of Service;[7] Policy, Safety, and Copyright Policy;[8] and Community Guidelines.[9] If you plan to monetize your channel (see "Making Money from YouTube," p. 387), you will need to agree with those terms[10] as well. And no: there is no negotiation with "The Tube." Their terms are "take it or leave it." The best you can do is understand what you are agreeing to.

Terms of Service

The YouTube Terms of Service change frequently. As of this writing, you can find them here: www.youtube.com/static?template=terms. They are quite extensive, so I can't go into everything here, but I'll flag some key issues.

- "YouTube is under no obligation to host or serve Content." Yup. No promises that you can post what you want to.
- You are not allowed to circumvent or disable content protection of the site's videos.

- No unsolicited promotions or mass solicitations. If you want to host a contest on the site, you must comply with YouTube's Contest Policies and Guidelines.[11]
- You must have permission to post other people's IP or be legally entitled to do so (here's where fair use comes in).
- When you post content, you not only give YouTube a right to distribute and perform it (duh!) but *you also give them a right to make derivative works* that promote YouTube from your content.
- You grant other users the right to play your content and to embed it on a website or blog.
- "You grant to YouTube the right to monetize your Content on the Service (and such monetization may include displaying ads on or within Content or charging users a fee for access). This Agreement does not entitle you to any payments." Yup. *YouTube* can still monetize your video and make money from it, even if you don't meet their monetization requirements for them to pay you.
- They can terminate your channel and account "if (a) you materially or repeatedly breach this Agreement; (b) we are required to do so to comply with a legal requirement or a court order; or (c) we believe there has been conduct that creates (or could create) liability or harm to any user, other third party, YouTube or our Affiliates."

Disclaimers

As you might guess, doctors, lawyers, and other professionals should include a disclaimer on their channel stating that the video content is not providing professional advice. But what if you're just a college student doing a product review or a how-to video on building a firepit? No need for disclaimers, right? Hold on . . . don't skip ahead just yet. . .

In general, if you are showing how to engage in activity or use a product that might be dangerous, you'll want to include a disclaimer of liability and state pretty clearly that anyone attempting to follow your instructions does so at their own risk. You should even call out what typical risks they might expect, like explosions, injury from fire, dangerous chemicals, etc. You should also disclaim liability for any product that you appear to be endorsing.

Furthermore, if you have been paid anything to review the product, you must state that in the video. For more on endorsements, see "Product Placement and Sponsorship," page 189. And yes, those of us who are doctors, lawyers, architects, pharmacists, and other professionals should include a disclaimer that are videos are not professional advice and do not create a professional relationship with the viewer.

The disclaimers ideally should appear prominently in the description of the video, within the video itself (at the beginning and at the end), and on any personal websites that your video links to. Disclaimers that apply to your entire channel, such as the ones disclaiming professional liability, should be placed in the description of your channel. It's also a good idea to put them in **bold** or ALL CAPS. The point is that they should appear in a place that is most likely to be seen, read, and heard by any viewer.

Music, Film Clips, and Other People's Content

Okay, if you've read this far in the book, this one is easy to understand. If you're using film clips, music, imagery, costumes, writing, or photographs owned by somebody else, you may be at risk of getting a takedown notice or worse. We've already studied at great length the concept of fair use and licensing . . . and all of that stuff applies here.

Keep in mind, however, that YouTube is not a court of law, and just because you don't get a takedown notice from YouTube, it doesn't mean that you posted content that's fair to use. Furthermore, the converse is also true: just because YouTube takes down your material, either on its own or in reaction to a notice and takedown from the owner of content you posted, it doesn't mean that you have violated somebody's rights. All it means is that somebody has identified their content on your site and wants it gone (or, more accurately, someone claims that they own the content that is on your site and wants it gone). Music poses special problems on YouTube, and YouTube's algorithms may identify the recording of a song you included in your video as owned by a third party and thus not allow it to be uploaded. We'll go into more depth on dealing with YouTube and copyright takedowns on p. 393.

Making Money From YouTube

These are the "Gold Rush" days of multimillion-dollar YouTube vloggers and online influencers, and just like in the historical Gold Rush, only a few will actually make money. As this is being written, there are about 51 million YouTube creators; only a small percentage will make any money, and even fewer will make enough money to generate a minimum living wage from ad revenue, which is the primary way that YouTube creators can make money from posting content.

I'm not trying to discourage you, just trying to set some realistic expectations. At least initially, you should consider the prospect of making money on YouTube icing on the cake, not the cake itself. Your moist chocolatey cake is the creative and promotional reward that comes from having your own YouTube channel.

Now that hopes have been dashed, let's pick up the pieces, glue them together with a little bit of optimism, put on our rose-colored glasses, and learn how YouTube creators can make money on the platform.

Because YouTube is an extremely flexible platform for nearly every type of audiovisual content imaginable, there are endless ways in which YouTube creators can make money: from promoting their own goods and services; to building a reputation for expertise in a particular area, thus bolstering their chances of being hired by an employer; to creating sample educational content to encourage viewers to sign up for more in-depth educational videos direct from the creator's website.

YouTube itself offers several different ways to monetize your channel:

1. Ad revenue (see: https://support.google.com/youtube/answer/2467968)
2. Paid channel memberships (see: https://www.youtube.com/intl/en_us/join/)
3. Selling merchandise through YouTube's "Merch Shelf" (https://support.google.com/youtube/answer/9454088)
4. "Super Chats" and "Super Stickers" (see: https://support.google.com/youtube/answer/7288782?hl=en)
5. Revenue from YouTube premium content that you post (see: https://support.google.com/youtube/answer/6306276?hl=en)
6. You can learn more about YouTube monetization policies here: https://support.google.com/youtube/answer/72857?hl=en
7. You can learn more about how YouTube revenue is calculated here: https://support.google.com/youtube/answer/9314489?visit_id=637537726025742504-1256154264&rd=1#YTR_compare
8. A helpful course on joining the YouTube partnership program is in their Creator Academy playlist: https://support.google.com/youtube/answer/72857?hl=en

YouTube itself has copious articles and videos on the whole process. A good jumping-off point is here: https://support.google.com/youtube/answer/72857?hl=en&ref_topic=9153826.

However, we're going to concentrate on two of the models most people think of when they think of YouTube content creators making bank: channel monetization from ad revenue and sponsorship.

Advertisement Revenue Monetization

Making money from commercials placed on their channels is probably the first thing people think of when they think about making money from YouTube. Here's how to get started:

1. You have to have an existing channel that meets YouTube's Advertiser-Friendly Content Guidelines; see: https://support.google.com/youtube/topic/9257894?hl=en&ref_topic=9257986. Briefly, if you hope to be monetized, you can't post content that contains the following:

   a. Inappropriate language.
   b. Violence.
   c. Adult content.
   d. Shocking content.
   e. Harmful or dangerous acts.
   f. Hateful and derogatory content.
   g. Recreational drugs and drug-related content.
   h. Firearms-related content.
   i. Controversial issues.
   j. Sensitive events.
   k. Incendiary and demeaning content.
   l. Tobacco-related content.
   m. Adult themes in family content.
2. Your channel must also meet a few threshold requirements to be eligible for monetization:
   a. The channel creator has to be 18 years old or older.
   b. The channel must have at least 1,000 subscribers.
   c. Within the past year, the viewing public must have watched 4,000 or more hours of your channel's content.
   d. You must make sure you comply with YouTube's community guidelines: www.youtube.com/howyoutubeworks/policies/community-guidelines/. Many of the restrictions here are common sense:
      i. No "fake engagement"—in other words, don't sign up for a bot service which artificially inflates your likes or subscribers.
      ii. No impersonation—don't try to pretend to be somebody you're not unless it's obviously satire or parody. Performing a celebrity impersonation is one thing; pretending to actually be that celebrity is another.
      iii. No nudity or sexual content—the key here is to avoid content designed to arouse, like pornography. And obviously—I hope it's obvious—nothing sexually explicit involving minors.
      iv. No links in your video to content that itself would violate YouTube's guidelines.
      v. Avoid hate speech, violent content, harassment and cyberbullying, and advocating suicide or self-injury.
      vi. No spam or deceptive practices.
   e. You must have a linked AdSense account. (see: https://support.google.com/youtube/answer/9914702?hl=en)

3. Finally, you must apply and be accepted to YouTube's Partnership Program ("YPP"), (see: https://support.google.com/youtube/answer/72851?hl=en), and you must live in a country where the YPP is available to you. So, if you live in Croatia, you have a shot; China or Vanuatu, you don't. That list is here: https://support.google.com/youtube/answer/7101720.

Demonetization

The dreaded "D" word: demonetization. You may have spent a lot of time and money creating an awesome video for your monetized channel and then suddenly find out that YouTube has flagged it for ad-inappropriate content or violations of community guidelines and thus demonetized it. That's right: even though your video may still be shown on YouTube (depending upon the nature of the infraction, obviously), you won't be making any money on it. YouTube has several levels of demonetization:

- Turning off ads on specific content that you post.
- Suspending your participation in YPP altogether.
- Suspending or terminating your YouTube channel.

If you really want to go "down the rabbit hole," a little Google research into the issue will show countless angry creators who have no idea what they did to trigger demonetization. Unfortunately, YouTube itself has been less than forthcoming about the issue. They haven't published a list of prohibited words or phrases that their AI algorithm uses to flag problem content, and to try to talk to a human at YouTube is all but impossible. They do, however, have a chat option in the YPP section of your YouTube account.

If you have been demonetized, YouTube says it will notify you on your channel or via email and provide options on how to return to their good graces.

Sponsorship and Influencers

Are you looking to build the channel and attract sponsors? If so, you need to make sure that you have a good sponsorship agreement in place. Furthermore, if you have a sponsor, or have received something of value like a free product to review, you must make sure you comply with federal guidelines relating to disclosures and truthful statements. For more on this, take a look at "Product Placement and Sponsorship," p. 189.

YouTube and Copyright Takedowns

YouTube tries to work very closely with content owners to protect the copyrighted material in their videos. To do so, it has several tools at its disposal to help it manage copyright protection for content owners. Perhaps the most famous—although infamous may be the better word—are the Content ID and the Copyright Strike, which strike fear into the heart of every YouTuber. If you have ever included a music or film clip that you don't have the rights to in your YouTube video, you've probably come into contact with one or both of these.

Content ID

The first thing to note is that Content ID is not really a legal remedy, it's more a dispute resolution process built into YouTube itself and is available only to copyright holders that qualify, apply for, and are accepted into the program enabling them to use it. If the rights holders are not members of the Content ID program, they may have no choice but to use takedown notice procedures. See "Takedowns and Copyright Strikes," p. 393.

Here's how the Content ID process works: let's say you include a piece of music in your video, but you didn't get permission from the record company that owned the copyright to the recording. If the record company has qualified for the Content ID program (the copyright owner must qualify and sign up for the Content ID program to be able to use it), YouTube's bots will likely identify the music on your video as owned by the record company and alert them to your video. At this point, the record company has a few options: it can block your video altogether, learn more about the engagement statistics of your video, or monetize your video and keep the revenue (although there is a way for music video creators[12] to possibly share in that revenue as well; see below).

If YouTube discovers content on one of your videos that triggers Content ID, they send you an email letting you know. You then need to log on to your YouTube Studio account and get details on the specifics of the Content ID claim in the "restrictions" section of your account page. If that Content ID holder is amenable, they may let you keep the video up, but with ads on it, which they get revenue from. They may choose to restrict geographic regions or devices where the video may not be shown, or they may block it altogether.

At this point, you can either:

1. Choose to do nothing and accept the Content ID claim as is, or
2. If you're in the YouTube Partner Program, you may be able to share ad revenue with the Content ID holder, or
3. Trim out the problem segment of your video, or
4. If the claim is an audio claim, you may remove or mute a particular song but leave the rest of the video as is, or
5. You may dispute the claim altogether.

CRITICISM OF CONTENT ID

On the surface, Content ID seems fair and reasonable: after all, most filmmakers would not want their work used in somebody else's without permission, so why not give copyright owners a chance to make money from unlicensed uses or block it altogether?

Well, a problem arises when we add the unreliability of AI algorithms[13] and takedown over-reach by over-zealous copyright owners protecting their work against otherwise permissible criticism, incidental use, or transformative uses of their work. Remember all that stuff about fair use of copyright we spent so much time on? Content ID often does a poor job of distinguishing between infringing uses and an otherwise clear fair use of a copyright. And because copyright owners can file takedown notices on YouTube much more cheaply and easily than filing a lawsuit (and without the risk of a judge hitting them with sanctions for filing suit over an obvious fair use), many copyright owners behave unscrupulously, submitting takedown notices for videos that criticize their work.

Here's just one example: In 2020, New York University Law School posted to YouTube a video of a copyright law conference they held where copyright law and music law experts discussed an important music copyright case. The video was flagged by the content ID system, despite the video being at the epicenter of what fair use was designed to protect. Even the experienced lawyers at NYU had difficulty navigating the YouTube appeals process. The video was finally restored but without any explanation to the professors as to why it was flagged in the first place.[14]

Disputing a Content ID Claim

If you want to dispute a content ID claim, you must provide a valid reason to do so. For instance, you may have the rights to use a song, or the video you included is in the public domain, or perhaps you're only using a small portion of somebody else's copyrighted work, and you are creating a review or critique video and relying on fair use. Either way, you need to think it through and be prepared to argue your point before you decide to dispute it.

To initiate the dispute, you do it from within your YouTube Studio (since YouTube may change its user interface, I'm not going to provide exact steps here. YouTube itself has helpful walk-throughs that will show you where to go). Once you have initiated your dispute, the copyright owner has 30 days in which to respond. They can:

1. Choose to remove the claim against your channel, or
2. Submit a copyright takedown to YouTube (in which case you get a copyright strike—more on this later), or
3. Uphold the claim (so they will continue to be able to restrict, learn from, or monetize your video as above), or
4. If they do nothing in response to your dispute, the claim expires after 30 days.

Appeals

Let's say the copyright owner is not willing to give up without a fight, but neither are you. If you've filed the dispute and they've responded by upholding the claim, you can appeal the decision. But don't think of it as a legal appeal where nuanced fair use arguments are made. This is more automated than that; an appeal on YouTube essentially repeats the process above but provides fewer options to the copyright holder. Once you file an appeal, they can either do nothing and the appeal will expire, release the claim (good luck), request immediate removal of your video, or schedule your video to be taken down within seven days if you don't remove the offending content.

Takedowns and Copyright Strikes

Content ID is not the only tool that copyright holders have to combat potential infringers. Perhaps the strongest tool—at least in the legal sense—is notice and takedown. And it is here that we must add to the realm of YouTube's own policies those required by the law, specifically the Digital Millennium Copyright Act (DMCA).[15]

The DMCA provides a way for copyright owners to compel a website to remove infringing material from their website. If a copyright owner has decided to issue a takedown of your video on YouTube, YouTube takes it down, and your account gets a "copyright strike."

Note: You do not receive copyright strikes from Content ID claims, only from takedowns.

When you get your first copyright strike, your specific video gets taken down, and YouTube sends you to "copyright school" on YouTube to learn more about copyright infringement. If you get three copyright strikes, your account may be terminated, with all your videos deleted, and you may be prohibited from creating new YouTube channels. Oh, and the copyright owner can still sue you in court.

To find out about your copyright takedowns, go to your YouTube Studio account online (everybody who creates a YouTube channel is given their own studio account) and research it in a manner similar to the way you did for Content ID. You can resolve a copyright strike in several ways:

1. Wait for it to expire (in 90 days).
2. Reach out directly to the content owner if you can find them and try to convince them to retract it.
3. Submit a **counter notification** telling YouTube and the copyright claimant that you believe you have a right to use the material included in your video.

The **counter notification** process requires much more of a legal response then the "appeals" process for Content ID. You can only submit a counter notification for three reasons:

1. You believe your video was mistakenly taken down,
2. You believe copyright in your video was misidentified as copyright protected, or
3. You are asserting a fair use defense.

To respond, you or your attorney will have to submit through your YouTube Studio portal the legal reasons you believe you are entitled to use the content that was objected to. Consider whether the following defenses are available to you:

1. The content you posted was in the public domain.
2. You're asserting a fair use defense (and yes, you have to lay out your argument, although perhaps not as formally as you would in a court of law. Still if you have a lawyer draft it, that's always a good idea).
3. You have a license or permission to use the work you posted (and yes, you should include that license).

Once you file your counter notice, the copyright claimant will have ten days to respond, asserting that—pursuant to the copyright statute—they are filing a lawsuit to keep your video from being restored on YouTube. Yes, you read that right: filing a lawsuit. When it comes to copyright takedowns, you're dancing on the edge of a lawsuit in a way that you aren't when you're only in Content ID territory (of course, keep in mind that at different stages of Content ID procedure, the claimant can opt to issue a notice and takedown).

It's important to reemphasize that notice and takedown procedures are not a creature of YouTube but of copyright law, which means that if you're posting videos on your own website that is not connected to YouTube, you may still receive a notice and takedown from copyright claimants.

Community Guidelines Strikes

Finally, let's say you have done your diligent best and avoided including unlicensed third-party copyrighted materials in your YouTube videos. No more strikes ahead, right?

BUZZZZ! Wrong answer. You can also get strikes against your account on YouTube by violating their community guidelines.[16] So if you include nudity, links to external content which also violates YouTube's policies (like porn), engage in deceptive or fraudulent practices, post videos which contain hate speech or graphic violence, or in any way violate YouTube's community guidelines,[17] you may receive a community guidelines strike. Seriously, read those community guidelines and internalize them.

If your first community guidelines offense is a relatively minor one, you may only get a warning and not an actual strike. This warning will remain associated with your channel. After that, you will get an actual **first strike**. In many ways, this can be more severe than a copyright strike. For one week following your first strike, you won't be able to upload videos or streams, effectively create custom thumbnails, or work with collaborators and playlists or show trailers during your YouTube Premieres. When that week is up, you will get your full privileges back, but the strike remains on your account for 90 days.

If you get a second strike within that 90-day period, you get hit with everything you did for your first strike, but now it's for two weeks instead of just one. And the third strike within 90 days means you're out. Not just you, but your entire channel will be removed from YouTube.

A couple of caveats here:

- Community guidelines strikes expire after 90 days.
- An especially severe community guidelines violation can still result in your channel being removed.
- There is an appeals process for community guidelines strikes, also accessed through your YouTube Studio dashboard. You may appeal each community guidelines strike only once.

Libel and Slander

There is so much drama on YouTube, and I'm not talking about the genre. YouTube shares a lot of its DNA with reality programming for the number of YouTubers who spend time insulting and trash-talking other YouTubers. Just keep in mind that if you want to produce a channel where that is the main feature, you should brush up on the section of the book dealing with defamation and libel laws. Know the line between being salty and being slanderous (technically libelous, but I couldn't resist the alliteration). For more on libel and slander, see that section in Appendix A, p. 449.

NOTES

[1] www.investopedia.com/articles/investing/062515/how-netflix-pays-movie-and-tv-show-licensing.asp (Accessed June 3, 2021).

[2] www.sebastiangibsonlaw.com/netflix-film-and-scripted-tv-series-streaming-contracts/ (Accessed June 4, 2021).

[3] www.cnbc.com/2018/08/15/netflix-cost-plus-model-tv-shows-revenue-upside.html (Accessed June 4, 2021).

[4] https://npfp.netflixstudios.com/#npfp-region-selector (Accessed November 30, 2021).

[5] https://en.wikipedia.org/wiki/Censorship_of_YouTube (Accessed April 12, 2021).

[6] YouTube policies and hyperlinks change frequently; like every tip in this section, make sure to verify the current status on YouTube itself.

[7] www.youtube.com/static?template=terms (Accessed April 16, 2021).

[8] https://support.google.com/youtube/topic/9223153 (Accessed April 16, 2021).

[9] www.youtube.com/howyoutubeworks/policies/community-guidelines/ (Accessed April 16, 2021).

[10] https://support.google.com/youtube/topic/9223152 (Accessed April 16, 2021).

[11] https://support.google.com/youtube/answer/1620498 (Accessed April 16, 2021).

[12] https://support.google.com/youtube/answer/3301938

[13] www.eff.org/wp/unfiltered-how-youtubes-content-id-discourages-fair-use-and-dictates-what-we-see-online#fn6

[14] www.eff.org/wp/unfiltered-how-youtubes-content-id-discourages-fair-use-and-dictates-what-we-see-online (Accessed April 26, 2021).

[15] 17 U.S.C. § 512.

[16] https://support.google.com/youtube/answer/2802032 (Accessed April 26, 2021).

[17] YouTube community guidelines: https://support.google.com/youtube/answer/9288567 (Accessed April 26, 2021).

9

CONCLUSION

If you find the prospect of dealing with so many legal issues daunting, take heart. You can do this.

Having worked with many different kinds of artists in my law practice, it has been my experience that producers, more than any other type of creator, tend to grasp legal concepts the most quickly. Perhaps it's because in many ways, a producer's job and a lawyer's job are similar: Both involve negotiating, lining up alternatives, creating contingency plans, and making the best of emergency situations.

If you can juggle the logistics of producing, you can manage all the law you need to keep your film in the clear. The trick is to realize that legal and business decisions are every bit as important to the success of your movie as the decisions you make regarding your script, camera angles, performances, and editing choices.

Remember—this book is not intended to replace a lawyer. However, it is designed to help you reduce your legal costs by giving you much of the information you need to make informed decisions about the legal aspects of your production. After all, the less time your attorney has to spend teaching you the law, the more time she can spend drafting contracts and negotiating on your behalf.

So, get yourself a good attorney, put this book in your bike messenger bag, and go make a great movie!

FINAL TIPS

To protect a film's assets, a filmmaker should:

- Establish a tight working relationship between your staff and a production attorney and accountant.
- Make sure your contracts protect your IP.
- Register and maintain your copyrights.
- Get permission to use any IP that is not yours.
- Keep a well-organized production book containing all the project's contracts and clearances.
- Maintain an E&O insurance policy.
- Decide whether you want to work with a distributor or to distribute by yourself.
- When in doubt, seek permission!

LAW LIBRARY

The remainder of this book contains your very own portable law library. Here you will find material that fleshes out and supplements the topics presented in the main part of the book.

The library is composed of two sections:

- **Appendix A**, "A Filmmaker's Guide to Intellectual Property Law" (p. 401). Learn more about copyright, rights of publicity, defamation, privacy law, and moral rights.
- **Appendix B**, "The Clause Companion" (p. 475). Learn more about typical contract clauses found in most film and video contracts.

A

A FILMMAKER'S GUIDE TO INTELLECTUAL PROPERTY LAW

This appendix provides you with a general background on the areas of intellectual property law, defamation, and privacy rights that most impact the filmmaking process. Here you will find resources to help your understanding of the following topics:

DOI: 10.4324/9781003228479-36

- Defenses to defamation (p. 452).
- Moral rights (p. 457).
- Avoiding trademark infringement (p. 460.).

A FEW WORDS OF CAUTION

This section is not intended to be an exhaustive treatment of intellectual property law. It is intended to highlight the areas of IP law most important to filmmakers. Copyright, trademark, rights of publicity, and idea protection laws are examined from the viewpoint of how they impact the filmmaker's ability to make and protect his or her movie:

- *Limited scope.* The areas of IP law that don't directly apply to the filmmaking process, such as patent, trade secret, and trademark registration, are not examined.
- *Limited jurisdiction. Only US laws are discussed in this book.* It is critical to keep in mind, especially when dealing with intellectual property, that the laws of other countries may differ significantly from those of the United States. Accordingly, a film that does not violate anybody's rights in the United States may violate somebody's rights in a foreign country! To help guard against this, make sure that your contracts are drafted to include the broadest possible grant of rights to the filmmaker.

Before distributing a film outside the United States, it is good practice to have your film viewed and your agreements analyzed by an attorney who is familiar with *international* intellectual property laws.

COPYRIGHT LAW

What Is a Copyright?

Copyright is actually a collection of legal rights, all of which protect "original works of authorship fixed in a tangible medium of expression."[1]

Copyright can protect:

- Literary works such as screenplays, novels, magazine articles, and poems.
- Motion pictures, television shows, and other audiovisual works.
- Musical works, including any accompanying words.
- Dramatic works such as plays, including any accompanying music.
- Pantomimes and choreographic works.

- Pictorial, graphic, and sculptural works.
- Sound recordings.
- Architectural works.
- Other works of original authorship.

Copyright is one of the easiest forms of intellectual property protection to obtain: Simply create an original work of authorship, write it down or record it in some way, and you automatically have a copyright in that work. Only a minimum amount of creativity is required in obtaining a copyright. You don't even have to fill out a form or put a "C" in a circle to get copyright protection, *but you will get more legal protections if you do.* (See "Copyright Registration," p. 164.)

> ***Example:*** You write a screenplay. If you've written it yourself and haven't based it on anybody else's work, it's original to you. Because you've written it down (or saved it to your hard drive), you've recorded it. Smile—you've automatically been granted a copyright in your work, without having to do anything else.

Copyright in Selection and Arrangement

When we think of what can be copyrighted, we often think of types of expression, such as paintings, sculptures, films, or screenplays. In addition to these works, a *particularly creative arrangement or selection of materials may also be copyrighted*, despite the fact that what is arranged or selected may be in the public domain. (See "Public Domain," p. 409.) Examples include:

- A collage made from scraps of 19th-century advertisements.
- A creative sequence of yoga poses.
- A selection of words; for example, in James Lipton's work "An Exaltation of Larks," Lipton was able to copyright the particular selection and arrangement of "terms of venery" (collective noun for a group of animals, like a "herd" of cows, or my favorite, a "murder" of crows).

It is important to note that it is because of the *creativity* of the selection and arrangement that it is granted copyright (as opposed to the public domain elements themselves), so the choices and organization of the elements must be sufficiently creative. For instance, an alphabetical listing of data is not creative enough to warrant copyright protection, nor is the chronological ordering of data.

Copyright Rights

For filmmakers and other authors, copyright law gives the copyright owner the *exclusive* right to take their work and:

- Make *copies* of it.
- *Distribute* it.

- *Perform* that work publicly.
- Publicly *display* the work.
- Make *derivative works* based on the original work.

Anyone who, without the copyright owner's permission, performs any of these actions may be infringing the copyright. (See "Copyright Infringement," p. 429.)

Copyright Terminology

Many of the following terms are taken directly from the federal copyright statute itself and may be helpful in interpreting copyright law. More definitions can be found in the US Copyright statute, 17 U.S.C.§101.[2]

AUTHOR

The *author* is the original copyright owner of a work. For instance, if you write a screenplay by yourself and it is completely original with you and no one has hired you to write it, you are the author. However, under the work-made-for-hire rules, if someone else hires you to write the screenplay, your employer would be considered the author, not you. (See "Work Made for Hire," p. 418.)

AUDIOVISUAL WORKS

Copyright law considers your film or video an *audiovisual* work:

> "'*Audiovisual works*' are works that consist of a series of related images that are intrinsically intended to be shown by the use of machines or devices such as projectors, viewers, or electronic equipment, together with accompanying sounds, if any, regardless of the nature of the material objects, such as films or tapes, in which the works are embodied."[3]

Common examples include:

- Movies.
- Television programs.
- DVDs, Blu-ray discs, and videocassettes.
- Streaming video.
- MP4 files.
- Animation in whatever format.

DERIVATIVE WORK

A *derivative work* is a work based on one or more preexisting works, such as a translation, musical arrangement, dramatization, fictionalization, motion picture version of a book, sound recording, art reproduction, abridgment, condensation, or any other form in which a work may be recast, transformed, or adapted. A work consisting of editorial revisions, annotations, elaborations, or other modifications that as a whole represents an original work of authorship is a derivative work.[4]

Examples of derivative works in the film and television industry include:

- A movie script based on a play.
- A movie is a derivative work of a script.
- A television series based on a movie.
- An action figure based on a movie character.
- A novel based on a movie.
- The recording of a song composition.

MOTION PICTURE

"'*Motion pictures*' are audiovisual works consisting of a series of related images which, when shown in succession, impart an impression of motion, together with accompanying sounds, if any."[5]

PERFORM

> "To '*perform*' a work means to recite, render, play, dance, or act it, either directly or by means of any device or process or, in the case of a motion picture or other audiovisual work, to show its images in any sequence or to make the sounds accompanying it audible."[6]

PUBLICATION

In copyright law, *publication* is the act of distributing a copyrighted work to the public. Specifically, it is "the distribution of copies [. . .] of a work to the public by sale or other transfer of ownership, or by rental, lease, or lending."[7]

The date of publication is a critical one in determining whether a work is still protected by copyright.

> ***Example:*** Many films are works made for hire. For any work made for hire that you create today, copyright protection will last for 95 years from the year of first *publication* or 120 years from the year of creation, whichever expires first.

Publication of a motion picture publishes all the components embodied in it, including the music, the script, and the sounds. Thus, if a motion picture made from a screenplay is published, the screenplay is published to the extent that it is contained in the published work.

The performance of a motion picture (e.g. showing it in a movie theater, on television, casting on a mobile device or computer, or in a schoolroom) does not always constitute publication. According to the US Copyright Office,[8] a motion picture *is* published when:

- "One or more copies are distributed to the public by sale, rental, lease or lending, or when an offering is made to distribute copies to a group of persons (wholesalers, retailers, broadcasters, motion picture distributors, and the like) for purposes of further distribution or public performance."
- "Offering to distribute a copy of a motion picture for exhibition during a film festival may be considered publication of that work. For an offering to constitute publication, copies must be made and be ready for distribution."
- "When a motion picture is published, all the components embodied in it are also considered to be published, including the music, the script, and the sounds. Thus, if a motion picture made from a screenplay is published, the screenplay is published to the extent it is contained in the published work."

Example: Petra the Producer uploads her film to YouTube and marks it "private." She shares the link only with the film's investors, cast, and crew. The film has not yet been "published." However, if she had uploaded it publicly so that anyone on YouTube could view it, it could constitute publication.

Copyright Duration

Like a gallon of milk, every copyright has a "use by" date. After that date (called the "*term of copyright*"), the copyright expires, and the work goes into the *public domain* (see below), where the work can be used by anybody, regardless of the wishes of the original creator (or their descendants). No permission is required in all to use the work at that point.[9] Public domain works are a great (and free) source of material to incorporate into your films. However, the life span of a copyright has changed so many times over the last hundred years, determining whether an older copyright is still alive can be tricky.

For the majority of the 20th century (pre-1978), a copyright was given an initial term, which could then be extended if the copyright was properly *renewed* with the government. Although the copyrights of modern works (created from 1978 on) no longer need to be registered or have that registration renewed, for older works, you will need to know a lot about how the copyright was created when you're determining their life span:

- What kind of work it is (**sound recordings have different terms**; see chart below)
- When the work was made.
- If the work has been published.
- If first publication was outside of the United States.
- If the copyright to the work needed to be renewed and whether the copyright was, in fact, renewed.

- When the author of the work died.
- Whether it was a work made for hire.
- If the work was first published in a country outside the United States that is not a party to certain international IP treaties.

To keep it simple, here are some of the more common copyright lifespans for works (other than sound recordings) a filmmaker may encounter.[10]

Copyright Duration of Works Originally Created on or After January 1, 1978

These works are protected the moment they are created and embodied in a tangible form.

- The copyright lasts until 70 years after the author dies.
- For joint works, the term lasts for 70 years after the last surviving author dies.
- For works made for hire, the duration of copyright will be 95 years from publication or 120 years from creation, whichever comes first.

Copyright Duration of Works Originally Created Before January 1, 1978, but *Not Published or Registered* by That Date

- The duration is the same as in the preceding section. The life-plus-70-year or 95/120-year terms will apply to these copyrights as well. An unpublished work by an author who died prior to 1950 is likely in the public domain.
- In no case will the term of copyright for works in this category expire before December 31, 2002.
- For works published on or before December 31, 2002, the term of copyright will not expire before December 31, 2047.

Copyright Duration of Works Originally Created and Published in the United States Between 1964 and 1977

- Protection started when the work was published with a copyright notice.
- The duration of protection is 95 years from date of publication with copyright notice.
- Copyright renewal was automatic.
- Registration was required.

Copyright Duration of Works Originally Created and Published in the United States Between 1927 and 1963

- Registration was required.
- Protection started when the work was published with a copyright notice.
- Protection is for 95 years from date of publication with copyright notice—but only if the copyright was properly renewed.

Copyright Duration of Works Originally Created and Published in the United States Before 1927

- The work is probably in the public domain.
- Registration was required.

KEY COPYRIGHT LIFESPANS

A work created 1/1/1978 or after	The lifespan of the last surviving author, plus 70 years
A work for hire created 1/1/1978 or after	95 years from publication or 120 years from creation, whichever comes first
Works published in the United States before 1927	95 years after publication date. In 2022, works published pre-1927 fell into the public domain; in 2023, pre-1928 works fall into the public domain, and so on until 2072 (or the law is changed)
Sound recordings first published in the United States before 1923	Public domain
Sound recordings first published in the United States 1923–1946	100 years from publication
Sound recordings first published in the United States 1947–1956	110 years from publication
Sound recordings first published in the United States 1956–02/14/1972	Copyright lasts until 02/15/2067

LIMITATIONS ON COPYRIGHT PROTECTION

While copyright can protect an infinite amount of creative expression, there are a few key categories that won't be covered by copyright law or over which copyright protection has been limited or extinguished:

- Expired copyrights.
- Public domain works.
- "Unfixed" works.
- Building blocks of expression.
- Creative Commons copyright.

WORKS IN THE PUBLIC DOMAIN

If a work is *not* protected by copyright, it is in the *public domain*. This means that it can be used by anybody without seeking permission from the original author. Some things are in the public domain by virtue of their nature—for example, facts, ideas, concepts, and works created by the federal government.

Even formerly copyrighted works can fall into the public domain for a number of reasons, including:

- ***Expiration of copyright***. Copyrights have a life span. When that span runs out, the copyright dies and the artwork becomes part of the public domain, where it can enrich the work of other artists. It's the karma of copyright, man.
- ***Copyright notice was not placed on the work***. Earlier versions of the copyright law required the © to be placed on the work when it was published. If a work was published prior to 1989 without proper copyright notice, the work may have fallen into the public domain. Be careful here; a number of exceptions to this rule apply. Don't automatically assume that a pre-1989 work published without notice is in the public domain.
- ***Failure to renew the copyright***. Earlier versions of the copyright law required authors to renew their copyright registrations with the federal government. If a copyright was not renewed, it died.
- ***Relinquished copyright***. Sometimes authors want their works to be public domain and have voluntarily given up their copyrights.

UNFIXED WORKS

An "unfixed work" is one which has not been embodied in a "tangible means of expression." Simply put: if you want to protect something by copyright, you have to write it down, record it, paint it, save it to a hard drive, and so forth.

> ***Example:*** If an actor improvises a speech on set, it will not be protected by copyright until it is captured on film or written down.

BASIC BUILDING BLOCKS OF EXPRESSION

From screenplays to soundtracks, from dailies to final cut, copyright law protects the majority of the components used to make a film and television program. However, there is a host of things copyright law simply will not protect.

In general, copyright law will not protect the "building blocks" required to make a work of art. For instance, though you can copyright a script, you cannot copyright a word. You can copyright a novel but not an idea. And so on.

BOTTOM LINE: **Copyright protects the particular way an author has expressed himself; it does not extend to any ideas, systems, or factual information conveyed in the work.**

TITLES, NAMES, SHORT PHRASES, AND SLOGANS

These are the domain of *trademark* law, not copyright law. Copyright will not protect them. Nor will it protect:

- The name of an individual (including pseudonyms, pen names, or stage names).
- The title or subtitle of a work, such as a book; a song; or a pictorial, graphic, or sculptural work.
- The name of a business or organization.
- The name of a band or performing group.
- The name of a product or service.
- A domain name or URL.
- The name of a character.
- Catchwords or catchphrases.
- Mottos, slogans, or other short expressions.[11]

  Example: You're trying to market your new vampire film using the phrase "The ultimate power drink—blood!" on all your posters and ad copy. Rather than turn to copyright law to protect that phrase, your best bet would be to try to register it as a trademark. Keep in mind that to be registered as a trademark, the phrase, word, or slogan would have to meet all the requirements of a trademark, such as identifying the source of a good or a service. However, the entire poster, phrase, and artwork *combined* could be copyrighted.

FAMILIAR SYMBOLS OR DESIGNS; MERE VARIATIONS OF TYPOGRAPHIC ORNAMENTATION, LETTERING, OR COLORING

In other words, you cannot copyright a plain blue circle. As in the previous example, you may be able to get trademark protection for a symbol that would otherwise not be copyrightable. However, if you made an animated film out of blue circles and the selection and arrangement of those simple shapes was *significantly creative*, you might be able to register the copyright to your animation (but not the blue triangles themselves). If you're confused, think of it this way: a blue dot might not be protectable under copyright law, but a pointillist painting is (unless it's from the 19th century, in which case any copyright it had has likely expired. Sorry, Seurat!).

RAW DATA

Copyright protection is unavailable for raw data. For instance, you will not be able to protect:

- Mere listings of ingredients or contents.
- "Works consisting entirely of information that is common property and containing no original authorship".
- "Standard calendars, height and weight charts, tape measures and rulers, and lists or tables taken from public documents or other common sources".[12]

HISTORICAL FACTS AND THEORIES

Despite the fact that the author may have invested a good deal of time and money researching a subject, historical facts and theories are also unprotectable under copyright law.

It might seem unfair, but just because you've spent time and effort laboriously researching a topic does not mean that you can copyright that research.[13] However, you certainly can copyright the text that contains that writing. As a result, you can't use copyright law to stop someone from reading your well-researched book or script and copying the facts and other data that you alone have uncovered. But you *can* sue for copyright infringement when that person copies the words, pictures, and structure that you've used to discuss your research.

> ***Example:*** Dana Documentarian has spent the past ten years researching her film *E.T. on the Grassy Knoll*, a groundbreaking documentary that demonstrates that Pres. Kennedy was actually killed by extraterrestrials. Although her film may be protected by copyright, her actual theory is not.

IDEAS, THEMES, CONCEPTS

Copyright law does not protect ideas. Let me state that again: ***Copyright law does not protect ideas!*** This is, perhaps, one of the hardest concepts for many artists to grasp. Copyright only protects an idea's *expression*, not the idea or concept itself.

One of the problems has always been how to determine where an "idea" stops and "copyrightable expression" begins. As one court pointed out: "The line [lies] somewhere between the author's idea and the precise form in which he wrote it down; protection covers the 'pattern' of the work the sequence of events, and the development of the interplay of characters."[14]

Example: The *idea* of a band of rebels who fight an evil Galactic Empire is not copyrightable. The fully expressed *screenplay* for *Star Wars* is copyrightable, however. The former is merely a concept and is capable of being expressed in any number of ways. George Lucas's screenplay, on the other hand, is a collection of specific scenes, dialogue, detailed characters, plot, and a sequence of events, all of which form a unique and copyrightable whole.

PROCEDURES, METHODS, SYSTEMS, PROCESSES, PRINCIPLES, DISCOVERIES, OR DEVICES

Systems, processes, methods, procedures, and devices may be protected, but not by copyright law. You need to turn to patent protection or trade secrets law, not copyright law, for help.

Example: Fiona Filmmaker invents a great new system for preparing film budgets. She cannot use copyright law to stop other people from using her system.

SCÈNES À FAIRE

Scènes à faire (French for "scenes to be made") are common themes typical of an artistic genre and thus appear in numerous works. "*Scènes à faire* are unprotectable elements that follow naturally from a work's theme rather than from an author's creativity."[15] "Incidents, characters or settings which are as a practical matter indispensable, or at least standard, in the treatment of a given topic are *Scènes à faire*."[16] Furthermore, "thematic concepts which necessarily must follow from certain plot situations" are not entitled to copyright protection.[17] In short, they're like ideas: "Under the *scènes à faire* doctrine, when certain commonplace expressions are indispensable and naturally associated with the treatment of a given idea, those expressions are treated like ideas and therefore not protected by copyright."[18]

Example: Molly is filming a Western, and she wants to shoot a scene involving a showdown between a sheriff and an outlaw. Because this scene is so common to the Western movie genre, she need not be concerned that she will infringe the copyright of *High Noon*. But although the *scènes à faire* doctrine will allow her to use the concept of a showdown without fear of copyright infringement, she must be careful not to use the same dialogue, characters, or choice of shots that are used in another Western, since these may be protected by copyright.

WORKS CREATED BY THE US GOVERNMENT

Works created by the US government are not protected by copyright.[19] A work of the US government is "a work prepared by an officer or employee of the United States government as part of that person's official duties."[20]

Example: Jolene wants to use photographs from NASA's Hubble telescope as a background to her music video. She may do so without seeking NASA's permission because NASA is a federal agency, and its images are generally not copyrighted. She must, however, be careful when using those images for commercial purposes, so as not to give the appearance that NASA is endorsing the particular product or service. Restrictions on endorsement fall outside copyright law and must be analyzed under right of publicity, trademark law, or particular federal statutes that may prohibit the appearance of commercial endorsement by a federal agency.

Be careful here. Even though the US government cannot create a copyrighted work, it can *hold* the copyright assigned to it by others. Nor does the law prevent independent contractors, working on behalf of the United States government, from owning the copyright to their works. This is why, when using material from the US government, you should still verify that the material is not copyrighted.

Additionally, unlike the federal government, *state* government works may (depending upon state law) be protected by copyright law. And to make matters worse for creators, if a state government infringes your copyright (Example: using portions of your documentary film without your permission on a state-controlled website), you are not allowed to sue that state for infringement unless it first consents to your lawsuit![21]

CREATIVE COMMONS COPYRIGHT LICENSES

Much of this book is designed to help you protect the monopoly rights in your copyright. And let me be clear: if you hope to sell your movie one day, you should maintain strong copyright protections over your work.

However, sometimes an artist wants to contribute their work to the public at large in a manner which encourages remixing, repurchasing, and its inclusion as a building block for other works. This is where Creative Commons (CC) copyright comes in. CC is a system of copyright licenses which allows for various degrees of public use of the protected work, often with far fewer restrictions than traditional copyright licenses. Filmmakers may benefit from CC copyright licensing by being able to use a work protected by the CC license without paying licensing fees to the original creator. A database of CC images may be found here: https://search.creativecommons.org/.

But don't just grab and go! *A few key points first*: CC is not the same thing as public domain! In fact, CC licenses require attribution for the original author and may limit the uses to which the Creative Commons-protected material may be used. It's important to identify the specific type of CC license that governs the protection of the work before a filmmaker includes it in their own.

There are currently six kinds of Creative Commons licenses, each with varying degrees of permission:

1. "CC BY 4.0": This kind of license allows both commercial and noncommercial use of the work. The scope of this license is quite broad: the work covered by the CC BY 4.0 may be used for purposes of distribution, remixing, adaptation, and building upon it, in any medium. The original creator must be credited, if their name is given, as well as notice of their copyright in the material, a link to their material, and various disclosures, such as whether you modify the original work and which CCC license[22] governs their work.
2. "CC BY-SA": This license has a similar scope to the CC BY license, above, with the added requirement that any derivative works created from CC BY-SA works must be distributed under the same or compatible license.[23]
3. "CC BY-NC": once more, the scope of use is similar; however, with the CC BY-NC license, the protected work may not be used for commercial purposes.[24]
4. "CC BY-NC-SA": this license is a remix of numbers 2 and 3: not only can you not use the final work for commercial purposes, but you must also allow your work to be governed by the same license as the work from which it is derived or uses.[25]
5. "CC BY-ND": this license curtails the scope of what you may do with the covered work: you may copy and redistribute it, even commercially. However, if you decide to use the work and remix it, transform it, or build upon it, you may *not* distribute your final product.[26]
6. "CC BY-NC-ND": the most restrictive CC license of all, this license allows only the *noncommercial* copying and distribution of the material.[27]

Earlier versions of many of these licenses had slightly different requirements. Before using any CC-covered work, make sure you understand the requirements of the license under which it was granted. For more information on Creative Commons licenses, see: https://creativecommons.org/.

Copyright Ownership

WHO IS THE OWNER?

The person or entity who creates a copyrighted work is considered the *author*.

- If two or more people jointly create a work, they may be *joint authors*.
- In addition to people, companies can also be authors.
- When an employee creates a work on behalf of a company, that company, and *not* the employee, is considered the author of the work. (See "Work Made for Hire," p. 418.)

Joint Authors and Joint Works

JOINT WORK, JOINT AUTHORS

Copyright law defines a joint work as "a work prepared by two or more authors with the intention that their contributions be merged into inseparable or interdependent parts of a unitary whole."[28] The authors of a joint work are, not surprisingly, called *joint authors*.

When two or more authors work together to create a screenplay or film, copyright law may consider them *joint authors*. To be considered a joint author, each coauthor must:

- Contribute expressive elements to the joint work, and
- At the time the work was created, intend to merge their own contributions inseparably or interdependently with the contributions of the other coauthors to form a unified whole.[29]
  - To figure out what the creators intended, courts may look to a variety of factors, including "whether the parties intended to be credited or billed as co-authors, the parties' view of decision-making and creative control, and the right to enter into third party contracts."[30]
- Have some degree of control over the creative work (only some courts require this).

Joint authors have certain rights under copyright law; if the authors want to change these rights, they need to do so by a contract between them, such as a writers' collaboration agreement. The contract must be in writing and signed by all authors.

COPYRIGHTABLE CONTRIBUTIONS REQUIRED FOR JOINT AUTHORSHIP

Generally speaking, each joint author's contributions must be copyrightable in their own right. If two people collaborate on a screenplay and one is doing the actual writing, but the other is just contributing ideas, you have only one author—the writer—unless the agreement specifies otherwise. "To be an author, one must supply more than mere direction or ideas: one must 'translate [. . .] an idea into a fixed, tangible expression entitled to copyright protection.'"[31]

As one court pointed out:

> "[. . .] the person with noncopyrightable material who proposes to join forces with a skilled writer to produce a copyrightable work is free to make a contract to disclose his or her material in return for assignment of part ownership of the resulting copyright."[32]

Example: Connor and Xander are working together on the screenplay *Hypno-Robot-Zombie-Vampires from Venus.* Connor just contributes the *idea* for the screenplay, and Xander does all the writing. Because ideas are not copyrightable, Connor cannot be considered a joint author. To share in the ownership of the copyright to the screenplay, Connor must enter into a contract with Xander in which Xander assigns part of the copyright to Connor.

However, not all courts agree that each joint author must contribute copyrightable work. The court handling the now-famous dispute between Neil Gaiman and Todd McFarlane over the question of joint authorship in the "Medieval Spawn" comic book character reasoned those ideas alone might be enough:

> "The contents of a comic book are typically the joint work of four artists—the writer, the penciller who creates the artwork (McFarlane), the inker (also McFarlane, in the case of Spawn No. 9, but it would often be a different person from the penciller) who makes a black and white plate of the artwork, and the colorist who colors it. The finished product is copyrightable, yet one can imagine cases in which none of the separate contributions of the four collaborating artists would be. The writer might have contributed merely a stock character (not copyrightable, as we're about to see) that achieved the distinctiveness required for copyrightability only by the combined contributions of the penciller, the inker, and the colorist, with each contributing too little to have by his contribution alone carried the stock character over the line into copyright land."[33]

On the other hand, other US courts have held that contributing ideas alone are not enough to make someone a joint author:

> a putative joint author's contribution must be independently copyrightable. As such, "ideas, refinements, and suggestions, standing alone," are not sufficient. Rather, a party asserting joint authorship must point to specific contributions that were fixed in a tangible medium.[34]

As a result, *where* in the United States the lawsuit is brought will often determine the extent each joint author must have contributed copyrightable content to the joint work. Hey, I don't make the rules. . .

WHAT ARE THE RIGHTS OF A JOINT AUTHOR?

When someone is a joint author, they have the following rights (again, unless a contract says otherwise):

- Each joint author is entitled to an equal and undivided interest in the copyright with the other joint authors. *Note:* The authors' contributions do not have to be equal; they will still share equally with other joint authors!
- Joint authors may grant nonexclusive licenses to the joint work. But *all* joint authors must agree to grant an exclusive copyright license to the joint work.

- Any joint author who sells or licenses the joint work must pay other joint authors an equal share of the money.
- Joint authors are not liable to each other for copyright infringement.
- Most courts require a signed contract to change a joint author's rights from those guaranteed by copyright law.

Example: Connor and Xander bring Natali in to write the screenplay with them—again, without a contract. This time, everybody contributes writing to the project, so everyone is a joint author. They are all excited and want to sell the screenplay. Connor and Xander go to Hollywood and submit the script to Big Film, Inc., a major Hollywood studio. Back at home, Natali gets a call from her uncle, the president of Fly-By-Night Pictures, a production company whose only claim to fame so far has been the production of several YouTube commercials for local car dealerships.

Fly-by-Night Pictures offers to purchase the motion picture rights to the screenplay for $100, and Natali accepts this offer over the phone without first talking to Connor or Xander. Can she do this?

Unfortunately, yes, she can. Natali has granted a nonexclusive license to her uncle for $100. This means that he can make the picture. Of course, the other joint authors can also grant nonexclusive licenses to other production companies to make their own versions of the picture. However, the practical effect of Natali's grant is that Big Film, Inc., will never make the picture—no studio will invest money in a film as long as someone else has the right to make the exact same picture as well. It is no consolation to her coauthors that Sally must split the $100 three ways with them.

To avoid this disaster, the three of them should have had a contract that specified that any and all licenses must be granted only with the unanimous (or at least a majority) approval of the joint authors. (See "Writing Collaboration," p. 108.)

IS EVERYBODY WHO CONTRIBUTES A JOINT AUTHOR?

Let's look at the converse question: is everyone who contributes to a movie a joint author? Nope. In a case involving the authorship of the film *Malcolm X*, the 9th Circuit held that a technical consultant was not a joint author, even though he "helped to rewrite, to make more authentic"[35] the script and the movie.

The court stressed that for a movie (in the absence of a contract), authorship was generally limited to the above-the-line cast and crew—in short, those who "mastermind" the movie:

> [The Author is] the person to whom the work owes its origin and who superintended the whole work, the "master mind." In a movie this definition, in the absence of a contract to the contrary, would generally limit authorship to someone at the top of the screen credits, sometimes the producer, sometimes the director, possibly the star, or the screenwriter—someone who has artistic control. [. . .] So many people might qualify as an "author" if the question were limited to whether they made a substantial creative contribution that that test would not distinguish one from another. Everyone from the producer and director to casting director, costumer, hairstylist, and "best boy" gets listed in the movie credits because all of their creative contributions really do matter. It is striking in *Malcolm X* how much the person who controlled the hue of the lighting contributed, yet no one would use the word "author" to denote that individual's relationship to the movie. ***A creative contribution does not suffice to establish authorship of the movie***. [emphasis added][36]

WORK MADE FOR HIRE

Copyright owners can license and assign their copyright to others—that's at the heart of every transaction related to the film property. It's the copyright to the screenplay that's being optioned, the distribution and exhibition rights under copyright that are in play when a film in distributed and played in a theater, etc. The cleanest way to obtain the copyright to the work created by a writer, director, or other artist is often through "work for hire."

Normally the person who creates a work is considered the author and will own the copyright as well. *Not so for a work made for hire*. The copyright to a work made for hire is initially owned by the employer or other hiring party, *not by the artist who created it*.

For any movie, TV show, script, song, or other expressive work created today in the United States, there are only two scenarios in which the copyright may be owned as a work made for hire:[37]

- ***Employees.*** Any copyrighted work created by employees within the scope of their employment is considered work made for hire and is automatically owned by the employer.

  Example: Artie the Animator is employed full-time by Rat Trap Productions, Inc., creating animations for the interstitial shorts they supply to the networks. Anytime Artie creates a work for his employers, the copyright to that work is automatically owned by Rat Trap. Even if Artie creates that work at home, if it is for a Rat Trap client, the copyright will vest initially with Rat Trap. However, if Artie works on his own anime feature film—a project that is separate and distinct from any Rat Trap projects—he will initially own the copyright to that anime film. To be on the safe side, Artie may want to document that his anime project is not connected with any Rat Trap project, nor does it use any elements that he created in the course of working on any Rat Trap project.

- ***Independent contractors.*** For an independent contractor's work on a motion picture to be considered a work made for hire, they must sign a written agreement explicitly stating that the work is a work made for hire. Without both the signed, written contract and the clause that says the work produced is "work made for hire," the independent contractor's work is *not* a work made for hire.

  Example: Artie the Animator quits Rat Trap Productions, Inc., and works as an independent contractor for several animation facilities. He picks up a project from Gertie and McCay Productions, Inc., creating backgrounds for a children's cartoon series. He does the work at his home studio on his own equipment and, with the exception of the delivery date, on his own schedule. Artie is clearly an independent contractor.

  To own Artie's work product as a work made for hire, Gertie and McCay Productions better have a written contract with Artie, which Artie must sign. The contract must expressly state that any work he produces for them is considered "work made for hire," a "work for hire," or a "specially ordered and commissioned work."

A CRITICAL ISSUE: WORK MADE FOR HIRE

This is one of the most important legal issues discussed in this book!

From a production company standpoint, *all* contributions of the artists, actors, writers, directors, other employees, and independent contractors should be created as works made for hire.

The contracts should do the following:

1. Explicitly state that the work these employees or contractors are performing for the production company is being done as a work made for hire.
2. The contracts should be signed by that employee or contractor.
3. The contracts should be written before the work is created. Although it's true that some jurisdictions, such as New York (2d Cir.), allow the contract to be written after the work has begun if and only if that written contract memorializes an agreement that the parties discussed and consented to before the work was started, some jurisdictions require the written contract first. Better to be safe and get it in writing right before the creative juices start flowing.

OFF
Work made by employee during scope of employment.
ON
Independent Contractor must sign a contract.
Contract must state that the work is a Work-Made-For-Hire.
The contract should be signed before the work starts.
Work for Hire

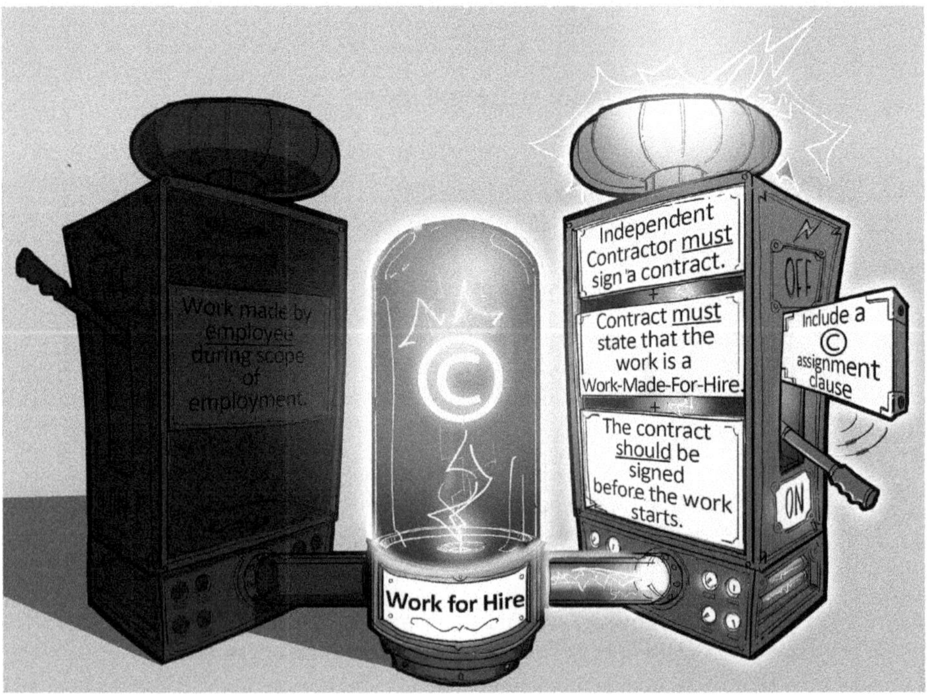
Work made by employee during scope of employment.
Independent Contractor must sign a contract.
+
Contract must state that the work is a Work-Made-For-Hire.
+
The contract should be signed before the work starts.
OFF
Include a © assignment clause
ON
Work for Hire

Duration of Work Made for Hire

Works made for hire have a shorter copyright life span than do works that are not made for hire. For any work made for hire created after January 1, 1978, copyright protection will last for 95 years from the year of first publication or 120 years from the year of creation, whichever expires first.

Who Is an Employee for Purposes of Works Made for Hire?

Because an employee's work product made within the scope of their employment is automatically a work made for hire, it is critical to determine just who is an employee. This might not be as easy as you think. Merely writing the word *employee* on a contract does not automatically create an employee/employer relationship.

In determining who is an employee for work-made-for-hire purposes, courts will look at the following factors:[38]

- The hiring party's right to control the manner and means by which the product is accomplished.
- The skill required to make the product.
- The source of the instrumentalities and tools.
- The location of the work.
- The duration of the relationship between the parties.
- Whether the hiring party has the right to assign additional projects to the hired party.
- The extent of the hired party's discretion over when and how long to work.
- The method of payment.
- The hired party's role in hiring and paying assistants.
- Whether the work is part of the regular business of the hiring party.
- Whether the hiring party is in business.
- The provision of employee benefits.
- The tax treatment of the hired party.

Determining the Scope of Employment

Let's face it, in today's world, most of us are gig workers with a side hustle. So, let's say you're employed by a production company to do whatever needs to be done on a particular day, which could mean anything from lighting, editing, and writing scripts for industrials to manning the phones when everybody else is on a shoot. In other words, whatever they need you to do. In a situation like that, how do you determine what your scope of employment is? If virtually everything is within the scope of employment, how do you know whether the feature film screenplay you're writing on the side would be owned as a work for hire by your employer? A court deciding on the issue might ask the following questions: (1) Is the work you made the kind that you are hired to make? In other words, were you hired to write screenplays for features? (2) When you created the screenplay, was it within the time and location that was controlled by your employer? (3) When you created the screenplay, were you at least in part motivated by helping your employer or furthering your employer's interests?[39]

Type of Works That Qualify as Work for Hire

All work made by an *employee* within the scope of his employment qualifies as a work for hire. However, making matters more complex, only certain types of *independent contractor*-produced work qualifies as work for hire:

- Contributions to a collective work.
- *Parts of a motion picture or other audiovisual work.*
- Translations.
- Supplementary works.
- Compilations.
- Instructional texts.
- Tests or as answer materials for a test.
- Atlases.[40]

This means that if you've hired an independent contractor to create a type of work that is not on this list, it is *not* a work for hire, despite there being a written, signed "work for hire" agreement.

If you're reading carefully, you've noticed that "part of a motion picture or other audiovisual work" is on that list, so as filmmakers, we're covered. However, if you want to have a make-up artist create zombie make-up for waiters serving finger sandwiches at your premier of *Hypno-Robot-Zombie-Vampires from Venus*, and you want to own the copyright to her makeup design,[41] you better have an alternate copyright assignment clause in her independent contractor's agreement.

Work for Hire in California

We've talked about the benefits of signing an independent contractor to a work-for-hire agreement. Now here's one potential drawback (at least in California). Under California law, when you sign an independent contractor to a work-for-hire agreement, *they become your employee.*[42] Yes, you read that correctly. If you sign a writer to an independent contractor work-for-hire agreement in California, you must treat him like an employee, which means you could be liable for unpaid taxes, disability payments, workers compensation, and other costs attendant on an employer/employee relationship. Furthermore, in California, the presumption is that any person providing labor for money (like a paid crew member) is an employee and not an independent contractor, unless the hiring party (e.g. the producer) can show:

(A) The person is free from the control and direction of the hiring entity in connection with the performance of the work, both under the contract for the performance of the work and in fact.

(B) The person performs work that is outside the usual course of the hiring entity's business.

(C) The person is customarily engaged in an independently established trade, occupation, or business of the same nature as that involved in the work performed.[43]

This is the infamous "AB5" law which took effect in 2020. Under it, a plumber called to fix the toilet on set would likely be an independent contractor, but any professional crew member or performer under the control of the director of producer (pretty much everybody else on set) should be classified as an employee. Which means in California, ensuring your film was created as a work for hire just got easier! It also means you really need to understand just what your obligations are as an employer.

Work Made for Hire/Copyright Assignment Clause

To be doubly sure that the copyright is effectively transferred from the creator to the hiring party, most work-made-for-hire agreements provide for an alternative copyright assignment. That way, if for some reason the work is not considered a work made for hire, the hiring party gets the copyright anyway by virtue of the alternate copyright assignment clause.

"But wait," you may be thinking, "if I can just get a copyright by the creator assigning it to me, why did I just read through all that stuff about work for hire?"

That's because a work-for-hire arrangement is often the cleanest way to acquire a copyright because of a counterintuitive provision of US copyright law: "Termination of Transfer" (see "Termination of Transfer," p. 427). In brief, any copyright assignment or license may be terminated after a certain period of time (often 35 years from the grant of the copyright), despite a contract which says otherwise! However, this is *not* true for works for hire: the author and original copyright owner in a work made for hire is the contracting party, not the artist herself.

But since work-for-hire arrangements are situational (and require key facts to be established), it is a good idea to include a copyright assignment clause, just in case. Perhaps something like this:

> ***Example:*** "Director acknowledges and agrees that all of their contributions to the Motion Picture, including, but not limited to writing, directing, storyboarding, gag creation, and any other result of the director's services provided under this contract (the 'Results and Proceeds'), are created as a 'Works Made for Hire,' with all copyright and other rights thereto vesting initially in the production company. Accordingly, the production company shall be considered the sole and exclusive author and copyright owner of the Results and Proceeds and of the Motion Picture. To the extent, if any, that ownership of the Motion Picture produced hereunder or the Results and Proceeds of Director's services do not immediately vest in production company by virtue of this Agreement, Director hereby immediately assigns to production company all rights (including all rights of copyright) of every kind and character in and to the Picture and the results and proceeds of Director's services. Director hereby waives all 'moral rights,' *'droit moral,'* and similar rights. All rights hereunder assigned shall be assigned in perpetuity, and such assignment shall be irrevocable. This effect of this clause shall survive any termination of this Agreement."

***TIP: Include a copyright assignment clause in every work-for-hire agreement.* To ensure that the copyright is fully transferred to your production company, make sure that the language of this clause transfers all material that was made for your film even *before* the contract was signed. A phrase such as "Writer assigns the copyright to the work performed under this Agreement" might not transfer a treatment written by the writer *prior* to the agreement being negotiated and signed.**[44]

LICENSING AND ASSIGNING THE COPYRIGHT

A copyright license is the grant of a portion of the copyright (usually limited by time, geography, medium, etc.). The person giving the license is the *licensor*; the person receiving the license is the *licensee*.

> ***Example:*** Dingo Distributors, LLC, the licensor, grants a license to Bandicoot Broadcasting, Inc., the licensee, to broadcast *Wombats in Love* in North America for a period of three years or for a total of nine runs, whichever comes first.

An *exclusive license*, also known as an *assignment*, is a license that gives the licensee the exclusive power to a certain right. It is a transfer of ownership of a copyright or any of the exclusive copyright rights. Even if it is called a *transfer of ownership*, that transfer may be limited in duration, scope, geography, or any other way you can think of. Once an exclusive license is granted, the licensor no longer has any power to grant another license to that right or to exercise that granted right herself. An exclusive copyright license must be in writing and signed by the licensor and the writing must clearly and unequivocally transfer the copyright.

> ***Example:*** Pickled Piper Productions is negotiating a distribution deal for its film, *Pickled Petunias*, with Dahlia Distributors, LLC. The distribution agreement grants the distributor the exclusive right to distribute the film in North America for five years. This is an assignment, because the right to distribute a copyrighted work is an exclusive copyright right. The assignment is limited by territory (North America) and duration (five years). Because it is a copyright assignment, it must be in writing and signed by Pickled Piper Productions to be effective.[45]

A ***nonexclusive license*** is a license that may be granted to any number of licensees at the same time. A nonexclusive license may be granted orally or may even be implied from conduct. The holder of a nonexclusive license may not grant licenses to the work to others without the copyright owner's permission.

TO TRANSFER A COPYRIGHT, YOU MUST GET IT IN WRITING

"17 U.S.C. § 204. Execution of transfers of copyright ownership

(a) A transfer of copyright ownership, other than by operation of law, is not valid unless an instrument of conveyance, or a note or memorandum of the transfer, is in writing and signed by the owner of the rights conveyed or such owner's duly authorized agent."

As one court put it: "The rule is really quite simple: If the copyright holder agrees to transfer ownership to another party, that party must get the copyright holder to sign a piece of paper saying so. It doesn't have to be the Magna Carta; a one-line *pro forma* statement will do."[46] However, that one-line statement must be unambiguous, clearly transferring the copyright.[47]

The Copyright License Request Letter

From literary characters to stock footage to musical recordings, some form of copyright license will be used in virtually every stage of the production's legal housekeeping.

The license and the request letter are the transactional workhorses of the production attorney. The two are often combined into one form—a letter of agreement that:

- Asks the owner's permission to use the copyrighted material.
- Offers the owner licensing terms for the requested material's use.

To accept the terms, the rights owner merely countersigns the letter and sends it back to the producer.

The request letter should be specific about how the producer intends to use the material, where the producer intends to exhibit the finished film or video, and the format of the film or video. Alternatively, depending on the owner's leverage, the producer may be sent the copyright owner's contracts and terms on a take-it-or-leave-it basis.

LICENSING TERMINOLOGY

Although copyright licenses differ depending on the type of material to be licensed, most licensing agreements share some common terminology:

- *The grant.* This is the critical clause of any licensing contract. It establishes exactly which material is being licensed and whether the license is exclusive. Because copyright is actually a bundle of rights—the right to reproduce a work, create derivative works, distribute copies of a work, perform a work publicly, or publicly display a work—a comprehensive license must outline the extent to which the licensee may exercise any of these rights.
- *Territory.* A description of where the film or video containing the copyrighted material can be performed or distributed.
- *Scope of use.* What media and method of distribution you can use the copyrighted material (Internet VOD? Broadcast TV? Movie theaters? etc.).
- *The Term.* The duration of the license. Most filmmakers want to have a license to use the material for the life of the copyright, including renewal terms, if any.
- *Advertising.* If the material the producer is licensing for the film will be included in the film's advertising, the producer will need to secure the right to include the work in the film's marketing and promotion.
- *Payments.* The rate of payment to the copyright holder and how it is calculated.
- *Credits.* How the copyright owner is to be credited in the film.
- *Representations and warranties.* Promises by the copyright owner that he has the right to enter into the license agreement and that nothing in the material infringes the rights of others. This section can be quite extensive.

- *Termination.* A statement that if the producer fails to pay the agreed-on rate or if the producer breaches the agreement in any other way, all granted rights revert back to the copyright owner.

Some other common terms include the right to audit a production company's accounts; a copyright owner's right to free samples of the finished work; and whether the licensee may, in turn, assign the rights it has been granted.

Termination of Transfer

One seemingly odd wrinkle in copyright law are the *termination of transfer* provisions, which allows a valid and otherwise irrevocable copyright assignment or license to be revoked after a certain time by the copyrighted work's author or her heirs. Once a copyright transfer has been terminated under this provision, no new derivative works can be made from the terminated copyright. However, works prepared while the copyright license or assignment was in effect can still be exploited as per the original agreement.

> ***Example:*** In 2020, Xander assigns the copyright to his screenplay *Two-Fingered Bob* to Despot Pictures, which, over a 35-year period, makes a movie and a television series based on Xander's work. Even though the screenplay acquisition agreement between Xander and Despot explicitly states that the copyright transfer is irrevocable and lasts for the duration of the copyright, *Xander can still revoke the copyright* starting at the end of 35 years from when it was transferred! Despot can still exploit the movie and the television series it had made prior to the termination, in accordance with the terms of the screenplay acquisition agreement, but once Xander revokes the copyright, Despot can't make any more derivative works from the screenplay (video games, books, merchandise, etc.) without relicensing the copyright from Xander.

It is important to note that a work created as a work for hire is not subject to the termination-of-transfer provisions. This is simply another reason that, for production companies, it is often better to get the copyright to the script as a work for hire rather than as an assignment.

> ***Example:*** Connor is hired by Despot Pictures on a work-for-hire basis to write his screenplay *Lilly Livered with Onions*. Thirty-five years later, he hears about Xander's success in terminating the transfer for *Two-Fingered Bob*, as described in the earlier example. Connor tries to terminate the transfer of rights to *Lilly Livered* but fails; unlike Xander, who assigned the rights in his screenplay, Connor created his screenplay as a *work for hire* for Despot. When a work is created as a work for hire, the copyright originally vests in the contracting party (here, Despot Pictures). The law considers Despot Pictures the author of *Lilly Livered with Onions* from the

moment of the script's creation. Since Connor never had any rights in the screenplay in the first place, he can't get the rights back.

TERMINATION OF TRANSFER STATUTORY PROVISIONS

The two sections of the copyright law that govern how and when a copyright transfer may be terminated are 17 USC §203 and 17 USC §304(c). Generally speaking, §203 deals with licenses and transfers of copyright which happened after January 1, 1978. §304(c) deals with licenses and transfers of copyright that occurred prior to January 1, 1978.[48]

Any work that you transfer now[49] and assign to a publishing company or other licensee or assignee may be terminated:

> During a period of five years beginning at the end of thirty-five years from the date of execution of the grant; or, if the grant covers the right of publication of the work, the period begins at the end of thirty-five years from the date of publication of the work under the grant or at the end of forty years from the date of execution of the grant, whichever term ends earlier.[50]

To terminate the transfer to copyright, the owners of such "termination interest" must send a signed notice to the licensee or assignee terminating the right to the transferred copyright.

It's important to note that it's not just the original author who can terminate the transfer: if the author is dead, the author's spouse, children, or grandchildren may also serve notice to get the copyright back.

To terminate a copyright interest under §203, the form of the notice must contain:

- "A statement that the termination is made under section 203;
- "The name of each grantee whose rights are being terminated, or the grantee's successor in title, and each address at which service of the notice is being made;
- "The date of execution of the grant being terminated and, if the grant covered the right of publication of a work, the date of publication of the work under the grant;
- "For each work to which the notice of termination applies, the title of the work and the name of the author or, in the case of a joint work, the authors who executed the grant being terminated; and, if possible and practicable, the original copyright registration number;

- "A brief statement reasonably identifying the grant to which the notice of termination applies;
- "The effective date of termination;
- "In the case of a termination of a grant executed by one or more of the authors of the work where the termination is exercised by the successors of a deceased author, a listing of the names and relationships to that deceased author [and pertinent information about the relationship to the deceased author]."[51]

Copyright Registration

To fully protect a copyright, it should be registered. The advantages of registration and the registration process are covered in the section "Copyright Registration" (p. 164).

Copyright Infringement

Anyone who violates any of the exclusive rights of a copyright owner may be liable for copyright infringement. Keep in mind that you don't have to *intend* to infringe a copyright to be liable for copyright infringement!

Proving Infringement

To prove copyright infringement, the copyright owner (the plaintiff) must prove both *ownership and copying:*

- *Ownership*. That they own a valid copyright.
- *Copying*. That the defendant copied copyrightable elements of the plaintiff's copyrighted work.

There must be copying of *copyrightable* material. Copying of unprotectable elements is not enough. For instance, if all that was taken was an idea (which is not copyrightable), that would not be enough to prove copyright infringement, even if the plaintiff could show that the idea was directly taken from his or her copyrighted work.

Copying is composed of two parts: *access* and *substantial similarity:*

- *Access*. Although it's great if you can actually prove that the defendant copied your work, evidence of copying is usually hard to come by. Recognizing that, courts will accept circumstantial evidence of the defendant's *access* to the copyrighted work. A plaintiff proves access by showing that the defendant had the opportunity to view or to copy the plaintiff's work.

- *Substantial similarity.* In addition to access, the two works (the plaintiff's copyrighted work and the defendant's work) must also be substantially similar. The test for "substantial similarity" is "whether an average lay observer would recognize the alleged copy as having been appropriated from the copyrighted work."[52]

PLAGIARISM IS NOT THE SAME THING AS COPYRIGHT INFRINGEMENT

Plagiarism is an ethical violation, not a legal cause of action. It is possible for a filmmaker to be guilty of plagiarizing another artist's work without being legally guilty of copyright infringement. For instance, plagiarism can occur when ideas are taken from a source without correct attribution. As indicated earlier, copyright law does not protect ideas.

Plagiarism can be a very fuzzy concept. If what was taken was an idea, it can often be hard to draw the line between plagiarism and inspiration.

CONTRIBUTORY COPYRIGHT INFRINGEMENT

Even if you did not do the copying yourself, you can still be liable for copyright infringement. For instance, if you have knowledge of somebody's infringing activity, and encourage, assist, materially contribute, or induce infringing conduct, you could be liable for **contributory copyright infringement**.[53]

VICARIOUS COPYRIGHT INFRINGEMENT

A somewhat related concept to contributory copyright infringement is the tort of **vicarious copyright infringement**. It's similar in that neither involves direct infringement by the wrongdoers, but here the relationship is one of a supervisor to a worker. Remember the concept of *respondeat superior* that we learned about when we were setting up our business entity? (See *"Respondeat Superior,"* p. 44.) If you recall, an employer is responsible for the tortious acts of its employee that are committed during the scope of the employee's job. In order to be liable for vicarious copyright infringement, you must have the right and ability to control a worker's infringing conduct, and you must directly benefit from your worker's infringing activity.

"One . . . infringes vicariously by profiting from direct infringement while declining to exercise a right to stop or limit it."[54]

Example: You're working with an animator to create your new superhero movie *Humongo-Phage—The World Devourer*, about a gigantic intergalactic being who eats planets. You encourage your animator to take a close look at the world-devouring Marvel comic villain, Galactus; give them copies of the character; and tell them to create a character that looks just like Galactus, but to "change the colors around a little bit." If the animator's final product is substantially similar to the copyrighted Galactus character, and Marvel sues you, you could be liable for contributory and vicarious copyright infringement even though you weren't the artist who drew the infringing character.

THREE-YEAR STATUTE OF LIMITATIONS

Lawsuits have a "shelf life," called a statute of limitations. If you don't sue within that time period, your time is up: no matter how favorable the evidence in your favor, you can no longer sue over that claim. For copyright law, the lawsuit must be "commenced within three years after the claim accrued."[55]

Of course, the question then becomes "when does the claim accrue?" And on that subject, the courts are split over two ways of interpreting when the clock starts, so it really does matter where you bring your case:

> Under the **injury rule**, [. . .] a claim accrues at the time of each act of infringement, regardless of the copyright holder's knowledge of the infringement. In contrast, under the **discovery rule**, a claim for copyright infringement does not accrue until the aggrieved party knows or has reason to know of the injury that forms the basis of the claim.[56]

PENALTIES FOR INFRINGEMENT

Courts have a plethora of punishments in store for the copyright infringe, for instance—*damages and profits*.[57] A court may order an infringer to pay either:

- The copyright owner's actual damages and any additional profits of the infringer, or
- Statutory damages in a sum of not less than $750 or more than $30,000 as the court considers just.
- For willful infringement, the court, at its discretion, may increase the award of statutory damages to a sum of not more than $150,000.

Costs and Attorneys' Fees.[58] The court, at its discretion, may allow the recovery of full costs by or against any party . . . and the court may also award a reasonable attorney's fee to the prevailing party as part of the costs.

Injunctions.[59] A court may issue injunctions halting the manufacture or distribution of infringing articles. Appendix B

Impounding and Disposition of Infringing Articles.[60] A court may order the destruction of all infringing copies of a copyrighted work. In addition to ordering the destruction of the copies, it can also order that the instruments that made the copies also be destroyed. This includes: "all plates, molds, matrices, masters, tapes, film negatives, or other articles by means of which such copies or phonorecords may be reproduced."

Criminal Penalties. Courts may also sentence willful copyright infringers to jail for periods ranging from one to ten years, depending upon the severity and amount of their willful infringement.[61]

The CASE Act

Protecting your copyright against infringers can be an expensive prospect involving the federal courts and tens of thousands of dollars in lawyers' fees. In fact, it's so expensive that many copyright holders choose not to sue if the amount that they could potentially recover is less than $30,000 or $40,000.

In 2020, Congress decided to address this issue by passing the Copyright Alternative in Small-Claims Enforcement Act of 2020 (CASE Act), which established the Copyright Claims Board (CCB). The CCB acts essentially as a "small claims court" for copyright issues. If you decide to enforce your copyright or defend your right to use someone else's copyrighted material using the CCB, here are some key elements you need to know:

- It is completely voluntary. You can use the CCB or bring your case in federal court. You can't file a claim in both venues at the same time. Furthermore, it's voluntary for all parties in a dispute. Either party can opt out of CCB adjudication and choose to file instead in federal court.
- Monetary damages are capped at $30,000.
- Unlike federal court, won't have to wait for a copyright registration to be issued before initiating a lawsuit under the CCB—as long as you have filed for copyright registration, that's enough.
- You don't need an attorney to file or defend a claim with the CCB (although it is a really good idea to get one).
- "The CCB will be able to consider the following:
  - "Claims for infringement of one of the exclusive rights in the Copyright Act.
  - "Claims for a declaration of noninfringement of an exclusive right (when a party accused of infringement wants a legal statement that they are not liable for infringement).
  - "Claims for misrepresentation during the notice and counter-notice process under section 512 of the Copyright Act.
  - "Counterclaims related to the same transaction or occurrence that is the subject of the original claim.

- "Legal or equitable defenses under copyright law or that are otherwise available."[62]
- It's important to keep in mind that if you disagree with the decision of the CCB, your right to appeal such decision is much more limited than if you had followed the process initially through the federal courts. In federal court, you can appeal a decision if you believe the court made a mistake of fact or law. However, if you disagree with the CCB decision. you're limited to:
  - "Request that the CCB reconsider a decision if it includes a technical mistake or a clear legal or factual error that is material to the decision.
  - "If the CCB denies your request for reconsideration, you will be able to ask the Register of Copyrights to review the decision to see if the CCB abused its discretion when denying the request for reconsideration.
  - "Ask a federal district court to vacate, modify, or correct a CCB determination if (1) the determination was issued as a result of fraud, corruption, misrepresentation, or other misconduct, (2) the CCB exceeded its authority or failed to issue a final determination, or (3) in the case of a default or failure to prosecute, excusable neglect was the cause of the default or failure to prosecute."[63]

FAIR USE AND OTHER DEFENSES TO COPYRIGHT INFRINGEMENT

FAIR USE

Among filmmakers, *fair use* of a copyright is one of the most widely known . . . and widely misunderstood copyright doctrines. Fair use allows a filmmaker to take a portion of copyrighted work owned by a third party without that filmmaker needing to secure the copyright owner's permission. The tricky part is figuring out *what part* and *how much* of a copyrighted work you can take without permission before it becomes copyright infringement. Of course, determining infringement is ultimately the job of a federal court, which means filmmakers often find out too late—after they've been sued—that their use was indeed fair use. And because it is a defense to copyright infringement, generally it is up to the defendant in an infringement lawsuit to prove that their use was fair use. (See "Copyright Infringement," p. 429.)

TOP FAIR-USE MYTHS

- You can use *any* text under 2,000 words.
- You can use *any* music clip under 5 seconds.

- It's okay to use *anybody's* work in yours if you don't sell the final product.
- As long as you give the author credit, you *don't* have to ask for permission.

All of these statements are *WRONG!* There are *no* bright-line tests for fair use. The distinction between fair use and infringement may be unclear and not easily defined. There is no specific number of words, lines, or notes that may safely be taken without permission. Acknowledging the source of the copyrighted material does not substitute for obtaining permission. Fair use is always determined on a case-by-case basis by the jury or the guy or gal in the black robe.

CATEGORIES OF FAIR USE

General categories of fair use include news reporting, criticism, comment, teaching (including multiple copies for classroom use), scholarship, or research. The 1961 *Report of the Register of Copyrights on the General Revision of the US Copyright Law* cites examples of activities courts have regarded as fair use:

- "Quotation of excerpts in a review or criticism for purposes of illustration or comment;
- "Quotation of short passages in a scholarly or technical work, for illustration or clarification of the author's observations;
- "Use in a parody of some of the content of the work parodied;
- "Summary of an address or article, with brief quotations, in a news report;
- "Reproduction by a library of a portion of a work to replace part of a damaged copy;
- "Reproduction by a teacher or student of a small part of a work to illustrate a lesson;
- "Reproduction of a work in legislative or judicial proceedings or reports;
- "Incidental and fortuitous reproduction, in a newsreel or broadcast, of a work located in the scene of an event being reported.[64]"

DETERMINING FAIR USE

Courts must give weight to the following four factors in determining fair use:

1. "The purpose and character of the use, including whether such use is of the commercial nature or is for nonprofit educational purposes;

2. "The nature of the copyrighted work;
3. "The amount and substantiality of the portion used in relation to the copyrighted work as a whole; and
4. "The effect of the use upon the potential market for or value of the copyrighted work."[65]

In analyzing the fair use factors, it's important to keep in mind just where the court is "looking" with respect to each one of the factors. To best understand what's going on here, I'm going to make up some definitions. The **Original Work** is what we are going to call the pre-existing copyrighted artwork from which a portion was taken without the permission. The **New Work** is art created by a second creator, partially utilizing a portion of the Original Work.

Fair Use Factor #1: "The Purpose and Character of the Use, Including Whether Such Use Is of the Commercial Nature or Is for Nonprofit Educational Purposes"

This first factor is often considered: "the heart of the fair use inquiry."[66] Here the court analyzes the New Work and asks a few questions:

- "Okay, so you took a portion of the Original Work. . . . What did you do with the portion you took?"
- "What kind of work is your New Work? Is it parody? Criticism? Commentary?"
- "Are you using this New Work for educational purposes, or is your use purely commercial?"

And, perhaps most importantly. . .

- "Did the New Work significantly transform the portion of the Original Work that it took? Did it recast or add new meaning to that portion of the Original Work?"

TRANSFORMATIVE USES

In analyzing the first fair-use factor ("The purpose and character of the use . . ."), a court will give greater weight to a defendant who is asserting a fair-use defense if she can show that her use is *transformative*. A transformative use "adds something new, with a further purpose or different character, altering the first with new expression, meaning, or message."[67] So, if instead of merely slavishly copying a film clip, a producer modifies it using digital effects and uses the clip to comment on its original source, creating new expression or meaning, the court may be more likely to find fair use. Filmmakers should take note that merely removing objectionable content from an unlicensed film without adding anything new is generally not considered transformative enough to justify a fair-use defense.[68] To be transformative, you have to do more than just repackage the old, unlicensed work into a new form. You have to use it to create new meaning, often by providing insightful commentary or criticism; otherwise, the court may find that you're "free riding" on another's creations.[69]

Findings that tip the balance of this first factor towards fair use include:

- The New Work is educational, informational, criticism, parody, or cultural commentary.
- The New Work is being used for nonprofit purposes rather than purely commercial purposes.
- The New Work significantly transforms the portion of the Original Work it took; it has created new meaning, "adds a further purpose or different character,"[70] and is not merely a minor variation of the Original Work.

Tips for understanding this factor:

- *Commercial use.* Courts disagree on the significance of the language: "whether such use is of the commercial nature." In fact, they also disagree as to just what is considered commercial nature. Some courts, for instance, feel that commercial use in this context should be limited to those situations where "repeated and exploitative unauthorized copies of copyrighted works were made to save the expense of purchasing authorized copies."[71] Ironically, even though the inquiry into the New Work's "commercial nature" is in the statute, courts by and large find it more helpful to center their inquiry around a term that is not in the statute—*transformative use.* One of the most important aspects of this first fair use factor is whether the New Work has significantly transformed the portion of the Original Work, the "central purpose of th[e] [first factor] investigation is to see whether the new work merely 'supersede[s] the objects' of the original creation . . . or instead adds something new, with a further purpose or character [. . .]."[72]

Fair Use Factor #2: "The Nature of the Copyrighted Work"

For the second fair use factor, the court now turns its attention away from the New Work and fixes its gaze[73] on the Original Work.

Here, the court asks the following questions:

- What kind of work is the Original Work?
- Does the Original Work have a lot of creative expression? Or,
- Is the Original Work primarily factually informative, like a news story?
- Has the Original Work been published?

Tipping the balance of this factor toward fair use would be:

- A finding which showed that the Original Works was primarily factual or informational, like a news story. News broadcasts, although protected by copyright, are themselves more prone to be used under fair use. As the US Supreme Court has stated: "Copying a news broadcast may have a stronger claim to fair use than copying a [creative work]."[74]
- A finding that the Original Work had been published. Unpublished works are subject to greater protection under copyright law; the reason being that an author should have the right to control the first publication of his or her work. While the fact that the Original Work was unpublished may weigh against a finding of fair use, it, in itself is not determinative.

Fair Use Factor #3: "The Amount and Substantiality of the Portion Used in Relation to the Copyrighted Work as a Whole"

To analyze the third fair use factor, the court holds both the Original Work and the New Work side by side and asks the following questions:

- How much of the Original Work was taken and incorporated into the New Work?
- What percentage of the Original Work was taken?
- The portion of the Original Work that was taken—was it the heart of the Original Work? Or, rather, was it a portion that was ancillary, or incidental to the Original Work?

Findings that tend to favor fair use on the third factor would include:

- Using a small or insignificant portion of the Original Work.
- Using part of the Original Work that was incidental or ancillary.
- Not using parts of the Original Work that are essential, critical, vital, or the "heart" of the Original Work.
- However, it does not help the fair use defense trying to prove how much you did *not* take. "No plagiarist can excuse the wrong by showing how much of his work he did not pirate."[75]

Fair Use Factor #4: "The Effect of the Use Upon the Potential Market for or Value of the Copyrighted Work"

Finally, the court examines the economic effect of the New Work on the Original Work. Unfortunately, this is one of the least uniformly interpreted factors.

The court may ask:

- Does the New Work attempt to substitute for the Original Work in the relevant marketplace?
- Is the primary economic harm done to the Original Work caused by the New Work's criticism or parody of the Original Work?
- Is the economic harm that is done to the Original Work substantial?

Findings that tend to favor fair use for the fourth factor would include:

- The New Work and the Original Work are sold to different types of consumers.
- The primary harm done to the Original Work is as a result of criticism or parody rather than the New Work substituting for the Original Work.
- The economic harm done to the Original Work is relatively minor.

Analyzing the Factors

Once the court has examined these four fair use factors, it steps back and looks at how they each interrelate and which ones, given the facts before the court, should be given the most weight.

And, while these four factors *must* be considered by a court when analyzing a fair use question, they are not the only factors a court can consider; in other words, other relevant findings may be considered, such as intent by the creator of the New Work to deceive consumers, willingness to give appropriate attribution to the creators of the Original Work, bad faith on the part of either party, etc.

In the past few years, many courts have expanded the kinds of uses that qualify as fair use. For instance, a video documentary posted on YouTube composed entirely of excerpts from another YouTube video was found to be fair use, despite the allegedly infringing video containing no explicit criticism or commentary. The court was satisfied that the manner in which the unlicensed excerpts were edited when shown on the alleged infringer's YouTube channel provided enough context that reasonable viewers would be aware that the resulting video was a working criticism and thus transformative enough to be considered fair use.[76] It's important to note that when the filmmaker whose work was taken lost her copyright infringement lawsuit, she was also ordered to pay the legal fees for the prevailing side.[77]

EXAMPLES OF FAIR USE

Two examples illustrate how a court will analyze whether an unauthorized use is fair or infringement.

Scenario #1: Daniel, a television commercial director, makes a commercial for a local car dealership. He uses a film clip from *Star Wars* showing Darth Vader swinging his light saber and cutting down Obi-Wan Kenobi. Over this, he puts a voiceover saying, "We slash prices and kill the competition." The film clip is used without permission, and the commercial airs. Disney sues for copyright infringement, and Daniel defends by asserting a fair-use defense.

- In determining whether his use was fair use, the court first looks to see "purpose and character of the use." Here, the court is analyzing what Daniel did with the clip he used. His use was clearly commercial and not educational, and therefore Daniel loses on this prong of the analysis.
- Second, the court turns to the clip itself and looks to "the nature of the copyrighted work." *Star Wars* is a work of fiction, not news or a documentary, and thus is afforded the highest protection under copyright law. This factor is also weighed against Daniel.
- Third, the court examines how much Daniel took and how important that clip was to *Star Wars* as a whole. Here, Daniel argues that his clip was only five seconds long—hardly significant given the movie's two-hour length. The attorney for Disney counters that though the clip may have been short, it was a critical moment in the movie, and thus its importance should not be judged by its length alone. The court will give weight to an argument like that one—and will look to see whether the "heart" of the work was appropriated. The court decides that this factor should also be counted against Daniel.
- Fourth, the court will look to see how Daniel's unauthorized use affects the market for the movie *Star Wars*. The court will take a look to see whether Daniel's use of the clip "usurps" the market for *Star Wars* clips.[78] The key here is whether the "defendant's use [acts] as a substitute for plaintiff's work in the marketplace."[79] Because Disney has licensed clips from *Star Wars* for use in other television commercials, this factor, like the others, is counted against Daniel. The court finds that Daniel has not made a successful fair-use defense and thus has infringed the copyright to *Star Wars*.

Scenario #2: Flaherty Filmmaker is shooting a documentary about the media's treatment of the issue of global warming and wants to use a few shots from an evening news story focusing on the world's biggest tire fire.

Flaherty tries to get permission from Nosey News Networks, Inc. (NNN), the company that produced the footage, but they turn him down. He decides to use it anyway, taking a 1-minute clip from the 6-minute story. The clip features a reporter who jokes about the impact on global warming the tire fire will cause, saying: "Will the fire warm the globe or just cause a few paranoid scientists to get hot under the collar? Over to you, Cathy." Flaherty adds "pop-up video"-style graphic bubbles with global warming statistics over the reporter's derisive commentary. The overall effect of Flaherty's editing and graphic additions makes the reporter seem extremely biased and ignorant of the issues. Even though Flaherty has been denied permission to use the clip, he nonetheless includes a copyright notice under the footage, properly attributing the clip to NNN.

Flaherty's documentary is released and he is sued by NNN. In court, he defends on the grounds that his use of NNN's clip was fair use. In its decision the court reasons as follows:

- In determining whether Flaherty's use was fair, the court first looks to see "purpose and character of the use." Flaherty used the clip as criticism of the news program and as social commentary. Furthermore, his use was educational. This factor is decided in his favor.
- Second, the court turns to the clip itself and looks to "the nature of the copyrighted work." News broadcasts, although protected by copyright, are themselves more prone to be used under fair use. As the US Supreme Court has stated: "Copying a news broadcast may have a stronger claim to fair use than copying a motion picture."[80] This factor is decided in Flaherty's favor as well.
- Third, the court examines how much Flaherty took and how important that clip was to the news broadcast as a whole. Flaherty took 1 minute of a 6-minute broadcast. The court decides that this was a substantial amount, and, because the clip contained the heart of the piece—the tire fire—the factor is decided in NNN's favor.
- Fourth, the court looks to see how Flaherty's unauthorized use affects the market for the NNN news segment. The court holds that because NNN does not license its clips, the nightly news market is NNN's primary market. Flaherty's use does not have any appreciable affect on the market, and this factor is decided in his favor as well.
- The court also points out that Flaherty's use was transformative—the "pop-up news bubbles" recast the clip. Furthermore, Flaherty acted in good faith by placing the NNN copyright notice below the clip.
- The court rules that Flaherty's unauthorized use was excused under fair-use principles.

CAUTION! It is up to the court to decide—after the fact—whether a use is "fair use."

The Copyright Office has a list of key fair use cases, which can be found here: www.copyright.gov/fair-use/fair-index.html.

De Minimis Taking

IP

De minimis is a fancy Latin phrase that means "of the least" or "of trifles." It refers to the taking of an insignificant amount of a copyrighted work—an amount so trifling that a court will rule that no harm was done even though what was taken was taken without permission. Although *de minimis* is a defense to infringement rather than an exception to copyrightability, it does underscore the fact that courts will rule that some infringement is just too harmless to worry about. Of course, it is up to the defendant to prove that the taking is *de minimis*. As the legal maxim goes, *de minimis non curat lex*—the law does not concern itself with trifles.[81]

> ***Example:*** Decades ago, a federal court was faced with the issue of potential copyright infringement within the movie *Seven*. In the movie there is a scene in which two police officers search a photographer's apartment, looking for clues to a murder. They enter the photographer's darkroom, which is filled with disturbing photographs. The copyrights to 10 of the photographs were owned by an artist who had never given his permission for the filmmaker to use them. However, in the final version of the film, the photographs are out of focus and only appear on screen for a matter of seconds. When the artist sued, the court ruled that the unpermitted use of the artist's photographs was a *de minimis* taking.[82]

THE LEGAL TEST FOR *DE MINIMIS* USE

For films, the court pointed out that whether the use was *de minimis* is based on:

> 1) the amount of the copyrighted work that is taken, as well as [. . .] 2) the observability of the copyrighted work in the allegedly infringing work. Observability is determined by the length of time the copyrighted work appears in the allegedly infringing work, and its prominence in that work as revealed by the lighting and positioning of the copyrighted work,[83]

as well as factors such as focus and camera angles.[84] Fair use is usually asserted as an alternative defense when a *de minimis* argument fails.[85] (See "Fair Use," p. 433.)

> ***CAUTION!*** Whether a taking was *de minimis* is something only a court can decide—after you have been dragged into a lawsuit. Remember: Every time you're sued, you have to pay an attorney to defend you, even if you win.[86] Copyright law does allow the winning side to ask for their attorney's fees to be paid by the loser, but it is not granted in many cases. A better practice is to secure permission for all copyrighted works used in your film rather than rolling the dice and gambling on the fact that a court will find an unpermitted taking to be *de minimis*.

The Doctrine of Independent Creation

This is not an exception to copyright law but rather a rule that allows two people to have copyright ownership in what is essentially the same work. The way it works is this: If two authors come up with the same work independently of each other and neither has copied the other's work, both works will be entitled to copyright protection—even though the two works are substantially similar to each other. This is true because copyright is based on originality rather than novelty. As long as the work originated with an author and is not copied from another author, that author may claim a copyright.

> ***Example:*** Wendy Writer spent two years writing her script *The Platypus Papers*. Because she doesn't have any contacts in Hollywood, her script sits on her hard drive without being seen by anyone but her mother. To her dismay, she opens up the paper one day and sees an ad for the new film *The Platypus Diaries*, produced by Monotreme Pictures, Inc. When she goes to see the film, she is even more upset. The film is substantially similar to her screenplay—so much so that if she could prove that Monotreme Pictures had seen her script, she would have a great claim for copyright infringement. However, because she can't prove that anyone has seen her script—let alone copied it—she has no claim. She owns a copyright in her script, and Monotreme Pictures has a copyright in their script and movie.[87]

THE RIGHT OF PUBLICITY AND OTHER PRIVACY RIGHTS

WHAT IS THE RIGHT OF PUBLICITY?

An offshoot of privacy law, the *right of publicity* is a person's right to benefit from the commercial exploitation of her own identity. Infringement of the right of publicity occurs from the unauthorized use of a person's identity (or likeness, voice, name, etc.) for commercial purposes (i.e., labeling goods and services with the unauthorized likeness or using the unauthorized identity in commercials and advertisements).

A celebrity's likeness is not the only part of her identity protected by her publicity rights. For instance, Johnny Carson won a suit against a company that was using the phrase "Here's Johnny" to advertise a toilet.[88]

Filmmakers tend to run into problems with right of publicity laws in two main areas:

- When they attempt to create merchandise, such as action figures, T-shirts, lunch-boxes, and so forth, that feature an actor whose publicity rights have not been obtained.
- When they create television commercials for products or services that use a celebrity's unlicensed likeness to help sell that product or service.

DURATION

Some states require a *signed writing* to convey the publicity right and the duration and extent of right of publicity protection differs from state to state.

- In California, your right of publicity lasts for 70 years after your death; lawsuits for misappropriation of your right of publicity therefore can be brought by your estate.
- In New York State, the right of publicity dies with you, unless you are a performer or personality with commercial value in their likeness (in which case that property right lasts 40 years)[89].
- Some states do not recognize rights of publicity.

The First Amendment and the Right of Publicity

The First Amendment greatly limits the extent to which the right of publicity can control areas outside commercial exploitation of an image. Movies, television, some art, news, literature, and educational uses are usually not considered commercial use of a person's right of publicity. Even TV commercials and other advertisements promoting movies and television shows do not infringe the rights of publicity of the actors who perform in the movies and television shows being advertised.

That being said, outside of obvious commercial use, such as featuring an unauthorized likeness in a television commercial, courts and state laws are literally all over the map with regard to what triggers infringement. For instance, using a celebrity's likeness in a videogame without their permission has been ruled a violation of their rights of publicity[90]—despite the fact that video games are protected by the First Amendment.

For instance:

- A television news station broadcast an entire human cannonball act without the performer's permission. The court held that this may misappropriate the right of publicity.[91]
- A movie recreated and fictionalized the events of *The Perfect Storm* and based its characters on real people. The court held that this did not infringe the rights of publicity in the people depicted.[92]
- A film portrayed Bobby Seales's participation in the Black Panthers without Mr. Seales's consent. In rejecting Mr. Seales's claim for infringement of the right of publicity, the court pointed out that a public figure had no exclusive right to his own life story. The court went on to state: "[I]n addressing right of publicity claims, courts have been mindful that the First Amendment provides greater protection to works of artistic expression such as movies, plays, books, and songs, than it provides to pure 'commercial' speech."[93]
- A commercial that depicted a robot turning letters in a game show violated Vanna White's right of publicity.[94]

One rule of thumb may be:

- "The use of a person's identity in news, entertainment, and creative works for the purpose of communicating information or expressive ideas may be protected [by the First Amendment], but
- "The use of a person's identity for purely commercial purposes, like advertising goods or services or the use of a person's name or likeness on merchandise, is rarely protected."[95]

TESTS TO DETERMINE INFRINGEMENT OF THE RIGHT OF PUBLICITY

The difficult part is determining where to draw the line between commercial and noncommercial use. Courts across the country have developed a variety of tests to determine whether a use is primarily commercial or primarily expressive.

- **Transformative Test**. Does the work which allegedly infringes a person's right of publicity contain significant transformative elements, so that the value of the work does not derive primarily from the celebrity's fame? In other words: "[a]n artist depicting a celebrity must contribute something more than a 'merely trivial' variation, [but must create] something recognizably 'his own,' in order to qualify for legal protection."[96]
- **Relatedness Test**. Is the work which allegedly infringes a person's right of publicity directly related to that person, like a life story? If so, then it may be protected under the First Amendment. However, if the name or likeness is used just to attract attention to that work and does not relate to the person himself, this may be a form of advertising and, therefore, require that person's permission.
- **Predominant Use Test**. If a product is being sold that predominantly exploits the commercial value of an individual's identity, under this test, that product should be held to violate the right of publicity and not be protected by the First Amendment, even if there is some "expressive" content in it that might qualify as "speech" in other circumstances. If, on the other hand, the predominant purpose of the product is to make an expressive comment on or about a celebrity, the expressive values could be given greater weight.[97]

At least as of the time of this writing, the use of the Transformative Test seems to be on the rise.

When a filmmaker is dealing with the gray area of rights of publicity, the best practice, as always, may be to seek permission.

VIOLATION OF OTHER PRIVACY RIGHTS

Producers need to be careful to avoid stepping on the privacy rights of people they film. The extent to which privacy rights are recognized differ drastically from state to state. What a producer may do freely in one state may be actionable in another. As with most torts, consent is a valid defense to these causes of action.

There are four basic kinds of invasions of privacy:

- Infringement of the right of publicity (previously discussed).
- Intrusion upon seclusion.
- Public disclosure of private facts.
- False light.

INTRUSION UPON SECLUSION

Intrusion upon seclusion[98] is, perhaps, what is typically thought of when we think of invasion of privacy. For a filmmaker to be liable for intrusion upon seclusion, all the following elements must be present:

- The filmmaker intrudes, physically or otherwise, on the privacy, solitude, or personal affairs of his subject.
- The intrusion must be of a kind that is objectionable to a reasonable person.
- The intrusion must occur where the subject has a reasonable expectation of privacy.

Example: Polly Producer is shooting a documentary about money laundering in the dry-cleaning industry. She tails Gus Grimes, CEO of Clean-as-a-Whistle, Inc., a dry-cleaning chain. Hoping to get some dirt on his money-laundering activities, she sets up her camera in an apartment across the street from his house. Using a video camera with a powerful telephoto lens and a powerful microphone, she peers into the window of his house, recording his secret business dealings. Mr. Grimes may be able to sue Polly for the tort of intrusion upon seclusion. However, if Polly waited until Mr. Grimes was in a public park before photographing him, she might have a successful defense against his lawsuit; she would argue that there is no reasonable expectation of privacy for conversations that occur in a public place.

PUBLIC DISCLOSURE OF PRIVATE FACTS

A producer can be sued if he publishes private facts about the subject. For a filmmaker to be liable for *public disclosure of private facts*,[99] all the following elements must be present:

- The filmmaker shoots a film that divulges private facts about the private life of the subject.
- The filmmaker exhibits or shows the film to others (this is referred to as *publication*, even though it is a movie).

- The publication of these facts would be highly offensive to a reasonable person.
- There is no legitimate public interest in the disclosure of these facts.

Example: Polly Producer wants her audience to know everything about Gus Grimes—including the fact that he is secretly a homosexual. Polly learned this fact from a friend of hers who works as a nurse in Mr. Grimes's doctor's office, where Mr. Grimes was tested last year for HIV. Polly photographs the lab report showing Mr. Grimes's medical condition and includes it in her movie. Once again, Mr. Grimes may be able to sue her for invasion of privacy, this time for public disclosure of private facts. However, if Polly had obtained facts concerning Mr. Grimes's sexual preference from a *public* record, she would have a good defense. Furthermore, if Mr. Grimes were a politician running on a platform in which he publicly attacked homosexuality, Polly would be able to defend the lawsuit brought against her on the grounds that "outing" Grimes and showing the hypocrisy of his platform was in the public interest.

Polly may have also violated the Federal HIPAA[100] law, which protects the privacy of medical records, and thus she may be looking at jail time.

FALSE LIGHT

False light[101] is similar to defamation in some respects. (See "Defamation," p. 449.) What is actionable here is publishing false information about somebody that attributes to that person viewpoints that they do not hold or actions that they did not take.

For a producer to be liable for the tort of publicly placing a person in a false light, all the following elements must be present:

- The filmmaker publishes *false* facts about the subject.
- A reasonable person would find these false facts highly offensive if the false facts were told about that person.
- The filmmaker had knowledge or acted in reckless disregard of the falsity of the published facts.
- If the published information is a matter of public interest or concerning a public figure, the producer must have acted maliciously.

In contrast to defamation, the false light tort requires a higher level of publicity not required by defamation. And, unlike the requirements for defamation, a person placed in a false light does not have to show harm to their reputation but may only need to show that they suffered mental distress or indignity from the false publication.

> ***Example:*** Polly Producer has tailed Grimes for days. Her camera catches him heading into a McDonald's restaurant to use the bathroom. Knowing

that Grimes is a strict vegetarian, she intercuts the shot of him going into the McDonald's with footage of hamburgers being fried and close-ups of a hand shoving a cheeseburger into a mouth. She finishes the sequence with a shot of Grimes leaving the restaurant and patting his stomach. People viewing her film assume that Grimes loves to stuff his face with cheeseburgers. When he discovers that people think he is a carnivore, Grimes suffers a nervous breakdown. The film is portraying him in a false light, and Grimes would be able to sue Polly yet again.

HIDDEN CAMERAS AND MICROPHONES

In addition to the privacy laws we've listed, filmmakers can run into problems when they use hidden cameras and microphones. Federal law prohibits using microphones and cameras to eavesdrop on a conversation unless the filmmaker has the consent of at least one of the parties to that conversation.[102]

Example: Polly Producer wants to catch Gus Grimes in the act of talking to his mob connection, Tony Turpentine. She hides a small video camera in a flower vase and puts it on the restaurant table of the secluded booth where the two are to meet for lunch. The camera records the conversation between the two evildoers and transmits it to Polly's laptop. Polly watches and listens to Gus and Tony's nefarious schemes while hiding in the restaurant kitchen. Polly has violated federal law, despite the fact that Gus and Tony were discussing criminal activities. Neither Gus nor Tony was aware of the camera, and Polly is not armed with a wiretap warrant.

Be careful here: While some states follow federal law and allow the use of hidden microphones if only *one* of the parties to the conversation consents, some states require (or may potentially require) *all the parties to consent* to having their conversations recorded. These "all party consent" states are: California, Connecticut, Delaware, Florida, Illinois, Maryland, Massachusetts, Michigan, Montana, Nevada, New Hampshire, Oregon, Pennsylvania, Vermont, and Washington.[103]

Example: Polly has lunch with Gus and Tony in a secluded luncheonette in Missoula, Montana. Unless she gets their permission to record the conversation, she may be violating Montana law—even though she would probably not be violating federal law.

LIBEL AND DEFAMATION

DEFAMATION DEFINED

There are two forms of *defamation:* slander and libel. *Slander* is the spoken form of defamation, and *libel* is a written, televised, filmed, or otherwise recorded form.

To be able to sue for defamation, the following elements must be present:

- A false and defamatory statement concerning another.
- An unprivileged publication of that statement to a third party.
- Fault amounting to at least negligence on the part of the publisher (fault amounting to "actual malice" in the case of a public figure; see "Public Figures," p. 451).
- Harm caused by the publication, or presumed harm because the statement falls within a special class of defamatory statements known as *defamation per se.*[104]

A film that contains false statements damaging to someone's reputation may expose the producer to claims of libel and defamation.

Defamatory Statement

A *defamatory statement* is one that is both false and that tends to "harm the reputation of another as to lower him in the estimation of the community or to deter third persons from associating or dealing with him."[105] Usually statements that are "merely unflattering, annoying, irksome, or embarrassing, or that hurt only the plaintiff's feelings"[106] do not support a defamation claim, nor does humor or parody.

Some kinds of defamatory statements are considered especially harmful. Examples include:

- Accusations that the plaintiff has committed a crime.
- Statements that hurt the plaintiff's business reputation.
- Allegations that the plaintiff has a "loathsome disease."
- Accusations that the plaintiff has engaged in sexual misconduct.

Statements "of or Concerning Another"

To sue somebody for libel, a plaintiff must prove that the libelous statement was aimed at herself. The test, known as the "*of or concerning another*" test, looks to whether a reasonable person would assume the statement was made about or concerned the plaintiff.

Example: A documentary film alleges that Chateau, MT, pharmacist Robert Martin poisoned all his customers by filling prescriptions while he was drunk. If the allegations were false, any Chateau pharmacist named Robert Martin might be able to successfully sue the film company. However, it would be unlikely that a San Francisco pharmacist with the same name would win such a suit, given how many pharmacists with that name may be in a large city like San Francisco.

Defamation in Narrative Films

Although most people associate motion picture defamation with documentaries, narrative films can create problems for filmmakers as well. It may seem surprising that a work of fiction can give rise to a defamation claim—after all, unlike in a documentary, the author is not trying to say that the story is real. Trouble usually occurs when a filmmaker fictionalizes an actual person's life or creates a character that closely resembles an actual person. When faced with such a claim, a court may satisfy the "of or concerning another" test by asking whether a reasonable person seeing the film would understand that the fictional character was, in actual fact, the plaintiff acting as described.[107]

To establish a connection between the fictional character and the real person of the plaintiff, a court may compare a host of characteristics, such as the names, backgrounds, physical characteristics, ethnic backgrounds, personalities, and ages of the plaintiff and the character. A court may place emphasis on whether the filmmaker or author knew and had a relationship with the plaintiff. A disclaimer stating that the film is a work of fiction and is not intended to represent actual persons may be given weight by the court but is not conclusive.[108]

Producers, take heart: In cases involving fictional characters, similarity of names between fictional characters and real people, by itself, is usually not enough to transform coincidence into defamation.

Publication of Defamatory Statement

For a statement to defame someone, the statement must be *published* to a third party. "Published" does not mean printed in a book, nor does "published" have the same meaning as it does under copyright law ("the distribution of copies of a work to the public by sale"). For a defamatory statement to be published, it must be seen, heard, read, and so forth by someone other than the person being defamed.

Example: Franco Filmmaker videos himself saying, "Barney Banker steals from the cash drawer at the First National Bank to fund his Hummel porcelain box collection." The allegation is false and defamatory. Franco shows the tape only to Barney. Even though it is upsetting, Barney has not been defamed. But the moment Franco uploads the video to YouTube or shows it to another person, Barney can sue for defamation.

Republication

If a defamatory statement is published again after its initial publication, it is considered *republished*. Generally, republishers may be sued for defamation as well. Filmmakers must be very cautious here! An interview in which a subject defames someone on camera may create republication liability when it is broadcast, when it is screened in theaters, viewed online, etc. Because the filmmaker has indemnified the broadcaster, exhibitor, and others, those parties' legal claims and expenses will be passed on to the filmmaker.

There are exceptions to this rule of republication liability, but it is best to nip the problems in the bud by avoiding libel publication altogether.

PUBLIC FIGURES

A public figure is a politician, celebrity, or other individual who has voluntarily placed himself in the midst of a public controversy. Public figures have a much more difficult time proving defamation. To prove defamation, public figures must show that the alleged defamatory statement was made with *actual malice.*

Actual Malice

In the context of defamation, *actual malice* is the knowledge that the statement was false or was made with a reckless disregard for its truth.

Example: Polly Producer shoots a "tell-all" television documentary alleging rock singer Opie Um's decline into drug abuse. The program shows Opie's police record: He was arrested once for carrying a small amount of marijuana, and his friends give interviews saying that he routinely went on benders. The program's voice-over uses phrases like "Opie slid into the dark depths of drug abuse and despair" and "There was a monkey on his back—a monkey named Addiction!"

Opie sues Polly for defamation. He produces evidence that the marijuana bust was the first and last time he ever used illegal drugs and that he was far from an addict. He proves that the "benders" his friends referred to were actually stories cooked up by his agent to cover up the fact that he was in South America doing missionary work—a fact that would hurt his public image with his hard-rockin' fans. In short, Opie demonstrates that the statements made in the documentary were false.

Will Opie automatically win his suit? Not necessarily. Because he is a public figure, Opie will still have to show that the statements were made with knowledge that they were false or that they were made with a reckless disregard for the truth. This may be tough, considering the producer relied on police records of a drug arrest and interviews with Opie's friends.

DEFENSES TO DEFAMATION

There are a number of possible defenses to a charge of defamation:

- ***Truth***. The most basic defense to defamation is truth. No matter how scandalous or injurious to a person's reputation a statement may be, it will not be considered defamatory if it is true.
  - ***Example:*** Freddy Filmmaker shoots a documentary film titled *Prostitutes and the Policemen Who Love Them*, which features interviews with prostitutes naming the cops with whom they have had sexual congress. Sergeant Lou Scivious, named in the film, sues Freddy for libel. At trial, Freddy shows footage of Officer Scivious handing money to and entering a hotel room with the call girl in question. Freddy produces evidence showing that Officer Scivious was not engaged in an undercover vice operation targeting prostitution. The court will most likely find that the film's statements about the officer were true, and therefore Freddy will not be liable for libel.
- ***Consent***. If someone consents to the publication of a defamatory statement, he will not be able to bring a claim for defamation. *This is why any time you film, video, or photograph somebody, you should get them to waive all claims of defamation.*
  - ***Example:*** Freddy Filmmaker shoots an interview with Dusty Rinkle, the owner of a retirement home under state investigation. Prior to the interview, Rinkle signs an interview release form in which he waives the right to sue for defamation. The final film intercuts footage of Rinkle discussing the benefits of his retirement home with cartoons showing Rinkle burying

little old ladies alive. If Rinkle sues, Freddy Filmmaker might win with a defense that Rinkle consented and waived his right to sue for defamation.

- ***Humor or parody***. Humor and parody are generally protected by the First Amendment and are considered a form of protected opinion (see the "Opinion" bullet). There is no libel when the material is clearly understood as parody, satire, humor, or fantasy and is not capable of a defamatory meaning.[109]
  - ***Example:*** *Saturday Night Live* does a sketch comedy routine about Gus Grimes, insinuating that he is a crook. Because this is a well-known humor and satire program, the skit will probably not be considered defamatory.
- ***Privilege***. Certain types of communications, such as judicial and legislative proceedings, are considered privileged and therefore immune from claims of defamation.
  - ***Example:*** Freddy Filmmaker films Congressional hearings in which Congressman Abe O'Lition accuses a tobacco industry lobbyist of having a second job of selling crack cocaine to children. The lobbyist sues the filmmaker. The filmmaker may successfully defend himself by the virtue of the fact that the statement was made during the course of a legislative proceeding.
- ***Fair comment***. In matters of public interest, many states require that a reputation-damaging false statement be made with certain amount of malice before it can be considered libel. However, this privilege does not extend to material that defames another and is not reasonably necessary to the development of the subject matter of the film.
  - ***Example:*** Jacob shoots a news story about a small dinner theater company's failure to pay the salaries it owes to its cast. He mistakenly says that dinner theater manager is "holding out" on the cast. In fact, the manager is withholding the money because the cast failed to show up for two shows, costing the theater money. The manager sues Jacob for defamation, claiming that the news story is one-sided. Since the story involves the public interest, if he can prove that he didn't shoot the story maliciously, Jacob may assert a fair comment defense.[110]
- ***Opinion***. Statements that reflect a point of view or opinion rather than specific allegations of fact are not considered defamatory. Also insulated from libel and slander are "vigorous epithets," "rhetorical hyperbole," "loose, figurative language," or "lusty and imaginative expressions."[111]

  Example: Freddy Filmmaker shoots a documentary about the history of New York pizza. In an interview with famous French chef, S. Cargo, the gourmet badmouths the owner of Pete's Za, a popular New York pizzeria. Cargo says: "Pete's pizza is the worst I've ever tasted. If you looked up the word 'disgusting' in the dictionary, you would find a picture of Pete. The man's an idiot!" Pete sues Freddy Filmmaker and Cargo for libel. The court will most likely find that Cargo's statements are opinion and, therefore, not actionable as libel.

Be careful here! Merely calling something "an opinion" does not insulate you from defamation. Whether a statement counts as an opinion depends on whether it is verifiable; in other words, can the statement be proven true or false? The statement, "In my opinion, Pete Za lied when he testified under oath," if false, may be defamatory, notwithstanding the use of the word "opinion," because it accuses Mr. Za of the crime of perjury, and whether he lied might be proven true or false.

In determining whether a statement is an opinion and therefore not defamatory, a court will take a look at the context in which the statement was made and the customary way in which the words used in the statement are typically uttered. The court may apply a "totality of circumstances" test to determine whether the statement is fact or opinion. This test will take into account (1) the specific language used, (2) whether the statement is verifiable, (3) the general context of the statement, and (4) the broader context in which the statement appeared.[112]

Examples of statements found to be opinion:

- Union officials are "willing to sacrifice the interests of the members of their union to further their own political aspirations and personal ambitions."[113]
- An attorney was a "very poor lawyer."[114]
- A university vice president was the "Director of Butt Licking."[115]

***BOTTOM LINE:* It may be counterintuitive, but the more inflammatory and hyperbolic a statement, the more likely a court will find it to be opinion and not defamatory language. So instead of saying, "Pete Za cheats on his taxes," you may be better off saying "Pete Za would cheat an orphan out of her last dime."**

MATTERS OF PUBLIC CONCERN: GROSS IRRESPONSIBILITY TEST

Thanks to the First Amendment, matters of public concern are given greater leeway when it comes to defamation claims. In New York, if the allegedly defamatory material is of public concern, the allegedly defamed person will have to show that a television news reporter, for example, acted with *gross irresponsibility* with regard to the accuracy of his or her reporting. Said one court:

> Under this "gross irresponsibility" standard, if an article is "arguably within the sphere of legitimate public concern" or "reasonably related to matters warranting public exposition," the party allegedly defamed can recover only by establishing, by a preponderance of the evidence, that "the publisher acted in a grossly irresponsible manner without due consideration for the standards of information gathering and dissemination ordinarily followed by responsible parties."[116]

In determining gross irresponsibility, courts look to whether the television news producer:

- Followed "sound journalistic practices" in preparing the allegedly defamatory piece.
- Followed "normal procedures," including editorial review of the piece.
- Had any reason to doubt the accuracy of the source relied on and thus had a duty to make further inquiry to verify the information.
- Could have easily verified the truth.[117]

SPECIAL RULES REGARDING DEFAMATION

- You can't defame a dead person.
- "Defamatory statements" are not limited to words alone. Pictures, videos, and film may also contain defamatory material.
- A filmmaker can be held liable for defamation even if they did not intend to defame somebody. The only intent that is required is the intent to publish a particular statement.
- Defamation requires publication: the unprivileged dissemination of the statement to a third party. In other words, an otherwise defamatory statement made only to the person it allegedly defames is not defamation. However, for filmmakers, a motion picture containing defamatory statements shown or distributed to the public would be considered "published."
- The liability for defamation extends beyond the initial publisher. Even parties who disseminate the defamatory material can be held liable if they should have known of the defamatory content.
- Corporations may also sue for defamation when a film's false statements prejudice it in the eyes of the business community by accusing it of criminal business practices, dishonest conduct, or lack of integrity.
- In general, a producer has greater leeway regarding the kinds of statements she may publish when the statements concern a public figure such

as a politician or actor than when they concern somebody who is not in the public eye.

- Many states have *retraction laws* that allow the defaming party to retract her statements within a certain time period. If the statement is retracted, the defendant will be liable for fewer damages should she ultimately lose her case.
- Groups of under 25 people can be libeled, and if so, they can each sue! For example, if you say, "Lawyers are all thieves," that's not libel. But if you say "All the lawyers living in Kalawao County, Hawaii, are crooks," you may be open to a libel claim. At 13 square miles, Kalawao County is the United States' smallest county and probably has fewer than 25 attorneys (one would hope).
- Generally, not defamatory are works "of fantasy, involving outlandish plot scenarios and characters with impossible powers. No reasonable reader of such a publication would take the events described as factual events."[118]

MORAL RIGHTS

Moral rights, sometimes referred to by the French name *droit moral*, are a collection of rights that allow the author of a work to have a say in how that work is used and whether it can be changed in any way.

- The author's right to be credited for the film or to refuse to be credited.
- The right of an author to prevent the film from being changed or altered in any way without the author's permission.
- The author's right to determine how the film is shown.
- The author's right to receive royalties from the film.
- The author's right to stop the film from being exploited in any way that damages the author's reputation.

In general, US laws do not protect moral rights in and of themselves. Although we don't recognize moral rights in the United States, we do have a statutory variation called the Visual Artists Rights Act (VARA; 17 USC §106A, et. seq.), but it only applies to "works of visual art," which—believe it or not—doesn't include audio-visual works, like film. They leave these sorts of protections to a combination of copyright, trademark, and unfair competition law. Other countries, notably France and other European countries, do protect moral rights. And, at least in France, they are inalienable and cannot be transferred or waived.[119] As a result, moral rights issues may come into play when the film is distributed in other countries.

Although moral rights generally cannot be transferred from one party to another, in the United States, an artist's rights under the VARA may be waived[120] (given up). To be on the safe side, production companies should include a clause that requires all writers, directors, actors, and other artists to waive their moral rights in their films.

TRADEMARK LAW

"Look up in the air: It's a bird! It's a plane! It's . . . a trademark!"

When most people think of a trademark, they think of logos for products, like the distinctive "3d" look of Superman's name[121] (Superman® comic books,[122] Superman® brand candy)[123] or services (Superman Ride of Steel®).[124] This is fairly accurate, since trademarks and service marks are used: (1) to identify and distinguish a trademark owner's goods and services from those sold by others and (2) to identify for consumers the source of those goods and services.

Furthermore, the images of cartoon comic book characters themselves can function as trademarks as long as they identify the source of the work of entertainment.[125]

A wide variety of things can be trademarked: colors, sounds, phrases, drawings, smells. What they all have in common is that all trademarks must be distinctive enough to act as a source identifier for their owners.[126]

The policy of copyright law is to protect authors; the policy behind trademark law is to protect business interests, specifically "goodwill." Because of this, trademark rights start with a trademark's *use*, not from its creation. Although every state has its own trademark law to protect intrastate trademarks, the strongest trademark protection in the United States is granted by the federal government. And that protection is only granted after a *lengthy* application and approval process with the US Patent Trademark Office (USPTO), after you prove to its satisfaction that:

1. The mark is distinct,
2. It is or will be used in commerce, and
3. It doesn't conflict with other registered marks (as well as a number of other factors).

Once registered, you can bring the mighty power of federal law to bear against anybody who tries to use a trademark that is confusingly similar to yours on goods or services similar to yours in commerce.[127]

Unlike a copyright, a trademark is potentially perpetual in nature—it exists as long as you continue to use it and it continues to identify its source. If it becomes a generic term—"aspirin," for instance, was once a trademark—then your trademark suffers the ignoble death of "genericide." To maintain a healthy trademark, you must police from infringement by others and maintain tight control over how it is used by your licensors. So, if you trademark your movie character's name and then license your character to be used on lunchboxes, you should have a quality control provision in your merchandiser's manufacturing agreement giving you the right to review and approve the trademark's appearance on those lunchboxes and to destroy any non-compliant merchandise.

It is beyond the scope of this book to go into ways to register your trademark, and for titles of a single artistic work, like a movie (as opposed to a movie series). So we're going to concentrate on the types of trademark use that get filmmakers into trouble: when they use or feature a trademark they don't own in their film and/or its marketing.

Trademark registration generally protects marks within specific classes of goods and services. So, if you register the mark "C.A.D. Berry" for your web series about a magical fruit that turns people into computer-animated versions of themselves, you will likely do it in "Class 41: Education and entertainment services." If Cadbury Ltd. wanted to sue you for infringing its mark, it would have a tough time, since its marks tend to be registered in Class 30, which includes goods like foods and chocolate. That is, unless it can prove that chocolate is sufficiently related to movies that their trademark rights would normally extend to movie titles, too (a bad argument, in my view), or that you are tarnishing or diluting their mark or making it appear that they've endorsed or sponsored your film. So let's dive in to those claims.

One of the strongest defenses against the charge of trademark infringement, tarnishment, or false endorsement (see "Injuries to a Trademark," p. 460) is the assertion of your First Amendment rights as a creator.

INJURIES TO A TRADEMARK

Copyrights can be infringed, but trademarks can be injured in a variety of different ways.

Trademark law protects commercial interests from a broad range of injuries: infringement, dilution, false endorsement, unfair competition, and more. We'll focus on a few of these here.

TRADEMARK INFRINGEMENT

If someone uses a mark that is the same or similar to yours, and that mark is *likely to cause confusion to your consumers*, you may be able to sue them for trademark infringement. What this means is that when your consumers (movie viewers and purchasers of related merchandise) encounter a mark that looks or sounds like yours but is being used without your permission by a junior user, and your viewers are or are likely to be confused as to whether that junior user's comics and toys are made by you, you may have a claim for trademark infringement.

EXAMPLE

You create a steampunk hero character called "The Chartreuse Chanteuse"—French cancan girl by night, hero by day; her skin was stained in a distinctive yellow-green paisley pattern after falling into a vat of magical absinthe. You register this distinctively featured character as a trademark for a TV series, as well as a line of handmade absinthe decanters featuring the image of the Chartreuse Chanteuse.

You sell your marked products online and at steampunk, gaming, and comic book conventions around the country. Your first-year sales are impressive; people love your character, so much so that when conventioneers see "The Chartreuse Chanteuse," they think of you and your company. In other words, it's acquired secondary meaning.

But the next year you do the convention circuit, you see that another merchandiser has come out with its own line of handmade absinthe decanters. However, these competing decanters are marked with the logo "The Shartreuse Shanteuse." On these shoddy, knockoff decanters is a similar yellow-green steampunk heroine. Not exactly the same as yours, mind you; there are differences. However, if consumers are likely to be confused and think that this new interloper's products are yours, or vice versa, you can sue for trademark infringement.

Trademark infringement turns on the "likelihood of consumer confusion." The more the following elements are present, the more likely consumers will be confused by the junior user's use of your mark:

- You have an inherently strong mark.
- Both marks were used on similar goods and services.
- The junior user's mark is very similar to yours.
- There's evidence that your consumers were actually confused as to whose mark is whose.
- The junior user used similar marketing channels as you use.
- Your consumers are not likely to exert a lot of care in selecting the goods and services both you and the junior user have marked (the thought being that the less a consumer typically cares about deciding whether to purchase your product or the junior user's, the more easily the consumer will be confused).
- There's evidence the junior user intended to use a mark that was similar to yours.
- If the junior user is using his mark on different type of good or service than the one you use your mark on, the likelihood that your business will expand to encompass those additional goods and services in the future.[128]

As in all trademark disputes, the timeliness of who *used* the mark first, as well as who *registered* the mark first, are key factors.

PENALTIES FOR TRADEMARK INFRINGEMENT

When the defendant is found liable for trademark infringement, a court can order a host of remedies for the successful plaintiff, including:

- **Injunctions**—the court can order the losing defendant to destroy all of the infringing merchandise it created, stop distributing merchandise, and take other steps as required to correct the problem.[129]
- **Money damages**—whatever profits the defendant made and loss of sales you, the plaintiff, may have suffered as a result of the infringing activity can be recovered by the successful plaintiff. The court even has the power to triple the amount of money the plaintiff should receive in egregious cases.[130]
- **Attorney's fees**—when federally registered trademarks are infringed, winning plaintiffs can also ask for their attorney's fees to be paid by the losing defendant.
- **Counterfeit[131] marks**—if the mark was not just infringed but was counterfeited (in other words, the defendant intended to create a confusing mark, like the makers of the Guc**c**ci bag), then the penalties are much higher. They include statutory damages,[132] *mandatory* treble damages,[133] and reasonable attorney's fees.[134]

INFECTED, POLLUTED . . . DILUTED!

"The term 'dilution' means the lessening of the capacity of a famous mark to identify and distinguish goods or services, regardless of the presence or absence of—(1) competition between the owner of the famous mark and other parties, or (2) likelihood of confusion, mistake, or deception."[135]

> "Confusion leads to immediate injury, while *dilution is an infection, which if allowed to spread, will inevitably destroy the advertising value of the mark*."[136]

No! NO! Not the spreading infection of dilution . . . EEEEEEEK!

DILUTION

If someone damages the distinctive quality of your trademark, you can sue them for diluting your mark . . . but only if you own a *famous* mark (e.g. Batman, the Hulk, etc.).

In dilution cases, the consumers often know that your mark and the junior user's mark represent different owners and maybe even different industries:

EXAMPLE

Batman is a comic book character protected by numerous trademarks; the character appears on merchandise and apparel, in movies, and, of course, in comic books, just to name a few categories. However, what if a sports manufacturer invented a special rack that held baseball bats and sold it under the title "Batman," but the manufacturer *did not use* any of the DC comic book character's distinctive logos or designs? Let's further assume that consumers do not think that DC Comics was the source or affiliated with the baseball rack manufacturer.

No infringement, right? Under those facts, probably not. However, DC could still sue the sports manufacturer for *trademark dilution*, the theory being that the more unaffiliated "Batman" marks there are out there, the less effective DC's registered Batman will be in identifying DC as its source.

To sue somebody for dilution, you need to show that:

1. "That you own a famous mark that is distinctive;
2. "that the defendant has commenced using a mark in commerce that allegedly is diluting your famous mark;
3. "that a similarity between the defendant's mark and your famous mark gives rise to an association between the marks; and
4. "that the association is likely to impair the distinctiveness of your famous mark or likely to harm the reputation of the famous mark."[137]

There are two "flavors" of dilution: *blurring* and *tarnishment*.

BLURRING

With trademark blurring, consumer confusion is not the problem. The problem is that the ability of your mark to identify you or your company is reduced—diluted—because there is *another similar mark* on the market that is identified with a different company.

EXAMPLE

Loony Lawncare, LLC, markets "Incredible Hulk" brand lawnmower bags but does not use the superhero design, just the name. Presumably, consumers know that Marvel/Disney is not in the lawn care business. But if Loony is allowed to keep this mark on its bags, when people see the phrase "Incredible Hulk," they might not think exclusively of Marvel but of Loony as well. In a sense, Loony is piggy-backing on the time, effort, and money Marvel expended in making that phrase distinctive for its superhero products. Marvel can sue for dilution through blurring. This is similar to the Batman/baseball bat rack example previously.

WHEN THE LINE IS BLURRED

"'Dilution by blurring' is association arising from the similarity between a mark or trade name and a famous mark that impairs the distinctiveness of the famous mark."[138]

TRADEMARK TARNISHMENT

When silver corrodes, it becomes tarnished. Your trademark can also become tarnished—its value is corroded—when someone uses your mark or a mark similar to yours in a scandalous or disparaging manner. It's almost like defamation of a trademark.

EXAMPLE

Let's step back to our C.A.D. Berry example, above. Even though your movie is about magical chocolate berries that turn people into animated characters, if you engage in advertising for your movie which uses the slogan "C.A.D. Berry chocolate is dangerous!" you will likely get hit with a tarnishment suit from the chocolate company with a similar name.

TARNISHED AND CORRODED

"'Dilution by tarnishment' is association arising from the similarity between a mark or trade name and a famous mark that harms the reputation of the famous mark."[139]

How Do You Know if a Mark Is Famous?
Only famous marks can be tarnished or diluted under federal law.[140] But how famous does a mark need to be?

"A mark is famous if it is widely recognized by the general consuming public of the United States as a designation of source of the goods or services of the mark's owner."[141]

FALSE DESIGNATION OF ORIGIN AND FALSE ENDORSEMENT

In addition to protecting trademark owners from blurring and tarnishment, that same section of the Lanham Act also gives trademark owners two more weapons to combat threats to their mark: *false designation of origin* or source, known as "product infringement," and *false description* or representation, known as "false advertising."[142]

EXAMPLE

Let's say you've changed your mind and want to avoid a trademark tarnishment claim, so you now decide to use a more chocolate-positive slogan for your movie: "C.A.D. Berry chocolate for everyone!"

The chocolate manufacturer might be able to argue that this conspicuous display of the words "CAD" and "Berry" sounds too close to their own mark and thus creates in the consumer's mind the impression that Cadbury Ltd. has played some kind of role in sponsoring or endorsing your film. However, as we will see below, in the United States, trademark owners must overcome additional hurdles when their marks are used in the title of a motion picture or other First Amendment-protected work.

FALSE ENDORSEMENT

If a trademark is used in such a manner as to create the erroneous impression that the product or service is being endorsed or sponsored by or is affiliated with another person or company, the trademark user can be sued for false endorsement.[143]

> "Trademark law is not limited to confusion of consumers as to the source of the goods, but also includes confusion as to sponsorship or affiliation."[144]

DEFENSES TO TRADEMARK INJURY

Maybe you want to comment on or criticize a company; maybe you want to reference another movie in yours—can you do it? Can you incorporate someone else's trademark into your film without getting the owner's permission?

Good news! In most cases, it is *not* infringement to use somebody else's trademark in your movie (as opposed to on your merchandise) for the following purposes:

- Parody.
- Comedy.
- Allusion.
- Criticism.

- News reporting.
- Commentary.[145]

In fact, to sue someone for trademark infringement, a plaintiff must show that the defendant used the plaintiff's mark "in commerce."

> "Only a 'person who, on or in connection with any goods or services, or any container for goods, uses in commerce' a trademark or false designation of origin, can be found liable for trademark infringement. [. . .]"[146]

Prominent *trademark disclaimers* can also be helpful to help guard against infringement claims. Since trademark infringement turns on consumer confusion, disclaimers in a movie's credits may alleviate confusion by alerting consumers to the fact that the trademark owner did not endorse or sponsor the use of their marks in your film.[147]

EXAMPLE

"The reference herein to any trade name, trademark, service mark, or manufacturer does not necessarily constitute or imply its endorsement, recommendation, or sponsorship by the owner(s) of such names and marks."

CONTEXT IS KEY

As in other areas of IP law, context is key: *how* a mark was used without the owner's permission determines liability—it is not the unpermitted use itself but the manner of the unpermitted use that is determinative.

TRADEMARKS AND THE FIRST AMENDMENT

The First Amendment can be a powerful defense to trademark infringement. For instance, a creator has a First Amendment right to reference the title of another creative work, as long as the reference is not misleading and is artistically relevant to the creator's work.[148]

Example

Moira directs a film called *Archetypes and The Avengers*, in which she tells the autobiographical story of a young woman falling in love with comic book heroes like Marvel Comics' "Avengers." The film's heroine becomes a hit in the cosplay scene and finally makes it as a successful comic book artist. Even though "The Avengers" is registered trademark,[149] it is directly and artistically relevant to Moira's narrative. As long as Moira steers clear of trademark tarnishment, false endorsement, or copyright infringement, she should be able to use The Avengers trademarked name in her title because it is artistically relevant to her subject matter and is not misleading.

TRADEMARK "FAIR USE"

Just as fair use is a defense to copyright infringement, trademark fair use is a defense to trademark infringement. Simple, right?

Not so fast. To begin with, there are actually *two* separate defenses to trademark infringement that fall under the heading "fair use," and, to make matters worse, neither of these trademark "fair use" defenses has anything to do with copyright's "fair use" defense.

CHECK YOUR DEFINITIONS

It's important to keep in mind that words can be defined very differently in different areas of law. "Fair use" of a trademark is a different doctrine altogether than "fair use" of copyright. The rules that apply to one don't apply to the other.

CLASSIC TRADEMARK FAIR USE

Classic trademark fair use occurs when the senior owner of a trademark has chosen a mark that contains commonly descriptive language and the junior user uses that descriptive language to describe their own product. For instance, a candy manufacturer selling "SweeTarts," brand candies cannot stop a juice maker from describing the flavor of its cranberry juice as "sweet-tart."

As the court in that case said: "That SweeTarts is an incontestable mark for sugar candy does not make [the candy manufacturer] the gatekeeper of these words for the whole food industry."[150]

When you use the descriptive terms of another mark to describe your goods, that is an example of classic trademark fair use.

EXAMPLE

You design a movie superhero character who is made of metal, and his superpowers include heating his body until its red-hot and shooting steam from his pores. You name him Man-Iron. Nothing about his design is reminiscent of the Marvel comics Iron Man character. Since he has the properties of a steam iron, using the terms "iron" and "man" would be permissible under classic trademark fair use (although, it probably wouldn't help your argument if you use those words in the same order that Marvel does).

NOMINATIVE FAIR USE

"Nominative" fair use is different from "classic" fair use. In nominative fair use, you are using somebody else's trademark to identify the mark owner's products or services.

EXAMPLES

- You shoot a TV commercial for a local comic book store in which you prominently display the trademarks of a variety of comic book publishers as they appear on the comic books, on the store shelves.
- In your movie, you shoot a scene which takes place in Times Square, NYC. You accurately depict portions of the many trademarks found on the billboards that stretch from horizon to horizon on 42nd Street. Your footage of these trademarks would probably be considered nominative fair use.

In order to mount a successful nominative fair use defense, you must not be using the plaintiff's trademark in a way that appears as if the plaintiff is endorsing you, your products, or your services.

PARODY

Nobody likes to be the butt of a joke, not even a trademark. However, parody is one more defense to trademark infringement.

In one case, a pet toy maker sold a handbag-shaped doggie chew toy marked "Chewy Vuiton." Luxury handbag manufacturer Louis Vuitton responded by suing the pet toy maker for trademark infringement and trademark dilution. The court threw the toy manufacturer a bone when it decided in its favor, finding the company not liable for dilution:

> For trademark purposes, [a] "parody" is defined as a simple form of entertainment conveyed by juxtaposing the irreverent representation of the trademark with the idealized image created by the mark's owner. [. . .] A parody must convey two simultaneous—and contradictory—messages: that it is the original, but also that it is *not* the original and is instead a parody.[151]

And the Hormel food company did not find it kosher when a puppet character in the movie *Muppet Treasure Island* was named "Spa'am, High Priest of the Boars," a name that sounded suspiciously like their product "Spam," America's favorite pork-based luncheon meat. When Hormel sued for trademark infringement, false advertising, and trademark dilution,[152] the court found for the parodical puppeteers, saying:

> No one likes to be the butt of a joke, not even a trademark. But the requirement of trademark law is that a likely confusion of source, sponsorship or affiliation must be proven, which is not the same thing as a "right" not to be made fun of.[153]

APPENDIX A: A FILMMAKER'S GUIDE TO INTELLECTUAL PROPERTY LAW

1 17 U.S.C. §102(a), (2021).
2 See at: www.copyright.gov/title17/92chap1.html.
3 17 U.S.C. §101, (2020).
4 Id.
5 Id.
6 Id.
7 Id.
8 www.copyright.gov/circs/circ45.pdf
9 For more on copyright duration, see the US Copyright Circular 15a, "Duration of Copyright" (https://www.copyright.gov/circs/circ15a.pdf).
10 For a deeper dive, take a look at Cornell University's helpful chart "Copyright Term and the Public Domain in the United States": https://copyright.cornell.edu/publicdomain. (Accessed December 8, 2020).
11 US Copyright Office Circular 33," Works Not Protected by Copyright," www.copyright.gov/circs/circ33.pdf, (Accessed October 6, 2020).
12 US Copyright Office Circular 1," Copyright Basics," www.copyright.gov/circs/circ01.pdf, (Accessed October 6, 2020).
13 See *Miller v. Universal Studios,* 650 F.2d 1365 (5th Cir. 1981).
14 *Hogan v. DC Comics,* 48 F.Supp.2d, 298 (S.D.N.Y. January 26, 1999).
15 *MyWebGrocer, LLC, v. Hometown Info, Inc.*, 375 F.3d 190, 194 (2d Cir. 2004).
16 *Williams v. Crichton*, 84 F3d 581, 587 (2d Cir. 1996).
17 *Reyher v. Children's Television Workshop*, 533 F2d 87, 91 (2d Cir. 1976).
18 *Swirsky v. Carey*, 376 F3d 841, 848 (9th Cir. 2004).
19 See 17 U.S.C § 105, (2010). Subject matter of copyright: "United States Government works: Copyright protection under this title is not available for any work of the United States Government, but the United States Government is not precluded from receiving and holding copyrights transferred to it by assignment, bequest, or otherwise."
20 17 U.S.C §101 (2021).
21 *Allen v Cooper,* 140 S Ct 994 (2020).
22 https://creativecommons.org/licenses/by/4.0/ (Accessed September 15, 2020).
23 https://creativecommons.org/licenses/by-sa/4.0/ (Accessed September 15, 2020).
24 https://creativecommons.org/licenses/by-nc/4.0/ (Accessed September 15, 2020).
25 https://creativecommons.org/licenses/by-nc-sa/4.0/ (Accessed September 15, 2020).

[26] https://creativecommons.org/licenses/by-nd/4.0/ (Accessed September 15, 2020).
[27] https://creativecommons.org/licenses/by-nc-nd/4.0/ (Accessed September 15, 2020).
[28] 17 USC 101.
[29] *Janky v. Lake County Convention And Visitors Bur.*, 576 F3d 356, 362 [7th Cir 2009]("intent [for joint authorship] does not have to do with the collaborators' intent to recognize each other as co-authors for purposes of copyright law; the focus is on the parties' intent to work together in the creation of a single product, not on the legal consequences of that collaboration").
[30] *Brooks v Dash*, 454 F Supp 3d 331, 337 [SDNY 2020].
[31] *Gaylord v. U.S.*, 595 F.3d 1364, 1377 (C.A.Fed., 2010).
[32] *Childress v. Taylor*, 945 F.2d 500, 507 (2d Cir. 1991).
[33] *Gaiman v. McFarlane*, 360 F.3d 644, 659 (7th Cir. 2004).
[34] *Corwin v. Quinonez*, 858 F. Supp. 2d 903, 910 (N.D. Ohio 2012) reconsideration denied, 3:10 CV 2163, 2013 WL 29806 (N.D. Ohio Jan. 2, 2013).
[35] *Aalmuhammed v. Lee*, 202 F.3d 1227 (9th Cir. 2000).
[36] *Aalmuhammed v. Lee*, 202 F.3d 1227 (9th Cir. 2000).
[37] 17 U.S.C. §101 (2010).
[38] *CCNV v. Reid*, 490 U.S. 730 (1989).
[39] "The Fourth Circuit, in a pair of decisions, developed a three-prong test to determine whether a work was created within the scope of an employment: (1) Is the work of a type the employee was hired to perform? (2) Was the work's creation substantially within the authorized time and space limits of the employee's job? (3) Was the creation of the work actuated at least in part by the purpose of serving the employer's interest?" § 5:69.Employee work made for hire—Post-CCNV interpretation of factors—Within the scope of employment, 2 Patry on Copyright § 5:69.
[40] 17 U.S.C. §101.
[41] *Carell v. Shubert Organization, Inc.*, 104 F. Supp. 2d 236, 243–244 (S.D.N.Y. 2000).
[42] Cal. Labor Code §3351.5; CA Unemployment Insurance Code Sections 686 & 621(d).
[43] Cal. Lab. Code Ann. § 2775 (West).
[44] *Gladwell Gov't Servs, Inc., v. County of Marin*, No. 05–17327, 2008 U.S. App. LEXIS 2291 (9th Cir. January 28, 2008).
[45] *Weinstein Co. v. Smokewood Entertainment Group, LLC*, 664 F.Supp.2d 332, 341 (S.D.N.Y.,2009) ("the intention of a copyright owner seeking to transfer an ownership interest must be clear and unequivocal").
[46] *Effects Associates, Inc., v. Cohen*, 908 F.2d 555 (1990).
[47] *Weinstein Co. v. Smokewood Entertainment Group, LLC*, 664 F.Supp.2d 332, 341 (S.D.N.Y.,2009).
[48] I realize that this runs the risk of being an overgeneralization, as these sections also deal differently with works depending upon their renewal terms and whether they were unpublished. Such distinctions are, unfortunately beyond the scope of this work.
[49] Or transferred any time after January 1, 1978.
[50] 17 USC §203(a)(3).
[51] 37 C.F.R. §201.10 (2013).
[52] *Warner Bros. Inc. American Broadcasting Companies*, 654 F.2d 204, 208 (2d Cir. 1981).
[53] *Perfect 10, Inc. v. Visa Intern. Serv. Ass'n*, 494 F.3d 788, 795 [9th Cir 2007].
[54] *Perfect 10, Inc. v. Visa Intern. Serv. Ass'n*, 494 F.3d 788, 802 [9th Cir 2007] (citing to *Metro-Goldwyn-Mayer Studios, Inc. v. Grokster, Ltd.*, 545 U.S. at 930, 125 S.Ct. 2764).
[55] 17 USC §507(b).

[56] *Urbont v. Sony Music Entm't*, 863 F. Supp. 2d 279, 281 (S.D.N.Y. 2012).
[57] See 17 USC §504 (2020).
[58] See 17 USC §505 (2010).
[59] See 17 USC §502 (2010).
[60] See 17 USC §503 (2010).
[61] See 17 USC §506 (2010); 18 USC §2319 (2010).
[62] www.copyright.gov/about/small-claims/faq.html (Accessed May 8, 2021).
[63] Ibid.
[64] House Committee on the Judiciary and Register of Copyrights. Report, Copyright Law Revision: REPORT OF THE REGISTER OF COPYRIGHTS ON THE GENERAL REVISION OF THE U.S. COPYRIGHT LAW, Ch.3 §3.B.1.a. (1961). See www.copyright.gov/history/1961_registers_report.pdf (Accessed June 6, 2021).
[65] 17 U.S.C. §107 (2020).
[66] "The purpose and character of the use, including whether such use is of a commercial nature or is for nonprofit educational purposes." Judge Leval has variously described the first factor as "the soul of fair use," and as the "heart of the fair use inquiry." Patry on Fair Use §3:1 (Quoting Judge Leval, Leval, 103 Harv. L. Rev. at 1116. See also *Blanch v. Koons*, 467 F.3d 244, 251 (2d Cir. 2006); *Davis v. The Gap, Inc.*, 246 F.3d 152, 174 (2d Cir. 2001) (Leval, J.)).
[67] *Campbell v. Acuff-Rose Music, Inc.*, 510 US 569, 579 (1994).
[68] *Clean Flicks of Colorado, LLC, v. Soderbergh*, 433 F.Supp.2d 1236, 1241 (D.Colo., 2006).
[69] Judge Pierre N. Leval, "Toward a Fair Use Standard," 103 *Harv. L. Rev.* 1105, 1116 (March 1990). "The first fair use factor calls for a careful evaluation whether the particular quotation is of the transformative type that advances knowledge and the progress of the arts or whether it merely repackages, free riding on another's creations."
[70] *Cariou v. Prince*, 11–1197-CV, 2013 WL 1760521 [2d Cir Apr. 25, 2013] (citing to *Campbell v. Acuff-Rose Music, Inc.*, 510 U.S. 569, 578–79, 114 S.Ct. 1164, 127 L.Ed.2d 500 (1994).
[71] *Cariou v. Prince*, 11–1197-CV, 2013 WL 1760521 [2d Cir Apr. 25, 2013] (citing to *Campbell v. Acuff-Rose Music, Inc.*, 510 U.S. 569, 578–79, 114 S.Ct. 1164, 127 L.Ed.2d 500 (1994).
[72] Judge Pierre N. Leval, "Toward A Fair Use Standard," 103 Harv. L. Rev. 1105, 1116 (March1990) "The first fair use factor calls for a careful evaluation whether the particular quotation is of the transformative type that advances knowledge and the progress of the arts or whether it merely repackages, free riding on another's creations."
[73] Although exactly how Lady Justice can gaze with that blindfold over her eyes has defied legal commentators for centuries.
[74] *Sony Corp. of America v. Universal City Studios, Inc.*, 464 U.S. 417, 455 n.40 (1984).
[75] *Harper & Row Publishers, Inc. v. Nation Enterprises*, 471 US 539, 565 [1985].
[76] *Hughes v. Benjamin*, 437 F. Supp. 3d 382, 391 (S.D.N.Y. 2020).
[77] *Hughes v. Benjamin*, 17-CV-6493 (RJS), 2020 WL 4500181, at *7 (S.D.N.Y. Aug. 5, 2020).
[78] *Lennon v. Premise Media Corp.*, 556 F.Supp.2d 310, 327 (S.D.N.Y., 2008) ("In considering the fourth factor, [the] concern is not whether the secondary use suppresses or even destroys the market for the original work or its potential derivatives, but whether the secondary use usurps the market of the original work. The market for potential derivative uses includes only those that creators of original works would in general develop or license others to develop").
[79] Patry on Copyright, §10:150, Westlaw, (2020).

[80] *Sony Corp. of America v. Universal City Studios, Inc.*, 464 U.S. 417, 455 n.40 (1984).
[81] *Gottlieb Development LLC v. Paramount Pictures Corp.*, 590 F.Supp.2d 625, 632 (2008).
[82] *Sandoval v. New Line Cinema Corp.*, 147 F.3d 215 (2d Cir. 1998).
[83] *Sandoval v. New Line Cinema Corp.*, 147 F.3d 215 (2d Cir. 1998).
[84] *Gottlieb Development LLC v. Paramount Pictures Corp.*, 590 F.Supp.2d 625, 632 (2008).
[85] Patry on Copyright, §10.10, "dismissal of the plaintiff's case on the ground it failed to establish a prima facie case on *de minimis* grounds avoids the more complicated fair use."
[86] Copyright law does allow the winning side to ask for their attorney's fees to be paid by the loser, but it is not granted in many cases.
[87] Or as the famous Judge Learned Hand put it: "If by some magic, a man who had never known it were to compose anew Keats' 'Ode to a Grecian Urn', he would be an author, and, if he copyrighted it, others may not copy that poem, though they might of course copy Keats." *Sheldon v. Metro-Goldwyn Pictures Corp.*, 801F.2d 49, 54 (2d Cir. 1936).
[88] *Carson v Reynolds*, 48 CPR (2d) 57 (1980).
[89] NY CIV RTS § 50-f (2020)
[90] *Hart v. Elec. Arts, Inc.*, 717 F.3d 141 (3d Cir. 2013); also *No Doubt v. Activision Publ'g, Inc.*, 122 Cal. Rptr. 3d 397 (Cal. Ct. App. 2011).
[91] *Zacchini v. Scripps-Howard Broadcasting Co.*, 433 U.S. 562 (1977).
[92] *Tyne v. Time Warner Entertainment*, 336 F.3d 1286 (11th Cir. 2003).
[93] *Seale v. Gramercy Pictures*, 949 F. Supp. 331, 337 (E.D. Penn. 1996).
[94] *White v. Samsung Electronics America, Inc.*, 971 F.2d 1395 (9th Cir. 1992).
[95] *Twist v. TCI Cablevision, Inc.* SC84856 (2003).
[96] *Hart v. Elec. Arts, Inc.*, 717 F.3d 141, 160 (3d Cir. 2013).
[97] *Doe v. TCI Cablevision*, 110 SW3d 363, 374 [Mo 2003].
[98] Restatement (Second) of Torts §652B.
[99] Restatement (Second) of Torts §652D.
[100] 42 U.S.C. 1320d-6.
[101] Restatement (Second) of Torts §652E.
[102] 18 U.S.C. §2511.
[103] www.justia.com/50-state-surveys/recording-phone-calls-and-conversations/ (Accessed June 4, 2021).
[104] Restatement (Second) of Torts §558.
[105] Restatement (Second) of Torts §559.
[106] Robert D. Sack, Sack on Defamation, §2.4.1, 2–12, (3d ed., PLI 2005).
[107] *Bindrim v. Mitchell*, 92 Cal. App. 3d 61, 78 (1979). The test of whether a fictional character so closely resembles an actual person as to satisfy the "of and concerning" test is "whether a reasonable person, reading the book, would understand that the fictional character therein pictured was, in actual fact, the plaintiff acting as described."
[108] For more on defamation in fictional characters, see Matthew Savare's excellent article, "Falsity, Fault, and Fiction: A New Standard for Defamation in Fiction" (Fall 2004). *UCLA Entertainment Law Review*, 12 (1).
[109] *Salek v. Passaic Collegiate School*, 255 N.J. Super. 355 (App. Div. 1992).
[110] *Bichler v. Union Bank & Trust Co. of Grand Rapids*, 745 F.2d 1006, 1012–15 (1984).
[111] Robert D. Sack, Sack on Defamation, §4.2.4, (3d ed., PLI 2005).
[112] *Milkovich v. Lorain Journal*, 497 US 1 (1990).
[113] *Gregory v. McDonnell Douglas Corp.*, 552 P. 2d 425 (1976).

[114] *Sullivan v. Conway,* 157 F.3d 1092 (7th Cir. 1998).

[115] *Yeagle v. Collegiate Times*, 255 Va. 293, 26 Media L. Rep. (BNA) 2337 (1998).

[116] *Chaiken v. VV Publishing Corp.*, 119 F.3d 1018 (2d Cir 1991).

[117] *Chaiken v. VV Publishing Corp.*, 119 F.3d 1018 (2d Cir 1991).

[118] *Netzer v. Continuity Graphic Assoc., Inc.*, 963 F Supp 1308, 1325 (S.D.N.Y. 1997).

[119] Hebette, Martine., Rep. Copyright Law in the EU: Salient Features of Copyright Law across the EU Member States., ¶X.2.1.1. "Moral Rights," EPRS | European Parliament, June 2018. www.europarl.europa.eu/RegData/etudes/STUD/2018/625126/EPRS_STU(2018)625126_EN.pdf

[120] 17 U.S. Code § 106A(e).

[121] USPTO serial number 71444138 (for magazine publishing).

[122] USPTO serial number 75432535.

[123] USPTO serial number 77578832.

[124] USPTO serial number 75543613, for entertainment in the nature of an amusement park ride.

[125] *Harvey Cartoons v. Columbia Pictures Indus.*, Inc., 645 F. Supp. 1564, 1573 (S.D.N.Y. 1986)("the image of a cartoon character and some indicia of that character can function as a trademark to identify the source of a work of entertainment.").

[126] 15 USC §1127.

[127] *DC Comics Inc. v. Unlimited Monkey Bus., Inc.*, 598 F.Supp. 110, 115 (N.D. Ga. 1984) ("Section 32 of the Lanham Act, 15 USC §1114(1), provides as follows:

"Any person who shall, without consent of the registrant—(a) use in commerce any reproduction, counterfeit, copy, or colorable imitation of a registered mark in connection with the sale, offering for sale, distribution, or advertising of any goods or services on or in connection with which such use is likely to cause confusion, or to cause mistake, or to deceive; or (b) reproduce, counterfeit, copy, or colorably imitate a registered mark and apply such reproduction, counterfeit, copy, or colorable imitation to labels, signs, prints, packages, wrappers, receptacles or advertisements intended to be used in commerce upon or in connection with the sale, offering for sale, distribution, or advertising of goods or services on or in connection with which such use is likely to cause confusion, or to cause mistake, or to deceive, shall be liable in a civil action. . .)."

[128] In NY, the courts apply a similar test, called the "Polaroid Test," taken from *Polaroid Corp. v. Polaroid Electronics Corp.*, 287 F.2d 492, 495 (2d Cir. 1961) ((i) the strength of plaintiff's mark; (ii) the similarity of the parties' marks; (iii) the proximity of the parties' products in the marketplace; (iv) the likelihood that the prior user will bridge the gap between the products; (v) actual confusion; (vi) the defendant's good or bad faith in adopting the mark; (vii) the quality of defendant's product; and (viii) the sophistication of the relevant consumer group.) *Polaroid Corp.*, 287 F.2d at 495.

[129] 5 McCarthy on Trademarks and Unfair Competition §30:5 (4th ed.)

[130] 15 USCA §1117 [West].

[131] 15 USCA §1116 [West] "(B) As used in this subsection the term 'counterfeit mark' means—(i) a counterfeit of a mark that is registered on the principal register in the United States Patent and Trademark Office for such goods or services sold, offered for sale, or distributed and that is in use, whether or not the person against whom relief is sought knew such mark was so registered; or (ii) a spurious designation that is identical with, or substantially indistinguishable from, a designation as to which the remedies of this chapter are made available by reason of section 220506 of Title 36."

[132] 15 USCA §1117(c) [West].

[133] 15 USCA §1117(b) [West] (treble damages are three times the amount of actual financial loss suffered).

[134] 15 USCA §1117(b) [West].

[135] *Moseley v. V Secret Catalogue, Inc.*, 537 US 418, 433, 123 S Ct 1115, 1124, 155 L Ed 2d 1 [2003] (citing to 15 USC §1127).

[136] H.R.Rep. No. 104–374, p. 3 (1995).

[137] *Louis Vuitton Malletier S.A. v. Haute Diggity Dog*, LLC, 507 F.3d 252, 264–65 [4th Cir 2007].

[138] 15 USCA §1125(c)2(b).

[139] 15 USCA §1125(c)2(c).

[140] 15 USCA §1125(c)1.

[141] 15 USCA §1125(c)2(a).

[142] *Resource Developers, Inc. v. Statue of Liberty-Ellis Is. Found., Inc.*, 926 F.2d 134, 139 [2d Cir 1991](citing to 15 USCA §1125(a).)

[143] 15 USCA §1125a(1).

[144] *Team Tires Plus, Ltd. v. Tires Plus, Inc.*, 394 F.3d 831, 835 [10th Cir 2005].

[145] *Charles Atlas, Ltd. v. DC Comics, Inc.*, 112 F.Supp 2d 330, 335–36 [S.D.N.Y. 2000].

[146] *Charles Atlas, Ltd. v. DC Comics, Inc.*, 112 F.Supp 2d 330, 336 [S.D.N.Y. 2000] (citing to Section 43(a) of the Lanham Act, 15 USC §1125(a).)

[147] *Home Box Off., Inc. v. Showtime/The Movie Channel Inc.*, 832 F.2d 1311, 1315 [2d Cir 1987]("We have found the use of disclaimers to be an adequate remedy when they are sufficient to avoid substantially the risk of consumer confusion.")

[148] *Rogers v. Grimaldi*, 875 F.2d 994, 998 [2d Cir 1989].

[149] U.S. Serial # 72278015.

[150] *Sunmark, Inc. v. Ocean Spray Cranberries, Inc.*, 64 F.3d 1055, 1058 [7th Cir 1995].

[151] *Louis Vuitton Malletier S.A. v. Haute Diggity Dog*, LLC, 507 F.3d 252, 260 [4th Cir 2007].

[152] (As well as a few other causes of action) *Hormel Foods Corp. v. Jim Henson Productions, Inc.*, 1995–2 Trade Cases P 71154 [S.D.N.Y. Sept. 25, 1995] affd, 73 F.3d 497 [2d Cir 1996].

[153] *Hormel Foods Corp. v. Jim Henson Productions, Inc.*, 1995–2 Trade Cases P 71154 [S.D.N.Y. Sept. 25, 1995] affd, 73 F.3d 497 [2d Cir 1996] (quoting 2 J. McCarthy, Trademarks and Unfair Competition §31:38 at 670 (2d ed. 1984)).

THE CLAUSE COMPANION

We've taken a look at the issues that shape a contract. Now it's time to take a brief look at the contract clauses that address those issues.

A *deal point* is any major or important term in a contract. It may be helpful to think of a contract as having both *major deal points* and *supporting deal points*.

Major deal points are those issues that everyone must agree on or there is no point in negotiating the rest of the contract. These major deal points are usually the points the producer negotiates first.

Supporting deal points are those issues that shore up and protect the rights of the parties and lay out the rules of the business relationship. These supporting points are usually left to the lawyers to hash out. In the interest of space, this book will not go into great detail on the supplemental deal points of each contract. But make no mistake—you will need clauses that cover *both* main and supporting deal points in your final contacts.

The sequence of clauses in a contract is not fixed in stone: You may see supporting provisions mixed in with major deal points. Some contracts will have all the clauses shown in this book, other contracts only a few. Here the clauses are presented alphabetically for ease of reference.

TIP: **You may want to bookmark this section**.

MAJOR DEAL POINTS

These points should be negotiated and agreed on before the contracts are drafted. Examples of these points include compensation, kinds of rights being granted, term and duration, and creative control.

Approval

How will creative differences be resolved? For instance, who has final say over the final cut, hiring of key or cast or crew, or script changes? There are several different ways to create a mechanism for resolving creative differences:

- ***Unilateral approval***. One party must approve the decision. This power is usually given to the producer or production company executive, and, unless

DOI: 10.4324/9781003228479-37

the director is also the rights holder, this is the most common method of resolving differences.

- ***Meaningful consultation right***. This is generally toothless, as the party consulted does not have final say but only a right to "meaningfully consult" with the decision makers.
- ***Mutual approval***. Both parties must approve the decision; if there is no tiebreaker provision, it is difficult to resolve differences with this method.
- ***Mutual approval with third-party tiebreaker***. Both parties must agree; if they can't agree, a predesignated third person decides which party prevails.
- ***Mutual approval with one-party tiebreaker over certain types of decisions***. Mutual approval with one party (e.g., the director) having final say over creative decisions. The director's power is limited by the restriction that a tiebreaker decision in their favor cannot cause production budget overages.

Tip: The production company should designate particular persons (such as the producer and the executive producer) who are the sole representatives responsible for authorizing approval on behalf of the production company.

Compensation

This is obviously a critical section, since it specifies how people get paid. It is usually the most heavily negotiated section of any contract. It is often broken down into subsections that deal with types of payment, such as contingent compensation, deferred compensation, fixed compensation, residuals, bonuses, and so forth. Common forms of compensation include:

- ***Fixed compensation.*** This is the money the party will be paid regardless of whether the movie makes any money or even makes it into the can. It is the only money the party can actually count on.
- ***Contingent compensation***. This is the money that a party will receive if the film is made and sold. Contingent compensation comes in many "flavors": deferred compensation, profit participation, residuals, and royalties. Bonuses can be contingent as well.
- ***Deferred compensation***. This is a sum, often representing a portion of a worker salary, which is paid out when the film production company repays the costs of making the film, after it has received the proceeds from the distribution company. (See Appendix B, "Deferred Compensation," p. 478.)
- ***Profit participation***. This is money drawn from the pool of the film's net profits. The definition of what constitutes "net profits" may be a closely negotiated issue. (See Appendix B, "Net Profits," p. 66.)
- ***Residuals***. These are fees payable to a performer when the motion picture is televised, broadcast, and so forth. Union contracts will set the minimum

rate for these as well. On a nonunion production, companies often have the actors waive these fees.

- ***Royalties***. These are monies paid to a party when the film property is exploited in other media. For instance, a writer may receive royalties from the license of the film property to a video game company.
- ***Bonus***. This is money paid to a party if a certain goal is reached, such as a script being filmed or box-office receipts reaching a specified target.

Audit and *accounting provisions* should always be included in any contract where one of the parties receives a net profit or other contingent compensation. (See Appendix B, "Audit and Accounting Provision," p. 485.)

Conditions Precedent

Requirements that must be satisfied, like the occurrence of an act or event, prior to a duty to perform arises. If the condition is not met, the promise by the other party does not have to be fulfilled.

> ***Example:*** Natali's performer's services agreement has as a condition precedent the requirement that she must pass a drug test on the first day of principal photography. If she fails the test, despite the existence of a pay-or-play agreement, the producers are not obligated to pay her and can treat her contract as though the contract had never been formed (subject, perhaps, to payment for any services she rendered prior to failing her drug test). (See "Pay or Play," p. 482.)

Credits

How credit is determined and the form it takes are integral parts of every film contract. This clause usually details when credit must be given; for instance, is the production company required to credit the party in just the film and its copies, or must the party's credit also appear in all paid advertisements for the film?

This clause may also specify the order in which the credit must appear and how large the credit must be in relation to the other credits. Production companies that are signatories to a union agreement, such as that of SAG-AFTRA or the WGA, need to make sure that they are complying with that union's crediting regulations.

Filmmakers should make sure that this clause prevents a party from suing them if there are any mistakes with the credits. The clause should expressly state that any failure of the credit provision is not a breach of the contract. The clause should also limit the injured party's sole remedy for a failure to provide credit on the film to a promise from the production company to correct the credits on future copies of the film.

Deferred Compensation

Many independent filmmakers attempt to save money for the production by deferring a portion of a worker's compensation. To quote Popeye's friend Wimpy, deferred compensation is like saying, "I'll gladly pay you Tuesday for a hamburger today." And, just like Wimpy's hamburger IOU, deferred compensation may never be paid; it requires the film to be distributed and the production company to receive the film's net profits prior to the compensation becoming due. (See Appendix B, "Net Profits," p. 66.) There is no guarantee that all the deferred compensation will be paid out to the worker; after all, the film might not make *any* money at all.

When the deferred compensation is to be paid is also the subject of negotiation, and the priority of payment will be driven by a production company's prior obligations to its investors. Deferred compensation may be paid out from the first dollar into the production company from the film's net profits or, alternatively, once the investors have recouped a certain amount over their investment; it all depends on the production company's deferred compensation definition. Accordingly, if a large percentage of a worker's fee is deferred, that worker may feel entitled to a higher overall salary to offset the risk of not recouping his or her fee.

Engagement

This clause occurs in every *services* contract. A services contract is a contract in which somebody is hired or commissioned to do something, such as perform in a film or write a screenplay. The Engagement clause lists the specific duties required of the party being hired and how those duties must be accomplished. You might want to draft the Engagement clause in general terms, such as:

> Ari Flecks agrees to provide the services of camera operator and such other services as are customarily provided on first-class features films produced in the United States. In addition, Mr. Flecks agrees to perform those duties specifically listed in Rider A to this contract, if one is attached, and any other duties Production Company may reasonably require from time to time during Mr. Fleck's engagement.

Be sure to state any additional or unusual duties on a separate rider. For instance, if you need your camera operator to pick up the rest of the crew in the production van every morning, you should state this in the rider to avoid any confusion over job duties.

The Engagement clause usually contains the *term* of the agreement. The term provides the time periods during which the writer, director, performer, crew members, and so on are obligated to provide their services to the production company. The term may also be defined as **exclusive** or **non-exclusive**; if the term is exclusive, the worker cannot perform services for anybody else during the term.

Exclusivity

When a party has an *exclusive* right to an IP right or a service, only that party is allowed to exploit that right or utilize that service. If a party has a *non-exclusive* right to an IP right or service, they can still exploit that right or utilize that service, but so can others that have been granted non-exclusive rights. Defining what rights and services are exclusive and non-exclusive is critical to ownership and use of copyrights, services of a performer or crew-member, scope of agency agreements, and virtually every aspect of filmmaking you can imagine.

> **Ex**: Jay grants exclusive distribution rights to her film to Ditzy Distributors, a third-tier distribution company. Diligent Distributors, a successful distributor, wants to distribute Jay's film as well (in other words, Diligent wants a non-exclusive distribution right). Jay must refuse because she granted an exclusive distribution right to Ditzy.

Ensuring that a performer is exclusive to the film during production is key—the shoot day would be ruined if the lead performer had a prior engagement. However, it is common to have performers on a non-exclusive basis for pre-production. But how do you ensure that a non-exclusive service provider will make time to come to a rehearsal if they are offered a better-paying job that same day? Make sure that even though they are engaged as non-exclusive to you during rehearsals, they are still on a *first-priority* basis with your production.

When someone is engaged as non-exclusive, first-priority, they can still accept other jobs, as long as those jobs don't conflict with your schedule. They must always give their first priority to you.

Most Favored Nations (MFN)

A Most *Favored Nations* clause says that no other party can receive a better deal or a more advantageous position than the person who has favored nations status. The clause is tied to a particular deal point, such as compensation or credits.

For instance, if a production company grants a most favored nations provision to a supporting actor with regard to their compensation, it will have to pay that supporting actor the same rate that it pays the principal actors, who presumably make more money.

Frozen Rights

In many agreements, a rights holder(s) is asked to suspend and not exercise rights they may have in a certain area; these rights are considered "frozen" for a certain period of time or indefinitely, as the contract specifies. If the rights are frozen for a period of time, that period of time is referred to as is referred to as the "holdback period" (see later in this section).

Ex: Jamie has optioned Alex's screenplay. During the option period, Jamie develops another draft of the screenplay and adds new material to Alex's narrative. The parties decide that if the option is never exercised (i.e., Jamie never purchases the script), the rights in the new material that Jamie added to Alex's work will be "frozen," and neither party will be able to use the new material.

Holdback Provisions

Reserved rights are often subject to holdback provisions. A *holdback provision* requires a copyright or other rights owner to refrain from licensing or exploiting certain rights for a limited period of time.

For example, as mentioned earlier, although production companies typically try to acquire the greatest number and scope of rights from a screenwriter, the screenwriter very often reserves certain rights for themselves, such as the right to turn the screenplay into a play for the theater. To ensure that the screenwriter does not execute their reserved rights in a manner that competes with the motion picture, the screenwriter's reserved rights are typically subject to a *holdback* period, which prevents the screenwriter from exploiting those rights for a certain number of years.

Key Person or Key Man Clause

Despite both the importance and prevalence of gender-neutral language in the film and television industry, this clause is sometimes still referred to as a *Key Man clause*. It designates one or more people as essential to the production, such that their absence from the project is either a breach of contract or allows the deal to be terminated by the other side.

Example: Shady Studios enters into a production services agreement with Poultice Productions in which Poultice will produce a 13-part medical documentary on the history of the use of leeches in medicine. Because Poultice producer Larry Lancet is known for his award-winning programming, Shady makes sure that Lancet is subject to a key man provision in the production services agreement. If Lancet quits the production, Shady Studios may void the contract or sue for breach, depending on the terms of the Key Man clause.

Kill Fee

Often a percentage of the full salary, a *kill fee* is a payment given to an employee (such as an actor, director, producer, etc.) if the project is cancelled in lieu of the money they would have made had the project gone forward. Once the kill fee is paid, the production company generally has no other obligations to pay the ex-employee. Kill fees are often offered as counterproposals to an actor or director seeking a pay-or-play deal. (See "Pay or Play," p. 482.)

Example: Burt Breathless, last decade's Hollywood-hunk-o'-the-month, has been offered the part of Wedgewood the werewolf-mummy in *Moon Me*. He wants a pay-or-play deal, which would obligate the producers to pay his full salary even if the film doesn't go into production. The producers counter with an offer to pay Burt a kill fee of 10% of his negotiated salary if the film doesn't shoot.

Net Profits

For non-studio-funded films, the film's net profits are the monies that are given to the production company after the distributors have deducted their expenses and have been paid their distribution fees. (See "Traditional Distribution," p. 355.) This is also the level at which investors and other net profit participants usually take their cuts. By contrast, the production company's net profits are what are left over after the production company has paid its investors, the profit participants (those people sharing in the net profits), deferred salaries, and other the costs of making and promoting the film. *Audit* and *accounting provisions* should always be included in any contract in which one of the parties receives a net profit or other contingent compensation. (See Appendix B, "Audit and Accounting Provisions," p. 485.)

For an overview of the subject, see "Net Profits" (p. 66) and "The Money Pipeline" (p. 358).

Option on Future Services

If the film is successful, the production company may want the option to hire the same actor, director, cinematographer, or producer again at a salary rate they can lock in now. The employee will usually require any future service obligations to be subject to their "professional availability" and will try to negotiate a step-up in payment or the ability to negotiate in good faith for an increase in pay when the option is exercised. It is always better from the production company's point of view to negotiate and agree on future compensation rates, since a failure to do so may result in a "worthless option." (See "Screenplay Option/Purchase," p. 124.)

Parties

Every contract starts by listing who is bound by its terms. These are the *parties* to a contract. A party could be a person or a company. One special type of company, called a *loan-out company*, provides the services of a particular person, such as an actor or director, to work on a film. (See "Loan-Out Companies," p. 51.)

Make sure that your contracts include the proper spelling of the parties' names. For instance, if you are contracting with FilmCo., LLC, make sure that goes in the contract, not "FilmCo., *Inc.*" or just "FilmCo." Remember, too, that a contract can have more than two parties.

Make sure to get full contact information, including Social Security numbers for individuals and federal ID numbers for companies—these will be necessary when you're handling payroll and other taxes. Also include contact information about the parties' attorneys or agents if they have them.

Pay or Play

The *Pay or Play* clause obligates the production company to pay the artist, actor, director, or crew member a certain sum regardless of whether their services are actually used. This clause is usually coupled with a *No Obligation to Produce* clause (see later).

Representations and Warranties

Representations and warranties are statements of fact and promises one party makes to another with the intention that the other party will rely on them. For instance, in a contract that transfers copyright from a screenwriter to a producer, one of the representations and warranties the screenwriter makes is that they have not infringed on anybody else's rights while creating the screenplay. For example, the writer promises that the screenplay is wholly original with them and that making it into a movie will not expose the production company to any claims of copyright infringement. (Representations and warranties for specific agreements can be found in the chapters that outline those contracts.)

The representations and warranties are usually coupled with an *Indemnification* clause so that a party who has misrepresented something must pay the other party's damages that stem from the misrepresentation.

Reserved Rights

The *reserved rights* are those rights that are *not* being granted under the agreement. For example, when granting the rights to a screenplay, a writer often reserves the right to adapt the screenplay to make a stage play. Because the stage rights are reserved by the writer, the production company, which may have the exclusive right to turn the screenplay into a film, does not have the right to make a play from the film.

Reversion of Rights

Screenwriters and other artists will want to get back those rights that they've granted if the production company has not exploited those rights within a certain period of time. This clause specifies how, if at all, those rights will automatically *revert* to the writer. This clause is often found in option agreements and provides that the rights will revert back to the writer or literary property owner if the option is not exercised within the option period.

Rights Granted

Rights Granted is one of the most critical clauses in any film contract because it does the work of transferring or licensing the intellectual property rights needed to create and protect the film property. (See "The Film Property," p. 25.) For instance, in a distribution contract, the filmmaker will assign the right to distribute the film (which is a copyright right) to the distributor. This clause occurs in virtually every single motion picture contract. For contracts with performers, crew, and creative staff, this section typically includes a Work-Made-for-Hire clause. (See "Work Made for Hire," p. 418.)

This clause should state:

- The rights granted—such as copyright, trademark, rights of publicity, etc.
- The territories (places) in which those rights can be used.
- The length of time those rights are granted.
- The media in which those rights are granted.
- The manner in which those rights will be exploited (e.g., distribution via theatrical release, cable, satellite, or free over-the-air television, Internet, VOD).

Term

The *term* is the period of time that a contract is in effect. During the term of the contract, its conditions must be met and the parties' duties must be performed.

In a services contract, the term is the period of time during which the hired party must perform their duties as specified in the Engagement clause. For instance, in a performer's services contract, the term usually covers some pre-production time for rehearsals; the shoot itself; and a period of time after principal photography to allow for reshoots, dubbing, publicity and press junkets, and so on.

Work Made for Hire

Under copyright law, when a work is a work made for hire, the hiring party and not the writer is treated as the author. In the case of employees who create a work as part of the scope of their duties, work-made-for-hire status is automatic. In the case of independent contractors, however, a work will only be considered a work made for hire if there is a signed contract that expressly says so. (See Appendix A, "Work Made for Hire," p. 418.)

The clause that is typically used to create a work made for hire in film contracts usually does double duty: (1) It first attempts to create a work made for hire, and then, in the alternative, (2) it says that in the event that the work is not considered a work made for hire by a court of competent jurisdiction, the copyright to the work is assigned to the hiring party.

Although most film crew members should probably be treated as employees rather than independent contractors, the best practice is to put a work-made-for-hire/copyright assignment provision in every contract used to hire cast and crew.[1]

In addition to dealing with copyright issues, the Work-Made-for-Hire clause usually attempts to give the hiring party the broadest grant of rights possible. For instance, the French intellectual property right *droit moral* is usually *waived* (given up), and "any and all other rights concerning the rights of authors" are typically *conveyed* (granted).

SUPPORTING DEAL POINTS

Some people refer to supporting deal points as the "boilerplate" terms. I don't. In fact, I hate that expression. It implies that the clause is not important or is a cookie-cutter one. Nothing could be further from the truth. These clauses, too often merely glanced at and forgotten, are quite powerful. For instance, they affect where you can sue the other party and what you have to do before you can sue them. They even determine whether you still have the right to sue in the first place—the clause may restrict the parties to using arbitration to settle disputes.

The point is that these provisions matter. The reason I've placed them in the "Supporting Deal Points" section is because they are either (1) not heavily negotiated by the filmmaker and left instead for the lawyers to hash out or (2) subject to a fairly common industry standard.

Arbitration

Arbitration clauses are very common in entertainment contracts. They require the parties go to binding arbitration rather than to a court to settle contract disputes. Unlike a court decision, it is very difficult to appeal an arbitrator's decision.

Assignment and Delegation

This clause lays out the rules by which the parties can substitute new parties into the contract.

Example: Pudgy Pangolin Productions, Inc. (PPP), has hired Walden Writer to write a screenplay. PPP may want to sell the film property to another production company, Angry Aardvark Associates (AAA). As part of that deal between PPP and AAA, PPP assigns Walden Writer's contract to AAA, according to the terms of the assignment and delegation provision of Walden Writer's contract with PPP. Now Walden must continue writing the script for AAA. The same terms apply to the Walden and Angry Aardvark relationship as applied to the relationship between Walden and Pudgy Pangolin—because it's the same contract. The only difference is that it has been assigned by one company to the other.

Typically, production companies have the right to assign their contracts to other companies. Production companies, however, should prohibit the artists from being able to assign their contracts to other artists. It may seem unfair at first glance, but consider that each artist is unique. The production company does not want to be in the position of hiring a hot new director only to have the director assign the director's services contract to their brother, who is still in film school.

Audit and Accounting Provisions

Audit and accounting provisions specify how frequently the parties must provide each other with a detailed accounting of profits, costs, and revenue streams. It also regulates how often a party can send a certified public accountant (CPA) to perform an audit of the other party's financial records. This is especially important for a film's profit participants (people who have a right to receive a portion of the net profits), who may need to audit the distributor to ensure that that the production company is receiving all monies due it by the distributor. One typical approach is that the profit participant must pay for the cost of an audit unless that audit shows a discrepancy of more than a certain amount specified in the agreement.

Choice of Law: Forum

This clause determines which state's laws apply to the contract and in which state the parties will bring any lawsuit or arbitration.

If a lawsuit is thought of as a battle, the *jurisdiction* is its battleground. Jurisdiction controls the location and kind of court that will hear a lawsuit. The laws can, and do, differ from state to state. Whether you sue in New York as opposed to California may make the difference between winning and losing your case.

The *Choice of Law* or *Forum* clause in the contract is the parties' attempt to control the jurisdiction of the lawsuit. There are tremendous advantages in having a lawsuit brought in the jurisdiction of your choice. Often, it's the home-court advantage.

But sometimes it's the other way around. For instance, a production company that's based outside California and New York might still want California or New York law to apply to the contract. Because many films are made in New York and California, courts in those states have generated a lot of case law that applies to motion picture and television contracts. By choosing one of these jurisdictions, both parties may benefit from an established body of entertainment law. This allows all parties to anticipate, to some degree, how a lawsuit might play out in the courts, its possible outcomes, and the measure of damages the loser will have to pay.

In addition to determining which state's laws apply, the Choice of Forum clause often lists the *venue* in which any dispute must be brought. Venue is the geographic region—such as a county—over which a trial court has jurisdiction. The venue answers the question: Within this state, which trial court will hear the dispute?

> ***CAUTION!*** Forum clauses are not always enforceable; however, they are a strong factor in the court's decision to allow a lawsuit to proceed in a particular court.

Counterparts

In the old days of contract law, each original copy of a contract had to be signed by all parties to the agreement for it to be valid. In today's email-friendly society, contracting parties may not live near each other, and in fact may never have met. Accordingly, a "counterparts" provision allows both parties to sign different physical copies of the contract, with both signed versions together being viewed as originals. Obviously, the copies must be the same version of the contract, but you can sit in New York City and sign your copy of the executable version of the contract, while the other party is sitting on a beach in Maui and signing their copy of the same version. Each signed version is considered an original.

Creative Control

It may seem odd to put a section on creative control in the "Minor Deal Points" section; it's here because it is a standard clause and is very rarely negotiated. Briefly, it says that the production company has creative control over all elements in the picture. The only time it is negotiated is when the director is vying for a final cut. (See "Director's Services Agreement," p. 214.)

Default and Cure or Notice and Cure

A lawsuit can halt production—a scenario in which nobody wins. A *notice-and-cure* provision gives the parties a chance to try to fix problems before they turn into lawsuits. This provision usually requires the injured party to send a notice to the party doing the damage (called the *defaulting party*). The defaulting party then has a period of time in which to *cure* the default—in other words, they are given time to fix the problem. If the problem is not fixed within a certain specified time period, only then can a lawsuit be filed or arbitration started.

Defined Terms

Defined terms are terms that are defined in the contract for the purpose of understanding the contract. They are always capitalized and defined in a "Definitions" section of a contract or defined immediately after their first use.

Be careful here! Once a term is a "defined term," it takes on the defined meaning, which may not necessarily be the meaning in the dictionary. For example, if the contract says: "'Rutabaga' shall mean any motion picture sequel derived from the Screenplay," *any* use of the word *Rutabaga* in the contract will mean a sequel (note the uppercase "R"). It will not mean "a turnip with a large yellow root" (which is, of course, a rutabaga with a lowercase "r".)

Of course, this is a silly example, but defined terms can be tricky, especially when the defined term is close to, but not exactly, the same as its dictionary definition. For example, everyone knows what a motion picture is, right? But what if a filmmaker uses the following definition in their contract: "'Motion Picture' shall mean the audiovisual feature film production, in whole or in part, produced by Film Prod, LLC, based on the screenplay *Script-o*, tentatively titled *Movie*, or any part thereof, and all derivatives of such production(s) and their or its parts, now or hereafter in existence, in any medium whatsoever, whether now known or hereafter in existence." Here the term *Motion Picture* means not just the film they're making but any sequel to that film, any television series, graphic novel, video game, and so forth!

SNEAKY TIP: **Watch out for the word *derivative*; it encompasses more than you may think. (See Appendix A, "Derivative Work," p. 404.)**

BOTTOM LINE: **If a term is not defined in the contract, a court may look to either: (1) the ordinary dictionary meaning of that term, (2) the meaning of the term as it is commonly used in the particular industry implicated by the contract (for our purposes, the film, television, or media industries, depending upon the deal), or (3) the meaning of the term in prior dealings between the parties.**

Force Majeure

A standard provision in any production contract, the *Force Majeure* clause is also known as the "Act of God" clause. It lists the kinds of events that can stop production but are beyond the parties' control (e.g., floods, earthquakes, terrorist acts, fire, pandemics, and riots). Among other things, this clause may determine how long the contract is put on hold when a *force majeure* event stops production. (See also Appendix B, "Right to Suspend or Terminate," p. 493.)

Further Documents

Whether it's a copyright assignment, a recordation of the transfer of ownership, or other legal document, no matter how well you plan the logistics of your legal deliverables, there's always a document or two that you may still need in the future. The further documents paragraph obligates the party or parties to execute additional documents that further the intent of the agreement at some unspecified future date.

Indemnification

Indemnification is the duty to compensate another person for their loss. It's kind of like saying, "Don't worry; I've got your back." Typically, rights holders and licensors (e.g., writers, filmmakers, and production companies) indemnify anybody who is licensing rights from them (called *licensees*). That way, if a licensee is sued over something they have been indemnified against, the licensor must pay the cost of defending the licensee and any damages the licensee is ordered to pay.

A licensee will typically asked to be indemnified for:

- IP infringement lawsuits arising out of their use of the licensor's material.
- Breaches of contract by the licensor.
- Falsehoods in the representations and warranties made by the licensor.

 Example: In a distribution agreement, Fatima Filmmaker indemnifies Dagmar Distributor against anyone suing Dagmar for copyright infringement stemming from Dagmar's copying and distribution of Fatima's movie. Fatima, however, used a pop song in her movie without getting permission from the song's copyright holders. The song's owners sue both Dagmar and Fatima. Because of the Indemnification clause, Fatima must pay to defend her own lawsuit, and because she has indemnified the distribution company, Fatima must pay Dagmar's legal costs as well.

Indemnification clauses are absolutely standard. No distribution company will pick up your film without being indemnified.

TIPS

If you are worried about your ability to indemnify a production company, you may want to try the following:

- Try to limit any knowledge-based indemnification to "best of knowledge and belief." For example, "To the best of Producer's knowledge and belief, Producer shall not include any infringing material in the program."
- Try to limit indemnification to payment of legal costs after the case has been lost and appeals exhausted. In other words, try to make sure you don't have to pay to defend frivolous lawsuits.
- Build in a cure period for those breaches that can be cured.
- Try to avoid absolute obligations ("Producer shall") and replace them with good faith obligations ("Producer shall use reasonable business efforts to").
- Make sure there is reciprocal indemnification; the production company should indemnify you as well!

Inducement Clause

This clause should be included in any contract between the production company and an artist's loan-out company. (See "Loan-Out Companies," p. 51.) Because the production company is contracting with the loan-out company and not the artist, the production company needs some assurances that the artist will abide by the terms of the contract between the production company and the loan-out company. This clause states that the artist will perform as though the artist (rather than their loan-out company) was the contracting party. It will also state that in the event of a default by the loan-out company, the artist will render services directly to the production company and indemnify the production company for any damages caused by the loan-out company.

Likeness Approval

Actors typically request some sort of approval rights over their likenesses prior to their image being used for movie posters or other publicity. This clause lays out how that approval is given and what percentage of photos, images, etc. the actor must approve. One typical formula is to require the performer to approve at least 50–75% of the images submitted to them by the production company.

Merger Clause

The *Merger* clause states that the written contract is the entire and complete agreement between the parties. In other words, if what you've been promised didn't make it into the written contract, don't sign the contract. Once you've put down your "John Hancock," the written agreement is what controls the relationship of the parties.

Morals Clause

A Morals clause provides a contractual mechanism for a production or studio to terminate a performer, director, or other crew member for bad acts like sexual harassment and substance abuse that create a hazardous work environment for the other performers and crew members or expose the production or studio to bad publicity. A filmmaker's best bet is to include in the suspension and termination rights clause the right for the production company to suspend the actor's services on a particular film for specific acts, such as criminal or tortious behavior or being intoxicated. For more, see p. 226

Negotiation points:

- What acts allow for termination? Clearly defined definitions are a must.
- When does the termination right vest? When is the act publicly known or when it occurs? Does notice and cure apply after it is publicly known?
- What level of proof is required to determine the triggering acts occurred? Who decides? Are allegations enough? Is the determination arrived at only through arbitration or litigation?
- To what extent does indemnification by the terminated party apply?

No Employment of Others

This clause prohibits the worker from hiring other workers (such as subcontractors) on the production.

No Encumbrances

Writers, directors, and other potential claimants to the film's copyright must promise not to "encumber" the copyright to a film. In other words, they will do nothing to impede or hamper the copyright or the clean transition of copyright from the production company to other companies to which the production company may be assigning the copyright.

No Injunction

An *injunction* is a court order commanding something to be done or preventing something from being done. For instance, a court could issue an injunction halting distribution of your movie or ordering that a copyright registration be amended to include another author.

To obtain an injunction, the person seeking an injunction must show that money alone will not compensate the injury and that irreparable injury will result unless the injunction is granted.

In a film contract, a *No-Injunction* clause limits the parties' ability to seek an injunction. To prevent the disruption to the film caused by an injunction, producers should always include a No-Injunction clause in every cast and crew contract and specify that the person working on the film (actor, crew, etc.) agrees to waive the right to injunctive relief and limit their remedies, if any, to suing for money damages.

No Obligation to Produce

This clause makes clear that although the filmmaker may have been granted the right to produce a film, they are not *obligated* to produce that film. Keep in mind, if any of the performers or crewmembers have a *Pay-or-Play* clause in the agreement, you will still have to pay them even if you didn't make the film.

No Third-Party Beneficiaries

A third-party beneficiary to a contract is someone who is not a party to a contract but who could nonetheless sue to enforce the contract. To become a third-party beneficiary, a person has to prove that the contract was made for their immediate benefit.

> ***Example:*** Acme Productions, Inc., is hired by the Poetry Channel to make a docudrama about Walt Whitman's little-known adventures as a gunfighter in the old West, entitled *Barbaric Yawp*. Acme hires Peter Performer to act in the program. In its performer's services contract with Peter, Acme specifies that Peter's services are for the benefit of the Poetry Channel. If Peter breaches his contract to Acme, the Poetry Channel, as a third-party beneficiary, may be able to sue Peter, even though the Poetry Channel is not a party to the contract.

The "No Third-Party Beneficiaries" clause specifically states that no other parties are beneficiaries to the contract (other than the contracting parties themselves).

Notice

Notice provisions govern how the parties must communicate with each other about issues relating to the contract. For instance, the clause may say that communication sent via e-mail does not constitute sufficient notice.

In drafting the notice provision, it is important to have the proper legal names of the parties. If you are dealing with Pariah Pictures, LLC, don't call them Pariah Pictures, Inc. It may sound obvious, but sending a letter to an "Inc." when the proper business form is "LLC" may mean the difference between giving proper notice and not giving proper notice.

Publicity

Filmmakers like to keep a tight rein on the publicity for their films. Accordingly, they typically demand that all cast, crew, and other creative personnel associated with the film refrain from giving interviews or engaging in other publicity about the movie unless it is preapproved and organized by the production company. This means no unauthorized tweeting or Facebook posts about the film!

The other side of the Publicity clause is the production company's right to use the biographies and likenesses of the cast, crew, and other creative personnel in the film's promotion. For lead cast members, the production company may also want the right to compel them to come to film festivals and premieres and to promote the film on press junkets (all on the production company's dime, of course).

Relationship of the Parties

This clause clarifies that the parties, while working together to make the film, are not partners. You want to be very careful becoming a general partner with somebody, as you may be liable for their debts and legal liabilities that they incur in furtherance of the partnership. (See "General Partnership," p. 46.)

Remedies

This clause details the remedies a party has if the other party breaches the contract. It usually severely limits the remedies for certain breaches, such as taking away any rights to injunctive relief a crew member or performer may have.

Right of First Negotiation

Whoever holds the *right of first negotiation* is saying, "You have to deal with me first!" For instance, if the owner of a copyright wants to sell or license that copyright, this clause requires the copyright owner to first negotiate the sale of the copyright with the party who holds the *Right of First Negotiation.* If, after good-faith negotiation, the parties can't reach an agreement or if the holder of the right of first negotiation doesn't want to buy the copyright, the copyright owner is free to try to sell the copyright to others. The Right of First Negotiation clause is often found in writers' agreements, screenplay options, and directors' and actors' services agreements.

> ***Example:*** Neville the novelist has transferred the right to make a motion picture from his novel *Two-Fisted Tales of Actuarial Science* to Paulina, a producer. Under the literary acquisition agreement he signed with Paulina, Neville reserves the right to make a play based on his novel. However,

Paulina has a right of first negotiation with respect to these theatrical rights. Bentley the Broadway financier has offered to purchase the rights to make a stage musical from Neville's novel. Before Neville can negotiate any deal with Bentley, he must first negotiate in good faith with Paulina, giving her the first opportunity to try to strike a deal with Neville. If Paulina passes or she and Neville cannot reach an agreement after good-faith bargaining, Neville is free to sell the rights to Bentley.

Right of Last Refusal

In a way, the *Right of Last Refusal* clause is like a bookend to the right of first negotiation (see previous discussion).

Effectively, the right of last refusal gives one party the "last bite at the apple." Like the Right of First Negotiation, this clause comes into play when the owner of copyright or any other rights wants to sell or license those rights.

After the copyright owner has negotiated a deal for the sale or license of the copyright, the owner must first offer those same deal terms to the person who holds the right of last refusal. The holder of the right of last refusal is given a time limit, typically two weeks to 30 days, in which they must accept the offer, or the offer will be deemed refused. Only after the holder of the right of last refusal has rejected the offer may the copyright owner sell or license the copyright to the party they were negotiating with originally. Like the Right of First Negotiation, the Right of Last Refusal clause is often found in writers' agreements, screenplay options, and directors' and actors' services agreements.

Example: Paulina the producer has a Right of Last Refusal clause in her literary acquisition agreement with Neville the novelist. Neville has negotiated with Bentley the Broadway financier for the sale of the rights to his novel to make a Broadway play, and Neville and Bentley have agreed on price and other terms; Bentley now has a firm offer off the table to Neville. Before Neville can accept Bentley's offer, he must first go back to Paulina and give her a chance to purchase the stage rights on the same terms as those that Bentley offered.

Right to Suspend or Terminate

This clause details how and when a production company may suspend or terminate a crew member, performer, or other worker's contract. Essentially, it allows the production company to put the worker's contract "on hold" for a certain period of time for events beyond the parties' control (such as *force majeure*). If the worker is ill, is incapacitated, engages in unprofessional behavior, or commits a crime, this clause also allows the production company to cancel the worker's contract altogether. Increasingly, the film industry is adding termination triggers based upon a workers' public statements and acts that are deemed racist, misogynistic, homophobic, and transphobic, even if those statements and acts occurred prior to the worker's engagement by the production company.

Right to Withhold

This clause gives the production company the right to withhold taxes, union pension and health payments, and other legally authorized deductions from the worker's paycheck.

Savings Clause

A *Savings* clause allows certain provisions to survive the termination of a contract. For instance, a production company will usually insert a Savings clause in the "Rights Granted" paragraph. This Savings clause will state that if the contract is terminated for any reason, the rights transferred to the production company under the agreement will remain with the production company.

Security Interest

A *security interest* is a property interest in collateral pledged to secure a loan or other obligation. For example, when you buy a car on credit, the loan company has a security interest in your automobile.

Often filmmakers are required to grant a security interest in their films as collateral for a loan. Sometimes filmmakers must grant a security interest to secure other obligations. For instance, producers who have agreed to work under SAG-AFTRA rules are required to grant a security interest in their film to SAG-AFTRA. If the production company fails to pay the performers' salaries, residuals, or other fees, SAG-AFTRA can seize the film, sell it, and repay the production company's debt to the actors. (See 253.)

Severability

If any clause in the contract violates the law, the Severability clause allows the offending paragraphs to be deleted from the contract without destroying the validity of the contract. The offending clause simply falls out of the contract, and the contract is interpreted as though the clause had never been included in the first place.

Step Payments

Production companies working with first-time writers or problematic scripts will often pay the screenwriter in incremental steps for each stage of the writing process. That way, if either the screenplay or the writer is not working out, the production company has not paid the full price of a completed screenplay. This deal is often referred to as a *step deal*. This clause outlines the stages and the amounts to be paid during each stage.

Survival

A survival clause allows certain provisions to survive the termination of a contract. For instance, a production company commissioning a screenwriter to develop a script on a work-for-hire basis will usually reference the "Work For Hire/Rights Granted" paragraph in the survival clause. This survival clause will state that if the contract is terminated for any reason, the rights transferred to the contracting party under the agreement will remain with the contractor.

Other clauses that are earmarked to "survive" contract termination: Grant of rights; Approvals and control; Promotion/name and likeness; Representations, warranties, and indemnifications; Remedies; Assignment; Choice of law; Severability; and Survival (because you have to have the survival clause survive, of course).

Waiver

This clause allows a party to a contract to be able to *waive*—to give up a legal right—guaranteed by the contract without waiving all the rights granted under the contract. It usually stipulates that all waivers must be in writing.

THE BOTTOM LINE: **Your final contracts should contain *BOTH* main and supplemental deal points**.

A NOTE ON "LEGALESE"

We attorneys take a lot of flak for confusing laypeople with our "legalese." It can be quite frustrating: A businessperson might make an offer to "sell" a widget, but a lawyer will "sell, convey, transfer, and assign all the rights in and to the widget, in perpetuity." You'd think we were being paid by the word. Quite honestly, some lawyers do use extraneous words. For instance, in this example, the single word "sell" would probably work just fine.

For most purposes, using clear, simple language in the contract is the best way to draft. In fact, there are very few "magic" legal words that are required in contract law. Much of the time, if you can express the party's intentions in plain language, it will do the trick.

However, there are times when a lot of seemingly duplicate words are necessary. Remember, the contract lawyer's job is to take the broad deal points and to render them as precisely as possible. The best contract is one that is *both* clear and precise. This is especially true for contracts dealing with intellectual property, such as those in the film industry. There are many different ways a copyright can be transferred from one person to another. It can be mortgaged, it can be sold, it can be licensed, it can be assigned, security interests can be granted in the copyright, and so on. And all those transfers are *not* the same.

When a lawyer is drafting a contract, the lawyer's greatest fear is that if they fail to be precise enough, that lack of precision will create a loophole that will be exploited when the parties decide they can no longer play nicely with each other. A contract that says only that "Ms. Jones hereby licenses the copyright to his screenplay to Mr. Smith" does not say anything about whether Ms. Jones may borrow money from a lender and use the copyright as collateral for the loan. If Mr. Smith wants to prevent that from happening, he needs to insert language into the contract that talks about mortgages, security interests, and so forth.

Okay, now you know what common clauses create contractual obligations, but what happens when a party to a contract doesn't live up to those obligations?

BREACH OF CONTRACT

Performance is the successful fulfillment of a contractual duty. If a party to a contract fails to perform his duties under that contract, they may have *breached the contract*.

There are two main kinds of breaches: *minor* and *material*.

A Minor Breach

A *minor breach* occurs when the damage to the aggrieved party is, well, minor. No surprise there. In the case of a minor breach, the contact still stands, and the non-breaching party must still perform their contractual duties (e.g. they must still pay the other party or must still deliver the goods or perform the services).

> ***Example:*** A laboratory that is contractually obligated to deliver an answer print to a producer by noon delivers that film at 1:00 p.m. If the contract does not stipulate that "time is of the essence," the breach may be considered a minor one.

Remedy for Minor Breaches

The breaching party must remedy the particular breach and compensate the aggrieved party for any damages. For a minor breach, the aggrieved party, however, is not relieved of their duties under the contract.

Example: In the previous scenario, the laboratory that was late in delivering the film must pay any expenses resulting from the one-hour delay. However, the producer must still pay the laboratory the agreed-on fee (perhaps minus costs that the producer incurred as a result of the laboratory's delay).

A Material Breach

Unlike the minor breach, a *material breach* substantially affects the benefit the aggrieved party expected to receive from the contract. If there has been a material breach, the damaged party may consider the contract terminated, with no further obligation on their part to perform the duties they were obligated to perform. Furthermore, the damaged party may pursue contract remedies in court.

Example: In the previous scenario, if the film laboratory failed to deliver the answer print within a reasonable time, a court would likely find that a major breach of the contract had occurred. Other examples of major breaches might be an actor failing to show up for production per her obligation under her performer's services contract or a production company failing to pay a salary per its obligation under a director's services contract.

Now let's say you've cast a teen actor to play the part of a 19th-century child laborer digging coal in England, and the actor was supposed to supply their own "clean wardrobe," but they show up on set with torn and disheveled pants. Would that be a minor minor miner breach or a material breach of breeches' material? Yeah, ignore this paragraph; my dad humor is showing.

REMEDIES FOR BREACH OF CONTRACT

A party that has been hurt because the other party to the contract has breached that contract may sue for *breach of contract*. The chief remedy for a breach of contract is the award of monetary *damages*. The primary kinds of damages awarded for breach of contract are *compensatory* and *consequential*.

Compensatory damages compensate the hurt party by paying them an amount of money that will:

- Put them in the position that they would have been in had the contract been performed as expected, or
- Put them in the position they would have been in if they had never entered into the contract in the first place (in other words, a repayment for any of the expenses they have incurred as a result of relying upon the contract).

Consequential damages compensate the damaged party for the reasonably foreseeable losses that occurred as a result of—as a *consequence* of—the breach.

Example: In the previous scenario, the reasonably foreseeable damages for the laboratory failing to deliver an answer print in a timely fashion might be the cost of booking a theater, if one had been booked. However, for consequential damages to be awarded, both parties must have been aware of the theater booking at the time that the laboratory contract is made.

***IMPORTANT TIP:* Regardless of the specific duties and obligations of either party, keep in mind that there is an implied condition in *every contract* that the parties will behave in good faith toward each other.**

REMEDIES FOR BREACH OF EMPLOYMENT CONTRACTS

If the *employer* breaches an employment contract with its employee, the damages may be the full contract price.

If the *employee* breaches an employment contract, the damages may be the employer's cost to replace the employee. The employee may have a right to deduct from the damages owed to the employer the amount of money owed to the employee up to the date of the breach.

Example: Andy Actor goes on a drug-fueled bender and fails to show up on set for an entire week. Per Andy's contract (see "Performer's Services Agreement," p. 256), Paula Producer sends notice of default to Andy's agent. Andy still fails to show up, and the default is not cured. Rather than cancel the shoot and lose thousands of dollars, Paula Producer hires the only other available actor of Andy's caliber, David Drama. Unfortunately, David's fee quote is 10% higher than Andy's. When Paula sues Andy for breach of contract, she may be able to recover the entire cost of hiring David, minus any moneys that Andy had earned to date.

In addition to damages, an aggrieved party may also be able to obtain injunctive relief. An *injunction* is a court order commanding something to be done.

Injunctions can also prevent something from being done. For example, a court can issue an injunction that compels a writer to transfer a copyright or that prevents a film from being distributed.

For employment and other service contracts, an injunction may not be used to force the employee who has breached the contract to continue to work for the employer. However, an injunction can be used to prevent the breaching employee from working for other employers during the term of the breached contract.

> ***Example:*** For instance, in the earlier example, Paula Producer may seek an injunction against Andy Actor working on another film during the term of his contract with Paula. Paula may not, however, get an injunction that compels Andy to continue to work on her film.

Note:

- The damaged party has a duty to *mitigate* damages, which means that they must try to keep down or reduce the amount of their losses.
- Contract breaches, like most legal issues in this book, are incredibly nuanced and complex matters. If you are involved in a breach of contract or other litigation, seek the advice of an attorney.

[1] Producers shooting in California may want to be careful here, as a work-for-hire agreement can create an employment relationship there. (See "DETERMINING WORKER STATUS UNDER CALIFORNIA LAW," p. 204.)

BIBLIOGRAPHY AND RESOURCES

STARTING AND RUNNING A BUSINESS

Anthony Mancuso, *Form Your Own Limited Liability Company* (Nolo Press, 2002).

Anthony Mancuso, *Your Limited Liability Company, an Operating Manual* (Nolo Press, 2002).

Fred S. Steingold, *The Employer's Legal Handbook* (Nolo Press, 2005).

Robert W. Emerson et al., *Business Law* (Barren's Educational Series, Inc., 1997).

FILM FINANCE

Bill Daniels et al., *Movie Money: Understanding Hollywood's Creative Accounting Practices* (Silman-James Press, 1998).

Daniel Harlow, *Making Movies Without Losing Money* (Routledge, 2020).

Glenda Cantrell and Daniel Wheatcroft, *Film & TV Tax Incentives in the US* (Focal Press, 2018).

Jeremy Juuso, *Getting the Money* (Michael Wise Productions, 2009).

John Durie et al., *Marketing and Selling Your Film Around the World* (Silman-James Press, 2000).

John J. Lee, Jr., *The Producer's Business Handbook* (Focal Press, 2000).

John W. Cones, *43 Ways to Finance Your Feature Film* (Southern Illinois University Press, 1995).

John W. Cones, *Film Finance and Distribution: A Dictionary of Terms* (Silman-James Press, 1992).

Louise Levison, *Filmmakers & Financing*, 8th ed., (Routledge, 2017).

Mark Litwak, *Risky Business: Financing and Distributing Independent Films* (Silman-James Press, 2004).

Schuyler M. Moore, *The Biz: The Basic Business, Legal, and Financial Aspects of the Film Industry* (Silman-James Press, 2002).

FILM AND TELEVISION LEGAL: CONTRACTS

Dina Appleton and Daniel Yankelevits, *Hollywood Dealmaking: Negotiating Talent Agreements* (Allworth Press, 2002).
John W. Cones, *The Feature Film Distribution Deal* (Southern Illinois University Press, 1997).
Mark Litwak, *Contracts for the Film and Television Industry* (Silman-James Press, 1998).
Mark Litwak, *Dealmaking in the Film and Television Industry* (Silman-James Press, 2002).
Scott Kirkpatrick, *Introduction to Media Distribution*, (Focal Press, 2019)
Stephen F. Breimer, Esq., *The Screenwriter's Legal Guide* (Allworth Press, 1999).

FILM AND TELEVISION BUSINESS AND LEGAL

Bob Levy, *The TV Showrunner's Roadmap* (Focal Press, 2019).
Gregory Bernstein, *Understanding the Business of Media and Entertainment*, 2nd ed. (Routledge, 2020).
Gunnar Erickson et al., *The Independent Film Producer's Survival Guide* (Schirmer Trade Books, 2002).
Jeffery C. Ulin, *This Business of Media Distribution*, 3rd ed. (Focal Press, 2019).
Jon M. Garon, *The Independent Filmmaker's Law and Business Guide*, 2nd ed. (Chicago Review Press, 2009).
Jon Reiss, *Think Outside the Box Office* (Hybrid Cinema, 2010).
Ken Basin, *This Business of Television* (Routledge, 2019).
Neil Landau, *The TV Showrunner's Roadmap* (Focal Press, 2014).
Neil Landau, *TV Outside the Box* (Focal Press, 2016).
Philip H. Miller, *Media Law*, 4th ed. (Focal Press, 2003).
Richard Botto, *Crowdsourcing for Filmmakers* (Focal Press, 2018)

INTELLECTUAL PROPERTY

Arnold P. Lutzker, *Content Rights for Creative Professionals* (Focal Press, 2003).
Bruce P. Keller et al., *Copyright Law: A Practitioner's Guide* (PLI Press, 2005).
Craig Joyce et al., *Copyright Law* (Lexis Publishing, 2000).
Donald S. Chisum et al., *Understanding Intellectual Property Law* (Matthew Bender Publishing, 1996).
Glenda Cantrell and Daniel Wheatcroft, *Archival Storytelling* (Focal Press, 2020).

Marshall Leaffer, *Understanding Copyright Law* (Lexis Publishing, 1999).
Melville B. Nimmer et al., *Nimmer on Copyright* (Matthew Bender, 2006).
Richard Stim, *Copyright Law* (West Legal Studies, 2000).
Richard Stim, *Getting Permission: How to License and Clear Copyrighted Materials Online and Off* (Nolo Press, 2000).
Richard Stim et al., *Nondisclosure Agreements* (Nolo Press, 2001).
Stephen Elias et al., *Patent, Copyright & Trademark* (Nolo Press, 2001).
Stephen Fishman, *The Public Domain: How to Find & Use Copyright-Free Writings, Music, Art & More* (Nolo Press, 2006).
Thomas J. McCarthy, *The Rights of Publicity and Privacy*, 2nd ed. (Thomson West, 2006).

MUSIC LAW

Al Kohn et al., *Kohn on Music Licensing* (Aspen Publishers, 2002).

WEBSITES

Attorneys

Attorney Ivan Saperstein, Esq.: www.ivansaperstein.com
Attorney Matthew Savare, Esq.: www.lowenstein.com/msavare/
Attorney Thomas A. Crowell, Esq.: www.thomascrowell.com; www.lanecrowell.com
Attorney Victoria Jade Bennett: www.jadeipc.com

Copyright, Intellectual Property, and Public Domain

The United States Copyright Office: www.copyright.gov
The United States Patent and Trademark Office: www.uspto.gov

Distribution

Filmfreeway.com

Education

Stage32.com

INDEX

Note: Page numbers in italics indicate figures and tables.

For Product Safety Concerns and Information please contact our EU representative GPSR@taylorandfrancis.com
Taylor & Francis Verlag GmbH, Kaufingerstraße 24, 80331 München, Germany

www.ingramcontent.com/pod-product-compliance
Ingram Content Group UK Ltd.
Pitfield, Milton Keynes, MK11 3LW, UK
UKHW022208190926
475702UK00003B/260

* 9 7 8 1 0 3 2 1 3 2 8 2 2 *